Working from Home

Also by Paul and Sarah Edwards

The Best Home Businesses for the 90's

The Computer Companion:
The Complete Computer Management System

Getting Business to Come to You

How to Use a Computer in Your Home Office
(with Hal Schuster)

Making It on Your Own

WORKING FROM HOME

EVERYTHING YOU NEED TO KNOW
ABOUT LIVING AND WORKING
UNDER THE SAME ROOF

PAUL and SARAH EDWARDS

Jeremy P. Tarcher/Perigee

Jeremy P. Tarcher/Perigee Books
are published by
The Putnam Publishing Group
200 Madison Avenue
New York, NY 10016

Library of Congress Cataloging in Publication Data

Edwards, Paul.
    Working from home: everything you need to know about living and
working under the same roof / Paul and Sarah Edwards.—3rd ed.
        p.   cm.
    Includes index.
    ISBN 0-87477-582-5
    1. Home-based businesses. 2. Self-employed. I. Edwards, Sarah (Sarah
(Sarah A.) II. Title.
HD62.5.E39   1990
658 ' .041—dc20   90-37626
                                                                        CIP

Jeremy P. Tarcher, Inc.
5858 Wilshire Blvd., Suite 200
Los Angeles, CA 90036

Cover design by Susan Shankin

Design by Robert Tinnon
Illustrations by Mike Cressy

Manufactured in the United States of America
10   9   8   7   6

CONTENTS

■■■■■■■■■■■■■■■■■■■■■■■

INTRODUCTION

■■■■■■■■■■■■■■■■■■■■■

This book is about living life to its fullest. It's about having your cake and eating it too, about having the best of all possible worlds.

It's a book for everyone who's tired of the daily commute and the pressures of the nine-to-five routine. It's for everyone who dreams of economic security, more free time, a healthier or more productive lifestyle, and a chance to be closer to family and friends. It's for people who want to take charge of their day-to-day lives and their futures.

This book took root at a time in our lives when our days were full and exciting. Paul was a chief executive officer for a corporation. Sarah was an administrator for a government agency. We both spent too many hours flying across the country, keeping tight schedules, and waving goodbye to each other in airports. We were smoking too much, sleeping too little, and leading the ulcer-prone lives that have come to characterize what our society calls success.

Sarah

In the late 1960s I didn't feel I had many choices as a working mother. Juggling a successful career and motherhood meant being dead tired most of the time and not being able to do either job with the dedication I wanted. I was determined, however, to have both a career and a family, so I did my best in a difficult situation.

Then, one day in the early 1970s, I visited the home of two consultants I worked with. They were doing what, at the time, seemed an unusual thing: operating their business from home. I took one look at their arrangement and knew with certainty, "This is for me!"

My parents grew up during the Great Depression, so I had been raised to think that nothing in the world was better than the security of a government

1

job. Still, two years, one master's degree, and first-time-ever home mortgage later, I left my secure government position and opened a psychotherapy practice in our new house.

Most people I knew predicted I would miss the benefits of a government career and regret my decision. But they were wrong. I haven't regretted my decision for one day in the sixteen years since I left the hallowed gray halls of the Federal Building.

Working at home was like having flowers delivered to me every day. I felt healthier immediately. For the first time in my son's young life, I could be a real mother and still pursue my career. I was more relaxed, and I relished working in an environment with windows and trees and the out-of-doors just a few steps away.

Paul

Initially I was hesitant about working from home. I had concerns about the image it might create and worried that I wouldn't get my work done. So when I started my own consulting firm, I opened a downtown office and hired a secretary.

I found I'd start working at home in the morning and go into the office later and later in the day. Many days I'd see no reason to drive in at all. Eventually I closed that downtown office and set up a workspace in our basement recreation room for my secretary. At first she was a bit uncomfortable with the idea of working in someone's home. But after thinking about it, she decided it was a wonderful opportunity. She could work within two miles of her own house and be closer to her children.

To me, working at home meant having all my files and books in one place. It meant saving a lot of time that used to be wasted commuting and a great deal of money that used to be spent in overhead. It meant being free to put those resources into making my home as pleasant as I wanted it to be. After all, I was working there! Most important, the saving on overhead has meant I can afford to pursue the kind of work I want to do instead of taking business just to pay the overhead.

A Joint Effort

When we were first married, we were both in college and spent most of every day together. On graduating, we discovered that "growing up" and going out into the world meant seeing very little of the ones we loved. How nice to find there's another way! We've been working from home for sixteen years and we see more of each other than ever before.

When we first began working from home it seemed somewhat unusual to our friends and neighbors. But soon the novelty aroused curiosity. People asked us many questions about how we did it and how they might do it too.

As the tempo of the questions intensified, curiosity about working from home has turned into a major social trend. Through this book, our column in *Home Office Computing* magazine, our radio shows, tapes, seminars and speeches, and The Working From Home Forum on the CompuServe Information Service, we've been able to reach hundreds of thousands of people from all over the country with our message: working from home is a good life, and you can do it too.

A Reference Book for People Working from Home

With this in mind we've created a reference book to help you at every stage of working from home—from the time you first begin considering it to the day you wonder if maybe you're outgrowing your home office. It's intended as a basic reference you can turn to any time a question arises or a problem develops.

If you're trying to decide whether working at home is for you, Part 1 should be helpful. In it we address the questions of who's doing it and why, what work is being done at home, the benefits and problems you can anticipate, and how you can tell whether it will be difficult or easy for you. If you think you'd like to work at home but need to figure out how you can earn a living doing it, you will find that in Part 1 we also provide concrete ideas for setting up your own home business or finding a job that enables you to work at home.

If you already know what you're going to do and are ready to set up your work at home, or if you are already in business from home, turn to Part 2. In it we give detailed suggestions about where to put your office, how to keep your work and personal life separate, what equipment you'll need, and how to arrange the most efficient workspace.

Another aspect of getting under way, but one we find many new or established home business people also need guidance on, is protecting yourself from legal regulators, tax authorities, and calamities. So in Part 3, we cover legal issues, tax matters, and insurance.

With the ever-increasing amount of paper in our lives and demands on our time, working efficiently and keeping clear of all kinds of clutter are challenges. In Part 4 we provide specific guidelines for such practical matters as managing your time, your money, and your paperwork.

Dealing with people and personnel is the subject of Part 5. Since you'll be your sole supervisor, solutions are given for problems like loneliness and staying out of the refrigerator. You'll discover strategies for dealing with children and family, and making sure your marriage survives. You'll also learn how to find employees and support services.

For home business people, pricing your services and finding customers or clients are important issues. That, together with what you can do if you find yourself outgrowing your home office and want to retain the benefits of working from home while you expand or move up the professional ladder, are covered in Part 6.

You'll find some of the topics we cover, such as interior design, time management, and computer technology, have been the subject of entire books that go beyond the scope of issues directly related to working from home. Throughout the book, we make mention of such resources and have included a Resource List at the end of each chapter so you can read further about those areas you would like to know more about.

Working *from* Home

You'll notice that our book is called **Working *from* Home**—not working *at* home. We chose to use the preposition *from* for two important reasons.

First, because "from" embraces not only those whose workplace is their home but also those for whom home is mainly a base of operations because much of their work is performed on others' premises. For example, home-based salespeople, contractors, consultants, and trainers do most of their actual work away from home.

The second reason we chose this broader definition is to communicate the importance of going out and reaching out to get business, of participating in the broader professional and business community. Having your office in your home doesn't mean withdrawing from life. On the contrary, it's a way to become more involved in living because you're in charge of your life, released from the fatigue of being trapped for hours in a car or bus. Freed of the limits placed on your entreprenurial spirit by traditional office structures, you become the creator of each and every day of your work life, shaping it instead of reacting to it. You can have a fuller sense of being your own person.

Sometimes we look at the days in our lives and marvel that we are living them. They are rich and varied and always full. For many years they were brightened by the sound of our son's feet as he ran in the door after school around four o'clock. Some afternoons were punctuated with a family trip to watch him play soccer. Last year he graduated from college and we're thankful our working lives were flexible enough to let us enjoy his growing up.

For us, that flexibility and variety is what makes life interesting and keeps us feeling young and vital. Yesterday was a typical day. We got up at 6:15 AM for a telephone interview on a radio show in Abilene, Texas. After the interview, we made long distance calls to the East Coast, read the paper, fed and exercised the dogs, and then headed off for a half-hour bike ride.

We had breakfast, got dressed and, at 9:00, Paul began making myriad phone calls while Sarah began planning an upcoming speech. We had lunch together and drove over to the outdoor farmer's market held each Wednesday here in Santa Monica to get in our produce for the week. We also dropped off the outgoing mail, made a bank deposit, and picked up some printing.

For Paul the rest of afternoon was filled with rewriting segments of this book and responding to incoming calls. Sarah met with a client about setting up his home-based business, and taped an interview with an author for an upcoming radio show. Later, she edited that tape and wrote an introduction for it.

Because work ran into the evening, we went out for a dinner of what we call Westside soul food—Sushi. Later we watched television, read, answered electronic mail, and got ready for bed. We were tired, but content. The day hadn't been perfect; there had been the ordinary mishaps. Answering the messages on CompuServe had taken longer than expected. Sarah hadn't finished as much of the speech as she'd wanted to. Paul couldn't find something he'd been looking for in the files. Still, the day was a good one. It ended with the satisfied feeling that comes from thinking about what you've accomplished, along with a twinge of excitement about all the next morning might bring.

Our goal in *Working from Home* is to have you feel like this too when the day is done. Whatever your ideal workday would be like, this book is designed to help you create it.

PART 1

....

New Freedom, New Choices:
Living and Working Under One Roof

CHAPTER
ONE

∎∎∎∎∎∎∎∎∎∎∎∎∎∎∎∎∎∎∎∎∎

Putting an End to Nine-to-Five

For most of us, going to work from nine to five, or a version thereof, has been the story of our lives. For some, it's no longer a very satisfying way to live. For others, like the handicapped, the elderly, or parents with small children, working away from home isn't always feasible. But until recently there haven't been many other choices.

In the past ten years, people have begun to explore new options for living and working. Today we can say goodbye to the daily commute, the dead-end job, the office politics, and the feeling that everyone else is in charge of our lives. Today we can work from home.

Your workday can begin with a brisk walk from the breakfast table to the den. The extra time you save every day by not commuting to work can be used doing whatever you want—sleeping late, jogging, taking care of your children, gardening, or getting a head start on the job that needs to be done. Think of it. Even if you only have a twenty-minute commute each way, working from home is like getting an additional four-week vacation every year.

Interested? You're not alone. According to repeated surveys, nearly one-third of American workers would prefer to earn their livelihoods at home. Today many of them have the choice, and more and more are exercising the option.

Almost 33 million people—more than the population of California or Canada—were found to be working from home in Link Resources' 1990 National Work-at-Home survey. This was 22 percent more people than were found the year before. A 1989 Roper survey for *The Wall Street Journal* found that 10 percent of all work done in the United States is done at home!

The New Dreams

Although our society has made giant strides in material well-being in the past forty years, the fast pace of the modern industrial world has not been kind to our personal lives. Work life and personal life have generally become two isolated worlds, separated in time and space by the daily commute.

Often people have to struggle to squeeze in a little "quality time" by themselves or with their loved ones—catching a few free moments between the late shuttle and the eleven o'clock news, between the extra load of laundry and the early-morning meeting. Divorce rates have soared. Stress-related illnesses like high blood pressure, chronic headaches, back pain, alcoholism, drug abuse, heart disease, and even cancer, are taking a heavy toll. In short, many workers need a change.

From this perspective, working from home holds the promise of a new American dream, opening the door to a better way of life while maintaining or even expanding our standard of living. Of course there are problems and adjustments to contend with, but in most cases they're outweighed by basic advantages.

We call today's home-based people "open-collar workers" because the comfort of being able to dress casually symbolizes the freedom, the convenience, and the flexibility of earning your living in your own home. This is in contrast to a Robert Half International survey that showed the vast majority of business establishments expect male employees to show up wearing neckties. Women's equivalents to neckties are, of course, high heels. Today's new open-collar workers, however, often can wear what we've been tempted to designate as the official work-from-home uniform—sweat suits, athletic shoes, and jeans.

Options for Earning a Living at Home

Working from home is actually not a modern invention. In the Middle Ages and Renaissance, European merchants located their shops and artisans their work areas on the main floors of their homes. Family living was done in a single shared room upstairs.

The mixture of work and home migrated to America. Paul Revere, like many of his time, did his silversmithing in the front of his home in Boston. You can see that on the Freedom Trail today. Some of you may have had grandparents who operated mom-and-pop businesses, living either upstairs or in the back of their store.

In the late 1800s, however, the Industrial Revolution's demand for workers drew people from their homes and farms to staff factories and offices. The advent of the automobile helped make work at home unfashionable except for writers, artists, and some salespeople. However, history has a way of repeating itself. So by 1980 when we began writing *Working from Home*, Alvin Toffler was predicting in his book *The Third Wave* an upsurge in what he called "electronic cottagers," people who would be working from home in a computerized information age. And indeed, today's information-centered society has opened many opportunities for people to work at home, with or without a computer.

After-Hours Work

The largest and fastest-growing number of people setting up home offices are being called after-hours workers because these corporate employees bring their work home after normal working hours. It's no wonder their numbers are swelling. A recent *Fortune* magazine poll of five hundred chief executive officers revealed that the majority expects their subordinates to put in more hours than they did ten years ago. Fifty- and sixty-hour weeks are common. The result is 16 million "after-hours" home offices and many overstressed employees who are thinking about another way of living and working.

Once someone starts taking work home and has set up a working office, it becomes tempting to spend more and more time there. So we find after-hours work often leads to taking office work home during the daylight hours as well, and, even more frequently, it leads to a growing number of sideline home businesses.

Ken Camp, a systems consultant for AT&T, is an example of this process. He began taking after-hours work home when AT&T offered substantial discounts on personal computers to its employees. He bought a computer and found he could leave the office around 5:00 PM, have dinner with his family, and put in a couple of hours of work before his favorite prime time television shows. He found he had fewer interruptions at home than at the office, so eventually he talked his supervisor into letting him work from home two days a week.

Before long he began moonlighting. For the past two years he has made a modest profit from a part-time consulting business helping small businesses on office automation. He envisions that one day he'll leave his job and run his consulting business full time.

Working a Salaried Job at Home

Three million employees now work at home during normal business hours, according to Link Resources. This fast-growing part of the working-from-home population is made up of salaried workers, sometimes called "telecommuters," who spend some portion of every workweek at home. This has many advantages for both employees and employers.

Jane Minogue, a technical writer for CompuCorp, is such a person. She began telecommuting when she was expecting her first child. "I didn't want the stress of driving to and from work every day while I was pregnant, and I wanted to be with my baby after he was born. My boss didn't want to lose me, so when I suggested working at home, he said okay."

Like many telecommuters, Jane works at home most of each week, at the office for the remainder.

You don't have to use a computer or work in a high-tech field, however, to work a job at home. "Low-tech" organizations are using the new work options as well. Pet Organics, which manufactures and distributes natural health products for pets, is entirely homebased. Founder Bob Baxter runs the company from his home, and his six sales representatives work from their homes too. "It's the most practical solution economically," Bob says. "Some of my people work full time, others work part time. Why pay for an office when you can just as easily get the job done from home?"

The future is bright for more such opportunities. Over half of companies surveyed in 1989 by the Conference Board, a business research organization, reported that they planned to begin offering home-based work options. In Chapter 4, "Working for Someone Else," we describe the best routes for taking your job home or, alternatively, finding a new job that lets you work from home.

Full- and Part-Time Home Businesses

The research firm of BIS CAP International finds that 18 million of America's 92 million households—nearly 20 percent—now have income-producing home offices. That number is growing too. You may be surprised to learn that twelve hundred new home businesses begin every day—that's one every 71 seconds! How many new home businesses have begun somewhere since you began reading this book?

Home-based business owners refer to themselves in a variety of ways: as small businesses, home businesses, self-employed, independent contractors, entrepreneurs, freelancers, or consultants.

Bill Spees of South Bend, Indiana, and Nancy and Mark Porter of Los Angeles are examples of this growing trend to strike out on your own.

A licensed professional engineer, Spees and four colleagues created Legendary Systems, Inc., a successful engineering consulting firm. "We started this business after we were forced into early retirement by the recent economic unpleasantness. Except when we're traveling to consult on site with clients, we all work at home," he reports.

The Porters' business, the Susquehanna Hat Company, imports Chinese sun hats. Nancy transforms the hats into brightly colored designer sunwear by dying them in her bathtub. Then she and Mark market them to department stores all over the country. Nancy sees this as just the beginning. "I was a starving artist struggling to feed two kids when I started this company," she says. "Now I'm doing so well, I plan to start manufacturing a second product, a rain hat."

In Chapter 3, "Working for Yourself," you'll meet others like Bill, and Nancy and Mark, who have started their own businesses. You'll find out how they developed the ideas for their businesses and what they do to keep them going and growing.

Why It's Possible Now

If you're already working from home or seriously thinking about it, you're definitely in the right place at the right time. That much is clear. But, you may be wondering, what happened? Why, all of a sudden, are there so many opportunities to work at home? Several factors account for the new options and suggest that working from home is not only here to stay, it's the wave of the future.

Restructuring of the Economy

The United States has changed from a society based on an industrial economy to one based on an information and service economy. By 1980, over half of U.S. workers held information- and service-related positions, employed as bank tellers, clerks, librarians, systems analysts, programmers, accountants, lawyers, therapists, managers, secretaries, doctors, nurses, journalists, trainers, salespersons, or advertising and public relations specialists.

This transformation has brought about significant changes in the way we work. Increasingly, well-educated managers and professionals seeking to climb the corporate pyramid have found mid-level positions disappearing as the corporate hierarchy begins looking less like a pyramid and more like a pancake. With the proper equipment, much of their work can be done as easily in a spare bedroom as in a downtown office.

Industrial and clerical workers are also feeling the squeeze. In the 1980s, over 10 million factory workers lost their jobs. Only three out of five of them found other work. Given frequent plant closings, layoffs, and automation, the specter of unemployment looms over many heads. Workers who are repeatedly downsized, reorganized, purged, and merged are eager to find ways to take control of their careers. As a result, starting a part- or full-time home business, or having a spouse start one, begins to look very attractive.

As futurist David Snyder has observed, there aren't many opportunities for working in your own backyard steel factory. Business didn't lend itself to working from home. By 1980, however, over half of U.S. workers held information- and service-related positions, employed as bank tellers, clerks, librarians, systems analysts, programmers, accountants, lawyers, therapists, managers, secretaries, doctors, nurses, journalists, trainers, salespersons, or advertising and public relations specialists. With the proper equipment, much of their work can be done as easily in a spare bedroom as in a downtown office.

So while economic restructuring is causing problems of dislocation and dissatisfaction, it's also creating the solutions. As industries consolidate into a few large corporations on the one hand and splinter into a multitude of smaller companies on the other, the mass market is narrowing into definable niche markets that can be easily served by small companies and even by self-employed individuals. And one result is that one out of three new businesses today is started at home.

Geologist Thomas Ballard was working for the Burlington Northern Railroad in Northglenn, Colorado, when the minerals industry took a downturn. Suddenly he had to fend for himself. Having what he calls a prospector's spirit, Ballard decided to stay in the mining business by creating a limited partnership that acquires properties and then leases them to large mining companies.

Lila Hexner was a manager for Northern Energy Corporation in Cambridge, Massachusetts, when the company's business outlook turned sour. She decided to explore an idea she had. Using the managerial skills she'd acquired, she began lining up experts in many fields and assembling a computer database of their names. She then approached corporations she thought would be interested in using their services and The Consulting Exchange was born. She's been in her home business seven years and earns over $50,000 a year.

Landscaping architect C. Thomas Fitzwilliam has a similar story. He was working for a large landscaping company that went under when the Texas economy took a downturn. He had always wanted to have his own business and being out of work provided the impetus to start. He now operates Fitzwilliam Landscaping and Irrigation from his home in Arlington, Texas.

Changing Demographics

As the bulk of today's population is entering its thirties and forties, these babyboomers have reached the age when people seek autonomy and promotion to higher levels of responsibility. But with American corporations cutting back and flattening out, advancement opportunities are shrinking. So achievement-minded babyboomers are striking out into their own business ventures. As a result, Tom Miller of Link Resources projects that the number of people working from home in all categories will swell to 35.8 million in 1992 and 38.8 million in 1993.

Harry Brawley had been an electrical engineer for twenty-five years when he decided his future could be brighter if he were on his own. His eight-year-old home-based company, Sigea Systems, produces software that automates electronic mail.

As Don Crescimanno neared forty, he began to feel tied down by corporate life. So he left it behind to start a clearinghouse that informs subscribers about upcoming events in Honolulu.

Like many women, market researcher Elizabeth Donovan bumped into the corporate "glass ceiling" in her early thirties. When she asked for a raise she was told she was earning enough for a woman of her age. At the encourage-ment of her accountant, she left her job to start her own market research firm. Over the past seven years she's turned her home-based business into a $600,000-a-year income working all by herself.

Sophisticated Information Technology

The availability and ever-decreasing cost of compact electronic office equip-ment in the form of computers and high-speed communications have made it possible to conduct business as easily from home as anywhere. When we began working from home, the most advanced equipment suitable for a home office was an IBM Selectric typewriter and an answering machine that half the callers hung up on. Since that time, personal computers, modems, fax machines, laser printers, and briefcase-sized copy machines make working from home as productive, efficient, and competitive as it is in any office.

Many manufacturers like AT&T, Canon, Fuji, IBM, Packard-Bell, Pana-sonic, and Sharp are designing products specifically for home offices. And you will find special home office sections in any number of retail stores today.

People can literally live anywhere and transact their business in style.

The owner of a skip-tracing agency does business from his home in the Virgin Islands, communicating daily by computer with his main office in Washington, D.C.

Thirty-year-old Steven Roberts, inventor, author, and computer specialist, has made his home on an "electronic bicycle." He bicycles across the country with two computers he uses to write and transmit his work to book and magazine publishers.

Thanks to a computer, Rohn Engh left the hassles of life in a large metro-politan area. Behind his barn in rural Osceola, Wisconsin, he now publishes *Photoletter*, an electronic newsletter that pairs photographers with photo edi-tors of magazines and other publications. The personal computer creates hun-dreds of business opportunities like Engh's that can easily be started and operated at home. With small computers, home businesses like these have many of the capabilities once reserved only for organizations with many em-ployees or large mainframe computers.

Larry Nickel, director of data processing for a publishing company, offers an example of how a computer can give birth to a home business. He says, "I started writing programs for myself for fun, but then someone at a computer club offered to hire me to help write a program. I did the job, and when I wanted to get a more powerful computer I decided I could make it pay for itself." He started moonlighting at home by creating N2 Data Serv, a com-pany providing data-processing services. His wife, Nancy, saw potential for a full-scale operation and quit her job in real estate to manage the company. They now have their new computer *and* what has become a thriving home business.

The computer and improving communications technology also offer job and business opportunities to those who cannot work outside the home because of physical or family limitations. Georgia Griffith, who is blind and deaf, uses her computer and a machine that prints computer Braille to work from her home in Lancaster, Ohio, as a music proofreader for the Library of Congress. Doing word processing for American Express, through the company's Project Homebound in New York, Joseph Wynn is able to make more than three times the money he received from Social Security disability. In tiny Reardan, Washington, Bruce Johnson produces computer graphics at home on his Apple computer. Confined to a wheelchair by a high school football injury, he finds this a feasible and satisfying way for him to work.

Work Force Trends

Another result of corporate mergers and downsizing is an increasing demand for part-time or freelance consultants, researchers, and designers. This demand has created a new category of employees collectively referred to as the "contingent work force."

Loosely defined, the contingent work force includes part-timers, leased employees, temporary workers, business services employees, and the self-employed. Their numbers have grown dramatically since 1980—up 28 percent. For some like Wendy Perkins, author of *Temporarily Yours,* "temping" has become a way of life, and a route to self-sufficiency. Wendy, who left her job as a stockbroker to seek greater self-expression, considers herself to be an independent contractor and has worked for over two hundred and fifty companies.

Beleaguered by the high cost of doing business, some corporations have actively helped the entrepreneurial exodus along. Rank Xerox, a London-based subsidiary of the Xerox Corporation, and Connecticut Mutual Life Insurance Company have developed programs to encourage middle managers in areas such as purchasing, personnel, and planning to quit their jobs and sign on as part-time outside contractors. A number of occupations such as medical transcription, instructional design, and notereader/scopist work are becoming largely cottage industries.

New Pressures/New Values

With growing numbers of two-career couples, singles, and single-parent families, both men and women are feeling the pressure of having to juggle many conflicting demands on their personal and professional lives. Almost a third of Americans say they feel rushed and two-thirds suffer from frequent stress. Many burn out on their jobs and on their lifestyles. And it's no wonder. Even weekends seem to be shrinking as job responsibilities, errands, and housekeeping all get squeezed into the two days that were once reserved for recreation and relaxation.

As a result of these pressures, people are looking for greater control over their time and more flexible work arrangements. Nearly eight out of ten American men and women would sacrifice rapid career advancement in order to spend more time with their families. A recent survey reported in *USA Today* showed that the love of one's family has become the value Americans cherish most. So they're opting for home and hearth—family, health, and personal satisfaction.

Today's workers are also looking for new rewards from their work. They want more meaningful, satisfying work and they want to work with people they respect. These priorities have come to matter more than money or opportunities to advance.

In search of a more rewarding life-style, increasing numbers of people are determined to become their own boss or to work more independently. Repeatedly as we travel across the country, we hear people saying things like: "I've been told 'It's none of your business,' so often that I've decided to start my own business." Or "I want to set my own hours and keep what I earn for myself. I'm tired of the rat race. I'm fed up with nine-to-five."

Gil Gordon's experience is not uncommon. After nine years, he left his position as a personnel manager to start his own management consulting firm; he had become disillusioned with corporate life. "The jobs I could be promoted to didn't look that attractive. They all involved managing rather than doing. Now I'm not working any less, but my attitude is different. I'm happy. The biggest satisfaction is knowing I'm doing something important."

Working from home holds the promise for having it all—meaningful work and more time to be with family and loved ones. The potential rewards are great, but what is it really like and would it be right for you? In the next chapter, we'll explore these issues and suggest ways to prepare yourself to work successfully from home.

Chapter Digest

1. Nearly twenty-seven million people are trading in the daily commute to work at least part time from the comfort of their home. And the number is growing every day. Over five million people began doing job-related work from home in 1989.

2. We call these home-based people "open-collar workers" because the comfort of being able to dress casually symbolizes the freedom, the convenience, and the flexibility of earning your living in your own home. This is in contrast to a Robert Half International survey that showed the vast majority of business establishments expect male employees to show up wearing neckties and women to wear high heels.

3. The options for working from home today range from bringing work home after hours to catch up on work and still be near your family to working full- or part-time at home for a salary or starting a full- or part-time business from your home.

4. This mass exodus home is occurring because of changes in the society that make working from home feasible and desirable.

5. The shift from an industrial to an information economy means the work we do can often be done from home as well as anywhere.

6. As industries consolidate into a few large corporations, on the one hand, and splinter into a multitude of smaller companies, on the other hand, the mass market is narrowing into definable niche markets that can be easily served by the small one-to-two-person business.

7. Sophisticated and compact communications technology like personal computers, faxes, modems, and copy machines can make the home office as productive and professional as any office environment.

8. Changing values toward more meaningful work and a desire for more personal and family time is fueling the drive to find an alternative to the 9:00 to 5:00 work regimen.

9. For growing numbers of people, working from home is becoming the new American Dream.

Resources

Books

Ideas and Information: Managing in a High Tech World. Arnold Penzias. New York: Simon & Schuster, 1989.

Information Payoff: The Transformation of Work in the Electronic Age. Paul A. Strassman. New York: The Free Press, 1985.

Megatrends 2000: Ten New Directions for the 1990s. John Naisbitt. New York: William Morrow and Company, 1990.

Audiotape

How to Succeed at Working From Home. Paul and Sarah Edwards. Harper Audio (60 mins.).

CHAPTER
TWO

■ ■

Is Working from Home
for You?

"It's the only way to go! I'd never go
back!" That's the spontaneous reaction many have to working from home.
But others can't wait to get back; they miss the office. Are such different
reactions surprising? Hardly. We've all been groomed to work in an office
setting, from the first day we started school. You got up, got dressed, ate
breakfast, and went to class. You sat at a desk all day long and worked at
various tasks and projects with others around you. When the bell rang you
packed up your things and went home. Without the bell, this description
could fit any day at the office.

When you venture into working from home, these familiar routines go the
way of the coal chute and the hitching post. You get up in the morning, and
you don't have to be anywhere. Do you get dressed? When do you start
working? Do you work at your desk or on the couch? There may be no one
there but you, unless your kids pop in or a neighbor drops by, and then what
do you do? In every case, it's up to you. No wonder people have such diverse
reactions! The whole experience is different from everything we're used to.

Some people flourish with the freedom from old structures, and other
people flounder. Some handle the change matter-of-factly, while others find it
profoundly upsetting. Tina Lenert took to working from home like a fish
returned to water. "I loved it from the moment I started. I never missed my
old job for a minute. And honestly, I can't think of any real problems I've had
working here."

Reporter Duane Tompkins's experience was quite different. "When the
editor told us we could work from home and send in our copy by computer, I was excited. It sounded great. But it wasn't what I expected. I became

disillusioned right away. I missed the hustle and bustle of the pressroom and everyone being up against the deadline together. Without anyone else around I found myself goofing off, and I was always at the refrigerator. I think I gained twenty pounds before I finally decided to move back downtown."

Carlin Stevenson had a similar experience when she left a real estate agency to create her own company at home. Her reaction was different, however. "I didn't want to go back. I really wanted to work at home. I just hung in there. It was a difficult year, but after a while I made the adjustment. Now I have many professional friends, and I certainly have accomplished more than I would have staying where I was. I had to learn a whole new way of operating, though, and it took some time."

What You Can Expect

For those with creative business minds, working from home can be the ticket to realizing their potential. For single parents and many women, working at home facilitates juggling family and career. For fathers, it can lead to more time and involvement with their children. For others, it's a step toward goals like gaining financial independence, or moving to a rural area, or simply escaping from the exhaust fumes, crowded trains, and crime-filled streets that bedevil the urban commuter.

Working from home can provide the means for stretching a tight budget or maintaining an accustomed life-style in the face of inflation. Couples who have invested time, energy, and money in building meaningful relationships find that when they work from home they see more of each other. For the retired, or the increasing number of people considering early retirement, working from home becomes a way of contributing, of staying alive and vibrant. And for many with handicaps or disabilities, it's the door to self-sufficiency and a productive future.

Working from home can be the answer to many dreams. But what can you really expect? What are the actual benefits you may enjoy and what problems might you encounter?

Most People Love It

While working from home is not for everyone, most people doing it are quick to recommend their life-styles. Tom Miller of Link Resources, who has been conducting the National Work-at-Home survey for years, finds that about one out of five people has a "complaint"; the rest are happy. *Home Office Computing* readers are even happier. Of 1,100 readers responding to a 1989 survey, 89 percent said they would recommend working from home to others, and 100 percent of the home-based business owners said they were happier at home than in a corporate office.

After giving a speech in Washington, D.C., we met a woman in the audience who does data entry at home. She told us enthusiastically, "It's the best thing that ever happened in my life." A man in the same audience piped in that after being self-employed for several years, "I'm unfit for employment now. I could never work for someone else again." These comments form a familiar refrain.

You Have Greater Freedom, Flexibility, and Control

When we ask people what they like about working from home, over and over again they tell us it's the freedom. They cherish the flexibility, convenience, and control it gives them over their lives. As Ann McIndoo of Computer Training Services says, "The bottom line is freedom. The side effect is I'm well paid."

Freedom means different things to different people, however. To Javier Ferrier, who transcribes court reporters' notes in Garden Grove, California, it means "the freedom to set my own hours. I work the hours I want." For Lewis Mann, a life and health insurance broker, freedom means "to work as hard or smart or casually as I want." Phoenix scriptwriter and audio/video producer Bill Burkett finds the freedom of working from home means "I can do it on my own terms." Or as Ivan Misner, founder of The Business Network Associates, says, it's "the freedom to make my own decisions and be in control of my professional destiny."

For designer Sandra Stratton of Kahului, Hawaii, and Robert F. Dobnick of Chicago, who does space planning for wholesale showrooms, it's the creative freedom they love about working from home. To David Chazin, who operates a Las Vegas laser cartridge remanufacturing company, it's freedom from the corporate world, "freedom to set my own direction." Washington, D.C., housing consultant David Freed prizes the "freedom, to be able to do socially meaningful work." And to Edward L. Svadlenka, who operates a carpet-cleaning and window-washing service in Hometown, Illinois, it "gives me the freedom to take time off."

Your control extends to when you work and to what you put first in importance. You no longer need react to a boss's urgency like a fire department responding to an alarm. You can create an office with the lighting, colors, furnishings, music, sound or silence you desire. You're not a captive of modular office systems that provide minimal privacy and require you to converse in hushed tones. And even though there are family and household distractions, for almost everyone there are many fewer interruptions than at an office. You're away from office politics, backbiting, and those disagreeable people you would never invite into your home.

You Get More Done:
Productivity Increases an Average of 20 Percent

Speaking of the growing trend of people working from home, President George Bush observed, "Millions have already found their productivity actually increases when they work nearer the people they're really working for—

their families at home." Indeed, research consistently indicates productivity rises 15 to 25 percent when work is done at home in telecommuting programs, according to telecommuting consultant Gil Gordon.

It's well established that the self-employed are the most productive people in the economy. With fewer interruptions, meetings, and office politics, it's not surprising that both the employed and the self-employed get more done at home. A study of 90,000 managers by Booz, Allen and Hamilton found that managers waste 25 percent of their time. Another study by Accountemps found 34 percent of the average employee's day was frittered away. Still another study indicated that employers lose no less than four and a half hours a week per employee as a result of lateness, long lunch hours, and working another job or business during office hours.

Psychological factors contribute to the productivity gains of working from home. People experience more of a sense of ownership of their work, gaining a new feeling of pride in accomplishment. They work at their own pace. If you're an early bird person, because of the flexible hours, you can begin your work early in the morning during your hours of peak performance. But if your body functions best after midnight, it's your choice to work then. When you feel better, you do better.

Lucy and Frank Knights, who both work from home for an Eastern utility company, agree with those findings: "We're surprised more companies aren't letting their people work at home. This is like owning your own business. You get more done. We're working harder than we did at the office, but we're enjoying it more."

When San Francisco computer consultant William Slavin started his business at home, he explained the gain this way: "The idea of being an entrepreneur is a real thrill to me. I really like it. I work more and I get more done. But instead of it being drudgery, I'm driven by pure joy."

Costs Go Down

At the same time that productivity goes up, costs go down. Think what you save if you don't drive to an office every day. You save wear and tear on your car, and you probably save on auto insurance. If you're putting 20,000 miles a year on your car, your mileage might drop to 12,000. Last year, Hertz calculated the cost of driving 20,000 miles a year in a Chevrolet Celebrity to be 28 cents a mile. So you'd be saving $2,200 a year, or almost $200 a month.

Pete Silver, a marketing consultant in Gainesville, Florida, told us he got a note from his dry cleaner asking, "Where are you?" As people go from white collars to open collars, the washing machine takes over for the dry cleaner.

If you operate your business from home you can usually keep your overhead down so you can break even more quickly in starting up. Some businesspeople use what they save on office rent to buy a house or an apartment building.

Working from home is also a legitimate way to keep more of the money you earn from the tax collector. You can also save money on the obligatory office collections, luncheons, and the purchase of candies and cookies from other people's children. Some people miss these social functions. For them, this is a trade-off. It's a matter of whether you think of them with fondness or as a pain in the neck.

Even when they cover equipment costs, companies usually save money by allowing employees to work at home. And for the self-employed it means only one monthly rent or mortgage payment. In cities, a cost of $12,000 a year for office space is not uncommon. Particularly when you're first starting, that expense can mean the difference between making a profit or closing the business.

Income Can Go Up

People who work from home on their own feel a sense of financial independence. They can say goodbye to what Mark Malone of the American Business Management Association calls the "40-40 plan"—forty minutes in traffic for forty hours a week. To that we add a third "40"—doing it for forty years. Joyce Brooks-Wiley, a computer graphics consultant and systems analyst, says, "My business has been good enough to allow me to improve my standard of living about threefold and meet lots of interesting people at the same time. I can run my office the way I like, hire and fire, and wine and dine, as well as be wined and dined." Greg Souser, who operates Tri-State Mobile Power Wash Company from his home in Grand Prairie, Texas, says, "I like the personal and financial freedom to have fun while I work and there's no ceiling on my income."

The sky's the limit when you're in a business from your home. How much you make depends on your own ingenuity, determination, and willingness to work at it. When Lynie Arden was doing research for a cover story for *Home Office Computing* on home-based millionaires, she found more home-based million-dollar businesses than she could include in the article.

While most home-based businesses don't reach six-figure incomes, the financial gains can nevertheless be substantial. When the White House asked us to talk about the issues concerning people who work from home, we asked members of the Working from Home Forum on CompuServe for their comments. This message from free-lance writer David Palmer gives a perspective on the importance to many people of what could be considered even modest income gains.

"I hope you can enlighten the folks on the Hill that self-employment is no longer synonymous with doctor, lawyer, or accountant. It also includes a growing number of displaced homemakers, single parents, factory workers, miners, and others whose skills are either no longer marketable in industry or who live in an area where self-employment is the only alternative to a service job stocking shelves in a chain drug store or flipping hamburgers. To a single parent with two or three kids, being self-employed and making $15,000 to $20,000 a year looks a whole lot better than being "employed" at $4.50 an hour."

You Save Time

How much time do you spend commuting to work every day? Look at the chart below to see how much of your irreplaceable time is spent driving in rush-hour traffic. The average commute in the United States is still about twenty minutes each way. That amounts to four forty-hour weeks a year! Many people in large cities and even those in small communities commute far greater distances. It's no longer unusual for people to tell us about one- to two-hour commutes each way. (In speaking recently to an audience of Los Angeles County employees, Paul cited a *Los Angeles Times* study that found the average commute in Los Angeles was twenty-two minutes. He never imagined that would be one of his bigger laugh lines.)

Then there's the time you spend getting dressed to go to work. It may add another five or ten hours a week to get dressed up so you can go sit in traffic. What would you do with the extra ten or fifteen hours a week you spend dressing and driving that no one is paying you for now?

What do people who work from home do with all this time they save? *Home Office Computing* found that two out of three people use it to get more work done. Three out of five spend it on exercising more. And, of course, many spend more time with their families.

And what do people do on their breaks at an office? Have a cigarette, a cup of coffee, eat a snack, go to the restroom. Taking a break at home means you can pet your dog, change the kitty litter box, water your plants, wash your hair, toss a load of laundry into the washing machine, exercise, have your lunch by the pool, start your dinner, watch part of a talk show or a soap, or read a paper or business magazine.

How Much of Your Life Do You Spend Commuting?

Daily One-Way Trip in Minutes	Round Trip	Hours Each Year	Equivalent Number of Forty-Hour Weeks
5	10	40	1
10	20	80	2
15	30	120	3
20	40	160	4
25	50	200	5
30	60	240	6
35	70	280	7
40	80	320	8
45	90	360	9
50	100	400	10
55	110	440	11
60	120	480	12

Stress Goes Down, Health Goes Up

A recent study indicated that heavy traffic is the number one cause of stress in daily life. Number two is frustration from interruptions at the office. Another survey indicated that the most frequent work-related stress for women is having to balance work and family demands. Work from home reduces or eliminates all these major causes of stress.

Other research indicates the more control we feel over our lives, the less stress we experience. Perhaps that's the reason the one quality people want most in a manager is someone who allows them autonomy. Being your own boss is the ultimate in autonomy. Despite working harder and longer hours, most people report their stress level goes down once they are in charge.

Recent medical studies confirm these reports. Despite the hard work and increased productivity involved, working at home produces less stress than working at similar tasks in the office. For example, Nancy Nickel finds that having the flexibility to adjust her hours and her work pace is relaxing. "It's almost like magic. I can tailor my work to what I want to do. I can stop and take a TV break and still get more done. I feel great at the end of the day."

As Jeremy Joan Hewes, author of *Worksteads,* has described, "If you have the safety valve of a walk around the block or a cup of hot homemade soup, you may not feel the pressure of deadlines as strongly as if you were in an office where the people and the energy level are often frantic."

You also avoid common office stress factors like fluorescent lights, ringing telephones, clattering equipment, buzzing conversation, and fighting rush-hour traffic. Financial consultant Michael Fey explains how the difference has affected him: "When I was commuting to and from work, I had to have a glass of wine when I got home to unwind." Now that he works from home he rarely has a drink outside social occasions.

Often it's small things that make big differences in reducing stress. Open-collar workers appreciate not having to put up with other people's smoking. Or, if they smoke, they enjoy the freedom to do so at home. People are glad to be rid of the negative attitudes of co-workers, the gossip, and the office politics that interfere with getting work done, not to mention the frequent meetings that consume a reported 45 percent of managerial and professional time.

It's well established that lower stress means better health. Stress lowers the white blood cell count and the immune system's resistance to disease. Heart disease and high blood pressure, which affect one in four Americans, are acknowledged to be stress-caused diseases. Not only do people working from home experience less of the major causes of stress, they also have more time to exercise and more control over what they eat. So better health is another benefit of working from home.

Family Members See More of One Another

We're in the midst of a mini babyboom right now and many new mothers want to raise their children themselves. By scheduling their work when the children are at school or when they're sleeping, some are able to be full-time parents.

The alternative in the workaday world is day care. Good day-care centers are in short supply and day care is expensive. Working from home may not completely eliminate child-care costs, but it can cut down on day-care costs that often run as much as $500 a month for each child. Because medical research finds toddlers are more at risk of getting serious infections in day-care centers, many parents feel safer having their young children at home.

Graphics designer Mary Stoddard finds having her studio at home makes playing two roles in life more manageable. "I used to have my business downtown, and the children would come there after school, but this is easier. I can stop and talk with them when they come home, and then they can go out to play with their friends. By being here where everything's in one central location, I save on baby-sitting costs and get work done in the time I used to spend driving my kids here and there."

Medical transcriptionist Glenda Noble loves being there when her children get home after school. "It may sound silly but I like being able to give them a snack and be there to answer their questions. Plus, I didn't miss all those 'firsts' that all of us mothers like to see."

For fathers, working at home means more time with family and loved ones. One parent jokingly told us he'd discovered children he'd forgotten he had. Gil Gordon says, "I feel closer to my children. Yes, it's a hassle sometimes, but I'm able to get involved with things other fathers can't."

With growing concerns about street gangs, teen suicide, drugs, and alcoholism, parents of teenagers are also finding working at home helps put their minds at ease. Tax specialist Alsey Graham of Kansas City had worked for the IRS while her daughter was in grade school, but she felt that the teen years were an important time to be there for her daughter. So she left her job to open a tax and bookkeeping service from her home. "If it weren't for my daughter I wouldn't be in business. But I'm glad I did it. You only get one chance with a child. I wanted to do it right." Sales trainer Ray Dunlop of Indianapolis would agree. He found running his business from home "made being a single parent of teenagers a lot easier."

Community Assumes New Importance

The rise of home offices makes a reemergence of community life possible. Three out of five *Home Office Computing* readers report they participate more in community activities as a result of working at home.

As Bob and Stephanie Wilson have found, the neighborhood takes on a new significance when you work at home. "The focus of our friendships and activities used to be in town. Now the focus has shifted. We find our friends and involvements right here in the neighborhood."

Working at home, you experience the events of life in the community. With someone on the block at home every day, the neighborhood becomes a safer place to live. It becomes a friendlier place too. Not having colleagues down the hall to meet at the coffee machine, you may find yourself talking over the back fence to somebody with whom you once had only a nodding acquaintance.

Suddenly, the neighborhood is no longer just a place to come and go from. It's now the center of your daily activities. Clients and customers, perhaps employers and co-workers, pass through it when they visit your office. You patronize nearby businesses like the post office, the print shop, the office-supply store. Perhaps you have business lunches or meetings in the area. As the condition of your community becomes more important to you, you may even find yourself becoming involved in civic activities.

And President George Bush believes working from home is helping communities in a number of other ways. It becomes easier for them to tackle air pollution and, in the process, forgo the impending gridlock on freeways and streets.

It's 100 Percent What You Make It

As you can see, working from home, whether you're salaried or self-employed, means more control over your schedule and your environment than ever before. You are in charge. There is no boss standing over your shoulder. There is no time clock to punch, no bell to tell you when to start and when to stop. There is no procedures manual for working at home—it's up to you. It can be either a dream come true or a nightmare, depending on what you do. It's 100 percent up to you!

Common Problems

Even with these many advantages, most people do report some problems working from home, at least initially. Below are the most common problems as shown by three studies: *The Wall Street Journal*'s American Way of Buying Survey conducted by the Roper Organization that identified *perceptions* about working from home held by 2,002 adults in the general population; the findings of 110 interviews we conducted with home-based business owners questioning them about their biggest problems in working from home; and a *Home Office Computing* survey of 1,100 readers.

Expectations and Reality May Vary

Often the problems people anticipate they will have in working from home are not the same as those they actually encounter. But the good news is that all types of problems occur much less frequently than people fear. For example, you'll notice that the top problem people were concerned about in the Roper study was not even included among the top problems people actually said they had working from home in the other two surveys. Whereas the largest concern expressed in the Roper study was not having necessary office supplies and equipment, this was not reported to be a problem for any of those who actually work from home. And the other anticipated problems that were reported were far less significant than expected.

Overall, the most common problems were these: not being taken seriously, feeling lonely or isolated, separating work and personal life, and self-management. Other problems included space limitations, lack of privacy, lack of time, missing support personnel, child care, and staying out of the refrigerator. You'll notice that many of the most common problems arise from the freedom, flexibility, and autonomy working from home provides.

Being Taken Seriously

In our survey, slightly fewer than one in five home-business people reported a problem with being taken seriously by customers, clients, supervisors, co-workers, colleagues, family, or friends. To some, working from home raises the fear of missing out on promotions, losing touch with the grapevine, and being forgotten when it comes to special projects that could advance a career. Entrepreneurs worry about their professional image and whether their clients will consider a home-based business a substantial one.

Top Problems of Working from Home

Roper Survey—July 1989—Problems *Perceived* by 2,002 Adults about Working from Home

Not having necessary supplies/equipment	51%
Family interruptions	38%
Mixing work and family life	37%
Distracted by household chores	32%
Lack of interaction with co-workers	27%
Not having a regular routine	23%

Edwards Interviews—Spring 1989, Problems Mentioned by 108 Full-Time Home Business Operators

Being taken seriously	18%
Separating work and personal life	13%
Space limitations	12%
Feeling isolated	11%
Lack of privacy	8%
Self-management	8%

Home Office Computing Magazine (HOCM) Survey—February 1989. Problems Mentioned by 1,100 Readers

Distractions from family and friends	21%
Working too much	15%
Finding new clients	13%
Lack of support services	12%
Feeling isolated	10%
Separating work and personal life	7%

Although a few horror stories of lost clients and missed promotions are enough to panic anyone, concerns over credibility are usually much more of a problem initially than in the long run. If you take yourself seriously and project a professional business image, others will take you seriously too. Many home-based businesses work successfully with *Fortune* 500 clients. Employees at home, like technical writer Jane Minogue, are usually pleasantly surprised to find that they continue to advance in their careers. Jane, who initially began working from home to care for her newborn baby, was promoted to a supervisory position while working from home.

In Chapter Three "Working for Yourself," you'll find a list of specific steps you can take to create a substantial business image. In Chapter Four, "Working for Someone Else," we talk about how to keep a high profile in your organization.

Separating Work from Personal Life

Since the whole day is sent under one roof, one to two out of ten people report they have a difficult time juggling the demands of both home and business. They're bothered by family interruptions, housework that needs doing, deliveries and service calls, friends who drop by, barking dogs, and not having a transition period between work and play. They find it hard to switch gears from the computer to Cuisinart and back again.

Although this may sound potentially chaotic, there are many creative solutions presented throughout this book for keeping your personal and professional lives in perspective. Setting up a schedule, finding the right place for your office, getting an answering machine, and arranging for proper child care are just a few you will learn about.

Self-Management

Although research consistently indicates that productivity goes up when people work from home, without the structure of a formal office routine about one in ten people in our survey has a hard time with self-discipline. They report problems with getting out of bed, getting to work, and sticking to business. Some find themselves sneaking in too much TV and taking too many trips to the refrigerator. At the other extreme, the HOCM survey shows that 15 percent have difficulty closing the door on work and leaving it behind at the end of the day. They find work becomes all-consuming because it's always there.

You'll be delighted to find many creative solutions throughout this book which people have developed to help them learn how to manage themselves successfully. We call it developing the "self-management muscle." It means learning to work on a schedule of your own making, putting personal time on your calendar, and having a separate office space that is out of sight and therefore out of mind.

Feeling Isolated

While nearly a third were *concerned* about isolation in the Roper study, only 10 to 12 percent of those in the other surveys actually reported feeling isolated and lonely. They said they missed the social contacts of an office setting. We've found problems with feeling lonely are more likely to occur under three circumstances:

1. A shaky start. Problems with isolation are more common initially, when new open-collar workers aren't fully clear about the direction they're going in with their work. They don't know whether their business or job at home will work out, and there's an initial lack of structure. Once business routines get going and they begin working with clients and colleagues, this problem disappears.

2. Solitary work. Sometimes problems of isolation are related to the fact that the nature of the work involves virtually no personal contact. Nancy Rabbitt, who operates Keyline Graphics, an electronic typesetting and graphic-design service, finds that "sometimes I may not leave the house all day. I mean, literally. If it's a really busy day I may not get out the door, even to get the mail. It can reach a point where grocery shopping is an adventure."

When your work demands long hours alone, however, feelings of isolation can arise whether you are working from home or in an outside office. As writer Marsha Seligson and career counselor Naomi Stephan found, moving into an office building didn't solve this problem. They both tried renting office space but eventually moved back home. The benefits in terms of contact in an impersonal building weren't sufficient to offset the added costs and commuting time.

When working from home, it's important to have this kind of "people break" even if there are not lots of friends or acquaintances right outside the door or down the hall. You need to replace these office contacts with routine phone calls and personal visits that you initiate yourself. Like many people working from home, both Marsha and Naomi created a support network of friends and colleagues they can call on. You'll find more information about how to create such a network in Chapter 16.

3. A social personality. About one-sixth of the American population is primarily motivated by the social interaction of their work. For these individuals, talking and dealing with others is the central focus and highlight of their day and working from home can become a problem indeed. Knowing this, few such people are attracted to working from home. They're only tempted to do so when illness, child-care needs, or some other necessity requires them to consider becoming home based. If you fall into this category, we recommend that you do whatever you can to stay in an office setting or, when that is not possible, arrange to have partners or employees who work with you at home.

Ten Tips for Avoiding the Common Problems of Working from Home

1. **Be sure all your printed material communicates that you're a serious business or professional.** This includes using professionally designed business cards, letterheads, and stationery.
2. **Have a separate business telephone line.** Keep your residential line for your personal use and for your family. Don't allow children to answer your business line.
3. **Answer the telephone with a pleasant, businesslike greeting** that communicates you're delighted to hear every caller.
4. **Have a physically separate space for your office**—a separate room if possible. Don't try to make the most intimate room in your home—your bedroom—also your office.
5. **Give yourself permission to treat household interruptions as if you were at the office.** If you need child care help, arrange it, particularly for children under five.
6. **Establish a work schedule.** You may work more hours at home than you would at an office, but don't work morning, noon, *and* night. Establish time for yourself and your family.
7. **Develop your self-management muscle by setting goals for every day.** Work on those goals first since there is never enough time to do everything. Don't get bogged down reacting to interruptions and demands. Think about what it means to separate the *important* from the *urgent*.
8. **Don't allow paperwork and office equipment to take over your home.** Use space-saving storage systems; if you need help, consult with a professional organizer.
9. **Have the attitude that you work *from* home, not *at* home.** Get out of the house at least once a day. Remember, your home is a base, not a prison.
10. **Get the support** of family members, clients, and, if you're employed, co-workers and your management.

Deciding Whether Working from Home Is for You

Despite facing these problems, experience clearly shows that the difficulties you may encounter need not be roadblocks if you are sufficiently motivated to find a way over, under, or around them.

So how will you know if working from home is for you? Who is suited to work from home? We've talked in depth with hundreds of individuals to determine the answer to this question and what we discovered surprised us.

Indeed there are certain personal qualities that seem to make working from home easier, particularly at first. As a general rule, those who are most successful are self-starters who like the line of work they're in, know what they want, and are determined to achieve it. They enjoy working independently and are comfortable with minimal structure and ambiguity. They are capable of establishing and following their own schedules and deadlines.

Surprisingly, however, we find that while these attributes make it easier and less stressful to begin working from home, they are not prerequisites for success. Many people working from home successfully and with great satisfaction did not initially have these attributes. Apparently the ability to work from home and to find it rewarding is not primarily a matter of being "suited" for it. It's more a matter of wanting to do it enough to find ways to make it work.

Like many others, home-based producer Ellie Kahn is not particularly well suited for working from home. She says, "Actually I would rather be employed and work in an office. I'm more suited for an office structure and a boss directing me and setting priorities, but my work as an oral historian is very important to me and I have yet to find anyone who will hire me to do it. So I'm learning how to be my own boss and it's worth it, because I love what I do." Had Ellie listened to conventional wisdom she might have decided she would be unable to work from home before giving herself a chance to see what she could do.

Actually, most of us not initially have the *mind set, skill set,* or *knowledge set* to work successfully on our own because we've had so little opportunity to acquire them. But research indicates that achievement is one human quality that's not determined by innate capacities. It's something we can learn from the experience of doing.

Since it's obvious that you too have some desire to work from your home or you wouldn't be reading this book, we suggest that instead of asking yourself whether you are already suited for work from home, ask instead how much you want to work from home and to what extent you are willing to learn how to do what it takes.

What Does It Take?

In addition to being a producer of a good product or a provider of a good service, working from home requires that you wear many other hats, some of which may be unfamiliar to you. Whether you are self-employed or working from home on a salary, you will undoubtedly need to carry out all the following roles at one time or another.

- **The Executive.** Plans for the future, defines and schedules what you will be doing, determines how and when you will do it, and monitors to see that you are doing it adequately.

- **The Supervisor.** Makes sure you get to work, stick to business, and don't burn yourself out overworking.
- **The Administrator and Purchasing Agent.** Equips and supplies your office, handles correspondence, answers the phone, schedules repairs, runs errands, files and manages financial record-keeping, obtains insurance, and so on.
- **The Security Guard.** Establishes clear boundaries between work and home so that family and friends don't interfere with your work and work doesn't interfere with your personal life.
- **Public Relations, Marketing, and Sales Manager.** Gets the word out about what you do, why people need you, and promotes you so your business thrives or your career advances.

And you may have to be the janitor too!

How Motivated Are You?

Since motivation and a willingness to learn seem to be the most important variables for success at working from home, first ask yourself on a scale of 1 to 10 (with 1 being "not at all" and 10 being "more than anything in the world"), "How much do you want to work from home?" The greater your desire above a 7, the more likely you will be motivated to do whatever it takes to master the many required roles mentioned above to succeed at working from home. The lower your score is below 7, the more important it will be that you already have the attitudes, skills, aptitudes, and knowledge you need before you start.

If you seriously want to work from home, you will probably be able to find a way to make it work for you. In fact, many people tell us that one of the greatest joys of having decided to go off on their own and work from home has been the satisfaction that comes from meeting new challenges and accomplishing things they never imagined they could do.

Assessing Your Potential for
Working Happily from Home

Here's a brief survey to help you identify what you could encounter, and some clues for minimizing problems, before you go to the trouble and expense of actually moving your office home. If you're already working at home, the survey will provide some insight into problems or ambivalent feelings you may be having and what you might need to do to improve the situation.

The survey takes only a few minutes to complete. Read the directions, make your choices, and then read on to interpret the results.

A Working-from-Home Suitability Survey

Below are descriptions of five offices. Choose the office you would most like to work in. Mark that office with the number 1. Then rank the other offices from 2 to 5 in order of their interest to you. Just be sure to include all the offices as you rank your preferences.

_____ **Office A:** Walking into this warm, comfortable environment, you feel right at home. This office has a friendly, lived-in feeling. Cushioned chairs and couches are gathered around a casual seating area. The hum of conversation fills the air.

_____ **Office B:** Everything about this office is unexpected. It's not like any workplace you've seen before. There's a sense of surprise and drama that makes just being here an adventure. The hustle and bustle of excitement fills the air.

_____ **Office C:** The first thing you notice about this office is that there's a place for everything, and everything is in its place. There is a sense of history and tradition about it. Everything down to the last detail is as it should be and exactly as you would expect it.

_____ **Office D:** This office is first-class. There has been no compromise in quality. Excellence is clearly the standard, and from the awards tastefully displayed around the room, you know it has been achieved. Whatever is done here is done extraordinarily well.

_____ **Office E:** This commanding office communicates a forcefulness that gets your attention. When you walk in the door you straighten up and take notice. It conveys a no-nonsense approach that demands results. The feeling of power in the office leaves a lasting impression.

Adapted from the *PSE Preference Survey and Motivation Profile,* © 1982, Paul and Sarah Edwards.

Interpreting Your Score

Each of the offices described in the survey represents one of the basic needs people seek to fill through work. By listing them in order of preference, you are indicating which needs are more important to you at this time in your life. Your choices provide some hints about how you're likely to respond to the most common concerns people have about working from home.

If Your Rating Was:

	1 or 2	4 or 5
Office A: *Will You Be Lonely?*	You may miss working with other people at an office. You'll probably like working from home better if your work brings people into your home or takes you out to work with others. You can create your own opportunities to get together with people. Schedule frequent meetings with customers and colleagues at meal times or get active in various organizations and associations. *See Chapter 16.*	You are probably well suited for working at home. Relating to others is not the most important part of your work. You will probably not be unduly stressed by leaving the social interaction of an office setting. But to maintain your social skills and to prevent becoming isolated from people in your field, you need to schedule face-to-face contacts with other people.
Office B: *Will You Be Bored?*	Your work itself had better be exciting and stimulating. Otherwise, you'll find working at home could be too dull. Running your own business, however, with the challenges and risks of entrepreneuring could keep you sufficiently stimulated. *See Chapter 3.*	You may enjoy escaping office pressures and hubbub by retreating to work in the quiet of a home/office. The demands and uncertainties of running your own business could be more stimulating than you want, however, so perhaps you'd be more comfortable working from home on a salary or a long-term contract. *See Chapter 4.*

If Your Rating Was:

	1 or 2	4 or 5
Office C: *Will You Be Disorganized?*	You probably like a well-organized environment and value the order that comes from attention to detail. If you're able to create and stick to your own schedules and organization, you may well enjoy working from home, where how you organize things is completely your responsibility. All the filing, scheduling, mailing, and cleaning will be up to . . . guess who?	You may enjoy the freedom from imposed schedules and rules that working from home offers. At home you can work anytime, day or night; the work's always there. You can leave things messy or organize them as you wish. Left entirely on your own, however, you may find your desire for order will increase somewhat, and you will need to motivate yourself to be sufficiently organized to get your work done. *See Chapters 11 through 15.*
Office D: *Will You Goof Off?*	You may be well suited for working from home because you're motivated to work hard and set high standards for yourself. You probably won't need a supervisor to keep you working all day. You may actually accomplish more with the independence of doing it all your own way. You could have a tendency to overwork, however, and if your other top choice was Office A, you may need to find a way to get recognition from others for doing a good job. *See Chapters 12 and 16.*	You may find it difficult to work at home. You may start working later in the morning and stop earlier in the afternoon. Your attention may drift away from your work to nearby attractions like the refrigerator, the garden, or the TV. You may not be as productive as you would be with the structure and supervision of an office setting. *See Chapter 12.*

	If Your Rating Was:	
	1 or 2	4 or 5
Office E: *Will You Feel Less Important?*	You could enjoy being in command of your work and your destiny without the encumbrances of an outside organization. But you might miss motivating and directing others to action and feel limited by the confines of a spare bedroom. If so, you may want to consider building a full-fledged organization that you can run from your own home. *See Chapter 15.*	You may feel relief from the power games and maneuvers of office politics and enjoy the freedom to work on your own.

As you can see, whether you'll find working at home a pain or a pleasure will depend primarily on you. While the survey may not determine whether working at home is right or wrong for you, it highlights some of the issues you may encounter and gives some direction on what to do about them.

Other Considerations

Here are some other questions to answer in deciding to make the move home:

Do you enjoy spending time in your home?
Is there adequate space for your work?
Do you like your neighborhood?
Do you get along with your neighbors?
Are the business resources you need available within a reasonable distance?
How will others you live with react to your working from home?
Will you enjoy being around them more often?
How will your customers or clients, your boss or co-workers feel about your working from home?

A strong negative response to any of these questions could mean that you may have serious adjustments to make. Fortunately, however, working from home affords great flexibility, so if you want to make the move, the chances are you will be able to find some way to accommodate your particular needs and circumstances.

A trial week or even a weekend of working at home can help you discover what you need to do to make it practical for you. Once you start experimenting, you may find you'd rather fight than switch back to an outside office. The rest of this book will help you deal with the problems that can arise and with how to make the necessary adjustments for success in working from home.

Chapter Digest

1. As a general rule, those who thrive on working from home are self-starters who like the line of work they are in and enjoy working independently. They're goal-directed achievers and are comfortable with minimal structure, capable of setting up and following their own schedules and deadlines.

2. The most important variable in whether you will work from home successfully, however, is how much you want to do it. Many people who do not initially have the proper characteristics work quite happily from home once they master the skills necessary.

3. The greatest rewards of working from home are freedom, flexibility, and control; increased productivity, lower costs, increased income potential; and times savings, reduced stress, and more time with families.

4. The problems people worry most about are often not the problems they actually encounter, and the number and extent of the problems are much lower than anticipated.

5. The most common problems people encounter are being taken seriously, being distracted by family and friends, feeling lonely or isolated, separating work and personal life, and self-management. Other problems include finding clients, space limitations, lack of privacy, lack of time, missing support personnel, child care, and staying out of the refrigerator.

6. The flexibility of working from home usually affords many alternatives for solving these problems to your satisfaction.

7. The Working-from-Home Suitability Survey highlights the issues you are most likely to experience and gives some direction as to what to do about them.

CHAPTER
THREE

■■■■■■■■■■■■■■■■■■■■■■■■

Working for Yourself:
Full Time and Part Time

Estimates are that for every person who actually starts a business, three to ten more are thinking about it. Perhaps we all have a little bit of the entrepreneur in us, a secret wish tucked away somewhere to become a consultant, write a book, open a little shop, sell our prize spaghetti sauce, or invent a better mousetrap.

In the comfort of your living space, you can now take your ideas and entrepreneurial desires out of the back rooms of your mind and start your own business. Actually, this is the easiest route to working from home, and the business advantages are encouraging:

- **The sky's the limit on your potential income** when you're your own boss. Your business can be anything from a part-time sideline effort that brings in several extra thousand dollars a year to a multimillion-dollar enterprise like Hewlett-Packard, a company that began at home in a garage.

- **Starting a business at home keeps the initial costs down** so you can get established more easily, turn a profit sooner, and increase your chances of success.

- **You can save $7,000 to $20,000 a year** on office rental at current rental rates.

- **You can turn personal expenses like rent, furniture, and telephone costs into tax-deductible items** if you meet IRS requirements (see Chapter 10).

- **You can test a new business idea,** or see whether you like running your own business, without much risk. In fact, by trying out the idea from home, you can tailor the amount of risk to your financial circumstances.

Going Out on Your Own: What It Takes

You've probably heard it said that entrepreneurs are a special breed. Some observers, like psychologist Alan Jacobwitz, have even gone so far as to say that entrepreneurs are born and not made, or at least that their early environment predisposes them to business success.

We agree that to succeed in your own business, you have to have the "right stuff." But today we live in an age of information and almost anyone can acquire the knowledge and skills of a successful entrepreneur. All you need is to be sufficiently committed to start and run a profitable business from home. Men and women of all ages and backgrounds have done it.

Some were successful corporate professionals before they started their businesses. They had confidence, and skills in selling, marketing, and managing a business when they began. But others were total novices, fearful of business basics like selling and negotiating.

So what was the "right stuff" for them? What did it take to achieve business success? We've met many people who found an answer, but there wasn't any one way. However, our interviews do indicate that by the time entrepreneurs achieve success, they have several things in common:

- They enjoy what they're doing enough to keep going when times are rough.
- They are good at what they do.
- They specialize, providing a product or service that a particular group of people wants or needs.
- They have learned how to sell themselves and their businesses. They know how they measure up to their competition, why their prospective customers should come to them, and how to let people know what they have to offer.
- They stay in charge of their money.
- They are flexible enough to adapt to unforeseen circumstances and adjust their workday to the demands of the business.
- They believe in themselves and are sufficiently committed to their work to persist until they get the job done right.

Success depends on finding the right combination of your personal preferences, talents, and skills to meet the needs of the marketplace, and then having clearly defined business goals and an effective plan for reaching them. It's like putting together the pieces of a puzzle, starting with selecting the right business for you.

Virtually any of hundreds of businesses can be started from home. In fact, a list of over five hundred of them appears in the Appendix. The only limitations are the space you have available and any legal restrictions that may apply. So the question is not so much "What's possible?" as "How do I select a business that has success potential and is right for me?" To answer this challenging question, here are three different roads you can take: starting a business on your own; buying a franchise you can start at home; or joining a direct sales organization. Let's consider each in more detail.

Starting a Business on Your Own

By far the majority of people who have a home business start their business from scratch. They select a business idea based on their unique interests, talents, contacts, and expertise and set out to serve customers and clients with their services or products.

We like to say that selecting a successful business requires that you tune in to the two most popular radio stations in the world: WPWPF ("What People Will Pay For") and WIIFM ("What's In It For Me?"). In selecting a business, you need to determine what you will enjoy and profit from as well as what people need and will pay you money for.

Market research will help you tune in to WPWPF. It doesn't need to be complicated or expensive. Your market research can be as simple as asking prospective customers what they need and investigating what the competition is like. Find out what people are paying now and what advantages you can offer over the competition. Can you compete on price, service, quality, variety, or ease of use? You may also find your competition even needs you to help cover their overload.

Honor Roll of Home-Originated Companies

Amway	Hershey Foods
Apple Computer	Hewlett-Packard
Ashton-Tate software	Liquid Paper
Baskin-Robbins ice cream	Lillian Vernon catalog
Ben & Jerry's ice cream	Marion Laboratories
Brookstone Company	Mrs. Field's Cookies
Cape Cod potato chips	Nike
Domino's Pizza	Pepperidge Farm
Day Runner	*Playboy*
Ford Motor Company	Purex
Estée Lauder cosmetics	*Reader's Digest*
Gillette razor	Walt Disney
Hallmark Cards	Welch's grape juice

To tune in to WIIFM, consider these factors:

- How much do you want to be involved with people? All the time? Some of the time? From a distance? Not at all?
- Do you want it to be a full-time or part-time business? Hobbies are more apt to become part-time or sideline businesses and some people report that by making their hobby their work, they kill it as a diversion or a source of entertainment.
- How many hours a week are you willing to invest in your business?
- How important is prestige and image to you? For example, will your self-esteem remain intact if you're making money as "Grunt and Dump Hauling"?
- How much money do you need to make? How much money do you want to make? Each week? Each month? Each year?
- What resources do you have available in terms of money, equipment, and know-how?
- How much risk do you want to take? How much money can you afford to lose—or write off as "an educational experience"—if the business is not successful?
- Do you prefer a proven type of business or are you willing to take the chances of a pioneer?
- Do you want to start a business from scratch or would you prefer to buy an existing business or franchise? A business that's been franchised is ten times more likely to succeed than one that's started from scratch, but most franchises require a larger investment because you're buying other people's experience, and many can't be operated from home.
- Will you and can you get help from other people, including your family?
- Who do you know or where can you find people who will help you?
- How big is your market? Are there enough buyers that you can reach to support the level of income you desire or need?
- Do you need any special licensing or training? For example, tax preparers, private investigators, and investment advisers often do.

With these considerations in mind, here are six possibilities for finding the ideal business for you:

Turn What You Most Enjoy into a Business

If possible, turn your favorite hobby or interest into a business. There's nothing better than getting paid to do what you most enjoy.

When teacher John Lewis neared retirement, he became interested in how people could remain vibrant and active after they retired. He found that

Options for Turning a Hobby or Interest into a Business

- Creating arts and crafts
- Becoming a travel guide
- Selling antiques or collectibles
- Selling cosmetics
- Doing interior decorating
- Teaching dance and exercise classes
- Offering tennis lessons
- Breeding, training, and grooming dogs
- Giving singing lessons
- Appraising collections (stamps, coins, art)
- Running a recording studio

knowing what to do was a problem for many retired people, so instead of retiring, he began doing retirement counseling.

Every free moment script supervisor Maureen Bender had away from her job she spent at an exercise salon. "Since I love exercising so much, I figured, why not share it with others? Instead of paying to exercise, why not get paid for it?" She set up her own exercise classes and was in business.

For years Clyde Glandon performed as an amateur magician while employed as a corporate executive. An unexpected illness woke him up to how important it is to do what you want to do while you have the chance. He became "Colonel Boone," a professional magician.

Here are some questions to help identify what you enjoy most:

- What do you get so involved in and intrigued with that you lose track of time?
- What do you do first when you get to a new city you've never been to before?
- What are you doing when you feel most like yourself?
- What are you doing when you like yourself the most?
- What are you doing when you feel most alive and energized?
- What do you like to talk about? What are other people talking about that draws you into the conversation?
- What do you take immediate action on? What do you delay?
- What do you do during your time off? When you're on vacation?
- What do you read? What newspaper or magazine headlines catch your eye?
- What do you collect? What mementos and photographs do you keep around your home and office?

Turn Your Existing Job Skills into a Business

Accountants, doctors, lawyers, psychotherapists, advertising or marketing specialists, auto mechanics, typesetters, editors, translators, gardeners—people from all walks of life—are turning their salaried jobs into profitable independent businesses. So whatever job you're doing now, consider how you could turn it into an entrepreneurial venture.

Gil Gordon was a personnel director. He became a management consultant. Larry Nickel is a director of data processing. He started a sideline business handling data-processing overload. Karen Youngblood was a full-time mother. She runs a day nursery. Peggy Glenn was a typist. She started a typing service, wrote a book about how others could do it, and is now a nationally known speaker, writer, and publisher.

Sometimes losing your job, or the threat of losing it, creates the momentum to start a home business. Kathryn Hubbell had been out of work and looking for a job in public relations for some time. One day she asked herself, "What am I doing begging people to let me work for them?" She stopped job hunting and opened her own public relations firm.

George Eagan had been with the auto workers' union for fifteen years when the layoffs began. At first he spent many a depressing day hoping he'd be called back. Finally he took charge of his life by setting up his own business custom-painting automobiles.

Sue Rugge started the highly successful research service, Information on Demand, after losing her job as a librarian owing to heavy cutbacks in the aerospace industry. In seven years, she and her partner turned the $250 they used to start the business into over half a million dollars' worth of sales. Reflecting back on the day she was laid off, Sue remembers, "I felt strongly that the only way I would ever have the job security and salary level I wanted was to work for myself. In other words, if you can't get a job, create one!"

Solve a Problem

Problems and complaints hold the seeds for many new businesses. People will pay to have someone do tasks they either hate or need help with. Career counselor Lynne Frances had been teaching this philosophy to her students at the center where she worked. When she decided to take her own advice, she opened a home-based cleaning service.

A thirteen-year-old boy heard people complaining at a local McDonald's about not getting their orders filled in the proper sequence. He went home, wrote a software program for cueing orders, and sold it, along with a computer to run it on, to the manager. Since that time he has sold his software and computer package to all the McDonald's franchises in the area.

While Marsha Zlotnick was fighting to survive a life-threatening disease, she discovered that recovering involved many changes in what she could eat and other daily habits, but there were few places for people like herself to turn for information, support, and assistance in making those changes. When she recovered, she turned her kitchen, dining room, and living room into a center for helping others conquer illnesses. She teaches cooking classes, offers courses in relaxation, acupressure, and massage, provides counseling, and has an extensive bookstore where people can get current information about getting and staying healthy.

Use a Hidden or Latent Talent

Sometimes the most obvious business to pursue is right under your nose, but too obvious to notice. Karen Nestler had always given outstanding parties. She never thought of being a party planner until a friend asked her to plan a party for a family occasion. She gladly agreed and loved doing it, but still didn't think of it as a business opportunity until her friend said, "That was so great I would have paid for it." Then the light went on, and her business was born.

Writing computer programs had been only a pastime for engineer Earl Patterson until someone in a local computer club hired him to write a program for a print shop. His sideline business, writing custom software, had begun.

Jill Connors thought of her cartoons as doodles until friends asked if she would decorate the wall of their nursery with her drawings. Seeing the finished nursery, another friend asked for her services, and then another. By the time she finished the third nursery, she had decided to start a business. Now in addition to custom-decorating nurseries, she is planning commercial lines of wallpaper, drapes, and toys that feature her designs.

Start a Business Doing Things Other People Hate to Do

- Income tax service
- Investment counseling
- Estate planning
- Real estate management
- Inventory or mailing-list management
- Selling (as an independent rep)
- Cleaning service
- Window washing
- Van and RV washing
- Shopping and gift-buying service
- Equipment repair and fix-it service
- Pickup and delivery service

Use Technology and Resources You Have Around the House

What you have lying around the house can become a business. Raymond Clark turned his VCR and video camera into a business taping weddings and other memorable events. Teacher Linda Hutton turned her 35-millimeter camera into a sideline photography business. Bonnie Moodyman used her typewriter to start first a part-time and then a full-time typing service. Ray Jones's pickup truck became We'll Haul, a pickup and delivery service. A van or pickup truck, in fact, can be used to start a number of home businesses.

Beverly Matthews is one of hundreds of people who have turned their spare bedrooms into bed-and-breakfast inns. Two women in Texas even use their washing machines to supplement the family budget. They created a business called Washer Women, a laundry service for the crews of ships that dock in the local harbor. Your kitchen is another room that can be transformed into a wide variety of businesses.

Because of their versatility, personal computers can literally become any one of hundreds of new businesses, from writing software or keeping mailing lists to helping people design personalized nutrition or exercise programs.

Bob Sherman has turned his love for computers into a family business. Bob runs a local bulletin board as a hobby and operates a computerized research service with his wife, Carol. Their twelve-year-old son writes programs and demonstrates the capabilities of computers for user groups. Bob helps market and distribute the software his son writes. Their most recent effort is marketing a security program called Padlock that protects information stored on a lap-top computer.

Dorothy Baranski used her computer to start an executive service providing word processing, accounting, and bookkeeping for small businesses. Others have used their computers to start electronic shopping or referral services.

Many people are using their mailboxes to start profitable businesses. Opening the mail each day to find a stack of cash orders feels great, and selling

---

Use Your Van or Pickup to Start a Business

- Gardening or yard service
- Carpentry or house painting
- Swimming-pool maintenance
- Home maintenance and repair
- Mobile lunch wagon
- Party-plan sales (clothing, cosmetics, computers, housewares)
- Plant-care service
- Hauling or moving service
- Mobile computer-repair service
- Mobile auto-repair service

Use Your Kitchen to Start a Business

- Catering services
- Homemade cakes and cookies
- Pet-food products
- Cooking service for specialized diets (macrobiotic, Pritikin)
- Cooking school
- Herb and spice packages
- Specialized candy
- Healthy snack food
- Canning gourmet fruits, jellies, and preserves

---

products through mail order is a growing business opportunity. Bud Weckesser actually turned a home-beermaking guide he wrote into a $700,000 mail-order enterprise. People spend over $17.5 billion a year on mail-order items, everything from books, clothing, and candy to housewares, plants, and sporting equipment.

Put What You Know to Work

Since this is an information age, you can turn virtually anything you know into a business if enough people want to know it too. Sandra Canter sold her recipes in a booket, *101+ Instant Hamburger Dishes*. It was the first item in what became a profitable mail-order business.

Having taken singing lessons all her life, Marie Moran knew how to use her voice effectively. Noticing that a major problem people have is not projecting their voices adequately, she started a speaker's training program teaching executives how to give dynamic presentations.

Having worked in a computer store, McCallister Merchant knew how to operate different kinds of computers. Noticing that new computer owners often had difficulty learning how to use their equipment, he offered his

---

Other Ideas for Putting Things Around the House to Work

- Use your piano for lessons, or rent practice time on it.
- Give swimming lessons in your pool.
- Turn a family room into a day-care center.
- Convert a side porch into a hothouse and sell exotic plants.
- Turn your yard into an organic vegetable garden and sell the produce.
- Dry the flowers growing in your yard and create gift sachets.

---

services as a consultant and was excited by the response. "I found many people will gladly pay me $40 an hour to come to their homes and show them what I know." So consider your particular expertise and the number of ways you can capitalize on it.

For more than five hundred business ideas, see the list of "Home Businesses from A–Z" in the Appendix.

If after reviewing so many business possibilities, you're still wondering just what would be the best business to pursue, here's a simple procedure; developed by Mark Kleinschmidt, a Maine computer consultant, for narrowing down your choices:

"Sit down and *honestly* write down what you can and can't do. Put down everything. Then write a letter to yourself really bragging up your strong points. There is no room for modesty in this step. Then start looking around your area and see what people are buying that you are able to provide. This will greatly cut down the list of options. If you are lucky, you will only have two or three choices. Then ask yourself if you can run one of these businesses professionally. If you think you can, sit down and draft a plan for how you'll proceed. Show your plan to colleagues and professionals, and get ready to make some changes in it. Once you have gotten this far, you will definitely know whether or not you want to follow through."

When you get to the stage of writing your business plan, there's computer software available to help you do it. A package of programs from Star Software called Venture, based on Tandy's Deskmate interface, enables you to develop your business plan and has a word processor spreadsheet, a simple database capability, a general ledger, a check writer, and templates for contracts and prospecting letters.

Below is a list of steps you need to take once you make a decision to proceed with a home business. In the upcoming chapters of this book you will find the details of how to carry out each step.

Turn What You Know into a Business

- Plan parties and weddings.
- Become a consultant (management consulting, wardrobe or color consulting, interior decorating, home and office organization consulting).
- Write and sell "how-to" books (how to find a job, how to grow prize-winning azaleas, how to coach little league soccer).
- Produce "how-to" tapes or video cassettes (how to buy investment property, how to sell your own home).
- Publish a specialty newsletter (backpacking news, organic gardening tips, guide to summer camps).
- Teach classes, give seminars, or tutor in your areas of expertise.

Seven Home Business Start-Up Steps

1. **Select a business** (usually a six- to nine-month process). Meeting WIIFM and WPWPF tests.
2. **Develop your business plan.**
3. **Deal with the legalities.** Check your zoning; determine the form of your business; select and register your business name; obtain and file needed licenses, permits, and registrations.
4. **Create your financial structure.** Establish a business bank account and credit; set up your bookkeeping and accounting systems; get needed insurance.
5. **Set up your office.** Select an adequate location in your home; get needed equipment, furniture, and supplies; establish your telephone service; set up your mail service.
6. **Develop your graphic identity.** Print business cards, stationery, and other necessary material.
7. **Establish your work schedule and start getting business.**

Buying a Franchise or License

If the idea of starting a business of your own from scratch feels too risky for you, one way to reduce your risk is to purchase a franchise or license from a company that has already established a track record of success and will teach you how to use their proven methods. There are more than 3,600 franchises available today and, since the fastest growing number of them are service-oriented, many of them can be easily run from home. In fact, the lower overhead of working from home makes starting a franchise even easier.

Examples of the types of service-business franchises that can be run from home include Binex-Automated Business Systems, which provides computerized accounting, financial planning, and tax preparation; bookkeeping services like Debit One and Advantage Payroll Services; cleaning services like TGIF domestic help; home inspection services like Housemasters; property tax reduction services like Communifax; direct mail advertising like Money Mailer; and directory publishing like Finderbinder.

When purchasing a franchise, you pay the franchiser for the right to use his or her trademark, trade name, products, and business system in exchange for an initial fee and ongoing royalties on your earnings.

In order to avoid the high costs of complying with franchising registration laws, small businesses will sometimes offer a license instead of a franchise. A license gives the start-up business person permission to use trademarks, proprietary methods, materials, or know-how and may also include training in using them in exchange for a fee and other ongoing costs of goods or materials. Licenses lack the extensive controls required of franchisees, and they do not provide the legal protection and disclosure requirements of the franchise laws. However, they can be good business opportunities. Here are some examples of licenses suitable for home-based businesses:

- The Boston Computer Exchange licenses people to use their approach for operating a business as a used-computer broker.
- Howard L. Shenson licenses the teaching of his training workshops in how to be consultants.
- Parent Effectiveness Training licenses people to teach its parent-education courses.

The major advantage of buying a franchise is that, statistically, your chances of success go up. According to the U.S. Department of Commerce, franchises have a far lower three-year failure rate than independently owned enterprises do. Reportedly, 95 percent of franchises succeed in the first three years compared with only 40 percent of independent businesses. So, statistically, a franchise more than doubles your chances for success.

And, although you are on your own, you're not alone. With a good franchise, you get the benefit of valuable business training and support. You have access to manuals with step-by-step instructions on procedures that have worked again and again. Some franchisers even offer financing for start-up fees and costs, specialized equipment and customized software, promotional materials, and the benefit of a national advertising campaign. Then, if you do well in your business, you can often sell it easily because the new owner will have not only your ongoing experience but the franchise name to help him or her get started.

In fact, buying a successful established business from an existing franchisee has several added advantages. You have an existing cash flow. How much you can make from the business is not at question because you can look directly at the books and see just how supportive the franchiser has been. In other words, even more of the guesswork is removed from starting a business.

Whether you buy a new or existing franchise, the expertise and support you receive can dramatically reduce the learning time involved in getting a business up and running. Walter Heidig of Binex Automated Business Systems, Inc., estimates that his franchisees are a full year ahead of consultants who try to run a computerized accounting and financial planning service on their own.

Starting a home-based franchise, however, is not always peaches and cream. It usually means acquiring a debt, and sometimes the franchise royalty is too high to justify the amount of money you can earn from running a one- or two-person business. You may find you're paying too much for a name that few people know. Low start-up fees that make entry easy may mean the parent company doesn't have the resources to provide you with as much support and training as you need. Lawsuits by franchisees against their franchisers for not delivering promised advertising and support are not uncommon. And if you're an independent-minded "my way" type of person, you may find the policies and procedures prescribed by the franchiser too restrictive and limiting to your creativity.

How to Determine Whether Franchising Is for You

Basically in buying a franchise you are buying a successful format and the assistance to use it effectively. So in deciding whether you are interested in owning a franchise, ask yourself:

- **How much structure do I need?** Are you already proficient at most aspects of running the type of business you are considering? Do you prefer to operate with a lot of flexibility and few rules? Do you work best when you make your own rules? Or are you new to this business and uncertain how you should proceed? Do you like to rely on the guidelines, policies, and procedures of someone with greater experience than you?

- **How much am I willing to pay for the support?** Could you almost as easily learn what you need to run the business from books, seminars, college programs, or consultants? Or does the franchise offer a superior or proprietary method of doing business that will give you a clear-cut advantage in attracting and satisfying your future customers and clients?

- **Do I have enough working capital to make the business work?** Generally you need at least three to six months to generate a profit. Could you start such a business for less than what the franchiser wants as a down payment? Many franchisers offer financing for a portion of the fee and the start-up costs. Others will provide you with assistance in developing a loan package. Would you be able to arrange for such financial backing if you were on your own? Franchise attorney Ira Nottonson of Sherman Oaks, California, advises that a good business opportunity should buy itself. In other words, after an initial down payment, the operating profit of the franchise should be enough to cover the payments on the balance of your loan.

For Herb and Linda Schulze, purchasing a home-based Chem-Dry franchise has worked well. Linda had been a nurse for twenty-five years; Herb a clergyman for twenty-three years. They were both feeling "burned out" when they met at a personal-growth seminar. They fell in love, married, and began dreaming about expanding their lives in a business together. Since neither had any business background, a franchise made sense to them and they borrowed the $4,000 they needed for fees and start-up costs from Linda's parents.

More than three years later, they're happy with their business. Looking back, Herb says, "A franchise means people who have never been in business can just follow the book and set up their business. We like the independence. The money is good. We made a profit immediately and paid back the loan within the first year. Best of all, we like to be of service to people."

He believes those interested in a franchise should talk with other franchisees about their experiences. For him the most important factors have been the integrity of the franchiser to follow through on promises; to provide strong initial training; and to supply immediate technical assistance when there's a problem.

52 Franchises You Can Run from Home
(from No Fee to $50,000)

Alarm and security service
Answering service
Balloon delivery
Bingo publications
Bookkeeping service
Business networking organizations
Carpet cleaning
Carpet restoration
Catering service
Ceiling cleaning
Chimney sweeping
Cleaning service
Companion service
Computer classes for children
Computer consulting
Computerized accounting
Dance classes for preschoolers
Direct mail advertising
Drapery cleaning service
Elder care
Environmental safety
Executive search
Financial planning
First-aid training
Handyman service
Holiday lighting and decoration

Home inspection service
House-sitting
Interior decorating
Laminated child ID tags
Lawncare service
Management training
Newborn announcements
Parent education
Party planning
Payroll services
Pet-sitting
Prenatal education
Publishing local resource directories
Real estate advertising
Refinishing and restoring
Securities and commodities brokering
Sewer cleaning
Skin-care products
Sports team photography
Tax preparation
Wedding planning
Window cleaning service
Windshield repair
Upholstery cleaning service
Video photography service
Video repair

For further information about franchises you can operate from home, refer to *101 Franchises You Can Run from Home,* by Lynie Arden (New York: Wiley, 1990).

Picking a Franchise or Licensing Program

The criteria you apply when picking a franchise or license should be similar to those you'd use to select any business. Ask yourself the following:

- **Is this business something I enjoy?** Just because someone else has made a franchise into a successful business doesn't mean you would enjoy doing it. Because you'll be trained, however, a franchise is an excellent way of making a career change into a field that's more to your liking. Over 75 percent of people who do it go into new fields.

- **Am I knowledgeable or interested in learning more about this field?** Just because the franchise will train you to apply its methods doesn't mean you won't need to have a proclivity for the business and the type of work involved. As more than one franchiser has said, "We provide support, but we don't run the business."

- **Is this a business that people in my community need and will pay for?** While the franchise may have worked elsewhere, it may not work in your area. There are strong differences in what people buy from region to region, even including such everyday items as mayonnaise and catsup. Also, a community may already have enough of one type of franchise—instant print shops, for example—so explore whether there are already more than enough businesses providing the service you're considering investing in.

- **Is the franchiser reliable, reputable, and financially solid?** We advise that you thoroughly investigate any franchise you are considering. Federal law requires all franchises to provide all prospective franchisees with a Uniform Franchise Offering Circular, or UFOC. This disclosure document will provide the basis for your investigation. Don't just talk with the franchisees the franchiser recommends; for a full picture that includes the good, the bad, and the ugly, talk with a number of other franchisees. Also, do talk with other franchisees and franchisers in the same field. Here are the kinds of questions you need to be able to answer:

  1. How long has the company been in business?
  2. How many franchisees does it have?
  3. What is its cash position or credit rating? You can do a computer search using Nexis or an information broker to gather this information.
  4. Are there any lawsuits pending from customers or franchisees?
  5. Is the product or service guaranteed? Can it be sold all year long? Does the U.S. Bureau of Labor Statistics indicate that this is a growing industry?
  6. Will you have an exclusive territory? Is the demand in that territory adequate to support another business?

7. Can your contract be renewed, sold, transferred, or terminated?
8. Does the company offer financing or assistance with developing a loan package?
9. What training does the franchiser provide? Is it ongoing? Can you call for help and expect to get it?
10. Does the franchise company have standards for screening applicants? If it is too eager to take anyone, makes big promises, and puts on the pressure for a quick decision, it's a bad sign.
11. Is the franchiser registered in your state?

Since there are so many franchise opportunities today, you will undoubtedly be able to find one you can run from home in a field that's suitable for you. In the resource list at the end of the chapter, you'll find resources for learning more about franchising.

Joining a Direct-Selling Organization

For more than 4 million people, working from home means being associated with companies like Amway, Avon, Mary Kay, Performax, Shaklee, Tupperware, and A. L. Williams. These companies sell products such as cleaning supplies, cosmetics, vitamins, insurance, and long-distance telephone service directly to consumers. Direct selling is a $30 billion a year worldwide industry based on door-to-door sales, home-party sales, and multi-level marketing (MLM) or what is now popularly being called "network marketing."

Direct selling has advantages. It's a way of getting into your own business with little capital or sales experience. A number of companies provide extensive sales training and motivational support. And there have been enough cases of people with little education becoming wealthy through building multi-level marketing organizations to make many others see their opportunity in direct selling.

From the perspective of product manufacturers, direct selling, and MLM in particular, is a relatively low-cost way of bringing products to market. They avoid the high cost of establishing store distribution systems and national advertising. Because it costs a company less to establish an MLM organization, many companies that are longer on hope than capital come into existence. An estimated 90 to 95 percent of them, however, are out of business within two years.

So before investing your time and money in a direct-selling organization, it's important to make sure the company you're joining is worth investing your time and your priceless energy in. This means being able to distinguish a sound business from an undercapitalized company or from an illegal pyramid scheme.

An illegal pyramid scheme exists if your profits are to come from signing people up rather than from product sales. An indicator that your profit comes from signing people up is that there is a cost, usually over $500, for obtaining the *right* to sell the product. If you have doubts about whether a plan is a pyramid scheme or you have questions about the soundness of the company, check out the company with the Better Business Bureau in your community or in the headquarters city of the company. You can also check with local and state consumer protection agencies, the assistant attorneys general responsible for consumer protection both in your state and in the headquarters state of the company, the regional office of the Federal Trade Commission, the U.S. Postal Inspection Service, and the Direct Selling Association in Washington, D.C. Be aware, however, that not finding a complaint does not mean the offer is legitimate. It may be new or people who have paid money for it may feel too embarrassed to complain.

Be skeptical of companies that promise you lifelong riches for a few hours of work a week in ads that feature well-dressed people standing in front of a Rolls-Royce, parked in front of a mansion with an Olympic-sized swimming pool. Neil Offen, president of the Direct Selling Association, says, "The opportunity in direct sales is real but it's hard, hard work to be successful. It takes forty to seventy hours a week." Recruiting other people into an organization takes endless meetings, phone calls, cajoling, counseling, and training.

If direct selling interests you, here are some questions to ask to help you find the right opportunity.

1. Is the company selling consumable products that appeal to most people? Because it takes many contacts to make sales, you want a product that large numbers of people desire and use often. Products should have some advantage, such as good price or high quality, over products available in stores or by mail. Quality products encourage repeat sales. That's important because it's easier to resell to people you've already sold to than find new customers.

2. How long has the company been in business? Companies that have been in business for several years are better risks. Eldon Beard, who has been involved with MLM companies for a number of years, advises, "While 'ground-floor' and 'start-up' opportunities can be good, there is a much greater risk involved."

3. Do you stand to lose much money? Beard says, "Most legitimate MLM companies only require you to pay a small fee for a distributor kit; initial purchase of a volume of product is not a requirement for getting started in the business." If you actually stock and deliver products, does the company have a buy-back policy for the products you stock? Beard says, "A good company should offer to buy back unsold inventory for at least 80 percent of what you paid. If the company has no such policy, you could be stuck with a lot of unsold inventory should you decide to quit selling the product." In fact, you may want to select a company that involves little stocking of products. Products consume your capital, take up space, and require records and inventory work.

4. Is the sales and marketing plan easy to understand? A complex plan with a hard-to-explain commission structure will make it difficult for many people to do well with it.

Direct sales is not for everyone. Common complaints are:

- Depending on your personality, it can be discouraging to encounter negativity from people who don't like direct sales or have themselves been involved with a failed MLM effort of one kind or another.
- With the exception of major companies that have lasted for decades, most companies and their products have short lifespans. Fewer than two hundred companies account for 90 percent of the sales volume in direct sales.
- With mature companies, finding potential customers can be difficult.
- The constant emphasis on recruiting new people can be disconcerting.
- Contact with sales "evangelists" who prod and spur, and classify those who do not perform as "losers," is offensive.
- Some companies restrict advertising and limit the way products can be sold, such as not permitting their sale in retail stores even if the distributor is the store owner.
- Having to attend many evening and weekend meetings and rallies can mean sacrificing home life and relations with friends and family members who, as a result, may not look favorably on your enterprise.

A Caveat: Business Opportunities That Aren't Opportunities

Lee Graham, who publishes the *Opportunity Review,* a newsletter containing his evaluations of what is being sold from "business opportunity" ads, says, "85 to 90 percent of what is advertised has no business value. Typically they're cheaply produced booklets eight to ten pages long containing little information of real value."

Sometimes classified ads lead to buying packaged work-from-home businesses that involve purchasing up to $10,000 worth of equipment and training. Occasionally there are worthwhile opportunities. For example, At-Home Professions trains people to become notereader/scopists and medical transcriptionists and then provides its graduates lifetime placement services. Most companies, however, cannot document any cases of individuals actually earning a living from the business plans they package. So *buyer beware!* Caution should be exercised when responding to ads that, as Graham says "focus on the financial rewards of a business opportunity and buying a lifestyle."

Roadblocks: Six Problems to Avoid

Our favorite questions to ask successful home business people are: "What surprises did you have? Did you encounter any detours? Were there any land mines hiding along your path?" And, indeed, whether they start a business from scratch, buy a franchise, or join a direct-sales organization, their answers indicate common surprises, detours, and roadblocks that all home-based entrepreneurs must contend with. Here are six of the most common problems and some ideas on how to avoid them.

Never Getting Started

Many who hope to start a business never get beyond the wishful thinking stage. In the press of our day-to-day responsibilities, some brilliant ideas and good intentions get put on the back burner and remain a matter of "Someday I'm going to . . ." Some ideas, of course, are best forgotten, but unless you give them a chance, you'll never know which ones would have worked—until one day you read in the paper or hear on TV about someone else who beat you to it by turning your idea into a success story.

To avoid the death of a good idea, plan to research and test yours as soon as you get it. Begin by reading up on the subject and talking with others who know about what you want to do. Find out who's already working in the field. Tell other people about your idea and get their reactions. If the idea still seems good, set out a step-by-step plan to test it, and establish target dates to complete each step. Then put your plan into action.

The Capital Squeeze and Money Mismanagement

Lack of capital and proper financial management is the most common reason small businesses fail. Some of the typical financial problems home businesses encounter are: not enough money to cover start-up and operating expenses; not enough money to grow; too much debt; cash-flow problems; inadequate financial planning; not charging enough to make a profit; poor credit and collection practices; inadequate bookkeeping. Here are some rules of thumb for avoiding these problems.

Start small.   Unless you have extensive experience in running a business like the one you plan to start and have major business contracts in hand, we advise that you keep your start-up expenses low. Peggy Glenn, founder of the International Professional Typists Network, started a successful typing service in her kitchen with $65. She rented a typewriter, bought a few supplies, and advertised by placing index cards on college bulletin boards. Within three months, she was earning a profit.

Your business may demand more of an initial investment. But try at least to keep it under $10,000, or preferably under $5,000. Norm Goode started the *MicroMoonlighter* newsletter three years ago by withdrawing $5,000 from his savings. He invested $3,000 in computer equipment and used the remaining $2,000 very frugally to get the business going.

If your resources are limited, start gradually. Use your brains instead of your checkbook. Find a college art class to design your logo, cards, and stationery. Have your business cards printed one month, your stationery the next.

Develop an entry plan. Depending on the business you're in, it can take from six months to a year to get under way, a year to three years to turn a profit, and three to five years to become self-sustaining. How to cover your costs of living and doing business until you're turning a profit is one of the biggest challenges a home entrepreneur faces.

If you have a job, keep it. Meanwhile, find out whether the business is viable. Do your homework. Figure out the bare minimum you need for living expenses and business expenses. Then establish an entry plan, a way to cover that minimum until your business is going.

Using the moonlighting plan, Sandra Oker started doing career counseling in the evenings and on weekends. When she had enough clients to pay for her rent, food, and gasoline, she quit her job. On the part-time plan, John Eldridge worked part time in a health-food store for several hours a week while building a community theater into a viable business. Gil Gordon used the spin-off plan. He got a six-month retainer from his previous employer before he left his job to begin doing management and personnel consulting. On the cushion plan, James Milburn used his personal savings to support himself after leaving his position as an accountant to become a computer programmer.

Avoid loans and investors. Finance start-up yourself. There are three principal ways to finance a business: You can use your own funds, you can find investors, or you can borrow. Although it's very tempting to find investors or borrow, we advise against both until there is evidence your business will be a winner and you need credit to expand it. In any case, it's difficult to find investors or secure a bank loan for the start-up of a home business unless you are beginning with lucrative contracts or purchase orders in hand or have

---

Five Plans for Starting a Home Business

1. **The Moonlighting Plan.** Keep your full-time job and develop your business as a sideline. When it takes off, you can go full-time. Be sure to work at least eight hours a week on a sideline business.
2. **The Part-Time Plan.** Work a part-time job to provide a base income while you're building up the business. When your business equals the base income, drop the part-time job.
3. **The Spin-Off Plan.** Turn your previous employer into your first major customer or, when ethically possible, take a major client with you from your previous job.
4. **The Cushion Plan.** Find a financial resource to support yourself with while you start your business. Your cushion should be large enough to cover your base expenses for at least six to twelve months.
5. **The Piggyback Plan.** If you have a working spouse or partner, cut back your expenses so you can live on one salary until your business gets going.

---

an outstanding reputation in your field or are buying a franchise that gives you a name to back you up. And borrowing, even from friends or relatives, puts your new business under the additional financial pressure of paying back the loans.

Instead, draw on earnings, savings, investment income, retirement funds, or insurance loans to start your business. If you're married and both partners are employable, consider living off one salary while the other spouse starts the business. Or start a business while on sabbatical or leave. We understand from those who have done it that it's even possible to start a business while receiving unemployment compensation, as long as you make the proper arrangements with the authorities.

Manage your cash flow. In a new home business you often must pay cash up front while waiting for your own customers to pay for your products or services. Covering expenses while waiting for income is the bane of small businesses.

Here are three basic strategies you can use for managing cash flow wisely:

1. **Minimize what others owe you.** Get deposits, retainers, and partial or progress payments. Take bank cards instead of giving credit. Ask for cash at the time of the sale.
2. **Get maximum benefit from cash on hand.** For example, deposit cash in interest-bearing accounts and use cash-management programs.
3. **Hold on to what you've got.** Ask for interest-free credit from suppliers. Charge your expenses on bank cards. Make timely, not immediate, payment of bills. Rent or lease equipment instead of buying it.

Inexperience

The second most common reason small businesses fail is their owners' lack of experience and knowledge. In the past this was often an unalterable limitation. Our knowledge was restricted to what we could learn at home, school, or work. But not today. Today information is available on virtually everything you might want to know.

If you're weak on sales skills, you can take courses, read books, or get private consultation on how to sell. If you're timid in negotiating contracts, you can use assertiveness training courses, personal growth seminars, or private counseling to improve your skills.

A recent survey of new businesses found that after three years of being in business, successful entrepreneurs had:

1. Taken six to ten months to research and to prepare for their business ventures.
2. Used professional advisers in setting up the business.
3. Taken business-related courses and read regularly about business management.

To increase the odds for success, become an information consumer in your field and in the general area of business. Read books, magazines, and newsletters. Attend seminars, conventions, and classes. Buy and listen to tapes by experts who have the skills you need. Talk with those who can advise you in business matters.

For specific information about your business area, contact professional or trade associations. Ask your local reference librarian to recommend a reading list. You can start with the resources listed at the end of this chapter.

Marketing Misconceptions

Accountant Susan Gwenn made the mistake so many people with new businesses make. After completing long and arduous training, she sent out announcements that she was opening her practice. Then she sat back, waiting in vain for the phone to ring. Similarly, potter Gloria Greene displayed her wares in one art fair after another only to carry most of her pots home again, wondering if she were as talented as she had thought.

The problem in both cases was marketing, or the lack of it. Thinking a good product or service will sell itself is the most common marketing misconception of new entrepreneurs. Often artists, writers, professionals, technicians, information specialists, and consultants start their businesses with little knowledge, interest, or skill in marketing and selling. Without it, you have no business and, let's face it, you aren't a business until you've got business.

As researcher Sue Rugge found in starting Information on Demand, "Marketing is the key to everything. Doing your work is the easy part. It's the selling that's the hard part. You can never sit back. Every day you have to sell yourself again." Starting with this philosophy, Sue made "house calls." She sold her research services door to door. She gave her card to everyone she knew. It was this effort that turned the $250 she and her partner started with into sales of half a million dollars.

Since most home businesses can't hire a marketing agency in the beginning, selling yourself and your product or service will probably become *your* task. Consequently, you'll need to develop what we call a "marketing mind-set," a way of thinking about business from a marketing viewpoint. This doesn't mean you have to take on a phony sales personality, but you do have to become good at letting the people who need your business know about it in a way that will convince them to buy. And you can. To learn the marketing mind-set and the skills you'll need, start with the books, tapes, and newsletters in the Resource List at the end of this chapter, and refer to Chapter 22: Successfully Marketing Your Home Business."

A Marginal Business Image

Think about the businesses you patronize. What do you expect from them? Of course, you want a good price, but people also want to feel confident that the business they're buying from is substantial, that it will be here tomorrow.

They want to believe they can count on buying a quality product or service that delivers what it offers.

How do you know whether a company has those qualities? Until you've bought from a business and tested it, all you have to go on is image. Image is where some home businesses fall down, however. Started on too tight a budget or operated too casually, a home business can look like an amateur effort.

Unfortunately, such a marginal business image creates a negative image for all home businesses and leaves the impression that a home business is not a real business. So in setting up your enterprise, pay attention to creating a professional image. It doesn't take a big budget. It only requires attention to detail. Avoid such indicators of an amateur operation as letters printed on a dot matrix printer, no one (or children) answering the phone during business hours, dirty clothes and dishes in business areas, irregular hours, unclear fee schedules, and a backlog of unpaid bills. Take conscious steps to make a professional impression.

Giving Up

For every three new businesses, two close their doors. Like the "golden hour" in emergency medical care, the first year is the most critical year for business survival. It can get long and lonely.

In starting his *MicroMoonlighter* newsletter, Norm Goode remembers the long and lonely periods, those times "when you've drained the bank account on a display ad that won't even appear for another three months, and there's only one paid subscription in today's mail." Those were the hard times, but he found it definitely paid off to weather them. "I could use such terms as creativity, luck, or just being in the right place at the right time to describe my success. Actually, though, I believe my success—and that of anyone beginning a business—lies in a single word, *persistence.*"

So keep going. Experiment, adjust, and test. As Thomas J. Watson, the founder of IBM, ironically advised, "The way to succeed is to double your failure rate." Persist until you find what works. In the meantime, make friends, and join relevant groups and organizations for support and encouragement through the rough spots. And listen to the advice of entrepreneurs who have been there and can make your way smoother.

Tips from Successful Entrepreneurs

In the long run, the successful entrepreneurs we talked with managed to avoid these problems and learn, not always the easy way, how to survive and grow. Here are a few of their conclusions:

■ **"You have to be the best at what you do.** You can't fake it. Even then, the phone doesn't always ring on the first day. You're always three months away from a new client. You have to develop your marketing plan to ensure that the phone does ring. You have to set aside time each week for PR. I try never to have lunch alone, for example. If I'm going to eat lunch, I eat with a business contact. I never know who a prospective client will be, so I treat everyone like a prospective client."—William Slavin, consultant, William Slavin and Associates.

■ **"A satisfied customer is always your best source of business.** When you advertise, though, you don't have to buy a big ad. In fact, the small ads I run regularly draw more business than the several-hundred-dollar ads I ran only once. I find running an ad regularly that has some kind of logo and catchy copy draws best."—Barbara Elman, writer and newsletter publisher.

Twelve Money-Saving Ways to Give Your Home Business a *Fortune* 500 Image

1. **Spring for a business telephone line.** An effective name doesn't help you a whole lot if people can't find it in the phone book or when calling for information.
2. **Answer the phone with finesse.** Answer after two rings with a positive professional greeting using your name or the name of your business. Have an answering service or answering machine take calls when you're not there. Call yourself periodically to listen for the impression you're making.
3. **Communicate quality with a custom-designed logo.** Use your own unique custom-designed logo on business cards, letterheads, envelopes, and invoices. Do not select a logo from among the standard designs offered by your printer. To keep your costs down, arrange to have a college class design your logo as a class project.
4. **Show substance with a federal ID number.** Use a Federal Identification Number for business purposes in place of your Social Security number. It's a no-cost way to dress your business for success. To obtain a Federal ID number, simply apply at the nearest Internal Revenue Service office.
5. **Select a strategic location for your office.** If you have business guests coming to your home, consider locating your office so you can have a separate business entrance, or locate your office near the front or side door so business guests don't have to walk through or past personal areas of the household. Make sure that any areas business guests must pass en route to your office are neat, clean, and clear of overly personal items like toiletries, children's toys, photographs, and household items. Use tasteful screens, drapes, or dividers if necessary to separate personal areas from business areas of the house.
6. **Let your checks speak for you.** Use full-sized checks on business stock with your business name printed on them. They cost no more than the smaller decorated personal checks. Use a check protector for entering the amount in large raised numerals, or use a computer with software like Quicken to print your checks.

■ **"Everything in business is a result of networking.** Whether it's getting an article published or finding a distributor, I keep in contact with old friends, past co-workers, and sales reps who used to call on me. I can't stress it enough—your friends and contacts are your best assets."—Gil Gordon, management consultant, Gil Gordon and Associates.

■ **"You have to really care about what you're doing.** Everything takes three times longer and costs five times more than you think it will. We wouldn't have kept going if we hadn't had a strong commitment to what we are doing."—Elizabeth Scott, developer and co-founder of Rhiannon, a software company.

■ **"As you travel down this path, discomfort is sometimes a companion,** though seldom for extensive periods. And on the other side of

---

7. **Use only top-quality paper.** Choose paper that looks and feels top grade for your letterhead, envelopes, and business cards. Fine paper doesn't cost that much more. We recommend 70-lb. bond for letterhead and envelopes. Buy the paper at a printer's supply house or directly from a paper company. You then supply it to your printer as "customer stock."

8. **Equip your office professionally.** The cost and size of electronic office equipment today makes it possible to equip your home office with the kind and quality of equipment you'd expect to find in any top-notch office in your field. Equipment that will enhance your image includes a photocopier that makes quality plain-paper copies, a letter-quality printer (preferably a laser printer), and a fax. Here's an added tip: Next time you reprint your business cards, include your fax number.

9. **Polish your correspondence.** A recent nationwide survey of executives by Communispond, Inc., showed that four out of five executives listed the ability to write as the most neglected skill in business. Even if your words don't flow magically from your fingers to your screen, your correspondence can be grammatically and stylistically correct using grammar-checking software.

10. **Incorporate for image.** Although there are several other reasons for incorporating, think about adding *Corporation* or *Inc.* to your company name to enhance your business image. Before making such a change, however, consult with a knowledgeable tax professional and an attorney to determine whether this would be a wise business decision. If you decide it is, have these professionals help you select one of several options for the way your corporation will be taxed.

11. **Dress for success.** Although the sweat suit may be the official uniform of the open-collar worker, dress like a successful person at the top of your field when meeting with customers, clients, and suppliers.

12. **Project a positive attitude.** Share good news. Radiate confidence. Remember, self-assurance attracts, self-doubt repels.

discomfort you will discover a new high that comes with a deeper sense of your own worth. To me that is the bottom line."—Sue Rugge, co-founder of Information on Demand.

Chapter Digest

1. Starting a business of your own is actually the easiest route to working from home, and the financial, tax, and psychological rewards are great.
2. Success in your own home business depends upon finding the right combination of your personal preferences, talents, and skills which meets the needs of the marketplace.
3. There are three routes to becoming your own boss. You can start a business on your own, you can buy a franchise, or you can join a direct sales organization. Each has its benefits and drawbacks.
4. There are over 500 businesses you can start in your home, everything from A to Z: answering services to zipper repair. To find the business for you, match up what you enjoy and are good at with what people need and will pay for.
5. There are thirty-six hundred franchises in the United States today and many of them can be run from home. Buying a franchise takes much of the risk out of starting a business by providing you with training, support, and a proven approach with a track-record of success.
6. For more than 4 million people, working from home means being associated with direct-sales organizations like Amway, Avon, Mary Kay, and A. L. Williams. These organizations enable you to get in business with very little capital and they provide you with training and support.
7. To avoid the most common problems that new home businesses face, start small, have a plan for financing your business for at least six months, and learn as much about your business as you can before you start. Make sure you have a plan for marketing your business adequately and always project a 100 percent professional business image.

Resources

Books

101 Franchises You Can Run From Home. Lynie Arden. New York: John Wiley & Sons, 1990.

The Best Home Businesses for the 90s. Paul and Sarah Edwards. New York: Tarcher/Perigee, 1991.

The Complete Handbook for the Entrepreneur. Gary Brenner, MBA, JD; Joel Ewan, MBA; and Henry Chuster, Ph.D, CPA. Englewood Cliffs, NJ: Prentice-Hall, 1990.

The Complete Work-at-Home Companion. Herman Holtz. Rocklin, CA: Prima Pub Communications, 1990.

Computer Entrepreneur. R. H. Morrison, P.O. Box 25130, Honolulu, HI 96825; (800) 528-3665, 1989.

Creative Cash: How to Sell Crafts, Needlework, Designs and Know-How. Barbara Brabec. Huntington Beach, CA: Aames-Allen Publishing, 1986.

Extra Cash for Women. Susan Gillenwater and Virginia Dennis. The New Careers Center, 6003 N. 51st St., Ste. 105, Boulder, CO 80301, 1982.

Freelance Food-Crafting. Jane Shown. Boulder, CO: Live Oak Publications, 1983.

Getting Business to Come to You. Paul and Sarah Edwards and Laura Clampitt Douglas. New York: Tarcher/Perigee, 1991.

Government Assistance Almanac: The Guide to All Federal Financial and Other Domestic Programs. J. Robert Dumouchel. Washington, D.C.: Foggy Bottom Publications. Annual.

Government Giveaways for Entrepreneurs. Matthew Lesko. Information USA, 10335 Kensington Pkwy., Kensington, MD 20895.

Growing a Business. Paul Hawken. New York: Simon & Schuster, 1987.

Homemade Money. Barbara Brabec, White Hall, VA: Betterway Publications, 1989.

Honest Business: A Superb Strategy for Starting and Managing Your Own Business. Michael Phillips and Salli Rasberry. New York: Random House, 1981.

How to Earn $15 to $50 an Hour & More With a Pickup Truck or Van. Don Lilly. Phoenix: Darian Books, 1987.

How to Make Money with Your Micro. Herman Holtz. New York: John Wiley & Sons, 1984.

How to Make Your Home-Based Business Grow: Getting Bigger Profits from Your Product. Valerie Bohigian. New York: New American Library, 1986.

How to Succeed as an Independent Consultant. Herman Holtz. New York: John Wiley & Sons, 1988.

Information for Sale: How to Start and Operate Your Own Data Research Service. John Everett and Elizabeth Crowe. Blue Ridge Summit, PA: TAB Books, 1988.

Making It on Your Own. Sarah and Paul Edwards. New York: Tarcher/Perigee, 1991.

Mancuso's Small Business Resource Guide. Joe Mancuso. New York: Prentice-Hall, 1988.

Moonlighting: 148 Great Ways to Make Money on the Side. Carl Hausman. New York: Avon Books, 1989.

Playing Hard Ball With Soft Skills: How to Prosper With Non-Technical Skills in a High-Tech World. Steve Bennett. New York: Bantam, 1985.

Running a One-Person Business. Claude Whitmyer, Salli Rasberry, and Michael Phillips. Berkeley, CA: Ten Speed Press, 1989.

Skills for Success. Adele Scheele. New York: Ballantine, 1987.

So You Want to Be an Innkeeper: The Complete Guide to Operating a Successful Bed & Breakfast Inn. M. Davies, P. Hardy, J. Bell and S. Brown. Professional Association of Innkeepers International, P.O. Box 90710, Santa Barbara, CA 93190.

Starting & Operating a Home-Based Business. David R. Eyler. New York: John Wiley & Sons, 1990.

A Whack on the Side of the Head—How to Unlock Your Mind for Innovation. Roger von Oech. New York: Warner Books, 1988.

What Color Is Your Parachute? Richard Nelson Bolles. Berkeley, CA: Ten Speed Press, 1989.

Word Processing Profits at Home. Peggy Glenn. Huntington Beach, CA: Aames-Allen Publishing, 1987.

Periodicals

Home Office Computing. Scholastic, Inc., 730 Broadway, New York, NY 10003.

Entrepreneur. 2392 Morse Ave., Irvine, CA 92714. **Entrepreneur** also periodically publishes **Entrepreneur Magazine's Guide to Home-based Business.**

In Business. Magna Publications, Inc., 2718 Dryden Dr., Madison, WI 53704.

Success. Success, Inc., 342 Madison Ave., New York, NY 10173.

Catalogs, Tapes, Newsletters, and Reports

Encyclopedia of Associations. Detroit: Gale Research Company. Published annually.

The Kessler Exchange. 8910 Quartz Ave., Northridge, CA 91324.

National Home Business Report. P.O. Box 2138, Naperville, IL 60556.

Thomas' Register of Manufacturers. Thomas Publishing Co., One Penn Plaza, New York, NY 10119; (212) 695-0500. A multi-volume affair listing the makers of many industrial products. Some companies have their product catalogs included. Useful in locating sources of supply, either for your own use, or for resale. Available at most libraries.

The Whole Work Catalog. The New Careers Center, P.O. Box 297, Boulder, CO 80306.

Government Publications

Small Business Administration:
The SBA offers many booklets on financing, planning, marketing, staffing, and other topics for new and established small businesses. Publications of note are:

Business Plans for Small Business Firms
Franchised Businesses (#SOS-0106)
Directory of Business Development Publications (#501W)
Directory of State Small Business Programs
Planning and Goal Setting for Small Business (#MA2010)

To order, write for free order forms 115A and 115B. SBA, P.O. Box 15434, Ft. Worth, TX 76119. Booklets will be mailed for a small processing fee.

Service Corps of Retired Executives (SCORE). The SBA also sponsors this program for small business consultation. To make an appointment, contact your local SBA office. Or to locate the nearest SCORE chapter, write SBA, Small Business Development Center Headquarters, 1129 20th St., NW, #410, Washington, D.C. 20036.

Publication from the Department of Defense
Operating Home-Based Businesses in Military Housing. Washington, D.C.: Department of Defense, 1988.

Internal Revenue Service:
New Business Tax Kit. Available in local IRS offices or phone (800) 424-3676 for further information.

Tips on Work-at-Home Schemes. Council of Better Business Bureaus, Inc., 1515 Wilson Blvd., Arlington, VA 22209. (Available for 25¢ and a self-addressed, stamped envelope)

Community Colleges Business Representatives
Many community colleges have a person or department whose job it is to further local business development. Contact the administration office of your nearest community college.

Radio

Home Office Show on the Business Radio Network.

Unless otherwise indicated, the show is broadcast live at 10 P.M. Eastern
"TD"—Tape Delay Sunday at 4:00 A.M. Eastern

Albuquerque, NM (Live and TD)	KMBA AM 1050
Atlanta, GA (Live and TD)	WPBE AM 1050
Binghamton, NY	WBNK AM 1360
Birmingham, AL (Live and TD)	WCEO AM 1260

Boston, MA	WXTK FM 94.9
Buffalo, NY	WWKB AM 1520
Charlotte, NC	WSTP AM 1490
Cincinatti, OH (Live and TD)	WCVG AM 1320
Ft. Myers/Naples, FL (TD)	WDCQ AM 1200
Grand Rapids, MI (Live and TD)	WGRD AM 1410
Greenville, SC (Live and TD)	WPCI AM 1490
Huntsville/Decatur, AL	WVNN AM 770
Kansas City, MO (Live and TD)	KBEA AM 1480
La Crosse/Eau Claire, WI	WOGO AM 680
Miami/Boca Raton, FL	WSBR AM 740
Minneapolis, MN (Live and TD)	KJJO AM 950
Nashville, TN (Live and TD)	WTTN FM 90.7
New Orleans, LA	WTIX AM 690
Portland, OR (Live and TD)	KBNP AM I410
Sacramento/Stockton, CA (Live and TD)	KWWN FM 92.1
St. Louis, MO	WRYT AM 1080
Salt Lake, UT (TD)	KCMR AM 1230
Santa Barbara/Santa Maria, CA	KSMA AM 1240
Seattle, OR (TD)	KEZX AM 1150
Spokane, WA (Live and TD)	KSBN AM 1230
Traverse City, MI (Live and TD)	WMKT AM 1270
Tucson, AZ	KTUC AM 1400
Washington, D.C. (TD)	WPCC AM 1580
Youngstown, OH (TD)	WYWR AM 1330

CHAPTER
FOUR

■■■■■■■■■■■■■■■■■■■■

Working for Someone Else:
Paychecks and Other Possibilities

Every three hours every day of the year, someone uses the "Working From Home Forum" on CompuServe to seek information about how to find a job they can do at home. Still others seek advice on how to get their management to let them take their job home. They want to combine the security and benefits of a job—health insurance, a pension plan, sick leave, paid holidays and, above all, a paycheck—with working from home. They tell us:

"I like my job, but with all the interruptions at the office it's hard to get anything done. I'd like to convince my supervisor we would all benefit if I could work at home part of every week."

"I'm the sole supporter of my kids. I need a steady income I can count on every week, but I'd sure like to be there when they get home from school."

"I've thought of starting my own business, but I think I would have a hard time getting customers. With my disability it's hard for me to get out of the house. I'm trained in keypunch, though, and if an employer could get the work to me I'd be in business."

"I'm in a bind. Next year my husband will be transferred to a city three hundred miles away. I'm going with him, but I hate to leave my job. I could do almost everything it calls for with a telephone and a computer terminal. Maybe I can arrange to stay on and work long distance."

"I hate losing one to two hours commuting in traffic and another hour getting dressed up every day. And I cannot say enough bad things about having to wear high heels to work."

Fortunately, there is a trend in many companies and government agencies to allow employees to work from home. This trend is a phenomenon in search of a name. Variously called telecommuting (substituting *commuting* for *communications*), teleworking (working from a distance), flexiplace (flexible workplace), each expression has its champions. Whatever you choose to call it, let's take a look at some of the many jobs being done from home.

Salaried Jobs You Can Hold at Home

Accountant
Actuary
Advertising copy writer
Advertising sales representative
Answering service operator
Architect
Assembly worker
Auditor
Booking agent
Bookkeeper
Budget analyst
Buyer
Computer programmer
Computer systems analyst
Computer technician
Cost estimator
Customer service representative
Data entry clerk
Database administrator
Desktop publisher
Economist
Editor
Environmental analyst
Financial analyst
Graphic designer
Illustrator
Indexer
Instructional designer
Insurance agent
Insurance claims adjuster
Interpreter
Interviewer
Inventory control clerk
Lawyer

Market research analyst
Marketing planner
Medical records technician
Medical reviewer
Medical transcriptionist
News reporter
Operations research analyst
Paralegal
Patent searcher
Personnel analyst
Pollster
Probation or parole officer
Public relations professional
Purchasing agent
Real estate agent
Records manager
Researcher
Reservation agent
Sales representative
Secretary
Social worker
Software engineer
Speechwriter
Stockbroker
Technical writer
Telemarketer
Telephone order taker
Transcriber
Translator
Travel agent
Typesetter
Urban planner
Utility rate forecaster
Word processor

The opportunity to work at home spans all levels of the office hierarchy, from vice-presidents to data-entry workers. Writers, artists, accountants, researchers, lawyers, and computer programmers can easily work from home. So can many clerical, data-processing, and communications personnel. Technical jobs that require a lot of reading and report writing are well suited for work at home, as are jobs that require large amounts of travel or field work. Even many managerial or supervisory positions in areas such as purchasing, pensions, sales, and planning can be done at home.

Although there are an ample number of jobs that can be done at home, finding one that is right for you is not necessarily easy. There are two primary routes to finding a job at home. You can convince your present employer to allow you to start working from home. Or, when that's not possible, you can start from scratch and find a new job as a work-at-homer.

Bringing Your Current Job Home

Senior Editor Nick Sullivan of *Home Office Computing* magazine, himself a telecommuter, says, "In general, I think it's easier to get a job and *then* talk about doing it at home." And we agree. Although it's still not the norm, more companies are allowing employees to work at least part time from home.

Salaried work at home has been growing at an estimated 20 to 30 percent a year during the 1980s. In a recent study of corporate plans for the nineties by the Conference Board, a business research firm, it was reported that 56 percent of corporations plan to allow home-based work in the future. Increasingly, companies are finding it makes more sense to move the work than to move people. Some companies institute formal work-at-home programs for which you apply in order to work at home. However, more than three out of four companies that allow employees to work at home do so on an informal basis.

The extent to which you can work from home without a formal program depends on what arrangement you can make with your supervisor. Whether done on a formal or an informal basis, being able to work at home means first proving that you are a capable and reliable self-starter. Even then, you can still expect to have some convincing to do.

Convincing Your Employer to Let You Work at Home

Even if your job can be done at home, why should your company allow you to work from home? What motivates a company to step outside convention and try something this new and revolutionary? Obviously companies need to see that the benefits will be worth the risks. Here are several of the primary reasons companies are having employees work from home. Think about which of the following will motivate your management.

- Increase productivity. After studying over two hundred companies with work-at-home projects, telecommuting consultant Gil Gordon reports that "company productivity rises from 15 to 25 percent when people work at home." These gains are possible because employees can work at their own pace and at their peak energy hours. They can work longer because of time saved commuting. Also, work gets done more quickly without office interruptions and socializing. Instead of taking "work breaks," as they might at the office, they take "rest breaks."

- Overcome staff shortages. Whenever the demand for workers exceeds the supply, as is currently the case with secretaries, medical transcriptionists, engineers, and software engineers, the alternative of working at home can become a way for companies to attract prospective employees not available for office work. Employees working at home can also reduce the cost of temporaries.

- Reduce turnover. Because of high job satisfaction, salaried at-home workers rarely quit their jobs. And by allowing valued employees to work at home, companies don't lose them if they move (or the company relocates), or if they decide to start a family, or need to care for someone who becomes ill. Not having to train new employees can result in considerable savings for a company.

- Decrease absenteeism. Employees can work at home despite illness, bad weather, sick children, waiting for home deliveries, or service calls that would otherwise cause them to miss work.

- Lower costs. Companies can save on space and parking. Savings of $5,000 or more per employee are not unusual. Growing companies do not need to have their growth limited by the cost and lost time involved in finding additional office and parking facilities. Companies with their own buildings can even consider leasing the space made available by employees who are working at home, and the rental income can increase profits.

- Use as an incentive. Allowing people to work at home is an alternative to promotion in companies where reorganization or downsizing provides fewer management positions. It can also be used to acknowledge and reward valued employees.

Once you are aware of what factors may motivate your company to let you work from home, your next step is to consider carefully the feasibility of doing your job at home. What tasks can be done at home? Which ones require you to be in the office? What difficulties might develop and how would you handle situations such as suddenly needing information that's only available at the office?

For most managers to consider having employees work at home, the work must be easily measured. You and the manager need to know without a doubt when the work you do has been completed. It should have a precise beginning and end and require minimal face-to-face contact with co-workers. Before proposing a permanent plan to work at home, build a track record of working from home informally. Occasionally ask to take your work home for the afternoon. Then try proposing to work at home on a specific project for a day or two.

Only take work home when you feel confident you can do an outstanding job. Keep in touch by phoning in each day to find out if anything has arisen that you need to handle. Follow up on all messages immediately, so no one will feel you are inaccessible.

Consultant Gil Gordon suggests that even after doing your homework and building a track record, "don't go for broke all at once. Approach management with the idea that you'll work at home on a small scale—perhaps starting one or two days a week at most—for the first two to three months."

Finding a New Job to Work at Home

Although taking your existing job home is your best chance of working from home on a salary, there are several ways to find a job to work at home.

Long-standing home-based jobs. Salespeople and repair and customer service personnel in some industries, such as publishing and pharmaceuticals, have long used their homes as their work headquarters. But these are generally work-*from*-home jobs as distinct from work-*at*-home jobs.

Personal contacts. Your most likely way to get a new job to work at home is through people you know or meet. Nearly two out of three people hired to

---

How to Determine Whether Your Job Can Be Done at Home

☐ Does your job require little face-to-face contact?
☐ Can needed face-to-face contact be scheduled into a weekly time at the office?
☐ Are the expectations for what you produce and when you produce it clear?
☐ Is your performance easily measurable?
☐ Can you work without physical access to resources and materials at the office?
☐ Can needed access to resources and materials be scheduled into a weekly time at the office?
☐ Does the job require a great deal of concentration without interruptions?
☐ Is there adequate security at your home for your work?

Each *yes* answer you can give increases the likelihood that your job can be done at home.

---

work at home are employed by firms with fewer than a hundred employees. Your best chance to work at home, therefore, is with a small company in your hometown. Such a job might be doing word-processing, typesetting, desktop publishing, billing for a doctor's office, taking telephone calls, or doing bookkeeping.

You find these jobs the same way you find any other kind of job. Research by the National Center for Career Strategies indicates that fully 70 percent of all jobs are obtained through personal contacts, or what is called "networking." As one employer who hires people to work at home told us, "The only way to get work is to ask for it." Networking is a way to make contact with the people you need to ask.

To locate the likely companies and get the interviews you need, tell everyone that you're looking for a job you can do at home and tell them the type of work you can do. Attend professional and trade association meetings in your field. Ask for ideas and suggestions. Follow up on any leads you get until you are successful.

To land the position you want, you might offer to work at home under contract on a specific project, or to provide overload services during emergencies. Do outstanding work and the company may call on you again and again, or even put you on salary.

Make your work at home a bargain. One of the most creative ways of getting to work at home was accomplished by a Los Angeles writer. In negotiating a job offer, her-soon-to-be employer asked her how much she expected to earn. She gave him two figures. The first was what she needed to earn to work at the company office. The second, although still a good salary, was $10,000 less—provided she could work at home. Her new employer developed a brand new attitude about the benefits of employees working at home.

Classified ads in newspapers. Newspapers regularly have ads for telemarketers in the "Help Wanted" section. Telemarketing includes selling by telephone as well as taking incoming phone calls. Many of the "800" numbers you see used for ordering products, making reservations, and contacting customer service are phoned into people's home offices. In fields such as medical transcription, in which there is a shortage of trained personnel, you will occasionally see a classified ad that indicates the job can be performed at home. Even if the ad doesn't say so, you may be able to persuade the prospective employer in fields like these to let you work from home.

Business opportunity ads in magazines. These ads may seem to offer jobs at home by using phrases like "Apply Now" for tasks like typing, sewing, arts and crafts, or assembly work on such items as models, earrings, and computer circuit boards. Despite the promises, these ads often state that you must buy a list of the names of companies that contract for work on a piece-rate basis. You then have to contact these companies yourself.

Another problem is that companies that operate with outside workers on a piece-rate basis often only want workers in their local area. Still others require "applicants" pay a nonrefundable membership or registration fee. What real employer ever asked you to do that? Lee Graham of the *Opportunity Review* says, "Companies that have work available virtually never advertise. If you find a company that wants to contract with you for assembly work at home, such as sewing pillows or dolls together, expect to earn less than the minimum wage." Remember, too, these are not jobs with salaries and benefits like health insurance, vacation, and sick leave.

A third type of classified ad is even less desirable; they are simply schemes to get your money.

Work-at-Home Schemes

Clouding the image of working from home are schemes that take millions of dollars a year from people through "Business Opportunity" ads that read as though they were offering jobs. They promise "Money beyond your wildest dreams," "Work in your spare time in your own home," "Anybody can do it," "Quick and easy," "Guaranteed earnings," and other enticements.

Envelope stuffing is the most common of these schemes. Stuffing envelopes sounds like easy work, but in actuality it is always a pyramid-like sales scheme in which you get a set of instructions telling you "to place ads similar to the one to which you responded."

Other schemes include making neckties, reading for pay, renting time on your computer, clipping coupons and newspapers, watching TV and listening to the radio. These are not even pyramid schemes; many of these simply take your money and send you nothing. Such schemes prey on people's hunger to make an income from home. They are neither a job nor a business opportunity.

How to Spot Work-at-Home Schemes

First, work-at-home schemes require you to send money before explaining how you are going to make money. An ad for a real job opening will not ask for money before you learn the details. Second, if an opportunity sounds too good to be true, it probably is. If you suspect a scheme, check it out with the Better Business Bureau, local consumer protection offices, state consumer protection and attorney general's offices, the Federal Trade Commission, and the U.S. Postal Inspection Service.

If you feel the urge to send in your money, follow the advice of Sidney Schwartz, who has made a study of these schemes. Here are his suggestions:

1. Keep copies of all ads, claims, and guarantees. If the only guarantee is on the order form, photocopy it before sending it in.
2. Pay with a charge card instead of by check or with cash. You can dispute the charge if you feel you're been taken.

3. Save the envelope or package the merchandise is shipped in so you will have a dated postmark.

4. Send all correspondence certified mail. Should you return the merchandise, always get a signed return receipt as proof of delivery.

5. Remember, when you respond to one of these ads, you're gambling. So don't bet more than you can afford to lose.

What Kinds of Companies Have At-Home Employees?

Companies with fewer than one hundred employees, and *Fortune* 500 corporations are the ones employing the most home-based workers. The reasons for this are that large companies and agencies are able to accommodate specialized work arrangements; and small companies are willing to be flexible in order to compete for qualified personnel and to save money.

Assuming your skills enable you to work in a job that can be done at home, let's consider the characteristics of the companies that are most likely to allow people to work at home.

Information-Intensive Organizations

Often, but not always, jobs in these information-intensive companies are computer or communications oriented and involve data entry, word processing, telemarketing, or teleordering. Representative industries and companies with employees working from home include:

- *Banks and financial institutions:* American Express, Citibank, First Chicago Corporation, Mellon Bank.
- *High-technology companies:* Control Data, Data General, Digital Equipment Corporation, DuPont, Hewlett-Packard, Honeywell, Hughes, IBM, Lanier Business Products, Xerox.
- *Governments:* City of Los Angeles, County of Los Angeles, states of California, Hawaii, and Washington, and various federal agencies.
- *Insurance companies:* Allstate, Blue Cross/Blue Shield of South Carolina, Blue Cross/Blue Shield of Maryland, Equitable Life Assurance, Hartford Insurance Group, John Hancock Mutual Life, New York Life, Travelers.
- *News organizations:* Time-Warner, Gannet, United Press International.
- *Retailers:* JC Penney (customer service), Bell Atlantic, Montgomery Ward, Sears.
- *Telephone companies:* AT&T, Bell Atlantic, GTE, New England Telephone, New York Telephone, Pacific Bell, US West.
- *Translation and transcription:* Berlitz Translation Services, Globalink Language Services, Journal Graphics.

Sales Organizations

Sales organizations have customarily allowed, or sometimes required, representatives to work from home. Businesses making extensive use of sales reps include insurance, publishing, real estate, printing, pharmaceuticals, and other product manufacturers.

Fast-Growing Small Businesses

Instead of renting office space or having employees come into the founder's home, growing businesses like Escrow Overload of Los Angeles and Letter Perfect of Baltimore, both of which began as home-based businesses, prefer to hire employees who will work from their homes. Such small businesses need employees to do secretarial jobs, sales, bookkeeping, product assembly and shipping, art, public relations, and computer programming.

Special Advice for the Handicapped

We have heard from dispirited and sometimes angry disabled people who, despite repeated attempts, have been unable to find work. And this, when they know that, thanks to personal computers and adaptation devices developed by companies like IBM and Apple, they can now work from anywhere. This could be discouraging for anyone. But the road to finding a job demands persistence. You have to become a "squeaky wheel." As Brian Wettlaufer, who operates a consulting practice in Miami called Handicap Placement Services Inc., advises, "Don't give up. There are opportunities."

In fact, the number of these opportunities is increasing. Owing to the shortage of entry-level workers as a result of the "baby bust" of the 1960s and '70s, job prospects for the nation's 10 million disabled citizens may be brighter than ever before. This includes jobs both at home and at traditional job sites. Companies that want to employ the disabled typically work through public and private agencies that serve the disabled. There is no predicting when a job or training opportunity will open up. That means staying in frequent contact with agency personnel so you will be the first in their minds when an opportunity does arise.

A marvelous resource for the disabled is the Handicapped Users Database on the CompuServe Information Service. Created and managed by Georgia Griffith, herself blind and deaf, this immense collection contains resources for employment arranged by state, and a list of local bulletin-board systems that enable local networking.

Problems You May Encounter as a Home-Based Employee

Aside from the general problems work-at-homers encounter, being a home-based employee introduces some other considerations.

Negotiating Satisfactory Compensation

Some critics, primarily from labor unions, fear that "electronic cottages" could become the sweatshops of the future, with low-paid employees slaving over computer terminals and being paid on a monitored piece-rate basis. Electronic Services Unlimited, which conducted a study to explore the potential of telecommuting, did not find this fear to be a reality, however.

In speaking across the United States we've met a wide variety of employees working from home, but never one who complained of abuse. To avoid problems with compensation and benefits, however, get a clear agreement about your employment status.

Among salaried positions at home there are differences in benefits, support services, and equipment and supplies provided by the employer. Let's discuss a variety of possible arrangements.

Telecommuters

When programmer Sharon Miller began working for National Computer Systems, she became one of the increasing number of employees who work at home through a computer or terminal on either a salary, hourly, or piece-rate basis.

Sharon's work as an applications programmer was well suited for working from home. It involved working on three-to-four-month projects that were one-person jobs. Although raising her three children kept her busy, she still got her work done. Her productivity didn't suffer. In fact she says, "They got more production out of me at home than they could ever have gotten at the office."

In most, but not all cases, needed equipment is provided by the employer. The majority of employees at home today are treated as regular employees with full benefits, though they may only work on a part-time basis.

Commissioned Positions

Gilda Silvani works from home, overlooking the blue Pacific at Laguna Beach, California. As an employment counselor for Escrow Overload, she specializes in providing temporary personnel to savings and loans, banks, and real estate companies.

Gilda interviews prospective overload personnel, checks out their backgrounds, and follows up on marketing done by the company's corporate office in Los Angeles county. As companies call her with needs for temporary workers, she matches the people from her files with the requirements of the job. She's one of the home-based workers paid on a commission.

When working on commission, alternative arrangements are possible. On straight commission, you simply receive a percentage of every sale you make. Sometimes you can get hired into a position that provides salary plus commission and fringe benefits. And some companies offer an advance, or "draw," against your future commissions so you will have some income while you are getting started or when business is slow. Ken Wasil, for example, works as a salesman for a wholesaler of housewares, hardware, and sporting goods. He receives an $1,800 draw each month toward his sales commission, which is 3 percent of the profits on what he sells, or 15 to 17 percent of the selling price.

The percentage of commission varies depending on the price of the product or service you are selling and your employment arrangement. Generally, when you are an independent contractor representing a company, the percentage of commission will be higher than if you work for a company that offers salary plus commission and fringe benefits. Bob Baxter of Pet Organics pays his independent sales reps a 20 to 25 percent commission plus an incentive if they reach their dollar sales goals. He says his commission is higher than most.

Owing to savings on overhead, some employers pay substantially more to commissioned employees who work at home. Escrow Overload, for example, can pay their employment counselors four to eight times the commission of their competitors because of the savings in overhead they realize by having the staff work at home. Customarily, temporary-help agencies pay commissions of 25 cents to 50 cents per hour of employment booked. Escrow Overload is able to pay $2 per hour booked, enabling some workers to make as much as $1,000 per week.

Benefits and support services also vary from employer to employer. Most certainly the company should provide you with a territory, sales leads, or a route to cover, as well as promotional materials, samples, and any back-up information you need in order to sell the product or service adequately. Although benefits often are not included, the better commissioned position will include group insurance coverage, a car, or travel expenses.

Contractual Arrangements and Networker Status

Another arrangement that is growing in popularity is to work as an independent consultant or networker, on contract with a company. In this status you are technically not an employee. Consequently you do not receive benefits or services, such as income-tax and Social Security withholding.

Contract consultants work at home for a company over a specified period of time for an agreed-upon fee. This time may be extended, and often is. Although contract consultants may work for only one company at a time, their services are available to other companies and they operate independently. Computer programmers frequently work under such arrangements, spending six months to a year working under contract with one company while also providing some services to other companies.

Networker status is an option pioneered in England by Rank Xerox, a 51 percent-owned subsidiary of the Xerox Corporation. Under this arrangement, existing employees are offered the opportunity to become consultants to their employer. They work from home, splitting their time between working for their former employer and finding and serving other clients.

This arrangement enables companies to continue using the services of an employee for whom a full-time role is no longer necessary. It also enables the company to save the cost of fringe benefits that may run as high as 50 percent of the salary. The networker gets the flexibility of working from home with more independence and the opportunity to ease into other business with the foundation of a steady client.

Negotiating a Work-from-Home Agreement

Whichever payment arrangement you negotiate, make sure to confirm such points as:

- The hours you will work, and how often you are expected in office.
- The method of payment: salary, hourly wage, piece rate, commission.
- What fringe benefits are included, such as health insurance and employer's share of Social Security.
- Whether you are covered under worker's compensation.
- What liability insurance you'll need on your home and who will pay for it.
- The process used to determine when work is completed.
- The amount of work expected.
- What equipment and supplies you'll need and who will pay for them.
- Method and degree of supervision and performance evaluation.
- The training available to you.
- Opportunities for wage increases and career advancement.
- Requirements and opportunities to return to work at the office.

Keeping in Contact

Feelings of isolation can be more of a problem for home-based employees than for home-based entrepreneurs. Those whose work requires them to sit at home and work alone all day at a computer terminal or typewriter are the most susceptible. Anyone, however, who is away from the office long enough can start to feel like an outsider. As time passes, company shop talk can begin to sound like a foreign language and you may discover you've missed out on special projects because no one thought of you when assignments were handed out. After all, out of sight, out of mind.

There are several solutions to this problem. Some lie with the employee, some with the organization and the supervisor.

To maintain contact, spend at least a part of each week in the office. Sharon Miller, who telecommuted for Northwest Computer Systems in Minneapolis, found that she "felt like I was in a vacuum all by myself. I had to use the manuals and the telephone instead of personal contact." She was concerned about being uninformed about company developments.

By going into the office once a week, however, and spending time on personal contacts, Sharon was able to maintain her work relationships. She did no work in the office that she could have done at home, but instead had her secretary fill up her time with appointments and meetings. She told us, "Not only did I enjoy talking with people when I went into the office, I enjoyed getting out of the house for a while."

Anyone working at home who wants to maintain contact needs to let people know it. Sharon Miller found that some people "had reservations about calling me at home." At the other extreme, employees like Gilda Salvini find that "when people know you're at home, they call early or late, any time of day or night."

Arranging Office Support

Working from home can feel like living on an island. Office support that used to be outside your door—supplies, secretaries, copy facilities, special equipment—is now ten to thirty minutes away. You end up missing a copy machine when you need one, handling all your appointments and phone calls yourself, and being your own file clerk.

Some of the support you need can be provided on your day in the office or perhaps by an expense allowance to cover the cost of buying stamps or having copies made in your neighborhood.

Getting Appropriate Supervision

Management consultant Marilyn Miller points out that in many offices, "You can be in the upper 50 percent of your field if you just show up at work, the upper 30 percent if you show up on time, and the upper 10 percent if you show up on time with your eyes open." Obviously, managing home-based workers requires something besides seeing them in the flesh.

Like other employees, work-at-homers need information, guidance, feedback, and support from their supervisors. Sometimes, however, since the supervisor can't see them in the hall or hear about it when they run into difficulty, at-home workers have to take a more active role by asking for the information and direction they need.

Being Aware of Possible Family Conflict

One survey showed that family conflict is more often a problem with those employed at home than with those who work for themselves. While the self-employed are more likely to list family closeness as one of the chief benefits of working from home, those on jobs at home are more likely to list it as a problem.

We suspect this may occur because more people working at home on a job are doing so out of necessity, while most people who start a business do so because they want to. Family conflicts are also more prevalent when the kind of work you do keeps you from getting out of the house, as is more usually the case if you're employed than if you work for yourself.

The best safeguard against family conflict is to be aware of how working at home will affect those you live with. Then set up your office and workday in the manner described in the subsequent chapters of this book to minimize or avoid problems.

If you plan your office space and work schedule with your family in mind and have honest family relationships, the period of adjustment can be brief and manageable. For example, the biggest problem telecommuter Sharon Miller faced was having to work when her family didn't want her to. But her husband would help out by fixing dinner or taking the family out to eat. Specific suggestions for easing family tensions when working at home are discussed in Chapters 18 and 19.

Certainly, working from home is not for every employee. There are workers like Sophie Wojicik, who tried working for a bank from home but eventually went back to the main office because she missed a traditional office environment. But there are also employees like Sharon Miller who will change jobs to spend more time working from home, and like Gilda Silvani, who describes her situation as "heaven on earth."

So while securing a job at home may be an uphill battle, if you think you're suited for it, persist in your efforts. Aside from the other advantages, the satisfaction of strolling from your desk out to your own mailbox where your paycheck lies waiting will make the effort worthwhile.

Chapter Digest

1. The number of traditional jobs that can be done from home is growing.
2. More employers are allowing employees to work from home.
3. Your best route to a job at home is to convince your employer to let you take your present job home.
4. To arrange to take your work home, focus on the benefits from your supervisor's, not your own, perspective. Demonstrate that you are a capable, reliable self-starter. Begin with a trial period.
5. To find a new job at home, personal contacts are your best bet. You may need to continue working at the office for an initial period of time.
6. Beware of the many work-at-home schemes that are advertised. They are neither a job nor a business opportunity.
7. When taking a job at home, get a clear written agreement up front as to the payment arrangement, job expectations, fringe benefits, equipment and training supplied, and so forth.
8. When working from home, go into the office weekly to keep in contact and arrange for adequate support and supervision.

Resources

Books

The One-Minute Commuter: How to Keep Your Job & Stay at Home Telecommuting. Lis Fleming. Davis, CA: Fleming Ltd., 1989.

The Telecommuter's Handbook: How to Work for a Salary Without Ever Leaving the House. Brad Schepp. New York: Pharos Books, 1990.

Telecommuting: How to Make It Work for You and Your Company. Gil Gordon and Marcia Kelly. Englewood Cliffs, NJ: Prentice-Hall, 1986.

Newsletters

Telecommuting Review: The Gordon Report. Gil Gordon Associates, 10 Donner Court, Monmouth Junction, NJ 08852.

PART 2

....

Making Your Home Office Convenient,
Functional, and Professional

CHAPTER
FIVE
■ ■

Keeping Your Work and Personal Life Separate

A peaceful marriage of home and office depends on establishing effective boundaries. The office, with its phone calls, mail, paper work, noisy equipment, and business visitors, can invade the sanctity of the home. In the same way, the friends, neighbors, kids, barking dogs, soap operas, and peanut butter sandwiches of home can clutter up the halls of business. Creating boundaries, however, preserves the character of each.

Fortunately, the boundaries you set up to maintain the privacy of your home will also help create a professional business atmosphere. Recognizing the boundaries you need to create is a first step in making practical decisions that will ultimately affect the success of your home office.

Keeping Your Home a Home and Your Office an Office

There are many tools and techniques for setting boundaries between your home and your work. Walls, doors, windows, lighting, furniture, and clothing are all material means you can use to define the boundaries you want to create. The way you use time and space—your office location, work schedules, and household rules—are other more subtle means you have at your disposal.

There are some general guidelines for using these tools and techniques. But obviously you'll be adapting the guidelines to your individual circumstances.

Financial consultant George Gaines separates work and home by a single door. He lives alone and detests housework. "My kitchen may be stacked with dishes and the bedroom a shambles. But that's okay. That's 'my' space. I keep it any way I want. On the other side of the living-room door, it's a different world. It's always neat as a pin, because that's where I meet with my clients. That's my office."

Programmer William Keen keeps work in bounds with a basement telephone. "I could work in the middle of a tornado. Nothing bothers me. I just tune it all out. Actually, I work best if two or three things are going on at a time. But if my boss or a business contact calls, they don't think so highly of the stereo blaring or the kids yelling in the background, so I have a little office in the basement for my business phone."

Joan Cullen creatively defines the boundaries between her work and home with a bedsheet. As an editor who works several days each week at home, she keeps her office on the dining-room table, which she has covered with a king-size sheet. The table is piled with manuscripts in various stages of editing. When she's ready to put the work away and claim her apartment for herself again, she stacks all her materials in the center of the table, carefully marking off each project with a rubber band or colored paper, folds and ties

---

Tips for Keeping Your Home and Office Space Separate

1. **Clearly demarcate your workspace** by using a separate room, partition, bookcase, screen, or room divider so you and everyone else will know precisely where the home stops and the office begins. Make sure you can close your office off when you're working.
2. **Set definite work hours** and let everyone know precisely when you will be available for business and when for personal activities.
3. **Have a signal** that makes clear when you do not want to be disturbed; for example, when the office door is closed or when you put up a Do Not Disturb sign.
4. **Learn how to say "No, I'm working now,"** firmly, but politely, and stick to it so everyone will know you mean what you say.
5. **Use a separate business telephone line** and have an answering machine or answering service to screen calls or capture messages when you are not available.
6. **Soundproof your office** by using a solid-core door and other materials and equipment that reduce noise.
7. **Dress in a particular way** when you're at work. You need not resort to coat and tie or hose and heels, but wearing work attire can help you and others know it's time for business if doing so becomes a problem.
8. **Organize your office** so you can keep work materials, paper, and equipment in clearly defined office spaces.
9. **Have a separate outside office entrance** for the ultimate in privacy or locate your office in a converted portion of a garage, in a guest house, or in a separate building.

---

the four corners of the sheet over the pile, and puts her whole "office" in a closet.

We use these examples because they illustrate how personal and how simple establishing useful boundaries can be. Whether you prefer the peace and harmony of a monastic retreat, the intensity and excitement of a politician's campaign office, or something in between, the essential task is to define boundaries that can keep both your household and workspace the way you want them.

Let's consider some of the basic decisions you need to make about the boundaries of your home office. As you make these decisions, what becomes clear are the boundaries you need to set for yourself and others.

How Much Privacy Do You Need to Work Productively?

We all need some degree of privacy to think, to concentrate, or to discuss sensitive material. But how much and what type of privacy do you need to get your work done? This privacy questionnaire has been adapted for the home-based worker from Franklin Becker's *The Successful Office*. We've designed it to help you identify the kinds of boundaries you need to create the right amount of privacy.

1. Do you close the door when you work?
2. Does the sound of music, television, or people talking in the background distract you from your work?
3. Do you prefer to work independently and autonomously?
4. While you're working, would you prefer not to see what's going on outside your office?
5. When you're concentrating on a particular task, do you ask people not to disturb you?
6. Do you have phone conversations or business meetings that should not be overheard by others in the house?
7. Do you have information in your files or records that must be kept confidential?
8. Is it important to your business visitors that they not be seen or overheard by one another while they are in your home?

If you answered "yes" to seven or eight of these questions, you'll want an office that is as separate as possible from the rest of your household. If it's feasible, you may wish to consider a separate structure or at least a separate entrance for business guests, or soundproofing your office in one of the ways suggested in Chapter 7. If you live with others, establish clear rules as to when they can and cannot interrupt you.

If you answered "yes" to just four to six of these questions, you'll probably want to have a separate workspace, but involvement with people and other activities is important to you. So you'll likely want a door to your office, but you'll also want ready access to what's going on outside the door at different times during the day. If you work alone at home, arrange at least weekly contact with colleagues, co-workers, friends, or clients.

If you answered "yes" to only one to three of the questions, you'll probably perfer your office in the midst of plenty of activity. In fact, you may prefer open office space in the heart of the household. If you work alone at home, occasionally try to take your work out to a public place like a restaurant, library, or hotel lobby, and try to have contact each day with customers, clients, co-workers, family, or neighbors. If there's nothing going on at home, you may even want to create some noise and activity there by turning on music or the TV.

If you answered "yes" to question 7, have locks put on your files and your office door. If you answered "yes" to question 8, arrange to have a double entrance into your office or schedule your appointments carefully.

Now let's consider the other basic decisions you'll need to make in setting up boundaries between your home and office.

Do You Let People Know You Work at Home?

Eighty percent of the people we've talked with say, "Sure, why not?" Essentially we agree that you needn't feel any stigma about working from home. It's growing in popularity, and today most people would respond with friendly curiosity and even a bit of envy.

But for some, not letting people know they're working at home can help solve problems. For example, when Jean Hilman first began doing calligraphy, some of her customers were hesitant to phone her at home. So, since she gets her work through local print shops, she just doesn't mention that her studio is at home until after customers know her better.

One consultant expressed his decision this way: "I work with *Fortune* 500 companies. They're used to working with consultants who have Madison Avenue addresses. I don't actually know what they would think if they knew I was talking with them in my bathrobe, but I'd just as soon not find out."

Jack Gibbs intermittently works at home so he can get away from office interruptions at the public relations firm that employs him. "The last thing I want is for people to know where I am. My secretary is the only one who knows—and my supervisor, of course."

If for these or any other reasons, you feel at all uncomfortable with people knowing you work from home, usually there's no need to tell them. By arranging outside business meetings, having a business phone and special mail service, you can just as easily appear to be working in a regular office setting.

Theresa Arnerich works with her husband, providing seminars and speeches for large business organizations. "We had an office before, but we find working from home much more enjoyable. As far as our clients know, we're still in an office. In fact most of them don't know I'm his wife. They know me by phone and by mail. I'm the business manager."

Do You Want Business Visitors Coming to Your Home?

Sooner or later most people who work from home are confronted with this decision. There are several points to consider in making the choice.

Security. Will you and your premises be safe if your business brings strangers into your home? Nancy Rabbitt decided that instead of having strangers deliver art work to her design studio, she would offer early-morning pickup at her customers' locations. Instead of having new psychotherapy clients come to her home office, Cheryl Smith arranged to do her initial interviews at a nearby clinic.

Privacy. Will you feel as though your inalienable right to privacy has been taken away or that your home is being invaded by strangers? How much space you have and how you arrange it will probably determine whether business visitors seem like an intrusion. For Kitty Friedman, who lives and writes in a one-room guest house, there is no way to close off her personal space from business guests. She makes most of her business contacts by phone or meets clients at a publisher's office.

When you have a little more space than Kitty does, closed doors or separate business entrances work to retain your privacy. Graphics designer Mary Stoddard didn't like having customers come into her office when it was in the living room. She felt her home had become too public. So she converted her garage into a studio/office and had a separate entrance installed. This created the boundaries she needed to keep business from invading her home.

Image. Is your office space appropriate for business meetings, and do you want to keep it looking presentable for clients or customers? Thomas Kerr thought not. He didn't feel his small apartment would convey the image he wanted to establish as a management consultant. His solution was to join a private club where he could hold business meetings. Some people join airline clubs for this purpose.

Word processor operator Barbara Bickford has her own prohibitive factors to contend with: five children from three to ten years old. "I couldn't have my customers in here. It's a three-ring circus! Sometimes I pick up and deliver, but whenever I can, I have them mail me their manuscripts or send them electronically."

Jeanett Eastman solved a similar problem when she had a photography studio in a small apartment. "There really wasn't room for guests, with all my equipment and my daughters' toys cluttering the living room. But the apartment building had a lovely porch that looked onto a garden, and, depending on the weather, I either met my customers on the porch or in the garden. It worked well. In fact, they told me they enjoyed it."

Another option should you decide your home office doesn't convey the right image for business meetings and appointments is to rent an office suite on a part-time basis from an organization like HQ, which provides all the professional office services you need, including conference facilities and office space, at a cost lower than renting an office full time. You use the facilities only when you need them. These office-rental organizations can also provide secretarial services, take phone calls, and receive mail for you.

How Do You Handle Business Phone Calls?

According to free-lance cameraman Steve Haines, the best thing about working from home is that he never misses a phone call. "Crews are notorious for calling at all times of day and night. Many times I've gotten the job because I was there to answer the phone no matter what time it was."

Not everyone is as willing as Steve to be available for business calls. Lynn Frances, for example, felt differently about taking customer calls for her cleaning service. "When you have your business at home, there's no respect for your personal life. People knew I would be at home, so they disregarded my business hours and called me anytime they wanted. For my own peace of mind, I had to find a way to limit business calls to business hours." She got a private line and hired an answering service for her business number.

As Lynne found out, the dilemma in setting up home-office phone service is how to make sure you don't miss important business calls without becoming a slave to the telephone twenty-four hours a day. The following is what we recommend.

1. Have a separate telephone line for business. We recommend this second line be a business line rather than a residential line so that:

- People who call Directory Assistance to ask for you by your business name will get your number.
- You will have a listing in the Yellow Pages; sometimes two listings.

What to Do When You Don't Want to Meet Business Visitors in Your Home

1. Offer pickup and delivery services.
2. Meet at the customer's, client's, or employer's location.
3. Transact business by mail or telephone.
4. Meet on neutral territory, such as a restaurant, hotel lobby, or club.
5. Communicate electronically by computer.
6. Rent a hotel suite or conference room.
7. Rent an executive office suite by the hour, day, or month. Such services provide office space, conference or meetings facilities as well as mail, phone, and secretarial services.
8. Use a fax machine.

- You comply with state utility commission rules that prohibit using residential lines for business purposes. If your phone company discovers you are using a residential line for business, it will likely request you to convert it to business service. If you refuse to do so, the penalty varies by state. Some allow the phone company simply to start charging you for a business line, others may fine you or allow the phone company to disconnect your phone service. So never answer a residential line with the name of your business.

Having both a residential and business line works because it:

- Enables you to avoid having to take personal phone calls during business hours.
- Lets you choose whether to take business calls after business hours, thereby protecting your private life.
- Leaves your residential line free for other family members to use without interfering with your business.
- Facilitates claiming business telephone costs as a tax deduction.

Switching a residential line to a business line usually costs about half of what it costs to install a new business line. Some people use one line for incoming calls and the other line for outgoing calls and, increasingly, people are installing separate lines for their fax and modem use. This keeps voice calls separate from "machine calls."

2. *Locate your business phone away from household noise.* Unless you're providing child care, pet care, or cleaning services, household noises that can be picked up over the receiver are a disaster during business conversations. Since you can't always predict when the neighbor's dog will bark or the kids will turn on the stereo, your best bet is locating the business phone away from such activity and using good sound-control techniques.

3. *Answer your business phone in a formal manner.* Use either your own name or your company name. The way you answer your business phone will often determine whether or not the caller perceives you as a professional who is at work.

If you don't have a secretary answering your phone, *you* will be the one to create the proper impression. To create a positive professional image, we greet callers with "Good morning" or "Good afternoon," followed by our name. It also works to our advantage to put a "smile" in our voices when we answer.

Do not have young children answer your business phone. If you want other adults in the household to answer business calls, instruct them to use the same professional procedure as you do.

4. *Use an answering machine, answering service, or voicemail.* Whether your goal is to free yourself of constant business calls or to be sure you don't miss any, your home business needs to use these resources to preserve your peace of mind.

Voicemail is an electronic substitute for a secretary. It's much like the systems proliferating in corporations. It turns a computer into a sophisticated answering machine that gives callers choices. Callers can select a number on their phone pad that instructs the computer to take a message, another number to obtain information you've recorded for them, or a third number to have the computer forward their call to you or someone else. The computer may also tell callers that all lines are currently busy and ask them to stay on the line until you're free.

If you use a service, check to be sure it is courteous, prompt in answering, and accurate in taking messages. We suggest periodically calling the service yourself, as if you were an unknown customer or client, to see how you are treated.

If you use an answering machine or voicemail, create a polite and businesslike message. Avoid the temptation to record anything "cutesy." Howard Shenson, publisher of *The Professional Consultant* newsletter, also gives a tip against starting an answer-machine message with "Hello," followed by a pause. This leaves callers feeling foolish when they realize they've responded to a greeting from a machine. An answering machine or voicemail message should:

- Begin by giving the name of your business (e.g., "You have reached...").
- State that you're away from the phone right now.
- Ask that the caller leave a name, number, and the time of the call.
- Assure the caller that you will return the call as soon as possible.
- Limit voicemail choices to no more than four and make instructions easy enough for any seventh-grader to follow.

In Chapter 8, we'll examine other new telephone features that can facilitate your work.

Do You Use Your Home Address for Business Purposes?

The majority of people who work from home use their home address for both personal and business mail. There are no special arrangements you need to make, nor should you encounter any difficulties with the post office regardless of how much business mail you receive.

However, if you're concerned about giving your home address to strangers or if you have an address on "Easy Street" or "Sleepy Hollow Lane" and don't like the business image it conveys, you can make other arrangements for mail delivery. If you're employed, use your employer's address and have your mail forwarded. If you're self-employed, rent a post office box or an address from an office-suite service like HQ, or use a mail-receiving service, such as Mail Boxes, Etc. Mail-receiving services provide you with a street address and a suite number instead of a P.O. Box number. This removes the doubt created in many people's minds when they see a P.O. Box as a business address. The cost is usually less than twenty dollars a month.

An advantage of a post office box for businesses that receive a high volume of mail is that mail is sorted and placed in postal boxes several times a day. However, courier services, such as Federal Express, will not deliver to a post office box. To get the advantage of a post office box and still get courier deliveries, include both your street address and post office box as follows:

> Your business name
> Your street address
> P.O. Box 415
> Anytown, NY 10222-0909

Using this format, approved by the U.S. Postal Service, your regular mail will be sent to the post office box, but your street address directs courier deliveries to your home address and shows you are not just a mail drop.

Private firms like United Parcel Service will, of course, provide door-to-door delivery to your residence. And for a small weekly fee, UPS will even pick up outgoing mail if your home is near a driver's established route.

How to Help Business Visitors Locate Your Home and Feel Welcome

1. If your residence is at all difficult to find, send directions by mail in advance describing how to get there. If possible, use a separate entrance for business visitors.
2. If you live in a multi-family dwelling, cut out the typeset name from your card or stationery; have it laminated and post it on your own door or on the building directory. If you live in a single-family home, hang a simple sign by your front walk displaying your name and address. Although business signs are usually prohibited in residential areas, signs like the one shown in Figure 5-1 should pose no problem and can greatly assist visitors.
3. Arrange for a convenient and easy-to-remember place to put guests' coats, hats, and packages. Since people are often unaccustomed to business meetings in the more relaxed atmosphere of a home office, be sure they've retrieved their belongings before they leave or you'll soon have a closet full of assorted wraps and umbrellas to return.
4. Have coffee, tea, or water available as you would in a traditional office, and offer it to guests when they arrive.
5. Keep bathroom facilities fresh and supplies available.
6. Keep the areas where your business visitors come clear of personal items like children's toys, family photographs, and clothing so that visitors don't feel they're intruding on your personal life.

Setting Boundaries for Other People

When you're working in a traditional office, the assumption is that while you're there, work has priority. This assumption generally defines how, when, and in what way people interact with you. When you're working at home, however, there is no single assumption about what you're there for. After all, it's a place where you play many roles: worker, neighbor, friend, mate, parent, citizen.

Under these circumstances, it isn't always easy for others to know how to interact with you. Therefore you need to set limits and define boundaries so they will know when you're working and when you're not. It's up to you to let them know what you expect and to help them feel comfortable with an unfamiliar situation. Here are some tips to help you accomplish this with various kinds of people.

Business Visitors

Let colleagues, co-workers, customers, and clients know specifically when they can call you. For example: "Call me on weekdays between nine and five." "Please call me after twelve o'clock." "Call me anytime and leave a message with my service. I check in every hour, and I'll call you back." To reinforce this boundary, do not answer your business phone after work hours. If you wish, you can put your answering machine or service on your business phone so you can return any calls you receive after hours.

If customers come to your home, clearly define business hours. We suggest having customers call before coming. Set a time to meet with them and give them an idea of how long the meeting should last. "We can meet from nine to

Figure 5-1.

ten tomorrow morning." "If you could simply drop the papers by, I would certainly appreciate it. I don't have much time right now." Again, to reinforce your limits, avoid making too many exceptions to transacting business before or after the hours you've set.

A study at the University of Southern California found that when you have regular business visitors, a separate outside entrance works best. Of course, a building will further separate your home life from your business life. For example, David Palmer erected a prefab building in his backyard for about one-fifth the cost of adding on to his home.

When having business visitors come to your home, be prepared for them. Once they arrive, make them feel welcome and comfortable. If family members are present when business visitors arrive or while you're meeting, take the initiative in introducing them briefly to your guests, and let them know you will be working and wish not to be disturbed.

Since you're not a traditional office setting, cueing guests that it's time to leave can be an awkward moment. Sometimes they wonder whether to stay and chat after the meeting. To ease the situation, stand up, or move toward the door to let visitors know it's time to leave. Thank them for coming and, when necessary, tactfully remind them you have more work to do.

Neighbors and Friends

As Mary Smith, a production manager for a telecommunications project, has found, "Sometimes it's hard to go into the study and shut the neighbors out."

Let friends and neighbors know your work hours and when you are available. "Come by after five," for example, or "Let's visit over lunch. I'll come over at noon." Tell them when they can call. If they call while you're working, politely say you'll call them back when you're finished. Do not start a conversation. If you wish, you can put your answering machine or service on your personal line while you work.

Of course, you don't want to antagonize people in the process of getting them to respect your work boundaries, but as writer David Goodfellow found, you do have to be hard-nosed about it. "My family and friends know that during business hours my office is strictly private, but I had to get downright unfriendly to make that happen. It worked, though, and with no lasting hard feelings."

To keep bad feelings from building up, and still be firm about boundaries, psychotherapist Ellen Barker uses the "not now, but when" approach to telling people not to bother her while she's working. Instead of just turning people away, she tells them exactly when she will be available.

Family

Plan your work schedule and go over it with your family to show them when you will and will not be available. Do not assume anything. Let them know at what times and for what reasons you can be interrupted.

Introducing Business Visitors to Family Members

Men are introduced to women. For example, introducing a male visitor to your wife you would say, "Margery, I'd like you to meet Jim Evans. Jim, this is my wife, Margery."

Or, introducing your female visitor to your husband, you would say, "Jill, this is my husband, George. George, this is my client, Jill Rose."

Younger persons are introduced to older persons. For example, you would introduce your son to a business visitor with "Jim, this is my son John. John, this is Mr. Evans."

People with less status are introduced to people with more status. For example, you introduce the vice-president of a company to your secretary like this: "Georgia, I would like you to meet my secretary, Susan Scott. Susan, this is Georgia McGuire of Holt Advertising."

Set rules for your family about your business telephone and your equipment. Let them know what help or support you need and expect. Discuss what noise you can and cannot tolerate, what areas must be left neat and tidy, and what they are to do when you have business guests.

Employees

If you have workers coming into your home, help them feel comfortable in what may be an unfamiliar arrangement by explaining exactly what you expect. Because working from home may feel much more informal than working in an office setting, it is particularly important to establish a businesslike manner.

Set clear hours. Define when employees can take breaks. Show them what areas of the house are open, and which bathroom to use. Make it clear whether or not they can use your business phone, your dishes, your refrigerator, or your food. Chapters 18–20 go into more detail about working at home successfully with family members and employees.

Special Considerations Regarding Pets

Managing pets while working from home can be a problem. First, if you have customers or clients coming to your home, a small but significant number of people are allergic to dogs and cats, and some people are afraid of dogs. In fact, a survey of three thousand Americans found that dogs were the tenth most common fear. So keeping your pets in a yard or a part of the house away from your business visitors makes good sense, even if your animals "wouldn't hurt a soul."

Another problem faced by dog owners who work at home is when the dog begins barking loudly right in the middle of an important phone conversation. So much for the professional business image!

Short of keeping your dog away from the work area, you can solve this problem by having a mute button or a hold button on your telephone, preferably both. The mute button allows you to hear the person you're talking with but prevents them from hearing you as long as you're holding the button down. The hold button keeps the caller on hold and frees you to leave the phone and take care of the disturbance. With these features, simply say, "Just a moment. There's a dog barking outside my window. Let me close it." They're also ideal for unexpected disruptions from children or other household emergencies.

Keeping Your Office Space in Bounds

By necessity, most home offices are confined to a relatively small space. But work projects don't always fit neatly in small spaces, especially as your business activities at home grow. Defining the boundaries helps you maintain the best aspects of a home and an office. Fortunately, as we'll discuss in the next chapter, you have options as to where you locate your office. And entire industries of products, supplies, and consultants are now available to help you keep your office space sufficiently organized to prevent its overtaking the rest of your home.

Chapter Digest

1. The degree of privacy an individual needs to work effectively and still preserve his or her home is a highly personal matter. Taking the time to define your ideal home office situation precisely enables you to establish the boundaries you need to work productively and still enjoy your home.

2. To keep the boundaries you need between work and home clear, you will need to communicate your needs and expectations to your family, neighbors, friends, clients, employees, and colleagues and help them feel at ease with your home-office arrangement.

3. With modern communications technology and new resources like private post office boxes and rentable office suite addresses, you are free to choose whether to let your clients and customers know you're working from your home.

4. You can also choose whether to let business visitors come into your home. In making the choice, consider your needs for security, privacy, and professional image.

5. Having a separate telephone line for your business calls with an answering machine, answering service, or voicemail will enable you to convey

professional image without disturbing your family. It also prevents you from missing valuable calls and provides you with needed time away from the phone.

Resources

Books

Feng Shui: The Chinese Art of Designing a Harmonious Environment. A Fireside Book. New York: Simon & Schuster, 1988.

CHAPTER
SIX
■ ■

Finding the Right Office Space

You can put a home office almost any-where—on a boat, in an RV, on the dining-room table, or in a converted basement. The critical question is, which place will maximize your potential for success and help you remove any obstacles to working from home?

In actuality, most home offices start out in the first place that comes to mind, and end up somewhere else.

Lynne Frances's cleaning service started out in her bedroom, but ended up in the living room. She didn't like waking up in the middle of the night and being reminded of the work she had to do.

Gary Eckart's stained-glass factory started out in the den and ended up in an RV parked beside his house. His toddlers were too interested in his tools and the brightly colored glass.

Mary Stoddard's graphics studio started out in the living room and ended up in the garage. She found she didn't like strangers entering the privacy of her home.

Tom Girard began his translation service on the kitchen table and ended up converting the basement into an office. He didn't like the breakfast table piled with his papers or his papers adorned with telltale jelly stains.

In fact, almost every problem people have in working from home—whether it's overeating, too many interruptions, or not getting enough work done—is either aggravated or alleviated by where they put their offices. The location of your office can even be the solution to problems that seem to have no relation to office location. The McNaughtons are a case in point.

Bill McNaughton is a professor and has worked at home part time for many years. As a high school teacher, his wife, Bonnie, had always worked away from the house. But when she left teaching, she completed a degree in instructional design and opened a business at home writing technical manuals.

She set up her office at the top of the stairs in a bedroom left vacant when the kids moved out. But from the very beginning, this arrangement didn't work. Two, three, or maybe four times a morning her husband would come into her office to ask a question, share some news, or just say hello. She kept urging him not to interrupt her, to please wait until lunch to talk. He would apologize and agree to leave her alone, but then interrupt again. She tried being tolerant, but once distracted from her work she would lose her momentum and find it hard to get started again.

On the verge of renting an office, she decided to have one last talk with her husband. The more they talked, the clearer the problem became. Because her office was right at the top of the stairs, he had to walk by it as he went to and from his office in the den. This happened quite often since he was used to pacing while thinking. Seeing her office, even with the door closed, was too much of a temptation for him. He couldn't resist dropping in to visit.

They solved the problem by trading offices. From the bedroom office, he could walk up and down the stairs freely, as many times as he wished. With his wife's office out of sight down the hall, it was also out of mind. She got her work done and they chatted over lunch.

Like so many of us, Bonnie hadn't really given much thought to where she'd put her office. The spare bedroom at the top of the stairs had seemed only natural. Yet this location created unnecessary problems, as unplanned office sites often do.

Finding the right space for your office is a matter of putting together several factors and coming up with the best possible location. The right space meets the demands of your particular job. It matches your personal work style and budget. And it fits in with your household environment. The object of this chapter is to help you identify the office location that will work best in your situation.

Minimum Home Office Space Requirements

To work effectively at home, most people need these basic work areas:

1. Space for a desk and chair, where you can do paperwork and make phone calls.
2. Space where you can work with a computer, typewriter, calculator, or other equipment.
3. Contemplation or conversation space with chairs or a couch, where you can collect your thoughts or hold business meetings.
4. Storage space for filing cabinets, books, and reference materials.
5. Shelf space for storing supplies and infrequently used equipment.
6. Large work space for activities like assembling or producing materials and doing mailings or shipping.

In addition to these basic work areas, consider your needs for specialized space. Do you need room for particular equipment? Workspace for employees? A waiting area for customers or clients?

All of these work areas needn't be in the same room. Attics, basements, garages, or an enclosed back porch are good for storage space. Closets will hold filing cabinets, and linen cabinets are adaptable for supplies. The living room makes a good meeting room. The dining room can serve as a conference room.

Plan, however, to choose areas that are arranged so you can use them conveniently. Everyday supplies should be as near as possible to your workspace, while less frequently used equipment and files can be kept in more remote areas.

Finding a Place for Everything

Since everything obviously can't be kept in your immediate desk area, use this formula adopted from Stephanie Winston's book *Getting Organized* to decide where to keep what. On a scale of 1 to 7, rate the item you're storing or filing in terms of how frequently you use it. Give items you use every day a 1; those you use once a year, a 7. Place the items in the following locations according to how you rate them:

1—place all items you rate as a 1 within arms reach of your desk area.

2–3—keep items you rate as a 2 or 3 within your immediate office space in files or cabinets, on counter tops or shelves.

4–5—store items you rate as a 4 or 5 in nearby cabinets or closets, or shelves outside your office space.

6–7—store those items you use only once or twice a year in remote locations like attic, basement, or garage.

From our experience, here's a final tip. Plan to add at least 10 percent of whatever office space you think you need for storage space. There are a number of places other than available closets and drawers for storing office supplies, equipment, and files.

Matching Your Work Style

It's very tempting to recommend locating your home office in a separate room with a sturdy door. This does seem to be the best and most obvious solution for many people. A separate office, however, is not always possible, and since we've found so many successful home offices that break this standard mold, we've come to another conclusion.

You've heard the saying, "Home is where the heart is." It applies equally to home offices. The best office space will be a space where you want to work.

We all have our idiosyncrasies and preferences, and the right place for one person can be a disaster for another. Elizabeth Forsythe Hailey, Noel Cavanaugh, and Marcia Seligson, for example, are all writers who work at home, but each prefers writing under quite different circumstances.

Elizabeth likes to write in the kitchen so she "can keep an eye on things." Noel locks himself away in a basement hideaway. "Everyone knows if I'm downstairs they'd better not interrupt me unless a new baby or a million-dollar check has just arrived. When I'm writing, I can stay down there for twenty-four hours at a time." Marcia Seligson likes to move around when she writes. She may type at her desk for a while in the sunny office she had built over her garage. Then she may get up and stroll outside to think and jot some notes, and afterward resume writing in the comfort of the living room.

So how can you know the best place for you? Here are several decisions you can make to help you match your office space to your personal preferences and work style. Mark where you fall on each of the folowing continua.

Private? _____ **or** _____ **Public?**

This is probably your most important space decision. Do you like or need to work in an exclusive private space away from all other noise and activity? Or do you like to work in the midst of it all? The privacy questionnaire in Chapter 5 should give you a good idea of where you are on this continuum.

At one extreme is Dr. Richard Ricardi, whose office is located in a separate building behind his garage. As a psychiatrist, he finds that "a separate location helps my clients feel this is definitely a professional office and not a social setting. I also find by walking back to the office in the morning I 'go to work' and then at night I close the door and I 'go home.' "

At the other extreme is Brenda Rosetta, who runs her cookie company entirely from her spacious kitchen. She says of her kitchen office, "I'm always in the heart of the action and never miss out on a thing that's going on."

Shared? _____ **or** _____ **Exclusive?**

Can your office space serve other household purposes when you're not using it for business? Too often we don't have a choice about this one. The question often becomes which room can be used both for an office and for household purposes, without totally disrupting the operations of either.

At one extreme is Mary Stoddard, who sets up and takes down her graphic-design studio every workday. Each morning she moves the cars out of the garage, pulls down tables that are hinged to the walls, and starts working. Every evening she puts her work away, folds the tables up, and drives the cars back into the garage. For her, sharing this space on a daily basis works out fine.

At the other extreme is William Lecker, who will not share office space with other household activities even on an infrequent basis. When he started creating handmade jewelry, he thought the guest room could easily serve as his workshop, since guests used it only once or twice a year. He found instead that his metals and stones could neither be put away nor moved without considerable difficulty, even for a weekend. He decided to move his workshop into an unused breakfast room where he could work and visit with his wife when she was in the kitchen.

Windows? _____ or _____ No Windows?

Some people find windows distracting. They can't keep their eyes and their minds on their work. Others feel almost claustrophobic in windowless rooms.

As a data-entry clerk, Helen Gilles sits at the computer most of the day. To minimize glare problems, she likes an interior room without windows.

Jack Gates works in sales so he's on the road most of the week. He doesn't look forward to the reports and other paperwork awaiting him on the weekend, but it becomes almost enjoyable as he does it near the large sliding glass door in his office, which looks out onto the backyard. "We have one of the most beautiful jacaranda trees I've ever seen. I like to look at that tree and see the sunlight flooding through it into the office. It relaxes me. I even enjoy watching the kids play out there with the dog."

Compact? _____ or _____ Spacious?

You may like a lot of elbow room, space to spread out your things while you work. Or you may prefer keeping everything close at hand.

When Sharon Kirkpatrick started working as a seamstress, she set up a sewing room on an enclosed porch off her living room. It was a big, open space and seemed ideal. She could spread out her patterns and tackle many projects at once. But she ended up feeling as if she were working in a giant wastebasket. Thread and scraps, patterns and half-cut garments, pins and tape were everywhere. She was embarrassed to bring people in there for a fitting.

So she decided to set up her sewing room in a large walk-in closet, where she sews on one piece of work at a time. The porch, which she put back into order, is a space she now uses to store her material, cut her patterns, hang finished garments, and have fittings.

Fitting into Your Household

Once you have a picture of the type of office most suitable for you, you can match your needs with what goes on in your household.

Engineer Jeff Knoghton set up his office in the den off the family room. The den was a natural place. In fact, one reason he bought the house was that he saw the den as the place he would use one day to start a consulting practice.

When that day finally arrived, he proudly set up his desk, files, and comfortable chair and went to work.

Everything was fine until 3:00 P.M. when the kids came home. From that hour on, the television was playing almost continuously, with the children laughing and carrying on nearby. At Jeff's request, they became pretty good about keeping the set turned down, but every once in a while, usually just as he was on an important call or in the midst of a crucial thought, he would be bombarded with the sounds of a highspeed chase, with police sirens and screeching brakes. Despite efforts at restricting viewing hours and other creative "solutions," household tensions increased until he finally moved his office to an upstairs bedroom.

A careful review of household activity patterns *before* deciding on his office location would have helped Jeff avoid the problem in the first place. Spend a day or even a week noticing what goes on in your home. Keep notes as to who does what during which hours.

Is the living room the most likely place for a romantic evening with a date? Would the answering machine and computer equipment interrupt the mood there? When and where do family members or roommates use noisy equipment like power tools, the lawn mower, the dishwasher, or the vacuum cleaner? What room do other people gravitate to when they come over? Where do the kids play? What are the traffic patterns through your home and the noise patterns outside your home? Does someone in the neighborhood practice the piano? Or even worse, the drums? Will the kids run down the hall past your office on the way from the living room to their bedrooms? Do you have to walk past your office on the way to your bedroom? With this kind of information, you're in a good position to decide what will be the best use of the space you have.

Making the Most of Your Available Space

We've known a few people who've moved to a new home just to have one that's better suited for a home office. But most of us are limited to what we've got. The space you have, however, is probably not as limiting as you think. As we've said, you can consider working in almost any part of your home. You can convert or remodel your space into something more suitable. And if all else fails, you may be able to expand or add on. Let's review some of these options, beginning with the most commonly used rooms.

The Spare Bedroom

The spare bedroom is the most popular candidate for a home office. Since it is a spare room, the workspace can generally be used without sacrificing a great deal of living area. In fact, you may find it possible to continue using the room for other purposes when you want to. If there's a sofa bed in the room, it can still be a guest room or, if it has ample bookshelves, it can serve as a library. Using the room for nonbusiness purposes, however, jeopardizes you home office tax deduction, as you will see in Chapter 10.

Spare bedrooms are often far enough away from the mainstream of household activities to offer some kind of privacy, yet accessible enough to make having business guests or running out for occasional household chores convenient. Most important, however, a spare bedroom is usually large enough to feel like a real office and not like a makeshift workspace.

The Living Room

Many executive offices today have been carefully designed and decorated to look like living rooms. Bookcases, casual conference tables, comfortable chairs and couches are standard office furnishings. So why not have a living room that's an office?

For the right business, a living-room office has many advantages. As long as you keep your desk neat, the living room can serve as your home office by day and return to its role as a living room after working hours.

The living room is usually the most spacious area of the home, making it more easily divisible into a separate office space with partitions, bookcases, screens, or furniture. It is almost always near the front entrance, which makes it accessible to business visitors. It is usually designed as the public part of the home, so personal areas are located away from it. It is often the most formal part of the home and as such is suitable for creating a business image. In addition, closets and guest bathrooms are usually found nearby.

In some homes with a family room or den, the living room is actually anything but a "living" room. It's reserved for holidays or the arrival of special guests. If this is your situation and you don't need a more isolated office area, the living room can be an excellent choice.

The Family Room

If you have both a family room and a living room, you can use the family room for your office, and move activities that used to take place there into the living room.

Family rooms are generally located near the kitchen and back entrances and therefore make good workshops, studios, or labs. They're somewhat removed from the sound of street traffic. But often they open onto other living areas. This can be an advantage if you like to be in the center of activity, but a disadvantage if you're seeking a more secluded workspace.

The Kitchen

Since the kitchen is such a central part of any home, locating your office there usually puts you in the heart of household activity. And since the kitchen probably has to be used, water, food, and cooking grease may gum up your

Figure 6-1. Breakfast room converted into an office.

office space. But if you need access to plumbing, electricity, or of course cooking equipment, this may be the right location.

A breakfast nook can often be turned into an office (see Figure 6-1). Sometimes the kitchen itself can be divided to create a separate office area.

Beware, though, of the temptation to snack your way through the day, and of a possible negative effect on your business image. A professional atmosphere in the kitchen is possible, but often difficult.

The Dining Room

Many people get along quite well without ever using their dining rooms, preferring to eat in the kitchen, family room, or breakfast nook. This infrequent use, along with the size and location of most dining rooms, makes them excellent candidates for home offices.

Sometimes the dining area is an alcove off the living room. For a business like consulting, this can be a particularly attractive setting, with the living room serving as a meeting room or waiting room for the office beyond. Or the dining room can become a second office for employees you hire, with your primary office located in the living room.

Closets, Dressing Rooms, and Storage Spaces

An area twenty-four to twenty-seven inches deep and five feet wide allows enough room for work or filing space. Therefore, walk-in closets, long closets with sliding or louvered doors, storage rooms, nurseries, guest bathrooms, or spaces beneath and along stairways are areas that can be transformed into home offices.

The advantages of these tiny, hidden areas are that they create a compact, self-contained workspace, and one that is out of the way when not in use. The disadvantages, of course, are that such work areas may be too small and outgrown too quickly.

The Bedroom

Sometimes bedrooms are large enough to be divided, partitioned, or screened off for separate office space (see Figure 6-2).

Generally, however, we discourage people from using their bedroom as a home office. Your bedroom is probably your most private and personal space, a place of retreat. Working in your bedroom, you may find you can't ever get away from business. Setting up an office in a bedroom you share may present even more problems, since your work is invading somebody's else's private space as well. Some couples we interviewed had declared the bedroom off limits for business, to preverve this one area of their home for intimacy and relaxation.

Converting or Remodeling

When existing space doesn't lend itself to a home office, you may be able to transform it into space that does. This transformation can be as simple as using screens, partitions, furniture, or wall units, or as complex as putting up or tearing down doorways and turning a dusty attic into a skylit studio. The costs can range from a $50 screen to thousands of dollars for a major renovation.

Ideas for simple and less expensive solutions are shown in Figure 6-3, which illustrates a variety of ways to carve out separate and private office space in the corner of any room.

New Space-Making/Space-Saving Resources

Products to Help You Organize Your Home Office. Manufacturers such as Rubbermaid and Rolodex are creating a rich array of clever products for the home office that provide innovative ways of organizing lots of material into cramped or underfurnished space. For example, the Design-a-Space helps you customize a system for handling mail, disks, files, business cards, etc., to suit your needs. Shelves and wall units like the Office Tower by Alumax Corp., or Basket Systems by Sculte, feature variable-sized floor-to-ceiling shelves. These products are available at office superstores, hardware stores, home center stores, and specialty stores like Containers & More, Function Junction, Conran's, Hold It!, the Container Store, and Placewares.

Integrated equipment. The trend in consumer electronics is toward combining functions once done by many pieces of equipment into one space-saving unit. Manufacturers like Canon and Panasonic are creating fax–phones, fax–copiers, answering machine–telephones and many other functional combinations. The Canon Navigator combines a computer, fax, copier, printer, scanner, and modem all in one.

Professional organizers. Over the past fifteen years a brand-new consulting specialty has emerged—the professional organizer. These information-age specialists offer space planning and design, paper management, storage systems, and general office organization. Often they specialize in home offices and they have access to many creative ideas and products that enable the person cramped for space to use every square inch to its maximum advantage. They charge from $50 to $125 an hour to help you set up your office in a way that maximizes your space.

Voice and communication coach Sandra McKnight, for example, hired a professional organizer when she found her growing business was taking over her one-bedroom apartment. She found the $475 she paid organizer Susan Rich to be worth every penny. Six hours and sixteen trash bags after Rich arrived Sandra discovered she actually had plenty of space. She just hadn't been using it well. She describes the process as follows; "Susan rearranged my desk, phone, and filing cabinets so I have easy access to everything. Then she turned some of my kitchen cabinets into an office supply area. Most importantly, however, she created a system for me to get my desk cleared off and keep it that way. Now I can immediately process the endless amounts of paper that come across my desk and quickly access what I need when I need it."

To locate professional organizers in your area, write to the National Association of Professional Organizers, 3824 Ocean View Blvd., Montrose, CA 91020, or consult your Yellow Pages.

Figure 6-2. Sometimes bedrooms are large enough to divide or partition off. A storage wall can create office space without disrupting the room.

One option is to use one of the open-plan modular systems so popular in today's offices. In the past, most of these systems were too cumbersome to use at home. The new Phoenix Design 20 from Tradex Corporation, of Zeeland, Michigan, has been described in *Business Week* as "the first office-quality unit we've seen that is suitable for the home." It includes a desktop, file drawer, shelves, and space for a personal computer, all built into a freestanding panel about five feet high and six feet wide. Short wing panels provide some privacy, and a sound-deadening fabric finish comes in four colors. The cost for the entire unit is about $1,500.

When ideas like these don't meet your needs, you might consider some of the more expensive remodeling options described below.

Figure 6-3.

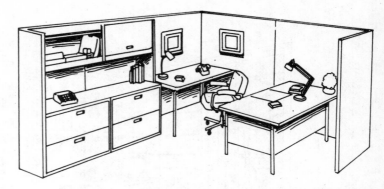

Modular panel systems

Wall units

Screens

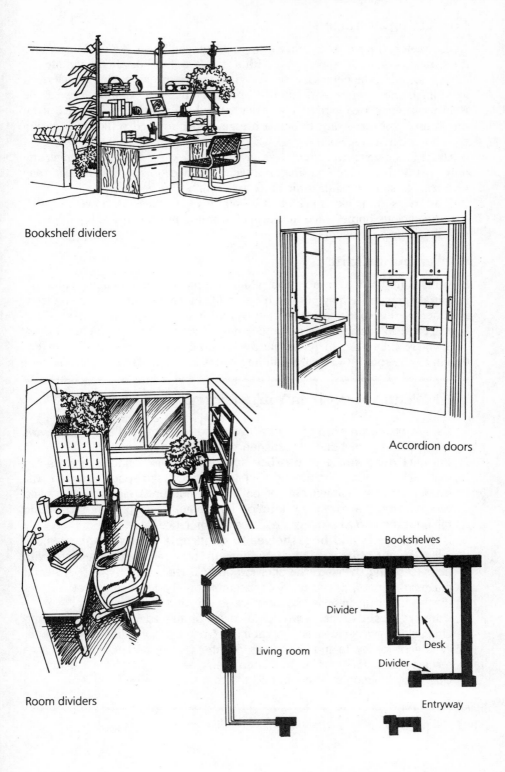

Bookshelf dividers

Accordion doors

Room dividers

Bookshelves

Divider

Desk

Living room

Divider

Entryway

Converting a Garage

To completely transform a garage into an office, you'll usually need to remove the garage door, build a new wall with a standard door installed, upgrade the floor, and put in the necessary insulation and waterproofing. Then you'll need to refinish the interior and exterior and add any necessary utilities. If the weather in your area is particularly severe and your garage is detached from the house, you may want to add a breezeway or covered walkway between your home and garage/office.

Usually, garage conversions mean giving up car space. However, converting only part of the garage or using an attached garage storage area instead may save enough space for a daytime office and a nighttime garage.

If all this sounds like a big job, it is. When you're finished, however, you'll have a spacious home office that provides ample privacy and a separate entrance for business visitors.

Converting an Attic

If you haven't used your attic in a while or removed the inevitable cobwebs, its initial appearance may put you off. But don't let appearances stop you from considering this space option. An attic/office is removed from the rest of the house, can provide a large work and storage area, and may even offer a view.

If you're interested in remodeling your attic, take a look at the current design of the room. Generally, building codes will allow you to convert your

---

Making Space When You're Renting or Can't Add On*

1. **Use your imagination.** If you start with the assumption that there's always more room somewhere, our experience is you'll find it.
2. **Convert dead space into office space.** The space under stairwells can make an excellent storage and supply closet. Unused space between wall supports can be carved out for built-in storage units. Space above filing cabinets also makes a great location for storage. A forty-eight-inch round table tucked into a corner can become a conference table.
3. **Use wall units and bookshelves to quadruple your storage area.** All walls in your office can be turned into usable space by lining them with floor-to-ceiling shelving. This shelving doesn't need to be expensive. Avatar makes reasonably priced ready-to-assemble units and there are retail stores that specialize in creative and inexpensive wall unit arrangements.
4. **Convert closet space.** A whole office can be tucked into a walk-in closet. Linen closets make ideal supply cabinets. Open up more space in the center of the office by taking the doors off the closets and using them as a recessed area for your or your employee's desk. Conceal file cabinets in closets by building a frame around the space and closing it off with sliding doors.

---

attic to living space if the ridgepole (the horizontal timber at the top of your roof to which the rafters are attached) is at least seven feet above the subfloor (the rough, unfinished floor of your attic).

The higher the ridgepole, the more comfortable your space will be. As a rule of thumb, at least one-half of the usable space needs to be seven feet high in order for the attic to be considered a viable home office option. The remaining less high areas can be used to create efficient storage space.

A frequent problem with attic conversions is access to the office. To build a stairway leading there, you need to have two feet by ten feet of space on the floor below and in the attic itself. A longer space would be needed if your

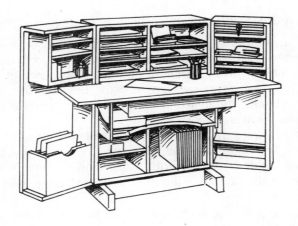

Figure 6-4. A Home Office in a Box. Manufactured by Nordisk, this desk—office unit expands to fit your needs. Closed, it measures only 32″ × 20½″ x 44½″. Opened, it measures 64″ wide. Available in walnut, teak, and redwood, it's priced at about $600.

5. **Divide an existing room with a room divider or screen.** Companies like Designer's Choice Shutter & Blind Company of Los Angeles will build a custom-designed wood divider with shutters that can be opened for light and visibility or closed to put your home office completely out of sight.
6. **Turn any existing room into an instant office with a folding desk unit,** like the one pictured in Figure 6-4 by Nordisk. Small when folded, when opened it becomes a full blown sixty-four-inch desk with lots of storage and filing space. A folding desk can also be built to fold down from a small closet with ample storage built in along the back wall of the closet.

*If you rent, remember to check your lease and talk with your landlord about any physical alterations.

ceiling is higher than eight feet. If you don't have this much space, you can consider a spiral staircase, which usually requires an area of four to five square feet. Remember, though, it may be difficult to get equipment up to the office on a spiral staircase.

Since the attic is subject to extreme temperatures in summer and winter, working conditions in an attic/office will be intolerable without proper insulation and an efficient means of heating and cooling. For both floor and ceiling, using fiberglass insulation batts, packed between the structural supports, is reported to be one of the most effective ways of controlling the room temperature. You can also use portable heaters and fans, but take safety into consideration before you purchase any portable appliance.

Converting a Basement

If you have a basement, that too can be turned into an office. Again, don't be put off by appearances. Clear it out, clean it up, and then look at the possibilities. Like attics, basements are removed from the flow of household activities and can offer you a quiet, private place to work. However, in addition to the inconvenience of stairs, the image of going "down" to see you could be less than desirable for business visitors.

The biggest problems in remodeling a basement are water leakage and humidity. You can waterproof the walls with commercial water sealants painted onto the inside of each exterior wall. Wood-textured board can then be placed between the exterior walls and a final covering of wall paneling or plasterboard.

If you decide to paint the walls, make sure you use waterproof paint and add a mildew retardant to the paint. If the room continues to feel damp, you may want to install one or two air vents that lead outside or to the house. Heaters, of course, will greatly help reduce the damp feeling, since the heat will cause the moisture to evaporate.

Since most basements have concrete floors, you may want to install a warmer-looking surface like a wood floor or carpeting. With proper padding and insulation, a carpet can enhance the atmosphere and provide further protection against cold and dampness.

Basements are notorious for exposed pipes, unconcealed wiring, and conspicuous utility meters. You can turn these eyesores into "architectural elements" using some bright paint over pipes, ducts, or other outcroppings to make them match the background or to create a colorfully pleasing design. Ceiling tiles, plasterboard, or textured wallboard can also be used. Make sure, however, that all the ducts and pipes are properly sealed and leakproof before you cover them.

You might set up a useful partition in front of the harder-to-hide heaters, meters, or wire boxes. Cabinets and freestanding closets can be cleverly placed to conceal a number of these unsightly objects, as can room dividers.

Converting a Patio or Porch

Patios and porches can become functional, attractive, and airy offices. These areas have the advantage of providing an exterior entrance and are usually set off from household activity. As with an attic, an enclosed porch or a patio requires insulation, heating, and cooling.

Adding On

When your home simply isn't big enough, you may have the option of adding on to what you've got. When adding on, you have three choices. You can build up, out, or down. The first step is to begin mentally breaking down walls, imagining rooms where there are none, figuratively digging out new foundations, and filling the yard or sky with a bigger house or perhaps separate structures.

You can begin by drawing a map of your house and the surrounding property, experimenting with different additions. Let your imagination go. Don't limit your ideas to office space. Consider adding on other areas that will free your existing space for office use. A master bedroom off the living room, for example, can become an ideal office when you've built a new (and improved, of course) bedroom in another part of the house.

To help plan changes in the layout of your home and office, you can use the Plan-A-Flex Office Designer kit, designed by an architect, which comes with a grid sheet and hundreds of reusable, peel-and-stick furniture and equipment syymbols for your to arrange and rearrange. Or you can use computer software like Design Your Own Home by Abracadata, Ltd., or Floorplan by ComputerEasy International, to try out various space-making alternatives.

After you've generated as many ideas as you can, check how feasible they are with more than one construction professional. Talk over your ideas with friends, relatives, or others who have added on.

When we realized we would have to add on, or move at least one of our offices out of the house, we began analyzing every possibility. We thought of building a second story over the garage, adding space off the living room, or constructing a separate building in back of the house. We weren't satisfied with anything until Sarah's mother suggestsed an ideal alternative we never would have thought of—leveling the redwood cathedral ceiling in our family room and building a second story over it.

A Dormer

If you have a steep roof, you can add workspace to existing rooms or create new rooms by building single, double, or full dormers (windowed projections built into the roof).

Figure 6-5.

Side porch became this sunny office.

Back porch off kitchen became this handy office.

Patio converted into studio

Loft office

Dormers

Raising the roof

Adding a wing

Raising the Roof

You can expand your available space by raising one or both sides of your roof. A small attic space can become a loft/office or a second floor over one or several rooms.

A Loft

A loft can make an ideal office space because it is usually removed from the mainstream of household activity. Since lofts typically involve raising the roof above existing space or opening ceiling space from rooms below, they do not afford privacy. Doors can be fashioned, however, to slide over a loft opening to solve this problem.

A Second Story

You can have a second story constructed over all or only a part of a single-level home. Of course, building a second story is a major project that is both costly and time consuming. Also, the living space below the new story will be out of use while building is going on. This can create considerable disruption to both your household and your work. So we recommend moving out of the house during construction, if possible.

Despite these drawbacks, adding a second story can double your space. When we built a second story over our family room, we created a bedroom and private bath for our teenage son, as well as a storage room. This addition freed our son's old bedroom, which was ideal for Sarah's office because it was right off the living room.

A Basement

If you have a partial basement, or a crawl space under your home, you can convert this area into a full basement and a viable home office. If you have no basement, you can create one under all or part of your house.

Creating a basement is another complicated and expensive option, but it *is* possible. It requires specialized knowledge of construction, so when considering this option locate a general contractor with previous experience and a proven track record doing such excavation.

A daylight basement can become a pleasant alternative to a damp and dingy underground basement/office. A daylight basement has all or part of one wall open to ground level, with windows that allow substantial light to enter into the office area. This windowed wall, which can be made of double-insulated glass, may also create an interesting entry. With sliding glass doors, it can even provide a patio extension to your office in warmer months.

The only requirement for a daylight basement is that there be a full-height foundation wall that is large enough for a door or at least a good-sized window at ground level. The amount of excavation and reconstruction of your foundation depends on the slope of your yard. Most homes can have at least a partial daylight basement built into the foundation.

A Separate Building

If you have the extra space, you can build or buy a separate structure. This structure can be attached to your house by a covered walkway or breezeway if you desire.

Because you're starting from scratch, building a separate structure can be more expensive than adding on. For some people, the advantages of adding a new, separate home office may be worth the investment, however. Construction doesn't disrupt the household, and when the building is finished you can have business visitors without their intruding into the privacy of your home. Your office will be completely self-contained.

If building a separate structure is outside your budget, your might consider prefabricated or precut construction kits. These kits cost anywhere from 20 to 40 percent less than comparable custom-built units—and they serve the purpose just as well. The sizes vary according to style and manufacturer, but most lines include models that are at least nine feet by twelve feet. To locate them, refer to the "Building" listings in your local Yellow Pages.

Mobile homes or recreational structures can also be relatively affordable office sites. Public relations consultant Jennifer Ash came up with one of the more creative office-space solutions we encountered. She occupies a two-room cottage with a large decked terrace off the living room. When she couldn't find a workable space for her desk in either room, she literally pitched a tent on the deck.

Her canvas gazebo, manufactured by Moss Tent Works, is totally self-contained and waterproof. By day it provides adequate workspace for her and one associate. At night, Jennifer merely zips up the tent and "comes home for the evening," carrying her phone along with her.

Getting a Professional Opinion

If your budget allows, consider getting advice from professional builders, designers, and architects. Lloyd and Suzanne Faulkner of Encino, California, are examples of designers who specialize in creating attractive and workable home-office spaces. They've helped clients with such innovative solutions as turning a pool table into a desk and finding a coffee table that can be raised, when needed, to desk level. They've even designed rolling desks for those who are confined to their beds. Aside from specialists like the Faulkners, various other professionals can be helpful.

Depending on your eye for design and the extent of your skills, you may be able to implement many of the ideas in this chapter yourself. Whenever remodeling or adding on to your home, however, contact your local city or county government to determine the permits and specifications required, and call on a licensed contractor of good reputation to carry out any extensive work. Also, recognize that finding the right office space may become an ongoing process, as it was for author-photographer David Goodfellow.

"Ten years ago I divided a twelve-by-twelve-foot spare bedroom in half and turned one half into an office for technical writing and the other half into a darkroom, but both areas soon became too small.

"Five years ago I sealed in our carport, the top of which doubled as a patio deck. It became a twelve-by-eighteen-foot office, a twelve-by-six darkroom, and a twelve-by-twelve junk room.

"To keep water from dripping down my neck when it rains, I had to have a composition roof put on the deck. Then our central heating didn't have enough selectivity to keep the office warm. So I bought a space heater.

"The advantages of the new arrangement are many, however. First, a nice percentage of my house is a tax write-off. Second, the new office is far enough away from the kitchen to make munching a real effort. Third, the office is bright and comfortable, which makes working there a joy."

A Guide to Professional Help
When Remodeling or Adding On

Architects
- prepare detailed plans and specifications for bids on the work to be done.
- draw up all plans in accordance with local health, safety, and engineering codes.
- provide workable plans to contractors.
- supervise all construction work.
- inspect the completed work.

Draftsmen or building designers
- draw up plans for straightforward and fairly simple remodeling.

General contractors
- work with the architect, designer, or owner in meeting all specifications for materials and construction of the work to be done.
- hire subcontractors to handle specific phases of the job and ensure that each phase is completed.
- set up all work schedules.
- secure all building permits and arrange for all necessary inspections.
- purchase all materials and supplies.
- furnish all tools and equipment required.

Interior designers or decorators
- assist you in utilizing your existing space more creatively or efficiently.
- assist you in furnishing and decorating the space.
- purchase furniture and decorator items at a discount.

So whether you find the right space for your home office immediately or, like David, create it over time, finding an arrangement that suits you can make a positive difference in your feeling about work. And remember, the costs involved in creating your office space are deductible, so keep your receipts. The next challenge becomes setting it up in the best way possible for your business.

Chapter Digest

1. Today's home office can literally be in any room of the house. Selecting the right location for your work activities is a matter of matching your work style and preferences with the limitations of your living space. To find the best space for you, begin by assessing your needs.

2. Minimum office-space requirements include adequate space for writing, telephone work, meetings, computing, assembling, storage, and office equipment.

3. A careful review of your household activity patterns during working hours will prevent unexpected problems with noise and interruptions.

4. Before selecting a location for your office, consider each room in your home—or the possibility of using a portion of it. You may be surprised that the best location is not the one you think of first.

5. Use the help of professional organizers, designers, and decorators when your own ideas run dry. Often they have solutions that will make even the most impossible space limitations workable.

6. Use integrated office equipment and the many creative new home-office organization products now on the market to make the most of your space.

Resources

Books

So This Is Where You Work! A Guide to Unconventional Working Environments. Charles A. Fracchia. The New Careers Center, 6003 N. 51st St., Ste. 105, Boulder, CO 80301.

The Successful Office, How to Create a Workspace That's Right for You. Franklin Becker. New York, NY: Addison Wesley Publishing Co., 1982.

Sunset Home Offices & Workspaces. Menlo Park, CA: Lane Publishing Co., 1986.

Sunset Home Remodeling Illustrations. Menlo Park, CA: Lane Publishing Co., 1988.

Sunset Complete Home Storage. Menlo Park, CA: Lane Publishing Co., 1988.

Other Resources

The American Society of Interior Designers. 1430 Broadway, New York, NY 10018. (212) 944-9220.

The National Design Center. 425 E. 53rd St., New York, NY 10022. Local retail stores; college and university design departments.

CHAPTER
SEVEN

■ ■

Outfitting Your Home Office
with Furnishings and Supplies

Most people take a "ready, fire, aim" approach to setting up a home office, according to Florence Feldman, a professional organizer based in Reston, Virginia. Too often when people buy furniture and equipment for their home office, they bring it home only to find it doesn't fit. Other people go after "bargains," which often have to be replaced, causing them to spend more money than if they had gotten proper items in the first place. Even more commonly, open-collar workers go on putting up with the mistakes they made in setting up their home offices— mistakes that now give them backaches, headaches, eyestrain, and even cauliflower ear!

But setting up a home office that works is not just a matter of avoiding problems. To establish what matters most to people about their home offices, we interviewed both veteran homeworkers and professional organizers, who get called in to help when a home office isn't working. Again and again, the veterans and experts listed four bottom-line criteria for making a home office work:

- Convenience—the setup needs to save you time and simplify your work; you should be able to come in and just start working.
- Comfort—the office needs to satisfy you physically and emotionally, and cause you no pain or strain while you're working.
- Functionality—work needs to flow smoothly, with items used everyday within arm's reach.
- Privacy—the office space needs to be free of intrusions and disturbances.

With these standards in mind, we organized this chapter like a department store, to offer as much variety as possible for addressing these major considerations, while taking into account both appearance and finding bargains in the process. We'll begin with the furniture department.

Choosing Your Furniture

Furniture is one of the things that home office workers tend to over-economize on, at least at first. Marge Abrams, who calls herself a Paper, Space, Possession, and Time Management consultant, says, "Until people are 'successful' in a home business, they don't spend a lot of money on furniture. They use what's in the house. I've done the same thing."

If you're like over half the office workers surveyed in a Louis Harris poll, you spend over 75 percent of your day sitting at your desk. This means there are some very good reasons not to use just any desk and chair. The wrong desk and chair can cause aches and pains in your back, neck, shoulders, arms, and even the undersides of your thighs or calves. Peggy Glenn reflects on her mistakes when setting up a home office: "I rented a typewriter and put it on the kitchen table. Now I tell everybody I know, don't put your typewriter there. You end up with a real crick in the neck. It can be very painful and literally put you out of business."

But the effects are not always so physical. Fatigue, loss of concentration, and irritability are some of the more subtle problems traced to the wrong furniture. On the other hand, productivity gains of up to 40 percent have been made once the right office furniture was found. More specifically, one-third of workers interviewed listed a comfortable chair as one of the top two contributors to their productivity. Designer William Strumpf suggests approaching chairs, desks, and other important office furniture as if the piece were a garment: "It should be proportioned to fit the person who's using it."

Not all designers are like Strumpf, however. According to a survey reported in *Interior Design* magazine, interior designers rank aesthetics over comfort in selecting office furniture (77% to 45%), so if you use a designer to help you select your office furniture, be sure you choose one who believes in comfort first.

The Desk

Desk surfaces need to be different heights for different tasks. While writing surfaces should generally be 30" off the ground, typing or computing surfaces are usually 26" inches high. Some desks are designed to include surfaces of more than one height. Others can be adjusted up and down or tilted to the position you desire as you change tasks. As an alternative, you can simply have both a writing desk and a separate typing or computer table.

Furniture Checklist: What Do You Need?

☐ Desk
   ☐ Different heights for different tasks
   ☐ Appropriate width and depth
   ☐ Suitable style
      ☐ Solid
      ☐ Cube
      ☐ Open table
☐ Chairs
   ☐ Desk Chair
      ☐ Supportive back
      ☐ Firm seat
      ☐ Breathable material
      ☐ Firm armrests
      ☐ Adjustable height
      ☐ Footrests
      ☐ Tilt mechanism
      ☐ Rollers
   ☐ Easy chair
   ☐ Side or conference table chairs

☐ Filing Cabinets
   ☐ Legal size
   ☐ Standard size
   ☐ Vertical cabinets
   ☐ Lateral cabinets
   ☐ Hanging files
   ☐ Non-hanging files
☐ Tables
   ☐ Work table
   ☐ Conference table
   ☐ End or coffee table
   ☐ Other:
☐ Couch
☐ Bookcases
☐ Storage racks
☐ Lamps
   ☐ Incandescent lighting
   ☐ Fluorescent lighting

Besides height, other features to be tailored to you and your home office are width and style. Unless the office is 20 feet or more across, choose a desk no wider than 7 feet. Larger desks will overpower and crowd the room. Even the style of your desk affects how large it will seem. Available choices are solid, cube, or open-style desks. In smaller offices, a table desk will appear to take less space than a cube desk of the same size.

The Desk Chair

An improper chair will cause muscle strain, swelling of lower legs, reduced blood circulation (which in turn diminishes your ability to think), and varicose veins. So plan to "test drive" your desk chair before using it in your office. Sit in it to evaluate the back, seat, arms, and optional features.

The back of the chair should provide support for the base of the spine, helping it hold a slight forward curve. The backrest should be high enough to allow you to relax against it, coming to at least the lower part of your shoulder blades.

Chairs with tilt mechanisms work with the seat and back fixed or with a separately adjustable seat and back. A five-pointed base to the chair, rather than the customary four legs, will help avoid tipping over if you lean back too far.

The seat of the chair should be rounded so it won't dig into your thighs and restrict blood flow in the legs. The seat should also be adjustable up and down over a range of six to nine inches, so you can adapt it to different work tasks. Preferably, you will be able to adjust the chair by gently pressing a button or lever under the seat from a sitting position.

When your chair is properly adjusted, your feet should be flat on the floor and the seat should be parallel to the floor. If you are short, you may need a footrest to keep your legs from dangling.

Often people assume that a soft seat is the most comfortable. Actually, this is only true for a short time, since too soft a seat limits the natural **S** curve of your spine. The seat material should be a rough, porous fabric that lets body heat dissipate.

The arms should have a hard surface that wears well and resists soiling, but preferably should not be made of metal, which feels cold and slick. As far as height goes, the arms should be low enough not to rub the underside of the desk or hit other furniture.

A chair with rollers will enable you to move from one work area to another. Make sure, however, that the rollers have self-locking casters that travel smoothly over carpeting but not too quickly over wood or linoleum. "Dual-wheel" casters are preferable to the "ball" type because they move more smoothly, distribute weight more evenly, and don't cut into the flooring.

Finally, whatever combination of features you choose, even the best chair isn't designed for long-term sitting, so get up and move around every twenty minutes or so while working!

Filing Cabinets

Just as you can never be too rich or too thin, you can also never have too many filing cabinets. Whether you need two file drawers or a bank of cabinets, you have several basic choices to make:

Size.   Because of Paul's law background, our files are legal-size, but the more convenient option is the standard letter-size.

Shape.   Although lateral files have gained in popularity, they can take up a substantial amount of floor space and we find them less convenient to use than vertical cabinets. A lateral cabinet can, however, be functional as a room divider as well as a spacious storage unit.

Filing features.   Hanging files fit on racks in a standard file drawer. While they make your folders easy to see and manipulate in the file drawer, the folders are clumsy to handle when removed from the cabinet.

Locking. If you have confidential material, locks are a requirement for your cabinets. In fact, you may want to get even stronger file cabinets that are burglar- and fireproof as well.

Quality. Whatever kind of file cabinet you buy, stick with recognized brands such as Shaw-Walker, Steelcase, and Litton. As Stephanie Winston points out in *The Organized Executive,* cheap cabinets jam easily. Their drawers may slip off the tracks or fall out completely, and their tendency to tip over makes them dangerous.

Noise Control

Noise, among all environmental factors, has the strongest correlation to job stress and dissatisfaction in an office, according to a Columbia University study. Even moderately high noise levels cause increased blood pressure, faster heartbeat, and other symptoms of stress, while excessive noise causes fatigue, distraction, and errors in work. Actually, noise may have consciously or unconsciously played a role in your choosing to work from home.

While too much noise certainly interferes with work, a total absence of sound is also stressful. As one person who moved his office home says, "The first thing I noticed was the silence. I never realized how much I appreciated the sounds of the office."

Just how much sound do you need to stay mentally alert? Probably not more than thirty decibels, about the sound of a normal air conditioner. Even better would be twenty decibels of sound, about equivalent to leaves rustling in the breeze.

The average office has a noise level of about fifty decibels. The sound of an average conversation is about sixty decibels, while the vacuum cleaner in your home runs at about eighty decibels. Prolonged exposure to over seventy decibels may result in hearing impairment.

To keep the sound levels in your office down to a comfortable level, you can simply increase the distance between your office and outside activity. Doubling the distance between your office and outside activity will decrease the noise that travels between the two points by six decibels. If this is impossible, you can use one or more of these sound-control techniques.

1. Draperies over windows. For maximum effectiveness, these need to be floor length and lined.
2. Ceiling treatments such as acoustical tile or commercially applied sound-absorbent material.
3. A thick pile carpet with an underpad to absorb noise in the room.
4. Heavily padded furniture.
5. Weather stripping on doors and windows.

6. Indoor barriers such as room dividers or screens; outdoor barriers such as a concrete block wall over five feet high.
7. Solid-core doors in place of hollow-core doors.
8. Double-glazed windows.
9. Wall coverings such as fabric or cork. Armstrong Soundsoak is a fabric over acoustical fiberboard that will absorb 60 percent of noise.
10. Acoustical drywall or paneling on top of your existing walls, with thick insulation placed between the studs of the new wall.

Before you spend a lot of money or time on any of these sound-control measures, however, find out if the noise is coming through a heat or air vent. If it is, using one of the sound "masking" techniques described below will be more effective.

To produce enough sound to keep yourself alert when working at home alone, you can create your own background noise. Consider using sounds like these while you work.

1. A stereo playing low.
2. A gurgling fish tank with a water filter and air pump.
3. A cage of songbirds, such as canaries.
4. A "white noise" generator.
5. One of the commercially available records or endless-loop tape cassettes that play office sounds or sounds from nature, such as the sound of the surf rolling in or the wind blowing.

Because these sounds are rhythmical, they will also help mask noise you can't screen out by other measures.

Lighting Your Home Office

According to the Harris poll for Steelcase we noted before, lighting is the number one contributor to productivity. The amount and type of light you need depends on your age, the kind of work you do, and your preferences.

Generally, the more detailed your work, the more light you need. So if you're a cartographer making maps, you'll need more light than someone taking notes while on the telephone. Also, as you age you need more light. A person over fifty may need 50 percent more light than a younger person, and a person over sixty may need 100 percent more light.

In using a computer at any age, however, you may need less light, not more, in order to avoid glare on your computer screen, because readability of a computer screen depends on the contrast between onscreen characters and the screen background.

Here are some general guidelines to follow when considering the best lighting for your office.

Use Natural Light When Possible

The best light for your office is also the cheapest—daylight. Daylight provides the truest color and is the least tiring and puts the least strain on your eyes of all light sources. This means you will be more productive in natural light. The quality of daylight, however, is affected by a number of factors: direction of exposure; the color and texture of your walls, ceiling, and furnishings; the arrangement of your workspace; and, of course, the time of day and the weather.

Daylight entering from the north is usually a soft, indirect light, shining steadily most of the day. Artists and craftspeople prefer this type of natural light, especially if it hits pale-colored interiors. Because of its lack of glare, northern light is best for operating a computer too. More direct light enters from an eastern or western source and, to a lesser degree, from the south, and will not only cause more glare but also an imbalanced illumination.

One way of getting nonglare daylight is to add clerestories, or windows that are installed high up on a wall. Clerestories throw diffused light into the center of a room, providing balanced illumination without glare, and because of their height they also provide privacy. Installing clerestories in an existing building, however, is likely to be expensive. Skylights are another attractive way of bringing additional daylight into offices where it is blocked or nonexistent. Various skylight styles enable you to direct light to a work area or diffuse light evenly throughout your office.

Supplement with Artificial Lighting

Of course, it's impossible to work by daylight all the time, even in an ideal room. At night or on gray days you have to turn on the lights. The most common types of artificial light are incandescent and fluorescent lighting. Both have their advantages and disadvantages.

Incandescent lights are usually small and have a high degree of intensity, so they can be used for task lighting—that is, supplementary lighting focused directly on your work. A desk lamp provides task lighting, as do track lights.

Comparison of Incandescent and Fluorescent Lighting

Light Source	Power Required	Light Output (Lumens)	Approximate Lifespan
Incandescent	150 watts	2,880 foot-candles	750 hours
Fluorescent	50 watts	3,200 foot-candles	12,000–20,000 hours

Used in conjunction with ceiling fixtures, a desk light can eliminate shadows on your work.

The color emitted by an incandescent bulb is warm-toned. It is softer, reflects better on the skin, and is gentler on the eyes than fluorescent light, although newer types of fluorescent lighting provide as good or better color rendition as incandescents. Incandescent light is also the most expensive form of lighting available, consuming the most electricity for the light produced, and it converts much of this energy into unwanted heat.

Fluorescent lighting is diffused, produces little heat, and provides a steady, highly efficient light source. It generally requires large, relatively expensive fixtures, however, and cannot easily be used to spotlight specific areas. Fluorescent lights also blink, and if you're near enough to the light source to notice the blinking, you're apt to experience eyestrain and fatigue.

Because incandescent and fluorescent lighting both have advantages, you may want a balance between the two. If you use fluorescent lighting, the most desirable kinds of bulbs for a home office are full-spectrum bulbs, which are most like natural daylight.

New products offer exciting solutions for home office lighting problems. Compact fluorescent bulbs are now being made that fit into standard lamps. These bulbs offer long life (approximately 7,000 hours) and use only about one-fourth the energy of a conventional incandescent bulb. Though compact by fluorescent standards, these bulbs are still more than twice the size of an incandescent bulb and may not fit within enclosed fixtures. Another innovation, halogen bulbs provide a white light, last about 2,000 hours, and use about 10 percent less electricity.

We are making use of Chromalux bulbs made with neodymium. These bulbs produce the color rendition of natural sunlight with a 99.6 percent rating. The bulbs fit standard lamps and last about 3,000 hours. You may be able to find these new bulbs only at stores specializing in lighting fixtures.

Use Light to the Best Advantage

Making the eye adjust to varying levels of light in a room is one cause of eye fatigue. Therefore, to avoid eye strain, have the general level of light in the room as near as possible to the level of light on your work.

One option for keeping this balance is to use dimmer-switches to adjust the level of light in the room. They also save on your electricity bill and can change the mood from a bright work setting to a softer conference-room atmosphere. Installing a dimmer-switch for incandescent lighting is simple and inexpensive, but for fluorescents it is costly. It's more economical to install a dimmer-switch on fluorescents when they are first put in, instead of at a later date.

Another cause of eyestrain is glare. The more illumination you have in an office, the greater the risk of glare. Therefore you need to find a balance between having too little light and too much. You can reduce glare by making sure light bulbs are not in your line of sight and by avoiding light

The Environmentally Conscious Home Office

We believe every open-collar worker is entitled to a bumper sticker that reads, "I save air, water, and energy—I work from home."

By not commuting to a job, you are not contributing to air pollution. As President George Bush pointed out to the California Chamber of Commerce on March 1, 1990, in the first speech in which a president endorsed working from home, ". . . if only 5 percent of the commuters in Los Angeles County telecommuted one day each week, they'd . . . keep 47,000 tons of pollutants from entering the atmosphere." By working at home, you're probably using less water than if you were at an office.

People working from home can also conveniently practice additional conservation measures. Here are fourteen things you can do:

1. Use halogen and compact fluorescent bulbs that produce more light, last longer than ordinary incandescent bulbs, and use less energy.
2. Install low-flush toilets. They use only one-third to one-fourth as much water as standard toilets.
3. Use word processing and desktop publishing software that previews what your printed page will look like. This will reduce the number of test copies you need to make.
4. Use personal information management software instead of making notes on paper.
5. Fax information instead of hand delivering it or using a messenger service or an air freight company. You'll save on fuel and energy.
6. Make use of an internal fax in your computer. You can send and receive faxed messages without having to produce printed pages.
7. Store information and documents on computer disks instead of in paper files.
8. Use outdated stationery to make notepads instead of throwing it away.
9. Buy products made from recycled paper.
10. When it will not create confusion, use the back sides of paper for lists and scratch paper.
11. Save for reuse shipping boxes, styrofoam balls, and other plastic packaging materials to avoid generating nonbiodegradable trash.
12. Consolidate as many errands as possible into one trip. Use your own shopping bags, rather than plastic bags.
13. Be environmentally conscious about the office products you use. Liquid Paper, for example, has a new environmentally safe line. Look for other nontoxic products that do not create environmental hazards.
14. Without decreasing your productivity, reduce air-conditioning by scheduling your work for other than the hottest hours of the day, using attic fans and skylights that open. Heat only the rooms you need to use in winter.

Best Ways to Deal with Static Electricity

1. Antistatic mats
2. Aerosol spray
3. Humidifier
4. Plants in your office
5. Uncarpeted floors

that reflects off shiny surfaces such as picture glass, mirrors, and the like. Another simple way of reducing glare is to have several small light sources rather than one bright light.

A simple way to enhance lighting in your office is using color to your advantage. Dark colors absorb light; light colors reflect it back into the room. One of Paul's previous offices had redwood paneling on about half of the wall area, while the other half was white. At night, there was a noticeable difference in the level of light needed in each area. Where the wall was darker, we had to increase the amount of electricity we used. So one way of cutting down your electric bill is to have light-colored walls and ceilings.

Providing Security and Fire Protection

Having a home office both increases and decreases your security risks. On one hand, you have added equipment and material to protect while you may be bringing strangers into your home. On the other hand, you are at home more often or at least away at irregular times. Either way, you reduce your chances of being burglarized, because thieves avoid houses where someone might be home.

Here are twelve ways to further protect yourself from theft and to safeguard confidential materials.

1. **Secure your doors and windows.** The more difficult you make entry into your home, the less chance there is someone will go to the trouble of breaking in. In addition, since thieves have often been in a house as visitors before they burglarize it, you can substantially reduce your risk by having prominent safety features like dead-bolts, and good locks. Even if potential burglars figure they can get into your home, getting things out will appear difficult.

2. **Light your premises well,** both inside and outside.

3. **Have a dog that barks at strangers.** Convicted burglars who were surveyed rate a dog as the most effective deterrent.

4. **When you're away from home, give the appearance that someone is there.** For example, leave lights on, keep a TV or radio playing, or have water sprinklers going.

5. **Hire a housesitter** when you're going out of town. At least be certain the newspapers and mail are picked up every day. Students at theological seminaries are reliable housesitters.

6. **Create environmental barriers around your home.** Research at the University of Utah has shown that creating a sense of privacy around your home is as important in preventing burglaries as the locks you use. Hedges, fences, shrubs, and trees act as psychological barriers to would-be burglars because your home looks less exposed. (The research has also shown that chances of burglaries are less if your home is on a cul-de-sac instead of a through street, in a suburb instead of a business area, and on a street without traffic signs.)

7. **Have a security inspection.** Some police departments offer free security inspections, or you can hire a security consultant.

8. **Hire a private patrol service,** or participate in a Neighborhood Watch program on your block. These operations have cut the crime in some areas by as much as 40 percent.

9. **Purchase a safe** for important papers, money, valuable tools, photographic plates, computer disks, and so on. Just having a safe may prevent theft, because the police estimate that most burglars are in and out of the house in six minutes, and breaking into a safe takes time. Safes can be fireproof, waterproof, and even explosion-proof.

10. **Install a burglar alarm system.** You can get "perimeter" systems that attach to your doors and windows and, if professionally installed, usually cost $2,000 to $3,000. More economical are "interior detection devices" or "space protectors" that can be used for monitoring a hall or stairway. These systems provide a warning only after someone has entered a home, however, and they can inhibit your own movement in the house or can be accidentally set off by a passing pet. To protect a specific object, such as a safe or file cabinet, you can use a "proximity device." The alarm in these devices is triggered only when an intruder gets within several inches of the object.

    You can also turn your computer into an alarm system. By adding magnetic switches to doors and windows or installing motion detectors and wiring these to your computer, it can sound alarms, blink lights, or dial a telephone number for help. Some people buy an inexpensive home computer, add the necessary wiring themselves and, for under $500, have as sophisticated a security system as one costing four to six times as much.

11. **Place a pair of size 16 work boots outside your door.**

12. **Install smoke detectors** and make sure to have your electrical service checked routinely to protect your home office against fire damage. When we moved into our first house and needed additional wiring for the porch we were enclosing, our horrified electrician discovered we had a slow fire in our fuse box.

Aside from these common precautions, you can also keep small fire extinguishers on hand and buy fireproof files. However, they are seven or eight times as expensive as conventional office files.

Creating the Image and Décor You Want

The way your office looks can make the difference between feeling productive and motivated or disorganized and demoralized while working. If employees, customers, co-workers, or clients come to the office, appearances can also be important for gaining their respect and trust. This is especially true in a home office, where establishing a professional atmosphere is more of a challenge than in a building full of other offices. Here are five basic steps you can take to achieve the image you want:

1. Take a fresh look at your office space. Imagine you're starting a new job and seeing your new office for the first time. Ask yourself if this is a place where you would feel like working and could be productive in. Decide if it looks too homey or too stark.

Rooms that look fine in a home may be too "busy" for an office, because of too many bright colors, too much clutter, or too little space. On the other hand, if you've cleared everything out of a room, attic, or basement, and all

---

Wall and Floor Coverings: What Are Your Options?

Wall Coverings
Paint. Quickest and cheapest way to change a color scheme. Quality of appearance depends on surface beneath the paint.

Wallpaper. Colors, textures, and patterns offer wide variety of looks; covers blemishes.

Foil. Shiny, bold, distinctive appearance, but possible glare problem.

Sheet vinyl. Durable and easily maintained.

Textured coverings (grasscloth, linen, wool, jute, felt, carpet, and other fabrics by the yard). Coverings give plush and homey look and disguise rough wall surfaces.

Wood paneling and boarding. Warm, durable, and insulating.

Cork. Warm, handsome, good noise absorption. Comes in tiles or paper-backed cork. Walls can double as bulletin boards.

Brick. Looks warm and solid.

Mirror paneling (glass, plastic, or acrylic). Creates the illusion of space, but possible noise and glare problems.

Murals. Photo wall-murals reproduce actual scenic photographs. Give life to a room without windows but may become tiring.

you have is a desk and a chair in an empty room, the space may be too large, drab, or cheerless for productive work.

Take a look at your office from the viewpoint of the people who will be coming there as clients, customers, employees, or business associates. Consider their expectations and the statement your office makes about you and your business. If you're an accountant, for example, does your office convey the attention to order and detail that suggests you give careful advice about money? If you're an artist, does your office look like a creative place?

2. Decide on the look you want. Choose the tone or overall impression you want to impart:

Practical	Elegant	Creative	Homespun
Classic	Casual	Contemporary	High-Tech

If you aren't sure about the look you want, think about the offices of people you respect and admire in your field. How do their offices look? Go through some decorating magazines and clip out photos you like. Remember offices you've worked in before and what you liked or disliked about them.

3. Coordinate your office. The furniture, the wall covering, the floor covering, the colors you use, the lamps, the ceiling, the window treatments, any wall decorations, and even the equipment and supplies should all work together to send the same message.

Floor Coverings

Hardwood. Looks good if in condition; warm; wears well; improves with age; can be refinished. Can be covered with polyurethane finish or treated with acrylic solution for greater wear. Dry heat may cause shrinking; dampness causes swelling; expensive.

Vinyl. Comes in both tiles and sheeting; waterproof; resistant to staining; cushioned vinyl is quiet and resilient underfoot; variety of colors and patterns; no-wax vinyls require less care. More casual than hardwood or carpeting.

Reinforced vinyl or vinyl-asbestos. Much like vinyl but less expensive.

Rubber tile. Doesn't conduct static electricity, wears well, quiet, waterproof, and soft. Recovers well from indentation but rubber heels make black marks and it stains easily.

Concrete, masonry, ceramic tiles. Tough, hard-wearing, can be washed or hosed down. Cold, hard, noisy, tiring to the feet.

Carpeting. Comfortable, and quiet. Available in wide variety of colors and textures. Wool carpet is longest wearing, but most expensive and builds static electrical charges. Nylon carpet is most popular, and least expensive, but even worse for static electricity unless blended or treated. Industrial carpeting with tight weave doesn't get as dirty and is very durable.

Color will have a particularly strong influence on the overall effect of your office. The colors you choose will affect you and those who come into your office both physiologically and psychologically. Color helps determine whether people feel their surroundings are cramped or spacious, and how hot or cool the room feels. For a sense of excitement, cheer, and relief from boredom, use warm colors. Reds, oranges, yellows, and browns increase heart rate and respiration. There are indications that yellow also results in higher productivity in the workplace, while reds contribute to tension.

If you want to create a calmer, more serene and restful environment, use cool colors. Blues, greens, and grays slow down bodily responses. There is evidence that natural wood reduces stress while the color gray is experienced as depressing. Gray carpeting, however, will hide dirt, lint, and spills better than other colors, so if you want to take advantage of gray carpeting, balance it by using warm colors elsewhere in your office.

4. Decide what has to go and what can stay. You don't have to start from scratch. Decide what present furnishings are consistent with the image you want. Often you can re-cover, refinish, repair, or repaint what you now have. Or you can leave it all as is and purchase items consistent with your new look piece by piece as your budget allows.

5. Consider consulting an interior decorator or designer. These professionals can not only help you select a new décor but can also show you how to make the most of what you have. In fact, they often will save you money by suggesting a few inexpensive accessories to tie in what you have available with the look you want. Of course, they can also guide you through the labyrinth of decorating options for major decisions like new floor and wall coverings.

How to Make a Small Room Look Larger

- Use one light color, such as an off-white or pastel, for walls as well as for drapes or curtains.
- Cover the floors with bright wall-to-wall carpeting.
- Keep the furnishings simple and uncluttered.
- Use mirrors (but remember they reflect light).

How to Make a Large Room Look Smaller

- Use bold colors and contrasting wall and floor coverings and furniture.
- Use large, heavy furniture.
- Use area rugs to define one or more sections of the room.

Maintaining Adequate Temperature, Humidity, and Air Quality

Studies show that people work better when temperature and humidity are at comfortable levels and the air is clear and fresh. You can usually maintain these optimal working conditions without much effort.

While climate is a matter of individual preference, people are most comfortable and productive in temperatures between 68 to 75 degrees, with the humidity between 40 to 50 percent. In other words, if you're sweating it out without an air conditioner during the summer, buying one can be good for your productivity as well as your comfort. Studies have shown that when the office temperature rises to the mid-eighties, mental performance becomes impaired.

If you have a problem room that's always too hot or too cold, there are a number of possible solutions.

The human brain works in such a way that even though the temperature remains constant, we can use color to make ourselves feel cooler or warmer.

To Warm Up a Home Office

1. Add solar panels to capture heat from the southern and/or western walls.
2. Install skylights and arrange your work area in their light path.
3. Carpet the home office and use ⅝-inch padding.
4. Plant deciduous trees outside windows for sunlight in the winter and shade in the summer.
5. Draw curtains, drapes, or blinds to retain heat when there is no direct sunlight.
6. Use insulated glass and make sure walls as well as ceilings are properly insulated to a standard of R-19.
7. Install a room heater.
8. Add a room humidifier to make the existing temperature seem warmer.

To Cool Off a Home Office

1. Place bookcases on all southern and western walls.
2. Use fluorescent lights.
3. Shut off appliances and lights when room is not in use.
4. Plant evergreens outside walls and windows with southern or western exposures.
5. Use indoor plants to shade direct sunlight.
6. Install a window air conditioner.
7. Use roof ventilating fans.
8. Arrange work areas in the direct path of circulating air.
9. Use blinds or curtains to block out direct sunlight.
10. Tint windows that receive the full glare of the sun.
11. Install heat-absorbing double windows.

You'll feel cooler in a room decorated with blues, greens, and grays, but warmer in a room decorated with pinks, reds, oranges, yellows, and browns. To get the effect you want, you needn't paint or paper your entire office with these colors. Use them in accessories like large wall-hangings, graphics, or pillows and even change them with the temperature of the season.

To keep the air in your office clean and fresh, you can install an electrostatic air filter, also called an electronic air cleaner. Adding these devices to most heating and air-conditioning systems costs approximately $500. Buying a portable air cleaner for the room will cost about $400. Either option removes smoke and cleans your air of microscopic particles that create a film on surfaces. The operating cost of an air cleaner is about the same as the cost of using a 60-watt light bulb.

According to research findings at the National Aeronautics and Space Administration, common houseplants can also help purify the air. Not only do plants such as English ivy, dracaenas, and palms freshen stale air, they also remove toxins such as benzene, formaldehyde, and carbon monoxide that can build up in any home office from the use of paper products, cigarette smoke, cleaning and office supplies, natural gas, and so forth. NASA researcher B. C. Wolverton recommends that plants should be included in your operating expenses, like pencils and fax machines. Although any plant will help, research has shown that Gerbera daisy, mother-in-laws tongue, pothos and spider plant absorb the most toxins. Wolverton claims that eight to fifteen plants will "significantly improve" the air quality in the average home. That's about one plant per 100 square feet.

An ionizing air filter can also improve air quality. These filters are useful in rooms without access to outside air, in areas where smog is a problem, or in rooms with electronic equipment such as office machines, television sets, and computers. For more information on these devices, see the Resource List at the end of the chapter.

Purchasing Office Supplies and Small Equipment

When you first set up your office, we suggest you generate a list of the minimum equipment and supplies you'll need. A good way to start, if you're currently working at a job, is to go through your office and list what you find on top of your desk, in your drawers, and in your cabinets. If you have a secretary, find out and list the common supplies he or she keeps on hand. Otherwise, review the equipment and supplies listed below.

Supplies and Small Equipment Checklist: The Basics

Supplies
☐ Accordion files
☐ Business cards
☐ Business envelopes
☐ Calendar

- [ ] Computer supplies:
  - [ ] Computer diskettes
    - [ ] Head cleaning kit
    - [ ] Printer paper and ribbons or cartridges
- [ ] Correction fluid
- [ ] Dust-Off air-spray cannister
- [ ] Envelopes and shipping boxes for air-express companies you use
- [ ] File folders
- [ ] File labels, tabs
- [ ] Glue, rubber cement
- [ ] Index cards
- [ ] Jiffy bags
- [ ] Large manila envelopes
- [ ] Paper
- [ ] Paper clips, fasteners
- [ ] Pens, pencils, erasers, markers
- [ ] Postage stamps
- [ ] Ring binders
- [ ] Rubber bands
- [ ] Rubber stamps
- [ ] Staples
- [ ] Stationery: letterhead, billhead
- [ ] Tape: cellophane, packaging
- [ ] Typewriter ribbons

Small Equipment
- [ ] Calculator
- [ ] Check protector (businesslike and inexpensive)
- [ ] Dictation equipment
- [ ] Flip chart (for brainstorming and planning)
- [ ] In and out boxes
- [ ] Letter opener
- [ ] Letter tray
- [ ] Paper cutter
- [ ] Paperweight
- [ ] Pencil holder
- [ ] Postage affixer or a digital postage meter (saves time)
- [ ] Postage scale (improves accuracy and saves money)
- [ ] Pencil sharpener
- [ ] Ruler
- [ ] Scissors
- [ ] Staple remover
- [ ] Stapler
- [ ] Typewriter pad, stand

Most of the items you'll need can be purchased from local stationery and office-supply stores, discount chain companies, or catalog suppliers. There are advantages and disadvantages in dealing with each.

Buying at Office Superstores

Office superstores and warehouse clubs specializing in office supplies, equipment, and furniture have spread rapidly across the country. The first of these, Staples, began in the mid-1980s, when it offered lower prices on office supplies than either local retailers or mail-order firms. Now there are several dozen chains of such stores, such as Bizmart, HQ, Office America, Office Club, Office Depot, Office Max, Office Place, Office Square, Office World, and Workplace. Products are grouped by category on high-stacked shelves and customers typically use shopping carts to load up with everything from paper clips to cleaning supplies.

Buying by Mail

If you buy from a mail-order catalog, you may find some products at bargain prices. Keep in mind, however, that you will also have to pay for shipping and, often, insurance. When these costs are added to the order, you may not save much money, particularly when compared with prices at office superstores.

Moreover, shipping can be delayed, especially during the holidays. If you have to return an item, it may take as long as two weeks before the return is processed. Finally, judging a product from a photograph is not quite the same as seeing it in person. Unless you're already familiar with the product, you may find it smaller, clumsier, or not quite the same color you had in mind. That's why it's important to read product descriptions, including measurements, and to check model numbers carefully before ordering.

Most catalog companies offer liberal return policies and will refund or exchange products to the customer's satisfaction. This, however, is not always the case, so review the return policy before buying. In other words, read the fine print, which should state the return policy next to, or on, the order form. When you have to pay return or exchange expenses, an item can end up costing more than if you had bought it locally.

Because of a lack of local suppliers or the specialized nature of an item, the only way to get some supplies may be through a catalog. Even in Los Angeles, we've found it easier to order some things by mail than to find a local supplier. In ordering such items, we suggest you keep a three months' supply on hand at all times and order quarterly.

For quick service, make sure to place your orders either before or considerably after a holiday rush. Actually, mail-order firms report that their busiest times are January 1–15, April 1–15, September 1–15, and the entire month of December.

A Dozen Little Things That Make a Big Difference

1. **Clear address labels** make mailings you send out look more like they're individually typed.
2. **A copy holder** holds paper with text or numbers while you're typing or entering information into a computer and saves awkwardly crooking your neck. A scanner is even better yet.
3. **Pre-moistened towels** clean your monitor screen, desktop, disk holders, and telephones—everything in your office that gets dusty and dirty. Fuji Photo Film makes premoistened towels for cleaning computer and other electronic components. Dow's Spifits and Fantastik S'Wipe's, Lysol, and Pine-Sol offer premoistened towels for cleaning work surfaces.
4. **An air-spray canister,** such as Dust-Off made by Falcon, sends pressurized air into nooks and crannies of electronic equipment where towels can't reach.
5. **A digital postage scale or postage meter** saves time waiting in post-office lines. Also keep on hand a supply of stamps in various denominations, along with Express Mail and Federal Express envelopes and certified and registered mail forms.
6. **Pre-inked and customized rubber stamps** for marking first class, priority, and fourth class mail as well as your return address can also save time and create a more professional image.
7. **Plastic silverware trays** keep pens, pencils, post-it pads, paper clips, rubber bands, scissors, stapler, and magic markers organized in your desk drawer.
8. **Plastic stacking trays** keep various types of stationery and documents you use too frequently to keep in a filing cabinet at your fingertips without cluttering your desk.
9. **Phone-dialer software** lets you use a few keystrokes on your computer to dial phone numbers. Hotline from General Information, in addition, comes with a telephone directory that enables you to dial 10,000 of the nation's largest corporations and government agencies. Additional specialized directories are also available.
10. **Logo-making and banner-making software,** such as Broderbund's BannerMania, lets you make an endless and exciting array of designs that can be used for banners, logos, business cards, and newsletter mastheads.
11. **Self-stick removable notes** such as Post-its and Avery note pads come in various sizes and special forms for faxes and tape flags for marking your place. You can stick them on your mailbox with instructions for delivery people, to display directions on your dashboard, and for countless other tasks.
12. **A postage stamp affixer** that feeds, moistens, cuts, and affixes postage stamps in all one motion to envelopes or packages saves time and energy. For other moistening tasks, we like a porcelain moistener.

Ordering by mail is a common cause of complaints to consumer agencies. To guard against having a problem yourself, order from a known firm with a good reputation. Before ordering, check out who's responsible for damage during shipment.

If you're responding to an advertisement, phone or write the magazine in which the advertisement appeared to find out if the mail-order business has a record of complaints. Other excellent places to check on a company as well as on a product you're considering buying are on the forums on an information service like CompuServe and on computer bulletin boards.

Unless the company has stated a specific time for delivery, it must ship within thirty days of receiving your order. If the company fails to do so, it must notify you and give you the choice of receiving a refund or agreeing to a new shipment date. You automatically have the right to cancel and get a refund if you don't receive your order within the required time. On the other hand, by ignoring the first notice of a delay, you imply that you are willing to accept later delivery. You must be notified of any further delays, however, and you must specifically agree to them.

To protect yourself from problems when returning unsatisfactory products, pay by credit card rather than by cash or check. Then should you have a prob-

How to Handle a Problem with a Mail-Order Company

Here are some agencies you can turn to with a complaint:

The Postal Inspection Service. You can locate the postal inspector in the seller's area by contacting your local postmaster or postal inspector. The post office has a mediation service for settling disputes.

Better Business Bureau. To find out the address and phone number of the bureau in the seller's area, contact the Council of Better Business Bureaus, 1515 Wilson Boulevard, Arlington, VA 22209.

Direct Mail/Marketing Association, Mail Order Action Line. This is the trade association of the mail-order business. It provides for self-policing of the industry and can be contacted at 6 East Forty-Third Street, New York, NY 10017.

In California, the agency responsible for consumer complaints is the Department of Consumer Affairs, Complaint Assistance Unit, 1020 N Street, Sacramento, CA 95814.

In New York City, contact the Complaints Division, Department of Consumer Affairs, 80 Lafayette Street, New York, NY 10013.

If you charged your purchase on a credit card, contact the issuer of the card in writing to get a credit on your account. You're entitled to withhold payment. Federal law and regulations provide extensive procedures for resolving disputes, and you will receive this information once you have notified the credit card issuer.

lem, you can often get the charge reversed. Sometimes when you can't get sellers to respond to your concerns, simply advising them that you will be asking their bank to credit your bill will spur them to action. While banks do not usually advertise this service, it is one which was brought about by the federal Fair Billing law, and the wise buyer takes advantage of it. The ability to protect yourself against problems of nondelivery or defective merchandise is reason enough to have at least one credit card.

One further tip: if the problem with a product is its quality, keep in mind that quality is always arguable and somewhat subjective. You will have more success by describing your problem as "not having been delivered in accordance with the agreement." Calling a problem a "billing error" rather than a "dispute" also increases the likelihood you'll get the charges reversed. And when the goods you've ordered by mail arrive, watch for any labels or stickers on the boxes that read Warranty Void. You may be wise to return the package unopened.

Among the people we have polled, these mail-order companies have the best reputations for prompt delivery and customer satisfaction.

Quill Corporation
100 S. Schelter Rd.
Lincolnshire, IL 60069
(312) 634-480 or
(714) 988-3200 (California)

Viking Office Products
13809 S. Figueroa St.
P.O. Box 61144
Los Angeles, CA 90061
(800) 421-1222

Reliable
1001 W. Van Buren St.
Chicago, IL 60607
(800) 735-4000

Buying by Computer

Buying by computer has become extremely popular and big business as well. The major electronic services—CompuServe, Delphi, Genie, and Prodigy— offer electronic shopping. For example, the Electronic Mall® on CompuServe offers goods and services in seventeen departments such as Computing and Office Supplies. One hundred and eight different merchants sell through the Mall. These include large companies, like AT&T selling home office products, to Waldenbooks selling books. Smaller merchants sell through the Mall as well. One of them is Computer Express, a home-based company operated by Phillip and Leslie Schier. The Schiers sell over $2 million worth of computers and computer accessories a year at 30 to 40 percent off list price.

Chapter Digest

1. Professional organizers and veteran open-collar workers find that the most important criteria in furnishing and supplying your home office are convenience, comfort, functionality, and privacy.

2. Investing in a high-quality desk and chair as well as in high-quality lighting can protect you from needless aches, pains, and eyestrain and boost your productivity, too.
3. Natural daylight is the best source of light. Today, however, there are a variety of new lighting solutions like Halogen and Chromalux bulbs that can simulate daylight when you must settle for artificial lighting.

Buying Bargains

1. Ask for a business discount. Usually you will need no more identification than a business card.
2. Shop at office furniture stores. In talking price, assume there is a discount and ask what it is.
3. Shop at business liquidation sales advertised in the classified section of most newspapers.
4. Shop at estate sales.
5. Go to police auctions.
6. Ask merchants for discounts for cash or early payment.
7. Look for moving sales when large companies change locations.
8. Shop at garage sales and bazaars.
9. Shop at second-hand stores, including veterans' rebuilt-merchandise shops.
10. Buy unfinished furniture, unassembled furniture, or furniture kits.
11. Build your own furniture with basic carpentry tools, using patterns or suggestions in popular "do-it-yourself" books and magazines.
12. Find out if you can buy slightly damaged furniture from shipping companies.
13. Investigate buying furniture that has been abandoned at storage companies.
14. Shop in rural or out-of-the-way sections of the country.
15. Buy seconds or furniture with manufacturers' errors.
16. Look for discontinued styles, specials, clearance sales, inventory sales, and "loss leaders" used to draw people into a store.
17. Shop in the want ads or in "bargain" newsletters for items being sold because a company is remodeling or redecorating.
18. Look for floor samples or demonstrator models sold at reduced prices.
19. Look for mill ends and remnants at carpet and flooring stores.
20. The federal government regularly auctions off surplus equipment and supplies. To learn about bidding on these items, write to the Federal Supply Service, General Services Administration, Washington, D.C. 20406, and to the Department of Defense Surplus Sales, P.O. Box 1370, Federal Center, Battle Creek, MI 49016.

4. A computer screen often requires less rather than more lighting. So instead of trying to light your entire office, use "task lighting": light each work area to meet the specific needs of the tasks to be done there.
5. Sometimes it's the little things that make the biggest difference in making your office work smoothly. So put accessories and supplies that save you time and energy high on your must-have list.
6. When working from home there are a variety of ways to keep the noise level in your office, so you are alert yet not distracted by street and household sounds.
7. The way your office looks can make the difference between feeling productive and motivated and feeling disorganized and demoralized. So select a décor and color scheme that projects the image you want to create and one in which you feel comfortable and productive.
8. Furniture, supplies, and accessories for the home office can be purchased economically and conveniently at office superstores, by mail, and, increasingly, by computer.

Resources

Books

Getting Organized. Stephanie Winston. New York: Warner Books, 1989.

Nontoxic, Natural, & Earthwise. Debra Lynn Dadd. Los Angeles: Jeremy P. Tarcher, 1990.

The Light Book: A Guide for Lighting Your Home. Cleveland: General Electric, 1988.

The Office Book. Judy Graf Klein. New York: Facts on File, 1982.

Organized to Be the Best. Susan Silver. Los Angeles: Adams Hall, 1989.

Video Display Terminals and Vision. Howard D. Kahn, OD, 1989. Optometric Extension Program Foundation, Inc., 2912 S. Daimler St., Santa Ana, CA 92705.

Magazines

Consumer Reports magazine (monthly) and **Consumer Reports Buying Guide Issue** (annual). Consumers Union, 256 Washington St., Mount Vernon, NY 10553.

Audiotapes

Office Chatter/Computer Chatter. Zable's Business Services, 156 Wall St., Kingston, NY 12401.

Productivity & Creativity Background Music. Halpern Sounds, 1775 Old Country Rd., #9, Belmont, CA 94002.

Catalogs

Seventh Generation. This catalog lists many products for operating an environmentally safe and sound home office, including the air ionizers mentioned in this chapter.

CHAPTER
EIGHT

■ ■

Equipping and Computerizing
the Up-to-Date Home Office

Hundreds of thousands of people have started home offices with nothing more than a desk, a telephone extension, and a filing cabinet. Some people begin with even less. When we began working from home in 1974, very little real office equipment was available or affordable. So we began operations with two desks, an answering machine, and an IBM Selectric typewriter. Consequently, we depended on outside services for photocopies and for turning our rough manuscripts into copy we could submit to clients and publishers. Now these are all things we routinely do ourselves because of the wealth of equipment that has become the heart of our home office.

The typical home office today has at least one personal computer, a printer, an answering machine, and a variety of special telephone features. Many home offices also have a copy machine, a fax machine, and a modem as well.

Why this high-tech transformation in home offices? First, the prices of electronic equipment have come way down. By shopping carefully, you can now get all of the equipment mentioned above for under $3,000. Second, equipment is increasingly more compact so it fits in small office spaces. Third, to be competitive today, a home business needs to use as much of the latest equipment as possible.

So what equipment do you need? You need enough to do business efficiently and remain competitive. But you should not and need not go into debt to equip your office adequately. Remember, as your business grows, you can and will invest in additional equipment.

In this chapter, we're going to take you on a verbal tour of the well-equipped home office and prepare you to shop confidently for your own home office equipment. You can actually take the Features-to-Look-For Checklists you'll find in this chapter with you when you shop to make the selection process easier.

We consider the items that appear on the checklists in boldface type to be important features of equipment that will be used at home for business purposes. Items in regular typeface are "nice to have," but not vital. We must caution you that the features and models of products for the home office change rapidly—faster even than those for automobiles or stereos! So keep in mind that the checklists are constructed as of this writing for 1990 models.

To get up-to-the-moment information and reviews of specific equipment, you need to check recent issues of magazines that conscientiously evaluate new products. These magazines are on the Resource List at the end of the chapter. Let's now imagine we're going shopping to equip your home office. We'll be taking a tour of the kind of equipment that you'll find either in successful people's home offices or on their wish lists.

Telephones

Research (ours and other people's) shows that people working from home spend more time on the telephone than on any other single activity.

In the past, all you had to decide about telephone service was whether to have a separate business line, whether to choose a desk or trimline model, and what color to order. Today you have many other choices. You must decide whether to lease or buy your equipment, which of a growing number of features and services you want, and what long-distance phone company to use.

AT&T and General Telephone cite these advantages in leasing or, more accurately, renting a phone from the phone company: free maintenance, the option to exchange your equipment, and the high quality of the phones. Phones today are priced so low, however, that free maintenance and exchangeability are less than compelling reasons for renting. And you can now purchase phones of the same quality you can rent.

So if you're like increasing numbers of people, you've decided to buy your own telephone equipment rather than rent it. Buying your own equipment, you can recoup your investment in a matter of months and take advantage of an ever-increasing number of choices in the style, material, and features available.

Telephone Services That Can Save You Time and Effort

Automatic Number Identification (ANI) allows a person receiving a phone call to see on a screen the phone number of the person calling. ANI is also called Caller ID in some states. Surrounded by controversy, ANI raises privacy issues that have filled many editorial columns. While ANI may be useful for being sure you note a caller's number correctly, it should not be used to screen out calls automatically. A call from a number you don't recognize may be from a stranger who will become one of your best clients, or one of your most important customers may be calling from the airport—and those are calls you certainly don't want to miss.

Call Forwarding allows you to be reached at a preselected number when you aren't home. Of course, if the call is forwarded outside your local area, you'll be responsible for any toll charges. In a home office with several lines and one answering machine, you can forward all the calls to the line with the answering machine.

Call Waiting signals you with a beep or a click if someone is trying to get through while you're talking. It means callers don't get a busy signal. Instead, you take the incoming call while holding the original call. Call Waiting is a way for a home office to make one phone line do the work of two. But many people passionately hate Call Waiting. Also, having Call Waiting on a line you use for computer or fax communications can disconnect your call or garble data. Some phone companies, however, have Cancel Call Waiting, with which you can temporarily disable Call Waiting. Remember, too, that answering machines can answer only one call at a time. So if your answering machine is turned on and responding to a call, someone else calling at the same time will get no answer instead of a busy signal.

Custom Ringing enables you to have two phone numbers on one line. Each number has a different ring, so you can differentiate between established customers and other callers. Or if you have more than one person or business in the same office, you can tell which calls are for whom.

Custom Ringing can also be used in conjunction with a device called Ring-Link made by Diamond Computer Solutions, which enables you to attach two separate answering machines to your phone line. For example, if you are getting by with one phone line for both business and residential use, Ring-Link may be what you need. It recognizes a business call by its ring and directs it to the business answering machine. If the call is for your home, it directs the call to your personal machine. Another use for Ring-Link is to route your fax calls automatically to the fax machine. By using Ring-Link, it will appear that you have a dedicated fax line because there are no codes for the caller to enter. Ring-Link costs under one hundred dollars.

Three-Way Calling permits you to talk with two other people simultaneously. This service differs from *Conference Calling*, which enables you to talk with an unlimited number of parties at the same time. Conference calls, however, must be arranged through an operator and are more expensive.

Some phone companies with older equipment don't offer these services, so check with the company servicing your area.

Choosing Telephone Hardware

In general, when you do decide to buy a phone, look for durability and reliability. You are more likely to find both in brand-name telephones from reputable stores. Beware of used or rebuilt instruments that are sold without

---

Features to Look for: Telephones

- **Mute button,** turns off your microphone to screen out sounds, like a dog's barking, while your caller continues talking.
- **Adjustable volume.**
- **Automatic redialing of last number.**
- Memory dialing of frequently called numbers.
- Speakerphone capability.

---

warranties. Even with a warranty, many phones have to be mailed to the manufacturer for repair. This could mean buying another phone to use in the meantime. So the wisest policy is to read the warranty and service policy before making a purchase.

Now let's consider other hardware you can buy to make your time on the telephone more convenient, comfortable, functional, and economical.

Telephone Headsets

A headset frees both your hands for writing or using your computer while you talk, prevents neck strain and, if you spend many hours on the phone, also prevents "cauliflower ear."

Cordless Telephones

A cordless telephone enables you to answer business calls anywhere around your home, indoors and out. That can be significant if you're working alone and need to attend to personal matters.

Features to Look for: Headsets

- **Lightweight and fully adjustable,** to conform to your head and hair.
- **Volume control,** so you don't have to hold the headset away from your ear when talking to someone with a loud voice.
- **Keypad,** so you can place outgoing calls without having to attach a separate handset.
- **High-quality microphone,** so your voice sounds clear. Try it out.
- Belt clip and long cod, to enable you to move about freely.
- Cordless.

Features to Look for: Cordless Phones

- **Transmits your voice clearly,** so people won't guess that you're using a cordless phone.
- **Range of quality transmission,** wide enough to cover your home and yard.
- **Light handset,** for convenience in carrying around.
- **Ten or more multiple-secured channels,** to offer you the best chance that other types of signals won't interfere with your phone.
- Two-way paging, to enable someone at the base set to beep the handset and vice versa.
- Intercom capability between base set and handset.
- Automatic standby, to avoid having to flip a switch from Standby to Talk.

Two-Line Telephones

Having a two-line phone allows you to have several lines available at your desk without the clutter of two phone sets. Two-line phones are available in both corded and cordless models.

Getting Your Phone Answered While You're Away

Your business phone needs to be answered at all times during business hours. You may not always be available to answer your phone yourself, however, since you may be away, on another phone line, or tied up with work that shouldn't be interrupted. So your phone must be answered for you. Your business phone may also need to be answered for you during nonbusiness hours because you never know when an incoming call is from a customer needing to communicate something vital or from a potential customer bringing you new business. Short of hiring your own receptionist, your choices for having your phone answered include using an answering service, an answering machine, or voicemail. Let's weigh the pros and cons of each.

Answering Services

Answering services provide a person to take your calls and, according to surveys, most people prefer a warm body on the other end of their telephone call. Nevertheless, we find most home-based businesspeople do not use answering services. The cost is one factor. An answering machine or voicemail is a one-time cost instead of a monthly fee that adds to your overhead each month. In addition, answering service personnel are sometimes rude and abrupt. Some people contend this is particularly true of services that handle doctors' offices, probably because doctors' offices are busier and their services put callers on hold longer.

Ten Ways to Save Money and Time on Your Telephone Bill

1. Dial direct. This can save you 60 percent of the costs of operator-assisted calls.
2. Place long-distance calls during off-hours whenever possible. The rates are lower when you call before 8:00 A.M. or after 5 P.M. on weekdays. Take advantage of time differences in placing calls to people in other areas. Remember, if your call extends beyond the off-hours, you pay the full day rate.
3. If your long-distance calls amount to more than $10 a month, use a discount calling plan, such as AT&T's Reach Out America, MCI's Prime Time, or Sprint's Sprint Plus.
4. To find out the current best rates for the major long-distance carriers, obtain the research of organizations like the Telecommunications Research and Action Center or *Consumer Reports,* which do impartial cost comparisons. Factor into your decision additional benefits like sign-up bonuses and getting frequent-flyer miles for using particular services.
5. To keep track of different types of calls, use more than one long-distance carrier. Then you can differentiate personal from business calls, one client from another, or one business from another. To gain access to the three major long-distance carriers, use these codes prior to dialing the long-distance number: AT&T, 10288; MCI, 10222; US Sprint, 10333. Calls will be listed by company on your telephone bill.
6. Use "800" numbers whenever possible. When you're calling an out-of-town business, it's a good idea to check an 800 directory or call information: 1 (800) 555-1212.
7. Check your telephone bills for errors. If you find them, call and get credit.
8. Use Touch-Tone phones. It takes four times as long to dial a number using a rotary dial.
9. If you spend more than six hours a week making phone calls, use an automatic phone dialer in the form of hardware or software.
10. There are alternatves to multiple phone lines. While we recommend that a home office have at least two phone lines—one for business calls and one for personal calls—with the increasing use of fax machines and modems, many home offices are getting a third and even a fourth line. But the more phone lines you get, the greater the cost, and some homes, like ours, are limited in the number of lines they can get. Two ways to make your phone lines serve for both voice and machine communications are (1) getting integrated equipment made by companies like Panasonic and Brother which combine phone, fax, and answering machine into one machine, and (2) using an automatic voice/data switch. There is a wide variety of these switches on the market today.

If you decide to use an answering service, locate a good one. Start with those you've enjoyed speaking to when you've called others. Here are a few ways to do some comparison shopping. Visit the answering service's office without an appointment. Notice how many times the phones ring before they're answered. Are the operators courteous? Do they personalize their conversations around their customers' businesses? Most services have many switchboards with different operators. Insist on an operator whose manner you like and be specific about how you want your phone answered.

Ask for the names of three or four of the service's customers, preferably people with businesses similar to yours. Call to find out if these customers are satisfied. Ask if they receive their messages reliably. Find out if their customers complain about the service and how well the service handles urgent phone calls.

Once you've started with the service, occasionally call your number to be certain your customers are receiving the treatment you want them to have. Stop by the service once a week and get to know your operator. And remember him or her on birthdays, Christmas, and other occasions. You'll be a sharp contrast to customers whose only contact with the service is to complain. The quality of your service should reflect this difference.

Answering Machines

Answering machines are economical, but as their prices have come down, our experience is that they are more prone to mechanical failure. An answering

---

Features to Look for: Answering Machines

- **Reputation for reliable performance.**
- **Outgoing message quality is clear and crisp,** faithfully reproducing your voice. Your outgoing message need not be limited to just 60 seconds.
- **Incoming messages can be recorded as long as the caller talks,** thus a caller leaving a long message is not cut off. This can be accomplished with a "voice-activated," or VOX, setting.
- **You can select the number of rings** before the machine answers. Two rings is best.
- **The machine is easy to rewind** and replays messages without erasing them.
- **The machine can be turned on from a remote location** at times when you forget to turn it on before leaving home. Other remote-control features enable you to play back messages and record a new message when you're not at home.
- **Easy-to-use controls.**
- A time-date stamp for messages so you know when people have called.
- Fast-forwarding or rewinding to a particular message.
- Built-in telephone.
- Security codes.
- The ability to answer two lines.

---

machine used for business has to perform day in and day out. It can't lose messages. It can't be temperamental. It has to be there when you're not. Even if a machine is under warranty, when something goes wrong with it, you either have to get a substitute machine or lose calls. The good news is that fewer people hang up on answering machines now than in the past. In fact, in some parts of the country, it is considered rude not to have an answering machine. So you shouldn't miss many messages as long as your machine is in working order.

Consulting the *Consumer Reports Buying Guide* will narrow your search for a machine that meets your needs. Once you have that machine, it's a good idea to call home periodically to make sure the machine is working properly and messages are being recorded.

Voicemail

Voicemail turns a computer with a hard disk into a telephone answering machine, a switchboard, and a phone-mail system like those you encounter when calling many corporations today. Callers are offered a choice of numbers to push on their phone pads, each of which answers a need of the caller. So essentially voicemail is a sophisticated answering machine that offers callers options beyond simply taking their messages. Voicemail can also be used to take dictation and can act as a calendaring system as well as a phone book that enables you to call in and get phone numbers when you're away from home.

A consultant described to us how he uses his voicemail system as a switchboard: "When a customer calls me up, my Watson voicemail system picks up the phone and relays my prerecorded message asking the customer to hold for a moment. The system then puts the caller on hold and dials me at whatever location I've designated, where I pick up the phone and talk to the customer as if I were at the office."

A voicemail system can also relay specific information that the caller is seeking, such as product descriptions or instructions for placing an order. When you're at home talking on another line, your voicemail system can tell your callers you're busy and take their messages or switch them to another line. This is an alternative to Call Waiting or to placing a caller on hold—both of which many people dislike intensely.

While voicemail has its detractors, it seems to have gained wider acceptance than answering machines in a comparable period of time. The key to making voicemail more acceptable is for the business owner to use his or her own voice for the recorded message and to keep the menu selections to a few short and uncomplicated choices. Although both answering machines and voicemail are technological substitutes for talking with a real person, voicemail has the edge because of its greater versatility.

A disadvantage of voicemail, however, is that it uses a great deal of hard disk space. Voicemail uses about 8 kilobytes per second of speech recorded at

---

Features to Look for: Voicemail

- **Will run in the background,** so you can use your computer for other purposes at the same time the voicemail system is operating. (This requires that the voicemail card have a coprocessor on board.)
- **Easy to install without extensive programming.**
- Handles multiple lines.
- Manages fax messages.
- Serves as a modem.

---

high quality and about 3 kilobytes per second to record at average quality. outgoing messages are best recorded at high quality, but you might economize your use of your hard disk by recording incoming messages at a lower quality.

Voicemail boards suitable for most home businesses with IBM-compatible computers include Watson by Natural Micro-Systems, Big Mouth by Talking Technology, and the Complete PC's Complete Communicator. Prices range from $200 upward.

Voicemail services are now being offered by telephone companies, too. For example, AT&T has a voicemail service priced at less than $2 a call. The number to call for more information about this service is (800) 562-6275.

A factor to weigh in choosing between an answering machine, an answering service, and voicemail is what your customers and potential customers expect during normal business hours. Answering a business phone with an answering machine immediately says to the caller, "This is a small operation." However, using voicemail, as increasing numbers of corporations and agencies do, communicates nothing about your size. Having your phone answered by a real live human being may communicate a higher level of personal service. But that depends on the quality of answering service you use. Another alternative to consider is hiring someone else who is home-based to take your calls. Such a person might be a mother raising children or a homebound handicapped person to whom you direct your calls using simple Call Forwarding.

One final note. If you often need to work without interruption, consider using an answering machine on your desk or voicemail in your computer for screening calls. You can thereby pick up essential calls immediately and return others at a more appropriate time.

Cellular Phones

More and more people who work from home are getting cellular phones installed as car phones or as portable phones so they will always be available to business callers. Cellular phones operate on radio bands and therefore can

What to Do About Telephone Tag

Fact: Two out of three business calls aren't completed on the first try. One party calls the other who is not available; the second party returns the call and the first party is not there; and so on. This back-and-forth calling has been calculated to amount to two years over a lifetime. To avoid playing telephone tag:

- Set up a telephone appointment, and agree on a specific time to call.
- Determine when the person you're calling will be in the office. State that you will call again at that time.
- Use alternatives to telephone conversation like voicemail, fax, or computer mail.

go wherever you go. Unfortunately, even though the price of many phones is now under $500, the price of service is expensive, with monthly bills easily mounting up to hundreds of dollars. You pay for both the calls you place and those you receive. Still, calls placed on cellular systems can be less expensive than hotel calls, on which high surcharges are sometimes placed. Many home-based businesspeople find that cellular phones have become a necessary time-saver. For example, it has been calculated that it takes an average of fifteen minutes to find a pay phone that works. To keep your costs down, don't give your car phone number out to everyone and avoid making personal calls on your cellular phone.

Fax

A fax, which is short for *facsimile*, allows you to transmit information over the phone lines instantly to another fax machine or to a computer that's capable of receiving fax. Using a fax saves time over conventional mail, costs a fraction of what messenger and overnight delivery services cost, and is easier to use than a computer plus modem. It takes less than twenty seconds to fax a page of text, so a three-page fax will require only a one-minute phone call even if sent to the other side of the world. After a computer and a telephone, a fax is probably the next most important piece of equipment to have in terms of enabling people to work effectively from home.

Fax technology comes in several forms—as a self-standing machine or as a board or card that's placed inside a personal computer. The advantages to a fax that's mounted on a computer board (such as the Intel Connection CoProcessor) is that it takes up no additional desk space, generally costs less, enables you to transmit documents created in your computer without first printing them out in hard copy and, because a document sent by your computer doesn't need to be scanned, the document received by the person you send it to looks better. However, you cannot transmit a document not stored inside your computer through a fax board. So if you want to fax a receipt or a

Features to Look for: Fax Machines

- **Resolution quality** sufficient for your needs—a graphic designer needs a fax capable of higher resolution than most other businesses do.
- **Size of documents transmitted** which should include the sizes you use—some fax machines will take documents 11″ wide (ledger sheets, for example).
- Data compression capability, to reduce telephone time used if you send documents at fine resolution or internationally.
- Automatic dialing (one-touch and speed dialing) of numbers stored in memory.
- Automatic re-try.
- **Sheet feeder,** so you don't have to feed in a multi-page document one page at a time.
- Document memory, which enables you to send the same document to multiple recipients without having to restart the calling process each time. It also enables you to receive documents when you are out of paper.
- Large paper roll size (over 100 ft.) means you won't have to change paper as frequently.
- **Automatic paper cutter.** Without one, documents you receive come out as one long sheet and must be cut by hand.
- Internal automatic voice/data switch, which recognizes the type of call and either rings for voice or produces a tone for fax.
- Plain paper. Thermal paper fades and feels slick to the touch, but plain-paper machines are much more expensive.

copy of a published article you've written, you must use someone else's fax or a separate scanner. A self-standing fax can also be used as a back-up photo-copier.

When using a fax, be careful to avoid problems that inferior paper can cause by always using high-quality paper. Name brand are Accufax, Labelon, and Mr. Fax.

Leading makers of stand-alone fax machines under $2,000 include Brother, Canon, Murata, NEC, Panasonic, Ricoh, Sharp, and Toshiba.

Computers

About half of all home-based businesspeople now have a personal computer, and many more are planning on having one, or thinking about it. If you're one of these people thinking about it, let us consider some reasons why computerizing your office makes sense.

Today you can think about computers the way you would think of any other modern convenience in your home office. They make your life easier. A computer extends your mind the way the automobile extends your legs, the telephone your ears, and the television your eyes.

Basically, computers increase your productivity. Our experience matches that of Peter McWilliams, author of *The Personal Computer Book*. He claims that a computer can keep overhead down and profits up in the following ways:

- If you're working alone, add a computer and you can double or even triple business without hiring staff.
- If you're working with a secretary as your only employee, add a computer and you may never need to hire additional staff.
- If you're working with a secretary and a bookkeeper, add a computer and your staff of two can do the work of three.

In the early eighties, when we first wrote about computerizing home offices, one of the reasons we gave for doing so was to gain credibility with clients and be able to compete better with larger, more established businesses. Today, the reasons for computerizing are even more compelling. Businesses without computers or those needing to upgrade older home computers run a serious risk of lagging behind their competition in terms of sheer productivity, capability, and professional image. Computers have become like telephones, a staple of office life.

Where to Begin

One of the first things you will need to decide in selecting a computer system for your home office is whether to enter the IBM world or the Macintosh world. Today we know that eight out of ten home-based businesses select an IBM or IBM-compatible (often called a clone), and about one in ten selects a Macintosh computer. The remainder choose some other system, like an Atari ST or a Commodore Amiga, which are decent computers, have some business software written for them, are reasonably priced, and are particularly suited for producing music, videos, and multimedia presentations.

While boards can be purchased that enable Atari, Amiga, and Macintosh computers to use software written for IBM-compatible computers, these cause the software to function slowly and generally cost as much as a lower-cost IBM-compatible computer itself. To have any real depth of selection in business software, however, it's necessary to consider an IBM (or IBM-compatible) or Macintosh computer, and more the IBM than the Macintosh.

Hal Schuster, who with his brother, Jack, operates a multimillion dollar publishing business from his home, says, "I am a Mac partisan, and if someone is going to do anything involving the graphic arts, I heartily endorse Mac. However, in the area of business software, there are a hundred good IBM programs for every excellent Mac program. The difference in the availability of specialized business software is startling!"

However, home-based computer consultant and former Egghead Software store manager Sidney Schwartz points out, "You're not looking for thousands of programs; you may just be looking for one. If you can find a Mac program

Features to Look for: Computer Hardware

We recommend that for business purposes, you need a computer with these characteristics:

- **Disk drives.** At least one floppy disk drive and one hard drive capable of storing a minimum of 40 megabytes of data.
- **Memory.** A random access memory (RAM) of no less than 640K, so you can take advantage of current versions of software.
- **Expandable memory.** Newer software is demanding increasing amounts of memory, so being able to expand your computer will undoubtedly be important as your business grows.
- **Speed.** The speed needs to be sufficient to enable the programs you plan to use to operate quickly, not sluggishly.
- **Ports.** At least two serial (RS 232) ports for communications and a mouse, and one parallel port for your printer.
- **Keyboard.** A comfortable feel, separate numeric keypad, separate function keys and separate cursor control keys, and a lighted cap-locks key.
- **Monitor.** You should be able to work in front of your monitor comfortably for several hours at a time. While a monochrome monitor is fine for most work, color is preferred by most people.
- **Expansion slots.** Vacant expansion slots so you can expand the capacity of the computer internally, thereby enabling you to keep pace with technological advances without having to buy an entirely new computer.
- **Service.** Everything that runs breaks, so select a computer that has local or on-site service.
- **Warranty.** Get a computer with a reputation for reliability, and one with a twelve-month or longer warranty. To double your warranty up to another twelve months, purchase your equipment with Gold MasterCard, Visa, or American Express. We advise doing this even if you have to pay an additional small percentage of the sales price to cover the dealer's bank charge.
- Graphics capability. Is this included with the computer or must you buy a separate graphics card?
- Low noise. Noise is caused by the cooling fan inside the systems unit and if it's too loud, it can become an ongoing subtle source of irritation.
- Sound capability.
- Software or peripherals, such as a modem or a mouse, that are included in the price.
- A toll-free hotline to manufacturer.
- Understandable and complete documentation that tells you how to set up and use the computer.
- Local users group.
- Total cost. Always get quotes in writing.

that works for you, what does it matter how many PC programs there are? Selection is nice, but quantity is no substitute for quality."

Schwartz, who owns both an IBM AT clone and a Macintosh SE says further, "Frankly, I don't see a clear and overwhelming advantage to either system. The conventional wisdom is that DOS machines offer more bang-for-the-buck and Macs offer greater ease of use. I've run across so many exceptions to this adage that I just don't give it much credence anymore."

Still another owner of both a Mac and an IBM says, "To me, the Mac has no advantage over the IBM PC, which is better priced and for which there is far more software available at basically lower prices." And that is the prevailing wisdom: the basic trade-off between IBM and Macintosh is lower cost versus ease of use. The choice is yours.

Whichever system you select, the keyboard and the monitor are the hardware you will interact with the most and therefore are the two elements to consider most carefully in your selection. Unless you're willing to spend additional money on a substitute keyboard, buying a computer with a keyboard you feel comfortable with is vital.

You must also determine whether the software you need is available for the system you're considering or you may find yourself frustrated like Hal Schuster, who has now found that the special software he needs for running the financial side of a publishing business is not available for his Macintosh.

You will also need to decide on the size of computer you want. Some people, particularly those in rural areas who are dependent on solar electrical power, or those who travel around a lot and need portability, are getting laptop computers as their sole computer. And, today, laptops certainly have ample computing power to serve as your primary computer. Their keyboards can feel cramped, however, and laptop screens can be less legible. There is another solution, too. If desk space is a limiting factor for you, but you would still prefer a desktop computer to a laptop, consider placing your systems unit in a tower on the floor to save the desk space you need.

Software

Selecting software is like buying ice cream from a store with 31 flavors, except this store has more like 31,000 flavors. You can grow old choosing! New programs and categories continue to be written, feeding a market in which computer owners spend several dollars on software for every dollar spent on hardware. However, it's estimated that 70 percent of us stay with the first business software we get because we don't want to start learning to use a new one. So if you invest time in selecting your software now and make a good choice in the beginning, you'll benefit from it for years to come.

First, before taking any software home, consider the popular and proven programs. Throughout this book, we identify popular software packages for the most common needs and uses. Softsel, a software distributor, publishes a chart of the best-selling software which is posted in many computer and software stores. Rather than trying to review the thousands of software packages that are available, try out these popular and proven programs because "bugs," or defects, have probably been eliminated. You'll find that sales personnel are also more knowledgeable and willing to assist you in exploring popular packages. Usually the instruction manuals for such software are better written. And finally, books, tapes, and classes are often available for learning to work with a popular program.

"User groups" have been formed around popular software in some parts of the country. These are groups of people who meet regularly to help one another learn and master particular software packages. They can be located through computer stores, software stores, and software publishers.

Second, read software reviews in computer magazines. You may wish to go to a library to read the reviews of the same software in several magazines. Different reviewers may notice and report on different characteristics that are important to you.

Third, don't depend on the short amount of time you have to try out a program in a store. Or worse, don't let a store clerk give you what instructional designer Michael Greer calls a "flying fingers" demonstration. Use the software for at least an hour, preferably two, with some of your own work. Later in this chapter we suggest guidelines for how to evaluate the software you're testing.

Fourth, buy from a store that allows you to return software for a full refund. It's not until you get home that you really get a sense of a program. If you don't damage anything or fill out the warranty card, you can usually return the software and the store will use its shrink-wrapping machine in the back room to make the program look like new again.

Fifth, once you have the new software at home, Sidney Schwartz, a former Egghead Software store manager, suggests taking several steps before you begin using the program for actual business functions. He advises, "A thorough 'road test' will help familiarize you with the product, and uncover potential problems and shortcomings.

"Be sure you know what you expect the software to do. If you haven't already, make a list of the features you consider most important, such as footnoting and indexing with a word processor, creating forms from a database, and so on.

"Review the documentation. If there's a tutorial or a 'getting started' section, read it first to familiarize yourself with the basic procedures. Then read all the documentation that applies to your use of the software, and at least glance through the rest. You may discover capabilities that you would never have stumbled across just using the software on your own. If you do find such capabilities, add them to your list. Make note of quick reference guides, keyboard templates, and other learning aids. Go ahead and install the software.

"Now start using the software, trying out each program feature that you plan on using. Concentrate first on the simple things—you usually wind up doing these the most. With a word processor, for example, enter some text and try the cursor-movement keys. Select, move, copy, and delete text. Try setting margins, indenting paragraphs, changing fonts, and other common formatting tasks. Then, go on to the more advanced functions like footnoting, outlining, indexing, and so forth. Don't get too involved with any particular feature. Refer to your list of important features, making sure each one works properly and is not confusing or difficult. Use this general procedure for whatever type of software you're testing, starting with the simple features and moving on to the more advanced.

"Call the company for technical support if you run across any problems. If you don't, make one up and call anyway. Good technical support can be critical, and if you can't get any help now, you probably won't when you really need it.

"If the software checks out okay so far, try making a 'model' of what you'll actually be using the program for. Keep it small, but incorporate all the important elements of the real thing. Create a one- or two-page newsletter, or a small database. Using your model, step through all the procedures you normally would carry out, from design to entering and editing data to printing output. If you need to import or export data, try it now. If you're testing accounting software, make sure the end-of-the-month and the end-of-year closings work properly. You may have to reinstall the program after you do this, but it's better than having a month's worth of real data disappear.

"If the software checks out okay now, it should work well for you in actual use."

For further information on testing software, see Alfred Glossbrenner's book *How to Buy Software*. Glossbrenner has developed quick reference checklists for evaluating how well a particular kind of software works. These lists tell you what features to evaluate in programs for word processing, spreadsheet, accounting, and so on.

User-Supported Software/Shareware

When free-lance software writer Andrew Fluegelman couldn't get a software company to buy his software, he engineered an innovative way of selling it. He made it available free. He asked that if people liked the free software, they send him a $25 donation, and so Freeware, Fluegelman's trademarked name for his products, was born. Many software authors now distribute their products in this way, calling it user-supported software or shareware. It is widely available from computer user groups, from bulletin board systems and on-line services like CompuServe, and from catalogs that specialize in this software. The catalogs charge a fee for duplicating and mailing the disk. People who go on to use the software are still expected to pay the author.

How to Keep Your Costs Low, and Other Ideas for Getting a Computer When You Can't Afford One

1. Buy a computer with bundled software, provided the software is what you need.
2. Order proven hardware by mail from reputable mail-order companies, but take into account shipping and other charges.
3. Buy a computer that includes peripherals, such as printer and modem, in the purchase price.
4. Buy last year's model, but be sure you will be able to get service, software, and peripheral devices locally.
5. Buy a used computer, after having it checked out. Disk drives are the most-likely sources of problems.
6. Shop the ads for special sales and introductory offers.
7. Comparison shop. Prices between stores and localities vary.
8. Ask your clients, customers, or employer to buy you a computer or give you one on a lease/purchase basis. Show them how such an arrangement could save them money or otherwise benefit them.
9. Buy or rent a computer or peripherals with colleagues or friends.
10. Buy at computer-show prices. Typically, exhibitors will offer special prices if you buy at the show, and these prices are often good.

Public Domain Software

Public domain software is free. It's been developed by computer enthusiasts who want to share their accomplishments. Alfred Glossbrenner describes public domain software and its availability in his book *How to Get Free Software*.

Buying Computer Hardware and Software by Mail Order

Many companies sell software through the mail. They fill the pages of computer magazines with ads. Although most popular software can be purchased by mail, sometimes at more than 50 percent off the list price, you may be taking a risk by buying this way. You usually won't have support in using the software, and if it doesn't work, you can only hope the seller will honor a "right of return" policy.

Check out both the software and the mail-order business before you order. Look in back issues of magazines to see if the company has been advertising for at least a year. Phone or write the magazine in which you've seen the advertisement to find out if the mail-order business has a record of complaints. Another excellent place to check on a company as well as on a product you're considering buying is on the forums on CompuServe or other

---

Four Top Mail-Order Sources

- Telemart. Generally has the lowest prices on software and small hardware (8804 N. 23rd Ave., Phoenix, AZ 85021. 1-800-426-6659).
- Compu-Add, which sells primarily hardware, has a growing chain of retail stores. The firm also sells at lower prices under the name Bentley Computer Products (12303 Technology Blvd., Austin, TX 78727. 1-800-456-3111).
- PC Connection sells IBM-compatible products (1-800-243-8088).
- Mac Connection sells Macintosh products. It has a reputation for providing more support than other companies (6 Mill St., Marlow, NH 03456. 1-800-MAC-LISA).
- 47th Street Computer sells all types of office equipment. (36 E. 19th St., New York, NY 10003. 1-800-221-7774). Retail stores in New York City at 67 W. 47th St. and 115 W. 45th St.

---

information services and bulletin boards. Pay by credit card rather than by cash or check. If you have a problem, you can often get the charge reversed.

Printers

Selection of a printer is one of the important ingredients in creating a professional image for yourself as a home business. For example, if you select the more economical dot matrix printer to use for producing letters, bills, and proposals, your documents will look as though they were printed on a computer and therefore convey a less professional image. Better 24-pin dot matrix printers produce nearly letter-quality type, but not quite. If you select a good laser printer, which prints documents that approach the appearance of typeset quality, the documents you produce may be virtually indistinguishable

---

Features to Look for: Printers

- **Quality output.** Select a printer offering the best possible quality that fits within your budget.
- **Printing speed.** Taking 65 characters per second (cps) as the equivalent of one page per minute, 24-pin dot matrix printers in near letter quality mode produce at the rate of about one page a minute. The Hewlett-Packard Deskjet prints at two pages per minute, the IIP at four pages per minute, the Laserjet III at eight pages a minute, and the IBM laser printer at ten pages a minute. A fast dot matrix printer, like the Hewlett-Packard Rugged Writer, prints at 480 cps in draft mode. That's almost as fast as the Laserjet III, but the sacrifice is quality and noise.

---

from those of the top floor executive suite of your community's largest corporation.

Today, printer prices almost form a staircase. Good 24-pin dot matrix printers are on the bottom stair and sell for around $300. Inkjet printers, such as Hewlett-Packard's Deskjet Plus, are one step up and cost a few hundred dollars more. A capable laser printer, such as Hewlett-Packard's Laserjet IIP, is yet another step up and costs several hundred dollars more. Then one more

---

- **Reliability.** Printers have a "duty cycle" rating, which is the maximum number of pages a printer is designed to print a month. Among laser printers priced under $2,000, the duty cycles range from 3,000 pages a month for Epson and Ricoh to 20,000 pages a month for IBM. Printers are also rated in terms of how long they operate before a breakdown. This is called "mean time between failures." Since you'll probably need to depend on a computer and printer almost as much as you do on your telephone, select a printer with a reputation for reliability.
- **Noise level.** Inkjet and laser printers are deliciously quiet compared with the clatter of impact printers and the wheezing of dot matrix printers. In a home office, a noisy impact printer can be more than an irritant; it can lessen your productivity.
- **Serviceability.** How long will it take to get a printer repaired? You may be able to get your printer repaired on a walk-in basis or you may have to ship it somewhere, leaving you printerless for weeks.
- **Convenience.** Easily readable printer controls in the form of buttons and lights on the front of the printer facilitate the operation. Laser printers that use cartridges containing the toner, which is ink in powder form, are much more convenient than lasers in which toner must be added from a bottle.
- **Memory.** A memory of 512 kilobytes is necessary for producing text with a laser printer. More kilobytes are necessary to print full pages of graphics.
- **Built-in fonts.** If you wish to have a variety of typestyles, the more fonts that come with the printer, the fewer you will have to purchase separately.
- **Compatibility** with Hewlett-Packard or Epson. Virtually all software is compatible with Hewlett-Packard laser printers and Epson dot matrix printers. If the printer you are selecting is not one of these, be sure to determine whether your software will be compatible with the printer you are considering.
- **Paper handling.** Some dot matrix printers allow for paper to be fed from both the top and the bottom. In selecting a printer, watch for any evidence that it produces paper jams. Paper jams are aggravating and lessen your productivity.

     Leading makers of dot matrix printers include Alps, Apple, Citizen, Epson, IBM, Hewlett-Packard, NEC, Okidata, Panasonic, Star, Tandy, and Toshiba.

     Leading makes of inkjet printers include Diconix and Hewlett-Packard.

     Leading makers of laser printers include Apple, Canon, Epson, IBM, Hewlett-Packard, Okidata, Ricoh, and QMS.

---

step up at around six hundred dollars more is Hewlett-Packard's Laserjet III with outstanding print quality. Several steps above that are Apple Computer's line of Laserwriter printers. As you mount this imaginary staircase, both quality and speed generally go up along with the price.

In addition to having the best printer they can afford, many home offices today also have additional printers for back-up and specialty work. For example, a dot matrix is useful for printing multi-part forms, a task a laser printer will not do. An inkjet printer, such as the Diconix 150 Plus, will operate on batteries. A Hewlett-Packard Paintjet produces color printing.

Modems

When you use a modem and communications software, your computer becomes both a library and a telephone to the world.

A modem translates the electronic signals from your computer into electric pulses of sound that can travel across telephone lines to another computer that also uses a modem to reconvert the acoustic signals back into a form it can process.

With a modem, you can gain immediate access to an estimated 95 percent of the information that's been published in the past fifteen years. You can do market research, check stock prices, find venture capital and personnel, investigate companies, and use the processing capabilities of mainframe computers.

Forty Ways You Can Benefit from Going On-Line

1. Getting and generating sales leads
2. Sending and receiving electronic mail
3. Banking by computer
4. Getting price quotes and ordering products
5. Learning about U.S. government procurement needs
6. Accessing a client's or employer's mainframe computer
7. Getting stock market quotes
8. Reading AP and UPI newswires
9. Reading stories from *The Wall Street Journal, Barron's,* and the Dow Jones News Service
10. Using the *Official Airline Guide*
11. Looking things up in encyclopedias
12. Making travel reservations
13. Buying, selling, exchanging, or financing real estate
14. Bartering for goods and services
15. Checking your personal account with your brokerage firm
16. Using the nation's 4,800 Yellow Pages directories
17. Holding meetings and conferences
18. Researching several thousand databases on almost any subject

You can save time and energy by running electronic errands—sending mail, doing banking or shopping, paying bills, getting airline schedules, and making reservations—all without leaving your desk. You can overcome the isolation of working alone by visiting the homes and offices of tens of thousands of people across the country and beyond, while still sitting in your chair. The connections you make on-line can be sources of new business, ways of learning from other peoples' experiences or mistakes, and an effective means for maintaining contact with clients, colleagues, and customers.

A modem also enables you to transmit information over the telephone lines via your computer even faster than on a fax machine. And the documents or data arrive in a form that can be edited or printed out by all types of computers. For example, you can send a document created on your IBM-compatible computer to someone who can read, change, or print it on a Macintosh computer.

Prices of speedy 2400-baud modems are now as low as $150; 1200-baud modems are available for under $100. And communications software is now available in the public domain. This means that transmitting information with your computer can be very cost effective.

An external modem is about the size of a book and plugs directly into the modular jack in your phone. If desk space is a problem, however, you can have an internal modem mounted on a card inside your computer.

---

19. Obtaining free public domain software
20. Sending telex messages to any of the 1.5 million telex subscribers around the world or fax messages to any fax owner
21. Getting IRS tax publications
22. Reading over 200 newsletters
23. Advertising
24. Calculating your net worth
25. Downloading software programs
26. Incorporating your business
27. Doing market research
28. Checking patents
29. Learning what proposals the government is seeking
30. Looking up 10,000 corporate SEC filings
31. Getting economic and marketing forecasts
32. Learning about foreign trade opportunities
33. Finding employment
34. Getting detailed demographic information
35. Doing credit investigations
36. Discovering investment opportunities
37. Getting medical information
38. Learning about pending congressional legislation
39. Finding venture capital
40. Locating personnel for your business

Features to Look for: Modems

- **Hayes compatibility.** Hayes is the leading maker of modems and its products create the standard.
- **Reliability.**
- **Ease of installation and use.**
- Error correction.
- Data compression.
- Switches located on the front of the modem for changing speaker volume and switching between voice and data.

Internal modems teamed up with a telephone line can also turn laptop computers into powerful communications devices. With our laptop, however, we still occasionally use a vintage acoustic modem when we want to communicate from a pay telephone. Instead of plugging an acoustic modem into a modular phone jack, you place the telephone receiver into rubber suction cups on the modem. However, acoustic modems, being limited to 300 bauds, or about 30 characters per second, are slow.

Leading makers of modems include Anchor, Hayes, Practical Peripherals (now a subsidiary of Hayes), Prometheus, Racal Vadic, and U.S. Robotics. Leading communications software programs for IBM-compatible computers are Procomm Plus, Crosstalk, Smartcom and, for Macintosh, White Knight, Microphone, and Smartcom. QModem and Boyan are established shareware programs for IBM-compatible computers.

Service and Support for Your Computer System

Media consultant Mary Ann Keats expressed what so many others have found about the importance of having good support for the computer systems they buy. "You get really dependent on your computer. I used to manage without one, of course, but now if something were to go out during one of my major projects, I don't know what I'd do. I've come to count on it. It's just the way I do business now."

In the world of computers, the quality of service and support you get depends on which computer you buy and where you buy it. The backup you receive—both in learning to use your computer and having it serviced—depends on what the manufacturer and dealer offer. To get the best possible backup, concentrate on the following:

Manufacturers and Dealers

Many computer manufacturers and dealers are falling by the wayside. Find out about a manufacturer's reputation and how the reliability of its products compare with other companies'. There are some good, relatively unknown computers you can get for excellent prices. But you have to decide how willing you are to take a chance, and whether there will be enough support for these computers to satisfy your needs.

Compare dealers on the basis of pricing, support, and service. Visit enough stores to get a feeling for when you're getting candid information and good service. If you get contrary information at different stores, do more home-work to clarify the contradictions. Too often sales personnel are misinformed or confused themselves.

Be aware that some dealers will try to steer you or switch you to a brand of computer on which they will make a high profit. Different manufacturers allow dealers different margins. The difference in profit from a brand offering a lower margin and one offering a higher margin may be $100 or more on a $1,300 computer.

Don't let someone who just changed jobs from selling used cars to selling computers use high-pressure techniques on you. And don't buy from a dealer who requires full payment before delivery. It's not customary, and experience has taught that this type of dealer is probably in financial trouble or worse. Even a 10 percent deposit should be viewed with some skepticism.

Also, find out whether people who have purchased computers from the dealers you're considering are satisfied. If you have any doubts, check with your Better Business Bureau.

Warranties

A ninety-day warranty is standard for computers, printers, and copiers. Many companies will offer up to a year. The basis for the ninety-day warranty is that if electronic parts are going to fail, they will usually do so within ninety days. To discover whether something will break down within the warranty period, you can "burn in" your equipment. To do this, turn your computer on and leave it on continuously for four days and nights. Better yet, have the dealer do this. This is a particularly good idea if you're like us and won't use the computer much while you're getting accustomed to it.

Check the wording of the warranty to see whether it covers labor as well as parts, and whether you must ship the computer elsewhere for repair. You can negotiate "nonstandard" warranties. Computer writer Ernest Mau, who works at home, bought an expensive computer system that began crashing, or breaking down, daily. The company notified him that they were cancelling his warranty because they wouldn't guarantee the computer's performance with "dirty power lines," and because he kept the computer on twenty-four hours a day. Fortunately, he had negotiated an addendum to the standard warranty, which the store had countersigned. It stated that the machine was to run on residential power, twenty-four hours a day, seven days a week. He thereby saved his warranty.

Service Contracts

When consultant Gil Gordon purchased a service contract for his computer, it seemed like a lot of money, but then a disk drive went out and he thanked the day he bought the contract. The bill for replacing the part would have been a hefty one, so he saved in the long run. If you're going to be giving your computer heavy use, a service contract can be a good investment. You can expect a service contract or extended warranty to cost about 1 percent of the computer's purchase price each month.

Service Availability

Find out where the computer equipment is serviced. Some computers must be sent to service centers, which may be a considerable distance from you. Others must be shipped back to the manufacturer. Still others are serviced by the dealer, and occasionally service personnel will come to your home office. IBM offers a 48-hour parts exchange for its new PS/1 computers.

Find out the turnaround time for service. Service while you wait is preferable. Twenty-four-hour turnaround is often a must for a home office computer. When it's longer than that, you should be able to get a loaner.

Telephone Hot Line

Some manufacturers have a telephone hot line you can call for guidance when you need it. This is highly desirable. Check to see that the line isn't always busy and that the people answering know what they're talking about.

Dealers offer telephone assistance too. Be sure the sales personnel at your dealer really know the computer you're buying. Since turnover is high among computer store personnel, also check to be sure more than one person there knows the ins and outs of your computer. One more option: companies are now coming into existence that sell hot line help for a fee.

Documentation

Documentation that accompanies both hardware and software should tell you how to set up and begin using your system. Some hardware and software is self-teaching, designed to train users without any outside help. This is called a "tutorial" and is great for the hurried businessperson who doesn't have time for a class.

Even with tutorials, however, you will want supporting manuals for reference. Skim the manuals before you buy to be sure you can understand them. Too often they have been written by technicians who assume that you are an engineer.

The best documentation is written in two sections: one that is like a tutorial, for learning to use the hardware or software, and the other indexed, for quick reference when you need to find something once you're using the computer. Also look to see if the documentation uses examples, has illustrations, and is adequately indexed. A rule of thumb is that the better the documentation, the better your chances that the system will be good.

Take a particularly close look at the instructions on imported computers and peripherals. Sometimes the translations leave a lot to be desired. For example, we heard about a booklet that stressed that the computer should be "earthed," which the owner finally concluded meant "grounded."

User Groups and Networks

In most areas, user groups or clubs have been started around the popular makes of computers. These are groups of people who get together to learn and master the capacities of their computers. User-group meetings can be a rich source of help and assistance, particularly when you are getting started. They are also an inexpensive way to get information, advice, and programming help. Some publish newsletters.

You can locate the user groups in your area by asking dealers who carry your computer, writing to the manufacturer, or checking the classified ads in computer magazines. A newspaper tabloid, *The Computer Shopper*, has regular listings of user groups. If you discover there is no group in your area, consider starting one.

Office Copiers

Having a personal copy machine is convenient and will save you the time of going back and forth to a copy store. With personal copiers now at prices beginning at about $400, it doesn't take many trips to a copy store to pay for one. If, for example, your time is worth $25 an hour and it takes you just half an hour to go to a store, wait in a line to make your copies, and then return home, and you do that three times a week, you'll pay for the copier in just over ten weeks. That doesn't include the cost of using your car, and you'll probably also get better-looking copies at less than a nickel each.

Buy a copier with the capacity to meet your needs. Someone producing training materials needs a heavier-duty, faster copier than home office workers making fifty copies a week. Leading makers of "mini" copiers for home offices include Canon, Mita, Panasonic, Ricoh, Sanyo, Sharp, and Xerox.

Rent, Lease, or Buy?

Virtually any piece of equipment you can buy can also be rented or leased. Like any purchasing decision, whether to buy, rent, or lease will depend on what you can afford, your cash flow, and your credit. There is no stock answer to the best method.

Features to Look for:
Copiers for Under 1,000 Copies a Month

- **High quality.** Copies on plain paper.
- **Ease of use.** The control panel and how you get toner into the copier are keys to ease of use. Copiers that use cartridges are much more convenient than those requiring you to load toner from a bottle.
- **Reliability.** Sources of information on reliability are the *User Ratings of Copiers* by Datapro Research Corporation, *Copier Selection Guide with Durability Ratings* by Buyers Laboratory, Inc., and *What to Buy for Business.*
- **Readily available service,** either on-site, which is more expensive, or carry-in.
- Stack feeding instead of manual single-sheet feeding.
- Reduction-enlargement capability.
- Multiple paper trays for different sizes of paper.
- Stationary platen, which takes less space than a platen that moves back and forth.
- Ability to copy larger than letter-sized documents.

When you rent on a daily, weekly, or monthly basis, you are incurring an ordinary business expense, while a purchase is an investment. When you no longer need the equipment, whatever you're rented obviously goes back. So if you need to rent equipment for three months or longer, consider buying or leasing it.

When you lease, unless it's just another name for a rental, you are actually financing the purchase of equipment. Ownership remains in the name of a third party (usually a leasing corporation) for the term of the lease. At the end, you can purchase the item for a nominal sum, such as 1 or 2 percent of the purchase price. From then on, it's yours.

There are tax consequences to consider in renting, leasing, or buying. Since Congress and the IRS are constantly revising the tax code, we suggest you

Buying a Used Copier

Be aware of some common buzzwords in selling used copiers. A "refurbished" copier has received a good cleaning and some new paint. A "reconditioned" machine has been newly painted and upgraded internally to match the manufacturers' new products. A "remanufactured" copier has gone back to the factory assembly line and had all worn parts replaced, in addition to getting a new paint job and internal enhancements. You decrease your chances of buying someone else's troubles with a remanufactured copier.

consult your accountant about which method will provide you the best tax advantage.

Leasing has a cash advantage over a purchase on credit because a lease usually requires little or no down payment, while a credit purchase may require 20 to 30 percent down. However, a disadvantage of leasing is that it's much more expensive than buying, since the leasing corporation includes charges to cover its overhead and make a profit. Another disadvantage stems from the fact that equipment is changing rapidly while costs are coming down, as is the case with computers and faxes. You could therefore find yourself at the end of a lease with obsolete equipment you can't resell for a reasonable price.

If you do decide to rent or lease, make certain you understand the contract—especially the fine print. Rental and lease agreements are printed so that customers will think the terms are fixed. But remember, everything is negotiable, even the terms of contracts with major corporations like IBM or Xerox. The contracts are written to their advantage, not yours. Elaine Ré, a national authority on negotiating, says that superior power in a negotiation isn't based on the size of the business, but on how attractive or unattractive it is for a party to make or not make a deal. Your contract may mean the difference between a salesperson's meeting a quota or qualifying for a bonus. So you do have some leverage in negotiating your contracts.

Here are some points to negotiate:

The exact nature of the financing agreement—does it have liens or restrictions?

The amount of each payment.

The disposition of the asset at the end of the lease.

Who is responsible for maintenance and taxes?

Renewal options.

Cancellation penalties, if any.

Disadvantageous terms and conditions.

Length of the lease period.

When you decide to buy rather than to lease or rent, you can use our twenty bargain strategies (in Chapter 7) for saving money in equipping and furnishing your home office.

No matter where you buy your furniture, equipment, and supplies, there are some cautions you should always exercise. For instance, don't buy broken or torn packages unless you have a chance to inspect the product or the opportunity to return it. Sometimes you can save money buying seconds or damaged merchandise, but be certain that the product is still usable. Since such items are generally sold as is, you probably won't be able to get a refund or make an exchange.

Quality and Getting Repairs

What first-time buyers often don't realize is that buying quality office equipment will save them money in lost downtime, repair, and replacement costs. How many home office workers can nod in agreement with Kathryn Acess, who runs a pension administration firm from her living room. She told us, "My biggest mistake was trying to cut costs buying used equipment that hadn't been thoroughly checked out, then spending more money than if I had gotten the proper machines in the first place."

However, even equipment with a reputation for reliability occasionally breaks or needs service. After the warranty runs out, getting equipment repaired by the manufacturer can be costly. One member of the Working from Home Forum found that the manufacturer of his office copier was going to charge him $245 for a repair that a manufacturer-authorized repair shop would do for $60. Another member was charged $300 by another manufacturer to replace a $30 battery. One wonders whether some companies charge overhead on their overhead. So check out prices before you take or ship a product for repair.

Chapter Digest

1. Although you can set up a home office with little more than a desk, a telephone extension, and a filing cabinet, today there is a wealth of small, cost-effective office equipment that can make your office as sophisticated and productive as any *Fortune* 500 company.

2. The typical home office today has at least one personal computer, a printer, an answering machine, and a variety of special telephone features. Many home offices also have a facsimile machine, a copier, and a modem as well.

3. You should be able to equip your office adequately for under $3,000 and should not need to go into debt to set up your office. Remember, as your business grows you can invest in additional equipment.

4. Throughout this chapter you will find Features-to-Look-For Checklists for each major type of office equipment. They highlight which features we consider to be important for effective home office use. You can take these checklists with you when you shop.

5. Virtually any piece of equipment you can buy can also be rented or leased. We suggest that if you need to use equipment for more than three months you should consider either buying or leasing it.

6. Make sure whatever equipment you buy is of good quality and has a reputation for reliability. Quality saves you money over time. When your equipment is down you're out of business, so make sure to purchase equipment with nearby or on-site (at your home) service and repair.

Resources

Books

The Book of FAX: An Impartial Guide to Buying & Using Facsimile Machines. Daniel Fishman & Elliot King. Chapel Hill, NC: Ventana Press, 1988.

The Complete Handbook of Personal Computer Communications. Alfred Glossbrenner. New York: St. Martin's Press, 1983.

Computer Workplace: Ergonomic Design for Computing at Home. Jan Wollman. Petersborough, NH: A BYTE Book, 1984.

How to Buy Software. Alfred Glossbrenner. New York: St. Martin's Press, 1984.

How to Get Free Software. Alfred Glossbrenner. New York: St. Martin's Press, 1989.

How to Look It Up On-Line. Alfred Glossbrenner. New York: St. Martin's Press, 1987.

How to Use a Computer in Your Home Office. Hal Schuster with Paul and Sarah Edwards. Las Vegas: Electronic Cottage Press, 1990.

Infomania: The Guide to Essential Electronic Services. Elizabeth M. Ferrarini. Boston: Houghton Mifflin Co., 1985.

InfoWorld Consumer Product Guide: A Year of Definitive PC Hardware and Software Reviews. Jeff Angus, ed. New York: Brady, 1989.

The Macintosh Small Business Companion. Cynthia W. Harriman. New York: Brady, 1989.

The Secret Guide to Computers. Russ Walter. 1988. Write to 22 Ashland St., Somerville, MA 02144.

Magazines, Newsletters, and Reports

Computer Shopper. Ziff-Davis Publishing Co., 1 Park Ave., New York, NY 10016.

Directory of Online Databases. Cuadra Associates, Inc., 2001 Wilshire Blvd., Santa Monica, CA 90403. Published by Elsevier Science Publication Co., Inc., P.O. Box 882, Madison Square Station, New York, NY 10159.

Home Office Computing. Scholastic, Inc., 730 Broadway, New York, NY 10003.

InfoWorld. IDG Communications, 1060 Marsh Rd., Ste. C-200, Menlo Park, CA 94025.

Link: Up. Learned Information, Inc., 143 Old Marlton Pike, Medford, NJ 08055.

MacUser. Ziff-Davis Publishing Co. (for full citation, see above, under **Computer Shopper**).

Macworld, the Macintosh Magazine. PCW Communications Inc., 501 2nd St., San Francisco, CA 94107.

Online Today. P.O. Box 639, Columbus, OH 43216-0639.

PC/Computing. Ziff-Davis Publishing Co. (see above).

PC Magazine. Ziff-Davis Publishing Co. (see above).

PC World. PCW Communications, Inc. (see above).

Personal Computing. VNU Business Publications, 10 Holland Dr., Hasbrouck Heights, NJ 07604.

Telecommunications Research & Action Center. P.O. Box 12038, Washington, D.C. 20005. Research on business long-distance costs.

What to Buy for Business. What to Buy Inc., 350 Theodore Fremd Ave., Rye, NY 10580.

Software

Bowker's Microcomputer Software in Print. Ann Arbor, MI: R. R. Bowker. Published annually.

Datapro—McGraw-Hill Guide to Microcomputer Software. Delran, NJ: Datapro Research Corporation. Updated monthly.

Shareware Express. 27601 Forbes Rd., Ste. 37, Laguna Niguel, CA 92677. Shareware catalog.

The Whole Earth Software Catalog. New York: Doubleday. Published annually.

On-line Services

CompuServe Information Service. 5000 Arlington Centre Blvd., Columbus, OH 43220; (800) 848-8199. Working from Home Forum. Enter "GO WORK."

Dialog Information Services. 3460 Hillview Ave., Palo Alto, CA 94304; (415) 852-3901.

Mead Data Central. 9393 Springboro Pike, P.O. Box 933, Dayton, OH 45401; (800) 227-4908. Full-text legal, medical, business, general.

Genie. General Electric Information Services, 401 N. Washington St., Rockville, MD 20850.

Prodigy. 15260 Ventura Blvd., Sherman Oaks, CA 91403.

PART 3

....

Protecting Your Assets:
Legal, Tax, and Insurance Matters

CHAPTER
NINE
■ ■

Zoning, Permits, Regulations,
and Your Legal Decisions

In this chapter, we'll discuss zoning or-
dinances, state laws, federal regulations, business permits, registrations, licenses, and contracts, and whether or not it would be beneficial for you to
incorporate your business. We'll also talk about how to select and when to
consult a lawyer. The terms we'll be using as we describe these legal issues
may be different in your state or locality, but the general principles will
be the same.

Is It Legal for You to Work at Home?—Zoning
Ordinances, Other Laws, and Restrictions

In too many cities and suburbs, the answer to whether it's legal for you to
work at home is no, because zoning ordinances often prohibit you from using
your home for business purposes. In a few situations, state or federal laws
and home association regulations may also limit the business use of your
home.

Although zoning originated in Roman times, current ordinances that restrict the business use of homes arose from a desire to protect neighborhoods
from the smokestacks of the Industrial Revolution. Some of today's zoning
ordinances were written back in Civil War times. Now, over a century later,
yesterday's good intentions often no longer apply.

No matter how outdated an ordinance or regulation may be, however,
violating one can be risky business. If you are operating illegally, you may be
forced to stop conducting your business, and you will certainly find yourself

faced with the discomfort of playing legal hide-and-seek. You may find yourself unable to complain about justifiable problems neighbors are creating, such as noise, for fear they'll retaliate by reporting you. So it's important for you to find out whether it is legal for you to work at home and what you can do about it if it's not.

How to Find Out Whether Zoning Ordinances Permit You to Work at Home

Zoning ordinances are created at the city or county level of government and vary widely from one locality to another. In Sierra Madre, California, for example, home businesses are permitted if you take out a business license. In adjacent Pasadena, however, you must apply for a home occupation permit before you can get a business license. And in nearby Bradbury, home businesses are not permitted at all. You can find out about your situation by answering these three questions:

1. Does your city or county have zoning ordinances? Some areas of the country, like the city of Houston, do not have zoning. To find out about your area, contact your city or county government. To figure out which unit of government is responsible for zoning, use this rule of thumb. If you would call the police in an emergency, you're governed by the city. If you would phone the sheriff, you deal with the county.

Within city or county government, zoning is usually handled by either the Building Inspector or the Planning Department. Otherwise, your area may have a special Zoning Administration you can contact.

2. How is your property zoned? Zoning ordinances divide the city or county into four basic classifications: Residential, Commercial, Industrial, and Agricultural. Each of these areas includes further distinctions, such as Residential–Single-Family Units, and Residential–Multiple-Family Units. Also, the types of activities that can be carried out in each area vary by locality. However, certain general observations can be made.

Most home businesses can be operated in an area zoned for agricultural use. After all, farming was the original "home business."

Many cities prohibit any residential use of buildings in an area zoned for industry. This causes problems for work-at-homers like artists who might want to rent warehouses or other industrial buildings to work and live in. A common exception to this restriction allows a guard to work and sleep on a building's premises in order to provide security. Consequently, some artists arrange to work as watchmen by night and painters or sculptors by day.

Most zoning codes allow buildings in commercially zoned areas to be used for both residential and business purposes. In fact, a familiar part of American tradition has been the neighborhood mom-and-pop shop, with the family living upstairs or in the back.

Residential zoning restrictions present the most problems for people working at home. Many localities either allow no business uses in residential areas or limit the nature and scope of business activities that can be done at home. Some communities allow more latitude in multiple-unit residential areas with apartment buildings and condominiums.

To find out which kind of zone you live in, locate your property on the official maps at the government office responsible for zoning. Chances are you live in a residential area and may be facing a number of possible restrictions.

3. Specifically, what is and is not allowed in your zone? Nine out of ten localities restrict using residences for offices or businesses in some way, according to a study entitled *Home Occupation Ordinances* done by Jo Ann Butler and Judith Getzels in 1985 for the American Planning Association. Some communities distinguish between a business and a profession.

In such cases, businesses generally cannot operate from a home, but recognized professionals like physicians, lawyers, dentists, musicians, artists, architects, and counselors can maintain home offices. What qualifies as a profession, however, may vary from one locality to another. For example, barber or beauty shops are considered professions in some places but not in others. Photography, real-estate brokerage, interior decorating, dance instruction, and roofing have been classified as businesses by some courts, while the giving of singing and music lessons have usually been found to be professions.

What particular zoning ordinances restrict and allow reflects the tastes of the local personalities responsible for the ordinances. As a result, contradictions between communities abound. For example, some communities prohibit a separate entrance for a home office; others require it. Irksome restrictions may limit the hours you can work; prohibit using your address in advertising, including Yellow Page listings; and using outside buildings, such as garages for your office. So before adding or remodeling an outside building for use as a home office, it's important to check your community's zoning and building codes.

Despite many variations in zoning codes, the American Planning Association study found some patterns. Following are the most common restrictions on home offices and home businesses (the percentages represent the percent of communities having the particular restriction):

- Restrictions limiting increases in vehicular traffic (46%)
- Restrictions on use or size of outside signs (42%)
- Restrictions on on-street parking (33%)
- Limitations on employees (33%)
- Limitations on the amount of floor space used (20%)
- Restrictions on selling retail times on the premises (13%)
- Prohibitions on outside storage of materials (11%)
- Restrictions on inside storage of materials (8%)

To find out specifically what is and is not permitted in your zone, read the ordinances, consult your lawyer, or ask a city or county zoning official. You don't have to tell anyone why you're asking. Zoning ordinances are public information, so you are simply exercising your right to know.

What You Can Do If You Aren't Zoned for Business

Many people living in areas that aren't zoned for business just ignore the law. They figure no one will know and there will probably be no problems. Often this is the case, because zoning officials usually don't have the time to go looking for violators. This is simply a fact, not encouragement to ignore zoning laws. There are many ways of solving zoning problems without violating the law. In any case, officials can find out about violations in a variety of ways.

Most commonly, zoning violations are reported by unhappy neighbors who call with complaints of too much noise, traffic congestion, or cars parked in front of their homes. Feuding neighbors might call just for spite, which happened to a man in the Pacific Northwest who was operating a contracting company from his home.

Each morning, four or five men would meet at his home office and he would send them out on their assignments for the day. They met inside, were not noisy, and did not congest parking. Yet the neighbors complained and zoning officials forced the contractor to stop doing business from his home. He

---

What Happens When You're Charged with a Zoning Violation

If authorities find you are in violation of a zoning ordinance, they will send you a notice ordering you to stop. After receiving such a notice you must stop, or file an appeal immediately, because each day you continue can be a separate violation.

If you do not comply with the order, authorities have two alternatives. Typically, they seek an injunction, an order from the civil court prohibiting you from continuing the violation. As in other civil lawsuits, you will be served with a notice of a hearing and have the opportunity to hire a lawyer or defend yourself. Violating an injunction, once it's issued, puts you in contempt of court, punishable by fine or imprisonment.

The authorities can also choose to prosecute the violation of a zoning ordinance as a municipal misdemeanor. This type of proceeding is usually a last resort, however. It begins with issuing a warrant or bill of complaint from the municipal court. If found in violation at the ensuing trial, the offender can be fined and/or imprisoned.

---

then sold his house, moved to another county, and began operating his business from his new home. Pursuing him, his old neighbors checked the zoning regulations, found he lived in another area not zoned for business, and reported him once more. Again he was stopped from doing business.

Obviously, good relations with neighbors are important in avoiding zoning problems. But there are other ways city officials find out about violations. Something as simple as an application for a business license or sales permit can call their attention to violators. A photographer who worked part time from his apartment discovered this the hard way when he tried to get a loan to buy new equipment. His bank required that he get a business license, which he did. Subsequently, a report of the license went to the zoning department and he was cited for a violation.

Similarly, the owner of a word-processing service discovered she had to pay state sales tax on some of her services. Applying for a sales tax permit meant the city would be notified of her home business, but failure to apply would put her in the position of violating state law. Too often, ignoring zoning ordinances leads to one of these legal double binds. A journalist even found the zoning inspector at his door within days of having a business telephone installed in his home.

Obviously the best strategy is to avoid zoning problems by taking preventive steps like these:

1. Establish and maintain good relations with neighbors. Find out how your neighbors feel about your working from home. Often neighbors feel safer knowing someone will be in the neighborhood during the day. Some are glad to have your business nearby. When your neighbors are supportive of your work, they can be valuable allies should you need special permits or a variance to work at home.

2. Know specifically what business activities you can and cannot do at home and adjust your business to meet the restrictions. If retail sales are prohibited on your premises, for example, distribute your wares through sales representatives or mail-order advertising. If employees other than your immediate family are prohibited from working in your home, contract with an outside secretarial service or have your employees work from their homes instead.

3. Rent a private mailing address or office suite to use as your official business address.

4. Apply for a use permit, which will allow you to use your home as a business. You may be able to get a use permit from community officials after an investigation of your business plans and facilities. Use permits usually do not require a public hearing.

5. Apply for a variance. You can ask the local zoning board for a waiver of zoning restrictions in your case.

6. Finally, work to amend local zoning ordinances to permit home office use in your area. These ordinances were created by political action and they can be changed by political action.

Applying for a variance. Variances are exceptions granted by a zoning board, a planning board, or an appeals board. Filing fees are charged to initiate the process. These fees may cost hundreds of dollars or more. Variances are escape valves built into the system. But no one has an inherent right to a variance, and zoning boards do not like granting them. In fact, boards will only consider variances under certain circumstances.

You may have a case if you can show that what you are doing is comparable to a permitted occupation. For example, someone tutoring children in how to use computers might be able to show how this new occupation is similar to teaching children to play the piano, which has traditionally been allowed at home.

You also may have a case if you can show that literal enforcement of the ordinance would deprive you of your livelihood and cause a hardship for you. For example, a single parent with three small children at home might be able to show that there is no other way either to provide or care for the children.

Finally, you may have a case if you can show there would be no harm done to the neighborhood or larger community. Since getting a variance requires a public hearing, such an approach is often your best bet. Poll your neighborhood. Find out how people feel about your working at home. Honor their concerns, get them on your side, and bring them to the hearing. If many neighbors come out to support you, and no one opposes you, it certainly will help.

Public support from people other than your neighbors can also make a difference. For six years after he retired as first violinist of the Boston Symphony, Herman Silberman taught violin in his condominium in San Diego, California. Then the homeowners' association reported his business to zoning authorities and they ordered him to cease and desist from teaching in his home.

Silberman's students, however, effectively used the appeals process and obtained a variance so he could continue offering his lessons. They circulated a petititon on his behalf and won over the six-person planning commission.

Learning the history and operations of the planning commission or zoning authority deserves your attention as well. Identify the members and review their voting records to discover what they usually allow and what they deny. Attend zoning board meetings on other cases to see how the hearings are conducted, how the board operates, who is most influential.

In larger communities, board members may represent special political or economic interests. In smaller communities, the people on the zoning boards are generally citizens like yourself. But whatever the size of your community, understanding the board members should help you build the best case for yourself.

Regardless of how well prepared you are, it's wise to consult an attorney. Legal expertise can help you in evaluating your situation and planning your appeal.

Reasonable Provisions for Zoning Regulations of Home Offices*

1. The home office or business is clearly secondary to the use of the dwelling as a residence and does not change the residential character of the dwelling or the lot in any visible manner.
2. The work done in the home office or business creates no objectionable odor, noticeable vibration, or offensive noise that increases the level of ambient sound at the property lines.
3. The home office or business does not cause unsightly conditions or waste visible off the property.
4. The home office or business does not cause interference with radio or television reception in the vicinity.
5. The home office or business has no more than two full-time employees who are not residents of the household. Special permits may be granted to allow more employees.
6. The home office or business has no signs visible from the street that are inconsistent with signs allowed elsewhere in the zoning regulations.
7. The home office or business sells no articles at retail on the premises which are not raised or grown on the premises.
8. The home office or business occupies less than half the floor area of the dwelling.
9. The home office or business has sufficient off-street parking for both the residential and the business uses of the dwelling.
10. The home office or business does not create a volume of passenger or commercial traffic that is inconsistent with the normal level of traffic on the street on which the dwelling is located.

*Adapted from a model ordinance developed by the National Alliance of Home Businesswomen, an organization that has contributed a great deal to the working-from-home movement.

Amending a zoning ordinance.   Since zoning ordinances are often anti-quated, you might consider mobilizing other home businesses in your community to get the ordinances amended. Artists in Los Angeles and New York, for example, successfully mobilized to get changes in zoning that allow them to live and work in studios located in industrial areas.

In another case, David Hughes of Colorado Springs, Colorado, began a community effort against a proposed ordinance that restricted home business activities in residential areas. Finding he was the only vocal dissenter, he put the text of the proposed regulation on his computer bulletin board, and nearly two hundred residents packed into the next city council meeting. The result was a substantially more permissive version of the original ordinance.

Other ways to locate fellow open-collar workers in your area are through civic organizations, professional and trade associations, Yellow Pages, or local newspaper advertising. You can join together to propose an amendment either through the zoning commission or directly to your city council or county legislature.

In drawing up the proposed amendment, enlist the help of a lawyer who believes in your cause.

The box below lists the types of provisions a reasonable zoning code might include. You can use these as guidelines for proposing an ordinance, or for reviewing a proposed ordinance or amendments to an existing code.

Homeowners' Association Regulations

Sometimes homeowners' and condominium association regulations are included as covenants that run with the land and restrict homes in the area from being used for business purposes. A deed with this kind of restriction can preclude your working from home if challenged by the association. So to ensure your ability to work from home, find out about any such limitations before buying a new home. If one exists, determine whether it can be waived and have your waiver acted upon as a condition of your purchase.

State Laws

A number of states have Industrial Homework laws. These laws were generally passed in the late 1930s to protect women and children from abusive labor practices. The laws are concerned with people employed in manufacturing products, and sometimes certain home businesses are prohibited entirely. For example, some states, such as California, Illinois, Pennsylvania, and New Jersey, prohibit the preparation at home of food and drink for commercial purposes, as well as articles used in serving food and drink. Such prohibitions make catering businesses in which the food is prepared at a home kitchen against the law. Other items that often cannot be manufactured at home include drugs, poisons, bandages, toys, and dolls. Illinois forbids the manufacture of metal springs, while Massachusetts doesn't allow the manufacture of clothing, except for women's hosiery and hats. California says "no" to making clothing for children under the age of ten, as well as to making toys and dolls.

Aside from prohibiting the manufacture of particular items, states with Industrial Homework laws require a potential employer to get a permit for such work; require the workers to get certificates; and require that homeowners permit inspection of their homes. New York specifically excludes clerical work, such as typing, transcribing, and bookkeeping from the requirements of its law. California has a law requiring talent agents to be licensed, but forbids granting a license if the business is to be conducted "in rooms used for living purposes." No doubt this was intended to curb exploitative "casting

States with Laws Regulating Home-Based Work

California	Ohio
Connecticut	Pennsylvania
Hawaii	Rhode Island
Illinois	Tennessee
Indiana	Texas
Maryland	Washington
Massachusetts	West Virginia
Michigan	Wisconsin
Missouri	
New Jersey	District of Columbia
New York	Puerto Rico

couch" situations. In all likelihood, these state laws should not affect you. To find out about such laws in your state, however, consult with your attorney, or if your state has an agency that helps small businesses, contact that agency.

Federal Regulations

Under the Fair Labor Standards Act, the federal government requires companies engaged in interstate commerce to provide all employees working at home, including clerical personnel, with "homework handbooks" in which the employee must keep detailed records of hours worked. Some states, such as California and New Jersey, also require the use of homework handbooks by businesses not covered by federal law. Also under federal law, the U.S. Department of Labor may prohibit categories of homework, and, since the 1940s, it has banned the manufacture of women's apparel in workers' homes. The rationale for this ban is to protect workers against minimum-wage violations, abuses of child labor laws, and the harrowing conditions of sweatshops.

The Wage and Hour Division of the Department of Labor enforces these regulations.

Business Permits, Registrations, and Licenses: What's Required?

Other than observing the ordinances, laws, and regulations governing business use of the home, operating a home business, on a full- or part-time basis, requires taking the same legal steps as operating a business anywhere else. The permits, registrations, and licenses vary greatly from locality to locality. They also depend on the nature of your business. So use the following checklist as a guide for identifying which legal steps you need to take. Then consult a lawyer or appropriate government agencies if you're not sure how these requirements apply to your business or locale.

Home Entrepreneur Checklist

Depending on the nature of your business and on state and local government regulations where you live, you may need to:
- ☐ Obtain a local business license.
- ☐ Register your business name with your county or state.
- ☐ Obtain a Seller's Permit, Resale Certificate, or Certificate of Authority for sales-tax purposes.
- ☐ Have an Employer's Identification Number; use Form SS-4.
- ☐ Obtain federal or state licenses.

Partnerships:
- ☐ File a statement of partnership.

Corporations:
- ☐ File articles of incorporation.
- ☐ Adopt by-laws.
- ☐ File a statement of domestic corporation.

Note: You may also wish to obtain a trademark or service mark.

Should You Incorporate Your Business?

A common legal question people ask when starting a business is "Do I need to incorporate?" Depending on whom you ask, you will get different answers. Even accountants and attorneys, the experts on this subject, disagree. You have three choices for setting up the legal structure of your business. You can operate as a sole proprietor, join with someone else in a partnership, or you can incorporate. The following outlines the pros and cons of each for a home business.

Sole Proprietorships

As a sole proprietor, you and the business are one and the same. You are the boss. What the business earns is your income; what you incur in business debts is money you owe. If you move to another city, the business moves. If you die, the business ends. Sole proprietorships are by far the most common form of small business, whether home-based or not, because sole proprietorships have a number of advantages. They cost the least amount of money to start because there are fewer legal filings and these usually do not involve drawing up legal documents. All this makes sole proprietorships the easiest type of business to start. It's also the easiest to discontinue and provides you with the greatest freedom from regulation.

However, sole proprietorships are limited to your lifetime and you will have difficulty raising money in the form of capital or loans.

Partnerships

Partnerships enable you to share the work and responsibility of a business with someone else. As a partnership, you may find it easier to raise capital. Parnerships cost less than corporations to start and, because there are few government regulations to contend with, they are also easy to start.

But there are some special risks involved in being in a partnership. First, you become legally responsible for the business actions of your partners, even for such things as damages should a partner become involved in an auto accident while doing business for the partnership. Anyone entering into a partnership should have an attorney draw up a partnership agreement first and obtain partnership insurance as soon as the agreement goes into effect. (For further details on insuring your business, see Chapter 11.) These precautions are important because it's as difficult to find a truly suitable partner as it is to find a good mate. Because partners have difficulty sharing authority or have clashing values, partnerships terminate at an even greater rate than marriages, 50 percent of which end in divorce.

Corporations

The words *corporation* and *incorporated* suggest strength, stability, and reliability. For a small business, this may mean having an easier time getting the attention of prospective customers and investors. The appearance of substantiality that comes with being incorporated is why even con artists often cover up their schemes as corporations.

In the past, many small businesses used to incorporate in order to take advantage of tax benefits. However, the Tax Reform Act of 1986 evened out the tax advantages of being incorporated. In fact, at some levels corporate tax rates are higher than individual tax rates. There are still certain tax deductions you may be able to take as a corporation that you could not take otherwise. These benefits, however, are not enough to offset the costs in time and money involved in becoming incorporated. So the decisions about whether to incorporate or not and the type of corporation for tax purposes you become, need to be made taking all factors into account and in consultation with experienced tax and legal professionals.

Factors to consider in making your decision include: The corporate form may limit your liability if something goes wrong. Being employed by your corporation may enable you to obtain Workers Compensation for yourself as a form of disability insurance. A corporation may have advantages for you for sheltering retirement benefits if your net income is high enough. It also offers better opportunities for raising capital if you choose to expand your business. Ownership can be more easily transferred. Because a corporation has a separate legal identity from your own, it can survive beyond your lifetime. If you are only using your home as a launching point for a company you plan to build into a much larger enterprise, it may cost much more to change an ongoing business into a corporation than its costs to incorporate at the outset of your operations.

On the other side of the ledger, corporations are much more expensive to start. They involve extensive paperwork and record keeping, are closely regulated, and may be subject to double taxation. For example, some states, like California, do not recognize S corporations (which, under federal law, allow you to avoid paying separate federal corporate income taxes). This means you may be paying state corporate taxes as well as state and federal individual income taxes.

Becoming a corporation may also raise your insurance costs. And, as a practical matter, whether you're incorporated or not, you need insurance in the event of a lawsuit. You can be sued in your own name as well as in the name of the corporation. Then there will be those legal bills to pay. So, incorporated or not, you need insurance to protect yourself against lawsuits. Even when you win a lawsuit, you lose because you have to pay the legal expenses of defending yourself. And attorneys fees are high!

We believe that when all factors are taken into consideration, most people starting a home business are best advised to begin as a sole proprietorship. However, if you decide to incorporate, we advise that you get the help of a lawyer experienced in small business start-ups. While it's relatively easy to set up a corporation with an incorporation kit (available in office supply stores), or by using a service such as Corporate Agents, Inc., it's even easier to make costly mistakes in attempting to make the legal and tax decisions involved in incorporating yourself.

Trademarks

A way of protecting your business identity is with a trademark or service mark. A trademark is a distinctive word, name, symbol, or combination of these used to distinguish a product or service from those of competitors. Historically, trademarks were developed to indicate the origin and authenticity of products. A *service mark* is simply a trademark for services.

Registering a trademark is different from registering a trade name. A trade name is used to identify a business and the laws and procedures are different. In some states, such as California, you cannot protect an unincorporated company name on a statewide basis, but you can protect a trademark. Trademarks can be registered either with the U.S. Patent and Trademark Office for nationwide protection or with your state government if state law permits.

In the past, you could only get a federal registration of your trademark if you were actually using it in interstate commerce. Now you only need to allege that you intend to use the mark in interstate or foreign commerce. A trademark registered with the federal government can use the 'small R in a circle' as a notice that your mark is protected. You can also serve notice to the world that you claim your mark by using the letters ™ prior to registering or without registering at all.

The current registration fee for federal trademark protection is $200, while state registrations range from $25 to $50. An additional advantage of federal registration is that it becomes "incontestable" after five years, which does not happen with state registrations.

Why and When You Need Contracts

Contracts are the job descriptions and pay scales of the self-employed. When you work from home, they are your most important safeguards against problems with customers and clients, and they help ensure that you are taken seriously as a business. Take heed from stories like these.

Artist Mary Kennelsworth was employed by a greeting card company when she decided to do sideline free-lance work at home. Having been employed with an established organization, she didn't realize that potential customers might not take her small business seriously.

"Perhaps it was because I was new at this or because I met customers in the living room with my two-year-old crawling around the floor. Whatever the reason, I did some work for several customers who didn't pay me. When one saw the work I'd done, she told me it wasn't what she had in mind. Another person never even came to pick up the work. When I called him, he said they had decided to have it done by their printer."

Management consultant Eric Paine had a similar experience. "When I first began consulting, I was so eager to get some business I didn't even think about a contract. The company I was talking with wanted to explore what I could do for them, and I was eager to show them. At first, things went very well. I completed the work over a three-month period, during which they seemed satisfied.

"When I submitted the final report with my bill, however, they asked for a few revisions. I made the revisions and resubmitted my bill. I didn't hear anything from them for a couple of months, and when I called they told me they were still reviewing it and might want more revisions. Now it's six months later. I haven't gotten any money and they aren't returning my phone calls."

Certainly Mary and Eric are not without any recourse, but the amount of time and energy spent trying to collect or entering into a lawsuit may be so great that it's not worth the effort. Better to offset such possibilities up front by signing a contract before taking the work.

Whatever your business, be it selling knickknacks, catering, or computer programming, create a standard contract to use with your clients or customers. In it, spell out your business agreement with specifics such as what you will provide, when you will provide it, what it will cost, and when they will pay you.

Contracts can be verbal or written, but written ones are certainly preferable. Psychotherapist Greg Rohan has clients fill out and sign a basic client information form (name, address, phone number, and so on) and at the bottom is a payment contract that reads this way:

"I understand I am to pay for services at the time they are rendered unless I have made other arrangements, and agree to pay for appointments I do not cancel at least 24 hours in advance."

He reviews this statement verbally to be sure the person understands and agrees. Whenever he makes other financial arrangements with clients, he writes these agreements on the form before they sign it. He attributes never having problems with collecting fees to this procedure.

Barbara Bickford has a printed order form that she uses for her word-processing services. On the form she lists the services ordered, the charge for each service, and the date and time she will have it to the customer. She has customers sign the order to confirm their agreement to all these items. Then, unless a company has previously established credit with her, she gets a 50 percent deposit on the work to be done.

Eric Paine now uses a "letter of agreement" for his management-consulting contracts. He meets with his clients to work out the specifics of the consulting he will do and afterward sends them a detailed letter indicating everything they agreed to in the meeting. He sends two copies and asks that one be signed and returned to him.

The best way to develop contract agreements that are customized to your needs is to consult a lawyer. You can also talk with colleagues about the contracts they use, ask your professional or trade association for information, or attend a workshop on contracting. Pro forma contracts are now available on computer software.

Sometimes your clients or suppliers will offer you a contract. When this happens, review the terms carefully. Usually these contracts are presented as a "standard form," so they appear to be unchangeable. Actually, a contract is always negotiable. Read the fine print and feel free to write in modifications.

In most cases, we suggest having a lawyer look over the contracts you negotiate at first. Later, you may feel familiar enough with the way contracts are written to make informed changes on your own.

Selecting a Lawyer

Some people only go to the dentist when they're in agony with a toothache. Then, too often they're faced with extensive, expensive, and time-consuming dental work. So it is with going to a lawyer. In either case, the better approach is to go in for periodic check-ups and avoid developing emergencies.

You can call on a lawyer to:

■ Help you decide upon and set up the form of business you want to establish (a sole proprietorship, partnership, or corporation).

- Advise you on regulations affecting your business and assist you in filing for necessary licenses, permits, and registrations.
- Advise you on insurance you need and refer you to a good agent.
- Review contracts and other legal documents.
- Help you with collection problems. Sometimes a letter on a lawyer's letterhead is enough to get payment from a debtor.
- Provide you with advice and help you take action to avoid lawsuits.
- Represent you in unavoidable lawsuits.

Whether you need a lawyer right now or not, find one you can trust who understands your business situation. You may actually consult your lawyer infrequently, but when those times come, you'll be a step ahead if that person already knows you and your business.

The best way to find a lawyer is through referrals from others with businesses like yours. If you don't already know such business owners, contact them through professional and trade associations or the Chamber of Commerce. Then talk with the lawyers you've been referred to. Tell them about your business situation and select the lawyer you feel best understands and reflects your business interests.

In some states you can join a prepaid legal plan that provides services to business. For an annual fee, often less than $200, you may get unlimited telephone consultation with an attorney, the writing of collection letters and letters to government agencies on your behalf, review of contracts and other documents, provision of partnership agreements and articles of incorporation, all at no additional charge. For more involved legal matters, you can obtain legal representation at greatly reduced rates. For example, the American Legal Network, to which we belong here in California, guarantees qualified specialists whose normal rates are $100–$200 an hour for no more than $70 an hour.

Once you've selected a lawyer, think of that person as an essential part of your business team. Get professional advice to avoid legal problems, just as you would call on an accountant to avoid an audit. Law, like taxes and insurance, is an area where you can use experts to help you keep your business on track.

Chapter Digest

1. Nine out of ten communities either restrict or prohibit using residences for business purposes. Contact the city or county government office that administers zoning to find out how your residence is zoned, and what limitations, if any, there are on your working from home.
2. Zoning ordinances usually reflect early twentieth-century efforts to prevent industrial activity from blighting residential neighborhoods. Today,

home offices don't disrupt neighborhoods. So if you encounter unduly limiting zoning restrictions, consider the variety of alternatives for gaining an exception.

3. Sometimes homeowner association regulations also limit business use of residences.

4. Eighteen states have laws governing work from home. While these laws don't affect most information-based home businesses, you may need to contact an attorney or the state agency that assists small businesses if you plan to prepare food at home.

5. Local permits, registrations, and licenses required to start a business vary greatly from community to community and depend on the nature of your business. An attorney or an agency that assists small businesses can help you identify what you must do in your locale.

6. One of the first decisions you must make in starting a business at home is what legal form your business will take: sole proprietorship, partnership, or corporation. Carefully weigh the pros and cons of each and, if in doubt, consult with legal and tax counsel to choose the best form for your business.

7. Contracts represent the job descriptions and pay scales of the self-employed. They are your most important safeguard against legal or financial problems with customers, clients, or suppliers. Get legal advice in drawing up contracts to ensure they represent your best interests.

8. Every home business should have access to legal counsel that understands the home office situation. To keep legal costs down, you can consider joining a prepaid program that offers counsel to businesses.

Resources

The Contract & Fee Setting Guide for Consultants & Professionals. Howard L. Shenson. New York, NY: John Wiley & Sons, 1990.

Independent Contractor Report. James R. Urquhart, ed., 2021 Business Center Drive, Ste. 112, Irvine, CA 92715; (714) 752-5544.

Selecting the Legal Structure for Your Business. SBA (#MA 6.004). See full citation under Chapter 3.

Various self-help law books from Nolo Press. 950 Parker St., Berkeley, CA 94710. Write for catalog.

Legal Barriers to Home-Based Work. National Center for Policy Analysis, 7701 N. Stemmons, Ste. 800, Dallas, TX 75247.

Trademark Management. Clark Boardman Company, Ltd., 375 Hudson, New York, NY 10014; 1-800-221-9428.

CHAPTER
TEN
■ ■

· Claiming Your Tax Benefits

The 1990s are likely to produce many changing and contradictory court decisions, perhaps even laws and regulations, affecting the tax status of home offices. On one side, the growing number of people working from home will result in less revenue for the IRS as people live more tax-deductible lives. On the other, the Executive Branch and Congress are coping with the federal deficit and are prodding the IRS to increase the amount it collects. Thus the IRS is becoming stingier in what it allows in self-employment and home-office deductions, and it can be expected to fight every court decision favorable to the home office. In other words, what the Tax Court giveth, the IRS taketh away. We expect to see this dynamic continue as more people opt for a tax-deductible lifestyle. It therefore becomes more important than ever that people in home offices know what their rights are, take great care to be able to prove their rightful deductions, and get the help they need to stay current on the fluctuating tax law.

Our intent in this chapter is not to make you a tax expert, but to let you know in general what you're entitled to under the law, so that you neither overlook items you should be deducting nor exaggerate your deductions recklessly—in other words, so that you operate from a smart, realistic middle ground. We'll discuss the types of deductions you may be able to take, how to qualify for them, and the records you need to keep. Because tax law is complex and there are many, many changes since Tax Reform, we recommend seeking professional tax advice concerning your particular situation.

In general, the deductions you can claim when working from home fall into one of two categories: *home-office expenses* and *regular business expenses*. Since the primary tax advantage the home-based worker has over other taxpayers is home-office deductions, let's turn first to how you can qualify for these deductions.

Meeting IRS Criteria for a Home-Office Deduction

As long as you meet the necessary criteria, whether you live and work in a house, an apartment, a condominium, a cooperative, a mobile home, or even a boat, you can deduct the cost of operating and maintaining the part of your home that you use for business. The Internal Revenue Service has two basic criteria your home office must meet in order to qualify as a tax write-off. The first is that *the portion of your home you wish to claim as a business expense must be used exclusively and regularly for business.*

Exclusive Use

"Exclusive use" means that the portion of your home you're claiming as a deduction is used only for business. Your home office may be an entire room you have given over to that purpose or it may be simply an alcove in your living room or a breakfast nook off your kitchen (one, however, that is not used for dining). It need not be separated from the room by a partition, but it must be a separately identifiable space. So for tax purposes, think of your home office—your business space—as an entity separate from the part of your home given over to personal use.

Currently there are two exceptions to the exclusive-use rule. You may take a deduction for space used to store inventory and for space used as a day-care facility.

As for the first exception, if you're in direct sales of cosmetics, gift baskets, health products, or household cleaning products, for example, and meet the following criteria, you can take a deduction on space used for inventory, even if that space is also used for personal activities or for storing nonbusiness items as well:

Your business must involve wholesale or retail sale of products.

The inventory must be kept for use in your business.

Your home must be the only fixed location of your business.

You must use the storage space on a regular basis.

The storage space must be easily identifiable as separate from space used for personal purposes.

As for the second exception, if you operate a licensed day-care facility in your living room, you are not excluded from claiming your living room because you also use it in the evening when the children have gone home. You calculate your deduction on the basis of the percentages of both space and time the room is used for day care.

Regular Use

"Regular use" refers to using the business segment of your home on a continuing basis. Let's say you have space set up as a photo lab in a bedroom and you use it exclusively for that purpose once every several months. This would be what the IRS calls "incidental or occasional use" and would not qualify you to take a home-office deduction.

You need to demonstrate that you are using your business space regularly for so many hours of each day or week. So if you set up a schedule for using the photo lab for business purposes every Monday, Wednesday, and Friday evening or every Saturday or Sunday, then you would be demonstrating "regular use."

The second criteria your home office must meet in order to qualify as a tax write-off is that *the portion of your home you use exclusively and regularly for business must be either your principal place of business or a place where you meet with customers or clients in the normal course of business.*

Principal Place of Business

In practical terms, *principal place of business* means that if you have more than one place where you conduct business, your home must be the principal place in order for you to be able to claim it as a deduction.

In 1990, the Tax Court liberalized the definition of what a principal place of business is by abandoning the 'focal point' test for determining the deductibility of home-office expenses. Under that old test, a taxpayer's principal place of business was the place where goods and services were provided to customers and revenues were generated. This prevented teachers, for example, from deducting a room where they graded papers at night and weekends because their work was principally at a school. In its place, the Tax Court considered the facts and circumstances of a case of an anesthesiologist who had no office in the hospitals in which he worked for keeping records, reading, or conducting various office activities. The Tax Court said that if a taxpayer's home office is essential to his business and he spends substantial time there and has no other location available to perform necessary office functions, the taxpayer is entitled to a home office-deduction. However, at this writing, the IRS has declared that it will not apply this test to other taxpayers, meaning others will need to take the IRS to court again.

A Place for Meeting

Even if your home office is not your *principal* place of business, you are also entitled to deduct home-office expenses if in the normal course of your work you see clients, patients, or customers face-to-face at home. Lawyers, doctors, psychotherapists, and management consultants are examples of people who might maintain outside offices yet also see clients at home. The space used for meeting clients, not for doing paperwork or other activities, is deductible.

Here's another exception. If your home isn't your principal place of business, but you have on your property a separate freestanding structure—a barn, a greenhouse, a workshop, a studio, a detached garage, a cabana, or anything physically detached from your home—and it is used exclusively and regularly for business, you can claim the home-office deduction for the use of that space. If a literary agent has a downtown office where she does most of her business, but has converted a guest house on her property into an office where she works every Monday and Friday, she will be able to take the deduction for her home-office space.

Deducting Home-Office Expenses

When you qualify for a home-office deduction, you can deduct a variety of expenses in addition to your regular business expenses.

Direct expenses for the business portion of your home—such as painting your office or fixing a leak in it—are fully deductible. But you should be aware that the IRS makes a distinction between capital improvements (like adding a room that you use for business, installing customized cabinets in your home office, or designing space for your computer) and repairs that you'd make in the normal course of maintenance (like fixing a broken window or repainting your office). Repairs are deductible. Capital improvements, however, are depreciated, which means that the deduction must be spread over a period of several years.

Indirect expenses related to the entire home—such as mortgage payments, insurance, utility bills, exterior painting, roof repair, depreciation—are deduct-

---

Possible Deductible Home-Office Expenses*

- Cleaning a home office
- Depreciation on home (partial)
- Household furniture converted to use in the home office
- Household supplies used in business space
- Interest on mortgage (partial)
- Real estate taxes (partial)
- Rent paid if you rent or lease (partial)
- Repair and maintenance of office portion of home
- Telephone, except the base local service for the first line into your home
- Trash collection
- Utilities attributable to business use of home (electricity, gas, water)

*Applicable to both the salaried and the self-employed.

ible in part. To calculate the part of these expenses you can deduct, divide the square footage of your office space by the total square footage of your home. Thus, if the office measures three hundred square feet and the whole home measures fifteen hundred square feet, your office takes up 20 percent of the total space and you can deduct 20 percent of your indirect expenses. (You can also calculate the deductible portion of your home by dividing the number of rooms used for business by the total number of rooms in your home if the rooms are of the approximate same size.)

Even when calculated at the proper percentage, however, the amount of home-office expenses you deduct cannot exceed the amount of gross income you've earned from your work at home. So to ensure that you will not be using a home-office deduction to offset income you've earned, you must calculate the deduction in a particular sequence of steps. This makes the calculation somewhat complicated, but it helps the government know you will not be misusing the deduction. Here are the steps you take:

1. Begin with the gross income from your home office.
2. Subtract your regular business expenses, which are described later in this chapter.
3. Subtract the expenses generated from the business use of your home, including the percentage of the mortgage interest and real estate tax deductions.
4. Deduct the business portion of your indirect expenses—such as cleaning, electricity, insurance.
5. Finally, deduct for your home-office space.

If at any time in this process your regular business and home-office expenses exceed your gross income, you can take no further deductions. For example, if you had a part-time income of $1,400 from your work at home, but your expenses were $1,600, you can still deduct no more than $1,400. *The home-office deduction can be used to bring the taxes on what you earn at home to zero, but it can't be used as a loss to reduce taxes on the income you earn at a full-time job or from other sources. However, you can carry forward to future years the home-office expenses you were not able to deduct.*

Finally, if you own your home, before taking a home-office deduction consider this possible pitfall. Suppose you paid $60,000 for your home and now plan to sell it for $100,000. Generally, if you purchase another home that costs $100,000 or more, the $40,000 increase in value will not be taxed if you "roll over" your money by buying and occupying the new home within 24 months. But let's say you've been taking a home-office deduction of 20 percent. When you sell your house, you will need to pay tax on 20 percent of the increase in value (on $8,000).

We've seen several people start businesses from their homes, find that they need more room, and then decide to move. So if you're thinking of taking the home-office deduction, be sure to weigh the value of that deduction against any taxes you'd have to pay upon selling. This is especially important if you plan to move soon. Even if after living in your home for ten years and only in the last year you took the home-office deduction, you would still be taxed on a percentage of the profit you made on selling.

If you disqualify your home-office deduction in the year of sale (and preferably the year before), you may be able to avoid paying income tax on the profit. Check with your accountant or attorney about your situation.

How to Calculate Your Home-Office Deduction

Gross Income from Work at Home	$20,000
Regular Business Deductions (Accounting, advertising, and so on, including direct expenses of your office, such as painting and repairs.)	– $ 5,000
Amount Remaining to Be Used for Home-Office Deduction	$15,000

Deductions Taken on Schedule A

	Total (100%)	Allowable to Home Office (20%)	
Mortgage Interest	$4,000	$800	
Real Estate Taxes	$1,000	$200	
Amount Deductible		–$ 1,000	
Amount Remaining to Be Used for Home-Office Deduction			$14,000

Other Indirect Home-Office Expenses

	Total (100%)	Allowable to Home Office (20%)	
Cleaning	$ 400	$ 80	
Electricity	1,000	200	
Gas	800	160	
Insurance	300	60	
Amount Deductible		–$ 500	
Amount Remaining for Home-Office Deduction			$13,500

	Total (100%)	Allowable to Home Office (20%)	
Depreciation	$3,000	$600	
		–$ 600	
Net Profit After Home-Office Deduction (Value of Home-Office Deduction: $2,100)			$12,900

Deducting Regular Business Expenses

Regular business deductions include expenses that are necessary for the operation of your business but are not included in the home-office deductions described above. If you are a salaried employee, these are expenses required for your employment but not reimbursed by your employer.

Now let's discuss such business expenses in more detail.

Everyday Expenses

The most common types of expenditures are items or services used in the day-to-day course of your work: the telephone, office supplies, postage and shipping costs, printing and duplicating expenses, advertising and promotion charges, fees for professional services. Not all deductible expenses are quite this obvious, however. A fashion consultant who subscribes to *Vogue* or a painter who buys books on art history can deduct these expenses because it's allowable to deduct the cost of books, magazines, and newspapers related to your work. Furthermore:

If you're a dance instructor, you can deduct the records and tapes you use for your classes.

If you're a psychotherapist, the cost of any personal-growth seminars you attend in order to evaluate their suitability for your clients is deductible. (So are the facial tissues your clients use.)

To a caterer, cookbooks are a business expense.

If you're a restaurant critic, your meals out are deductible.

If you hold sales meetings at your home, the coffee you serve—and the paper cups—are write-offs.

A color or wardrobe consultant can deduct the cost of mirrors in the office.

If you're a journalist, you can deduct the daily newspaper.

A swimming teacher giving lessons at home can claim a portion of the pool expenses.

If you are a professional speaker, you can deduct your audio and video equipment.

In fact, an entertainment-industry musician can deduct the cost of going to movies, subscribing to cable television, buying records, and attending entertainment-industry seminars. These are all research-related expenses that enable such a musician to keep abreast of the profession and get ideas for future work.

Travel

Whenever you leave home to meet with business contacts, do work-related research at the library, buy office supplies or postage, negotiate a contract, or attend a work-related class or meeting, you are making a business trip. If you

Deductible Business Expenses

Accounting and bookkeeping fees

Advertising expenses used for prizes and contests

Attorney fees

Automobile expenses including
—Auto club membership
—Garage rental
—Loss on sale of auto

Bad debts

Bank service charges

Bankruptcy

Books and periodicals related to business

Business conventions including those on a cruise ship

Business meals (80%)

Business start-up expenses

Capital expenditures (Section 179, Internal Revenue Code)

Career counseling costs

Commissions paid to agents and sales reps

Consultant fees paid to reduce cost of business

Copyright costs

Corporate organization expenses with election to amortize

Depreciation

Dues for
—Clubs and fraternal organizations that are business related
—Professional and trade associations

Education expenses for maintaining or improving required skills

Electronic mail services

Financial counseling fees

Furniture and equipment (office)

Gifts (business), but limited to $25 per recipient per year

Insurance expenses (including portion of homeowners')

Interest on trade or business debts

Legal fees

License fees and taxes

Lobbying expense of appearing before legislative bodies

Messenger services

Office furniture and equipment

Office supplies

Operating losses in a prior year

Organization expenses of corporation (amortizable over not less than 60 months)

Passport fee for a business trip

Pension/retirement plan contributions

Postage and shipping

Printing and duplicating

Professional association dues

Professional books and journals

Repair and maintenance of business property

Social Security taxes (50%), as of 1990

Tax preparation of business tax return

Taxes, state and local taxes on business

Theft losses of business property

Travel expenses

---

happen to stop at the dry cleaner or grocery store en route, the entire trip still counts as business. You will, however, need to keep a log of your business and nonbusiness travel if you also use your car for trips that are just personal.

If you use public transportation such as buses, subways, or taxis (a taxi driver will give you a receipt if asked), record the date, destination, cost, and purpose of each trip in a travel diary. If you mainly travel in your own vehicle, log all business-related mileage. Then deduct the cost in miles (in 1990), the IRS is allowing 26 cents per mile, plus parking and toll fees).

The alternative is to calculate what percentage of your overall car use is devoted to business, and take that percentage of your total automobile expenses (including gasoline, repairs, maintenance, insurance, and depreciation) as your deduction.

Entertainment

Home-based workers can deduct not only restaurant meals, drinks, and tickets to events such as concerts and plays—but also expenses incurred while entertaining business associates at home, such as wages for hired help, the cost of flowers, and the cost of food and drink. However, this deduction is limited to 80 percent of their cost, and there are strict rules for deducting business meals, such as the requirement that the business discussion be directly preceding, during, or directly following consuming the meal or beverage. Besides these typical entertainment expenses, business gifts are also deductible, at the current limit of up to $25 per business associate.

The IRS will disallow any expense that you can't substantiate, however, so be sure to keep receipts as well as a record of people in attendance at each event, their business relationship to you, a summary of the business discussion of the event, and the date. In other words, saving a credit card receipt from a restaurant is not enough; you must fill out the reverse side with the names of the people you entertained and a summary of the business discussion, in order for the IRS to accept it as a deduction.

Business Property: To Deduct or Depreciate?

When it comes to the way tax law deals with business property, we're in the arena of depreciation and capital-expense deductions. These are terms of confusion to many people who are innocent of our labyrinthine tax system. Our purpose in the next few paragraphs is to help you think about these things so you can take maximum advantage of them.

If furniture in your home office and the equipment you use in the course of your work can be used for three years or more, you can depreciate the property. To depreciate means that rather than deducting the entire cost of your new printing equipment in a single tax year, you spread the deduction over the life of the equipment. You can also take furniture that was previously for personal use, put it to use in the business portion of your home, and depreciate it.

The decision to depreciate is a strategic one. Suppose you spend $2,000 on a laser printer for your business. If you buy it in a year when your earnings are high, you may want to take the large deduction all at once in order to bring your taxable-income level down. If, on the other hand, you have a year when your earnings are low, you might be better off spreading out the deduction over a period of years. (The IRS, by the way, has guidelines for the amount of time over which you depreciate particular kinds of property.) Also consider that because depreciation expenses lower your gross income they may lower the amount of Social Security tax you pay too.

Because a computer may be the most expensive item of business equipment you buy, we'll use it as an example of how to deduct business property costing more than $100.

If you use your computer more than 50 percent of the time for business, you have two options for deducting the cost of your computer. You can deduct the cost in the year you purchase the computer, as a Section 179 capital expense, or you can depreciate it over five years. You are allowed up to $10,000 as a Section 179 capital-expense deduction. If you spend more than the maximum amount eligible for a capital-expense deduction, the excess amount can be depreciated. But the amount of property that can be taken as a capital expense cannot exceed the taxable income from a business. In other words, you cannot offset income from a job or other source using the capital-expense deduction.

Your other option is to depreciate your computer. You can use the Modified Accelerated Cost Recovery System (MACRS). Or you can use straight-line depreciation. This method spreads out the time you depreciate your equipment. Since Tax Reform in 1986, automobiles and light trucks must be depreciated over five years and stringent limits are placed on automobile deductions each year. This was done to keep luxury cars from being paid for by Uncle Sam.

A word of caution is in order here. If you use your equipment partly for business and partly for personal reasons, you will need to substantiate your deduction with adequate records proving business usage.

This is a subject of some current controversy and increasing complexity as the IRS attempts to prevent Uncle Sam from paying for home computers that are not explicitly used for business. IRS Publications 529 and 534 contain the current IRS positions on and formulas for deducting home computers.

Tax Responsibilities of the Self-Employed

Estimated Tax Payments

If you are a sole proprietor, a partnership, or a shareholder in a Subchapter S corporation, you are considered self-employed. Since you don't have an employer deducting taxes from your pay throughout the year, you are responsible for making advance payments of your estimated federal income tax. Estimated tax payments are due quarterly—on April 15, June 15, September 15, and January 15—and are filed on a Form 1040-ES. At the end of the tax year, you will file a final Form 1040 with a Schedule C, which itemizes your business expenses for the whole year.

If by the end of the year you have not paid at least 90 percent of the tax you owe or as much as you paid the year before, you may be charged substantial penalties, so it's in your interest to make your estimated tax payments during the year. This system also keeps you from owing a large sum of money all at once, which can be overwhelming when you're running a small business. If your state of residence has income taxes, as most do, you will have to make estimated tax payments throughout the year for state taxes as well.

Social Security Payments

Your estimated tax payments will also include the Federal Self-Employment Tax—Social Security. If you were employed by another person, your employer would pay half of your Social Security and the other half would come out of your paycheck. Self-employed people must pay the full amount themselves. However, as of 1990, 50 percent of Social Security taxes are deductible.

Employment Taxes

Home-based workers who employ others must comply with many additional tax requirements. IRS Circular E, *Employer's Tax Guide*, covers the federal regulations, and your state tax agency can inform you of state requirements for employers.

If you employ your children or grandchildren, their earnings are deductible. Family businesses do not need to pay Social Security or unemployment taxes on minor children, and the children pay no income taxes on the first $3,000 of earned income. To substantiate this claim, keep time records of their work (the records will be more believable to the IRS if a nonrelative keeps them), note the work done, and pay family at the rate you would pay a nonfamily member for the same work.

Reminders for Moonlighters

What if you are a salaried employee *and* you operate a home-based business as a sideline? In this case, you'll be filing both the usual Form 1040 and a Schedule C for your home-business deductions; you may also have to pay additional Social Security tax. No matter how little your sideline income is, you should be aware that it is subject to tax—although by taking advantage of the home-office deduction, you may find you owe little or no taxes.

The IRS presumes an enterprise is a hobby (and not eligible for deducting losses to offset income from other sources) if it does not show a profit for 3 years out of 5. So to meet IRS standards, the business needs to be showing a profit by its third year. However, this is a rebuttable presumption. If you are showing steady progress each year but are continuing to operate at a deficit, you may still be able to claim business deductions. Be prepared, however, to prove to the IRS that yours is a serious business and not a hobby.

The Home-Office Deduction for
Salaried and Commissioned Employees

If you are a salaried or commissioned employee of someone else but work from home, you may still be eligible for the home-office deduction. Tax Reform has made an employee's home-office expenses, like other unreimbursed employee business expenses, deductible only to the extent that they exceed 2 percent of adjusted gross income. Like anyone claiming a home-office deduction, you must meet the exclusive and regular-use tests, and your home must be your principal place of business or a client meeting place. In addition, however, the *business use of your home must be required and expected by your employer*. Using your home must be *for your employer's convenience*. To support this claim, get a statement in writing to this effect from your employer.

What does this mean in practical terms? A concert musician needs a practice room 30 hours a week but, because the orchestra does not provide a space for individual practice, he uses a room at home as a studio. The studio qualifies for a home-office deduction. If, on the other hand, you merely take your briefcase home at night and do some work in the evenings, you are not entitled to the deduction.

Requirements for Selling
Taxable Goods and Services

If you sell taxable goods and services from a home-based business, you must pay state sales tax. Handicrafts, antiques, silk flowers, and pet products are all examples of taxable goods; if you operate a repair service, the parts you use may be taxable.

Taxable services are difficult to pinpoint and vary greatly from state to state. In California, for instance, taxable services include printing, audio tape duplication, videotape rental, and some aspects of word-processing services. This is a tricky area; you may think the services you are providing are not taxable, when in fact they are. And since state tax authorities are very serious about collecting their sales taxes, it's important to check with your local agency to find out whether your work falls into a taxable category.

One woman we met ran a graphics business without being aware that her work was subject to sales tax. After five years in business, she was audited— and the amount she owed for five years' worth of sales tax plus penalties and interest was so high that it forced her to close up shop.

Keeping Adequate Tax Records

Clear, complete records of your income, expenses, assets (such as a computer or typewriter), and liabilities (such as loans or notes) enable you to minimize your taxes and to defend yourself in the event you're audited. The IRS does not specify what form your records should take, but you must be able to substantiate any claim you make.

Think of your records as footprints; the written documents—invoices, bank statements, canceled checks, deposit slips, and especially receipts—are the paper trail that your business operation leaves behind. You can either maintain your records yourself, hand over the task to a professional, or use some combination of the two.

Receipts are particularly crucial because they back up your claims for business expenses. Get in the habit of obtaining receipts by paying with a check or credit card (there's automatically a paper record), asking for a receipt, or creating one immediately upon expenditure. Suppose you make a long-distance business call from a pay phone—no receipt. Then create your own, writing down the expense and its business purpose on a piece of paper, in a logbook, or on an appointment calendar.

Some people consider it sufficient to place all their receipts and tax records in one box or envelope. Then they try to sort things out at the end of the year. We discourage this shoebox approach to record keeping.

First, the shoebox gives you no sense of where you stand financially during the year, and it provides no help in calculating your estimated taxes each quarter. You're forced to accomplish all your tax organizing at tax time, taking valuable hours and energy away from your daily business. In addition, it's too easy for some things to miss the box. Keeping track of your expenses as they occur increases the likelihood that you'll claim all your deductions and thereby minimize your taxes.

Whatever record-keeping system you develop, the important thing is finding one that's comfortable and effective enough so you will use it routinely. If you don't want to do it all yourself, get the help you need during the year to keep on top of your financial records.

Getting the Help You Need

Tax law is not only complicated, it's also constantly changing. So unless you're a trained tax expert, we recommend getting professional help in preparing your taxes. When tax time arrives you'll want to continue carrying out your work as productively and enjoyably as possible. You certainly don't need to get bogged down in tax complexities.

In fact, if your tax return is at all complex, having tax help is not only desirable but essential. In one case, the IRS actually leveled a negligence penalty against someone on the grounds that his tax return was too complicated to complete himself.

For tax help, you need someone who keeps up with the continually changing law, IRS code, tax rulings, and cases. The IRS alone issues a new ruling every two hours of each workday. You also need someone who has experience and empathy with home-based businesses in general and your type of business in particular. Too often we've heard tales of home-based workers selecting professionals whose experience has been only with large traditional businesses. As a result, these open-collar workers have received advice that was either inaccurate for their situation or contrary to their best interests.

Although there are other alternatives, including tax attorneys and tax consultants, we believe an accountant is generally your best choice for tax help. Accountants not only prepare your tax returns at filing time but also can be considered, along with your lawyer, as part of a team of professional advisers to whom you can turn throughout the year. They can set up your record-keeping system, perform certified audits, represent you to the IRS, prepare financial reports or statements, and help you with tax-planning decisions.

Accountants may be one of the more expensive sources of tax help, but in the long run their assistance can save you more than they cost. A Certified Public Accountant, or CPA, has had formal training in accounting, earned a college degree, and passed a tough state certification examination.

Accountants who are not certified are called Public Accountants and may or may not be licensed by the state. They are qualified by experience and perhaps have had special training. They generally cannot represent you before the IRS as your tax preparer.

To find an accountant, ask your lawyer, banker, or people in work similar to yours for recommendations. You can also contact the American Institute of Certified Public Accountants society in your state for the names of accountants who serve on the Small Business Committee or its equivalent. Then contact firms on that list until you find an accountant who understands your tax situation and with whom you're comfortable.

A less expensive option is to have an "enrolled agent" prepare your return. Enrolled agents are not only able to prepare returns but also are eligible to represent you before the IRS and the tax court as your tax preparer. These agents have received their "enrolled" status either by passing a two-day examination given by the IRS or by working for the IRS full time for at least five years. You can locate enrolled agents in the Yellow Pages, or the National Association of Enrolled Agents will give you the name of one in your area.

For even less costly tax help, you can go to a tax preparation service. The level of service you receive, however, is also limited. Tax preparation services are often so conservative and routine that they may advise against legitimate deductions. For example, we know of one service that trains its tax preparers to advise routinely against home-office deductions.

Using Your Computer to Do Your Taxes

While we recommend using computer software for your business accounting, the records you create with your software are not sufficient to satisfy the IRS. So paper records are essential. However, tax-preparation software has gotten so easy to use that some home-based businesspeople are using it to calculate their own taxes. Among the best tax preparation programs are Chipsoft's

Considerations When Interviewing a Tax Specialist

- What is the specialist's training and experience in preparing tax returns?
- How much will it cost and how is the fee calculated?
- How does the specialist check returns for accuracy?
- Is the tax specialist available throughout the year or just during tax season?
- Are the specialist's clients never audited (the tax specialist is probably being too conservative) or audited too often (exceeding one chance out of seventy for all returns, and about one chance out of twenty if your income exceeds $50,000)?
- How often does the specialist quote the tax code to you rather than figuring the best solution to your tax situation?
- Does the specialist seem too good to be true?
- Does the specialist belong to a professional association?
- Can the specialist represent you in reference to your return before the IRS if you're audited?
- Has the specialist had experience appearing in IRS appeals?
- Will the specialist pay any penalties and interest resulting from his or her errors, and has this ever happened? Have they ever paid a negligence penalty to the IRS for their own negligence?

Turbo Tax and Andrew Tobias' Tax Cut and, for the Macintosh, Softview's Macintax. The programs must be changed each year to reflect changes in the tax laws, and each February or March, computer magazines review the various revised programs.

Remember, accounting programs and tax-preparation programs are not the same. As New York CPA Irvin Feldman explains, "Tax rules and accounting rules are very different. Accounting rules have some logical basis as opposed to tax rules, which are designed simply to raise money and perform some social purpose." This means that there are no software packages that will do both. You must know the possible tax consequences of treating something a particular way before you do it.

What If You're Audited?

In the past, taking a deduction for a home office was an audit flag—it called attention to your tax return and increased the possibility of your being audited. The IRS says this is no longer true. Nevertheless, if you claim that deduction, you will want to take care in meeting the criteria we've outlined above and substantiate your claims fully. If you exaggerate the amount you deduct, you may be liable not only for back taxes and interest but also for a penalty.

Some Difficult, or Impossible, Deductions

- You can't rent part of your home to your own corporation or to your employer in order to qualify it as income property eligible for deductions that you ordinarily would not qualify for as a home office.
- You can't claim your family dog as a watchdog because you have inventory stored at home.
- You can't take a home-office deduction for managing your stock portfolio.
- The IRS frowns on deducting landscaping and lawn care expenses, but if customers and clients come to your home regularly, a case can be made for their deductibility.

Some items that will invite IRS audits are:

High Schedule C losses from a part-time business.

Farfetched business deductions, like claiming nylons because you must dress up for business meetings.

Payments to family members as employees. Remember to keep records of when family members work and what they do.

Items on the tax form preceded by solid black darts. These items are viewed with particular care by the IRS.

You can head off an audit by providing lots of documentation with your return. You tax preparer should be able to warn you if an item is likely to raise IRS scrutiny. Then you can include documentation such as notes of explanation and copies of canceled checks to circumvent the difficulty of locating records several years later and, more important, to avoid the time and trouble of an audit.

If the IRS challenges your home-office deduction, an agent may actually visit, yardstick in hand, to measure the space you have claimed. As soon as you receive an audit notice, get good advice from your accountant or lawyer. If you decide to handle things on your own, provide the IRS with information only about the items they're questioning. It's not in your interest to arouse an agent's curiosity about items not being questioned or about past years. For all practical purposes, the job of IRS personnel is to collect money, and consequently their position is an adversarial one. It is therefore to your advantage to get the best advice you can from the moment there might be difficulty.

Letting Congress Hear from Us

We estimate that there are some seven million people in the "underground" economy today—people who are engaged in legal business activities but who are not filing or paying income taxes.

We believe that two principal reasons for evading taxes are the complexity of the tax system and the heavy burden of the higher Social Security tax that is imposed on the self-employed.

The laws and interpretations of the IRS relative to home-office deductions, however, may change as a home-office constituency begins to exert its influence on Congress and the executive branch. Squeaky wheels *do* produce reform. We have been told that each letter received by a representative or senator is perceived as equaling the sentiments of 27,000 constituents. Thus it is clearly in your interest to express your views on the tax system and to suggest ways it can be altered to improve the situation of home-based workers.

Chapter Digest

1. Owing to fluctuating economic and political conditions, we can expect the IRS to become tightfisted in what it allows in the form of home-office and self-employment deductions. It therefore becomes all the more important that you know your tax rights, take care in documenting your rightful deductions, and get the help you need to keep current on changing tax laws that affect you.

2. As long as you meet the necessary criteria or fit one of the exceptions, you can deduct the cost of operating and maintaining the part of your home that you use for business purposes.

3. In addition to deductions for your regular business expenses, possible home-office deductions include portions of your rent, interest on mortgage payments, real estate taxes, and other expenses like cleaning, repair, and trash collection.

4. Self-employed individuals will need to make quarterly estimated income tax payments and will be required to pay the full amount of their Social Security payments. However, half of Social Security taxes are now deductible.

5. Salaried employees may deduct expenses for the business use of their homes if they qualify to the extent that the expenses, together with other employee business expenses and miscellaneous deductions, exceed 2 percent of their adjusted gross income.

6. Clear, complete records of your income, expenses, assets, and liabilities are necessary to minimize your taxes and to defend yourself should you be audited.

7. Unless you are a trained tax expert, we advise that you get professional help in preparing your taxes. Computer software can assist you as well.

Resources

American Business Management Association. P.O. Box 111, West Hyannis, MA 02672; (800) 333-4508.

Home-Office Tax Deductions. Thomas Vickman. Enterprise Publishing, Wilmington, DE 19801. 1988.

Income Tax Examination Handbook; Tax Audit Guidelines—Individuals, Partnerships, Estates and Trusts, and Corporations. Freedom of Information Reading Room, Internal Revenue Service, 1111 Constitution Ave., NW, Washington, D.C. 20224.

Taxsaver Home Office. Jay Knepp. Menlo Park, CA: Sunset Books, 1987.

Reports

Steps in Meeting Your Tax Obligations. SBA. See full citation under Chapter 3.

U.S. Internal Revenue Service. Publications of interest include:
Tax Guide for Small Business (#334)
Self Employment Tax (#533)
Business Use of Your Home (#587)
Index to Tax Publications (#900)
Depreciation (#534)
Tax Withholding & Declaration of Estimated Tax (#505)
Tax Information for Direct Sellers (#911)
Recordkeeping for a Small Business (#552)
Determining Whether a Worker Is an Employee (#SS-8)
Taxpayers Starting a Business (#583)

CHAPTER
ELEVEN
■ ■

Insurance: What You Need
and How to Find It

Whether you are salaried or self-employed, working from home does present the possibility of some risks that adequate insurance coverage can help you avoid. The good news is that you can usually protect yourself from the risks of working from home for significantly less money than if you were operating a business outside the home.

Attorney Arnold Goldstein states in his book *Starting a Business on a Shoestring* that the average cost of conventional business insurance can run from $8,000 to $10,000 a year. Only rarely would a home-based operation require such an investment. Some types of coverage will cost only a few additional dollars a year on top of your regular insurance. Despite these considerable savings, however, we were surprised to discover that, with the exception of health insurance, home-based businesses often have little or no insurance at all.

While five out of six of those we surveyed had some form of personal health insurance, under half had no protection for their business property or for liability on or off their premises. And only one in six had any disability insurance. Often the reason open-collar workers had no business insurance was because they didn't realize they weren't covered for business activities as part of their existing homeowner's and auto insurance policies. Sometimes they judged their risks to be too small to justify the cost of added insurance and sometimes the cost of available insurance was simply beyond their budgets.

We think about insurance as one of three approaches open-collar workers can take to risk-management. Avoiding risks in the first place is, of course, the best method. Staying healthy, keeping up your property, doing a quality job, and maintaining valuable equipment are a few examples of good risk-prevention. Planning to absorb any risk that occurs is another alternative. If you virtually never have business visitors come to your home, for example, or if you never carry business equipment in your car and don't have inventory, your needs for the specialized insurance that would protect you from the risks inherent in these practices would be so low that you might opt to "take your chances."

But let's consider a few all-too-real examples to illustrate why being insured can not only save you money but also put your mind to rest and, in some cases, save your business. Free-lance photographer Mary Holt had her camera equipment locked in the trunk of her parked car while she was running an errand on the way home from a shoot. The car was stolen. Mary's equipment was not covered under her auto insurance policy because it was used for business purposes. She had to bear the entire loss.

Thirty-seven-year-old marriage and family counselor Nadine Barney, a single woman and head of her household, was stricken with the Epstein-Barr virus after five years of managing a successful counseling practice. She was unable to work and lost her business, her savings and, ultimately, her apartment. She lived with her mother while she recovered and after three years was able to rebuild her business. She wishes she'd had disability insurance, but admits she had never even thought about it.

When an electrical fire swept through publicist George Craighton's garage, the home office he'd carved out in the back was destroyed along with it. He thought his homeowner's insurance would cover the loss of his personal computer, printer, and software. It didn't. Like most homeowner's policies it excluded any property used for business purposes. And, since his files were lost as well, his business was at a standstill. Fortunately, none of his clients sued him for failing to complete his contracts on schedule. But what if they had? This possibility hadn't occurred to him until after the fire.

In this chapter, we'll discuss the variety of insurance needs people working from home should investigate to protect themselves from these and other risks. Reviewing them will give you an understanding of what risks there are and how you can avoid those which might threaten you.

Liability to Customers and Other Business Visitors

The standard homeowner's or apartment dweller's policy protects you from personal liability if a guest is injured while visiting your home. It doesn't protect you, however, if the visitor is coming to your home for business purposes. In that case, you need added coverage. Most homeowner's or apartment dweller's policies can be broadened to protect you by covering injuries to business visitors should a customer, client, colleague, delivery person, or supervisor fall, for example, while visiting.

This broadened coverage is available to most occupations and businesses that are conducted at home. In fact, liability coverage for home business activity is available even if you live in an area not zoned for home office use. You can usually get the coverage you need by adding an endorsement to your homeowner's policy for a few extra dollars a year. Such an endorsement is often referred to as an Incidental Business Option or a Business Pursuits Rider. Typical arcane language for such an endorsement is, "The residence premises shall not be considered a business property because an insured occupies a part thereof as an office, school, or studio."

Excluded from coverage through a homeowner's policy are claims for injuries or damage that result from the actual rendering of services or sale of products. Protection for these kinds of claims requires additional coverage, such as malpractice or product liability insurance, depending on your particular business, and is discussed later in this chapter.

General Liability

Insurance broker Toby Haynes of Pasadena, California, considers the risks of liability for home-based entrepreneurs to be greater when they're working away from their offices than when they're working at home. If you do any of your work in the homes of your customers, for example, you might accidentally knock over and break an heirloom vase. Or suppose you're sponsoring a training program in a conference facility at a hotel. A participant could slip and break a leg on a polished floor, and you would probably be named as a defendant along with the hotel in any resulting lawsuit.

General liability insurance will protect you from risks such as these for several hundred dollars a year. So if you are self-employed and do any part of your work away from home, the coverage is a wise investment, even if you're thinking, "I'm not going to injure anyone or damage anything enough to justify the cost of extra insurance." That may be true, but you're not just protecting yourself from your own clumsiness or oversights. In today's litigious environment, you're protecting yourself from situations over which you may have no control, like slick floors or fragile chairs.

But do exercise caution when you shop for a general liability policy. You need to be certain it will pay for attorney's fees and other costs of defending yourself in case you are sued. Unfortunately, anybody can sue someone in today's world, but not everyone can afford an adequate defense.

Business Property

Basic homeowner's or apartment dweller's policies protect you from damage or loss to your personal property but often exclude coverage for business uses of your premises. When you begin working at home, check the restrictions and limits on your policy to make sure you have ample coverage for damage or loss to your business property. The standard form for homeowner's coverage lists as an exclusion "business property pertaining to a business being conducted on the residence proper."

You could even find that running a business from your home voids the coverage of your policy altogether or that there are limits as low as $200 on what you can recover in case of loss from fire, burglary, or other damage to "property used or intended for use in a business." By the time you add up the value of a personal computer, printer, telephone-answering machine, filing cabinets, fax, and copy machine, you will have thousands of dollars' worth of business property to protect. In such circumstances, the limits on your policy could mean negligible compensation.

If you can't get insurance without such limitations, you can broaden your coverage either by getting an endorsement that raises the amount of coverage and includes your business equipment or by buying a separate policy to cover business equipment. A separate policy has the advantage of covering "mysterious disappearance" of property, while homeowner's policies do not allow for this contingency in the event of theft. Also, a separate policy can pay off at the stated value or the replacement cost of an item without figuring in the depreciation factor included in many homeowner's policies.

If you own a computer, you may want to get a special "floater" policy covering risks unique to computer owners or an endorsement to your homeowner's policy. In the event that a power surge wipes out your $600 software or destroys six months of work on disk, this kind of policy can be well worth the expense. Special computer insurance costs between $50 and $200 a year and also includes protection against fire and theft of hardware, software, and temporary rental items. However, policies covering data loss will be more expensive.

Adequate Homeowner's Coverage

Since your home is probably your most valuable asset, and even more valuable now because it is also your office, you should keep your homeowner's coverage current with inflation. Most insurance companies automatically adjust homeowner's policies upward, but people often find themselves terribly underinsured at a time of loss. A policy issued to cover the mortgage when the original loan was made on a home, even with automatic increases, may not provide enough to cover a loss equal to the value of the home today.

Insurance companies require that buildings be insured at current replacement value in order to pay off fully for a loss. If a home is not covered for at least 80 percent of its replacement value, the insurance company may only pay a percentage of the cost to repair or rebuild. While 99 percent of losses are partial, at today's construction costs few losses are small, and the percentage paid can easily amount to less than the policyholder's expenses.

To discover the current replacement value of your home, you can have it professionally appraised. This may cost $75 to $200 and involves a personal visit to your premises. You can also get a telephone appraisal from an evaluation service for as little as $10. In either case, your insurance agent can help you locate the expertise you need.

Protection Against Business Interruption

If, like George Craighton's, your home office is damaged by fire or another disaster, you'll be faced with closing, relocating, or cutting back on your business activities while you recover. Business interruption insurance protects you from the consequent losses of these disruptions. This kind of coverage provides the money you would need for expenses such as payroll, loan payments on equipment, and costs of relocating or making arrangements to continue operations.

A Small-Business Policy

A basic small-business policy provides more extensive coverage than you can get from adding a business endorsement or rider to your homeowner's policy. It will compensate you for property damage from disasters like fire, theft, vandalism, and lightning but will also cover loss of business data and lost income from such events, which riders do not. It also protects you from lawsuits claiming personal injury or injuries arising from defective goods, or breach of contract.

Of course, such a policy costs more. According to *Money Magazine,* a policy for a low-risk business with $300,000 limits on liability and damage will cost from $250 to $350 a year. That compares with a cost of anywhere from $15 to $25 a year for adding a business endorsement or rider to your homeowner's coverage.

Discuss which would be the best choice for your business with your insurance agent, particularly when more than 20 percent of your residence is used for business or when your business activity has a high risk of liability, such as catering or manufacturing handmade toys for children. Also if you have over $3,000 in business inventory on hand, you should consider a small-business policy or separate business-inventory insurance.

Auto Insurance

Sometimes people are surprised to discover that if they have an automobile accident while on a business trip or if business property is stolen from their car, the damage or loss may not be covered under their personal auto insurance policy. So review your policy with your agent and determine the best way to cover yourself and your business property while in your car.

Health Insurance

If you are self-employed or your employer's fringe benefits do not include health insurance, you will need to locate an adequate and affordable plan. This is an increasingly difficult but not impossible challenge for individuals and small businesses.

Although as many as one-third of self-employed individuals in California reportedly have no health insurance, our survey of home-based businesses showed that over 80 percent of those we interviewed had found a way to cover at least health emergencies, despite the cost. Others, however, have found themselve priced out or closed out of health insurance.

Working from Home Forum member Warren Whitlock told us that since his premiums rose to $500 a month, health insurance is no longer in his budget, so he's been what he calls "self-insured." Owing to preexisting conditions, consultant Sharon Connell couldn't get coverage after leaving her tenured position at a state university. And the company that bookkeeper Chellie Campbell purchased health insurance from went out of business.

While stories like these are not uncommon, our agent, Chartered Financial Consultant Dan Silverman of the Silverman Group, assures us that with adequate information and some ingenuity and persistence you can usually find protection.

Health insurance can be purchased individually or as a part of a group policy. Group policies have several advantages. They often offer higher limits and more benefits than you can get on an individual policy. And sometimes they cost less than individual plans. This varies widely, however, so you will want to compare a variety of sources. You may also be able to get coverage as part of a group when you are not able to get insurance as an individual. And a group insurance plan is tailored to the particular needs and interests of your group rather than to the "average" person.

If you are already self-employed but want to be covered under a group plan, here are several options you have:

1. You may arrange to be carried by the group policy of a company with which you are affiliated. Some sales organizations offer insurance to their independent sales personnel, for example.

2. Group hospitalization insurance is available to members through professional and trade associations, college alumni associations, and trade unions.

3. Some insurance agents specialize in placing small businesses in what are known as "multiple employer trusts." Such trusts enable the small employer to get group rates and are available through companies like Mutual Benefit Life.

4. You may be able to get coverage under a company policy of an employed spouse.

5. Some Chambers of Commerce now make health insurance available to their members.

If you are currently employed and covered under a company group policy, find out before you become self-employed whether you can convert that coverage into an individual policy when you leave. Before taking this option, however, compare the benefits you will get with other policies. Conversion policies are typically not as good as the original group plan, and in some cases may cost more than what you could buy on the open market.

The cost of health insurance is climbing astronomically owing to advancing technology and an aging population. Some of those we interviewed were paying more than twice what they once paid. But consider this. The average amount an employer paid per employee for health insurance coverage in 1989 rose to $2,600. And medical costs now constitute 12 percent of the gross national product. Therefore, it's not surprising that your costs will also be considerable when you pick up the full cost of your health insurance.

Beware of companies offering too-good-to-be-true policies. Some health insurance companies, organized as Multiple Employer Welfare Arrangements under federal law, amount to nothing more than pyramid schemes. Still other companies are not financially sound, having invested heavily in junk bonds, and either may not pay on your claims or may end up going out of business. The result is the number of insurance companies that fail is increasing, leaving you unprotected if you enroll with the wrong company.

To protect yourself from such problems, Mark Weinberg, Executive Vice-President of Individual, Small Group, and Government Services for Blue Cross of California, advises that, before selecting a health insurance company, find out from the state insurance commissioner if the company has a certificate of authority to operate in your state.

Blue Cross is taking a lead in making policies available to self-employed individuals. And in eleven states, Blue Cross will accept individuals regardless of their health status during their "open enrollment" drives. These periods usually last only a few weeks, so contact your local Blue Cross for further information.

Weinberg assured us that there are still lots of insurers who will sell health insurance to individuals and small groups. He advises that if you want to find the best price for your coverage, you should ask the following two questions:

1. What are the rates? He suggests that the company should have a rate sheet that tells you the rate based on your age and location, and how long that rate will be in effect. If the company requires other information about you in order to give you the rate, that's probably not the answer you want. You want to be assured that you and everyone like you is going to pay the same price. This will take lots of insurers off your list.

2. What assurance do I have that a year from now, you won't raise my rates by some absurd amount? Some companies will offer an initial rate far below their cost and then double, triple, or even quadruple your premiums the next year. You want to hear that your rate is being pooled with a sizable population and that the experience of that entire population will be the basis for any new rates. This means you're unlikely to see a 60 to 80 percent rate increase within the year. You might see a 20 percent increase if that's what the trend is, but you've satisfied yourself that your experience is being pooled with a large enough population to preclude your particular rate from being substantially affected if you or one of your employees gets ill.

So in shopping for health insurance, consider not only the cost of premiums but also the benefits included, the health of the company, and how the company sets its rates. To minimize your health insurance costs, you might also consider health maintenance organizations (HMOs) and preferred-provider organizations (PPOs) in addition to traditional fee-for-service health insurance plans. To find out which PPOs and HMOs accept individual members, contact your local medical society or your city's office of consumer affairs.

In addition, many states have high-risk pools that insure individuals who are not otherwise insurable. Premiums are usually high and normally there is a delay in reimbursements for pre-existing conditions, but contact your state insurance commissioner to find out if this resource is available to you.

Disability Insurance

Statistically, an executive at age thirty has a 48 percent chance of being disabled for ninety days or more before reaching the age of sixty-five. While working at home should lessen the chances of a disabling accident or illness, the possibility of being disabled without income is sufficient motivation to get self-employed people to pay for the protection disability insurance provides. Also known as loss-of-income insurance, it's particularly important to the self-employed who have no sick leave to draw on in case they do face illness or accident.

There are a number of factors to consider in selecting a disability plan. They include:

1. **How "disabled" you must be to receive benefits.** If a plan defines disabled to mean "totally disabled," you need to be unfit for any kind of work. If you are highly trained, you may consider yourself disabled if you cannot pursue your chosen career. You might not want to work at something you would be "able" to do, such as telephone solicitation. Therefore, a more advantageous definition of disability is "unable to engage in any gainful occupation for which the insured is suited by education, training, or experience."

2. **How long after a disability you must wait before payments begin.** The waiting period may range from seven days to six months. The longer the waiting period, the less you should have to pay for the policy.

3. **How long after disability the payments continue.** Payments may continue for any time from thirteen weeks to throughout one's lifetime. But statistics indicate the average disability lasts for five years.

4. **How much it will cost.** Cost of disability insurance depends on the factors stated above, the company you choose, and how much the policy will pay you. You can calculate how much coverage you need by adding up your costs of living and subtracting any income from investments, royalty payments, Social Security, or spouse's earnings.

5. **Is the policy both "noncancelable" and "guaranteed renewable"?** Both these terms refer to whether the policy can be terminated after you become sick or make a claim. A policy that is noncancelable and guaranteed renewable can only be canceled if you fail to pay the premiums. The premiums can't be increased so long as you are current in your payments, and the policy must be renewed by the company but not necessarily at the same rate.

Another type of disability insurance is credit disability insurance. It's usually designed to continue loan payments should you become disabled.

The cost of disability coverage can seem high, but that's because with other forms of insurance, claims are paid in one lump sum. Disability payments, should you need them, can stretch out over many years. So here are several ways you can reduce the cost of disability protection:

■ The longer the period after disability before the insurer begins payments, the lower the premium.

■ Costs can be halved if you cover the possibility of being disabled only up to age 65, rather than for your lifetime.

■ Some credit card suppliers, like American Express, which issues a special Corporate Card, provide lump sum benefits of $10,000 to $50,000 for small-business owners for an annual tax-deductible fee of $45.

■ Buying yourself a Worker's Compensation policy if you're incorporated can be a low-cost form of disability insurance for work-related disabilities.

We have encountered cases in which companies refused to write a disability policy for a self-employed individual who is working from home. Should you encounter this, keep looking, because there are companies that don't discriminate against people who work from home.

Employee-Related Insurance

If you have employees, there are various kinds of insurance you may be required to provide for them. For example, you may need to provide worker's compensation insurance, employee insurance benefits plans, or non-owned auto insurance.

Worker's compensation protects workers should they be injured on the job. Whether this coverage is required for a small business varies widely from state to state. For example, California requires an employer to have worker's compensation coverage if one person comes in to work only a few hours a week, while some states don't require this insurance until an employer has more than ten employees. So if you hire people to help you in your business, check with your insurance agent, your attorney, or the appropriate state agency to find out what's required in your state.

At the same time, you can consult your attorney or agent regarding other benefits you may need to give your employees. There are federal regulations for providing employee benefits like pension plans, retirement plans, group life and health insurance plans, and employee welfare benefits. These regulations may apply to your business, too.

If your employees ever use their own cars while working for you, your family or personal automobile insurance policy will not cover accidents. However, you can get non-owned auto insurance to protect yourself in this situation. This kind of policy covers you against damages that result while employees are driving for any purpose related to your business and is particularly important for businesses with sales representatives or delivery personnel. This insurance is also necessary for a nanny or a child-care helper who drives your car for any purpose connected with her work for you.

Protection Against Suits Related to Your Product or Service

You may need to insure yourself against claims for injuries or damages that arise out of the services or products you offer. For example, health professionals may give advice that their clients perceive as leading to illness. An error in a computer program may lead to loss of business for a client. And a glass product can inflict injury on a buyer or on those shipping or handling the product.

Depending on the nature of your work, you may protect yourself against such risks by obtaining malpractice insurance, errors and omissions insurance, product liability insurance, or commercial liability insurance. Consult with your attorney and insurance agent to determine the coverage you need.

Partnership Insurance

Under the law, you are liable for the actions of your business partners. This is true in both formal and informal partnership arrangements. So if you are operating a business in partnership with anyone else, it is wise to consider having partnership insurance to protect yourself against lawsuits arising from the actions of your partner or partners.

Life Insurance, Retirement, and Financial Planning

Even though you're working from home, you probably won't want to work full time forever. Often in the prime of one's career, that time seems far away. Studies show, however, that by the time people reach fifty, more than half of them begin to worry that inflation will reduce their standard of living when they retire, and 40 percent worry about becoming financially dependent on others. So thinking about a financial and retirement plan is another form of insurance open-collar workers should consider, because when you work from home on your own, any plans for your retirement will be entirely up to you.

We were startled to read that consumer health experts are now predicting that anyone who expects to be 65 years old by the year 2000 should plan to have from $50,000 to $200,000 in savings just to pay for long-term health care. That's a lot of money to accumulate after you're fifty, and that's for medical care alone. So setting up and following a comprehensive financial and preretirement plan that begins well before the age of fifty is all the more important.

Retirement plans for the self-employed, also known as Keogh or HR-10 plans, are available to sole proprietors and partnerships under a special rule that permits them to be treated as employees. Another approach to accumulating retirement benefits is the Simplified Employee Pension (SEP). It allows an employer to contribute up to $30,000 or 15 percent of an employee's compensation, whichever is less, to an IRA or annuity. Again for this purpose, the sole proprietor or partner is treated as an employee.

If you are a single parent, the primary breadwinner in a two-career family, or a person supporting anyone other than yourself, life insurance is also a must. Dan Silverman recommends beginning with a basic term insurance policy, which provides benefits if you die during the term of the policy. Then as your revenues grow, he suggests adding equity or whole life insurance in which part of your premium goes toward that insurance and part is set aside as savings that you can cash in or borrow against. Robert Hunter, president of the National Insurance Consumer Organization in Washington, D.C., recommends that for most families with young children the rule of thumb is to purchase insurance equivalent to five times your annual income.

Phasing Your Insurance with Your Growth

Even though insurance is less costly when you operate a business from your home, getting all the insurance you ideally need can be a considerable expense for a start-up business. Therefore we asked Dan Silverman to recommend a plan that phases in your overall insurance needs. He recommended the following for each of three business periods:

- **Start-up.** If your budget is limited, get only the essential coverage at first: property, liability, auto, and medical.

- **Growing and expanding.** As your business grows, increase the limits on the essential coverage and add disability, term life insurance, and basic financial planning.

- **Established and profitable.** Maximize limits on all essential coverage and obtain equity life insurance, retirement planning, and a complete financial plan.

Keeping Adequate Insurance Records

In the case of loss, it is always the burden of the insured to prove the value of what is lost. Some insurance companies can be very rigid about this, requiring bills of sale and receipts. After a theft or fire, it's difficult to itemize everything that is missing and document what you paid for it. So here are several methods for keeping a current inventory:

- **Retain receipts of every durable item you purchase.** If you depreciate business property for tax purposes, you'll already have some of these records.

- **Keep a written inventory.** Organize the inventory room by room. List each item in a room, its date of purchase, its price, and its present value. Insurance companies give away booklets that will help you organize this information.

- **Make a visual record of your home office and possessions.** You can videotape or photograph the contents of each room yourself, or use a service that will make a visual record for you. If you do it yourself, make an oral record of what's on the videotape or in the photographs. Your narrative will need to indicate when you bought the items pictured and how much they cost, as well as their make, model, and serial numbers.

A good agent can direct you to companies that are reasonable in processing claims, and in the event of a loss, the agent can run interference for you in collecting on your policy. A complete and accurate inventory of your property, however, is needed to make sure you can collect what you're entitled to.

Finding the Professional Help You Need

Insurance is a highly competitive industry. Companies differ in their rates, premium payments plans, and insurance packages, so it's important to find an agent who is willing to investigate all your options until the best ones have been located.

Insurance agents do not charge you for their service; they receive their compensation from the insurance companies for whom they write policies.

Therefore we suggest talking to several insurance agents and comparing the different plans they propose. There are independent agents who deal with multiple companies and there are agents employed by a given company who write policies only for it. We have a preference for independent agents because they are not tied to any one company and can therefore combine policies into the best total package tailored to your budget.

Agents are listed under "Insurance" in the Yellow Pages, or you can ask your attorney, accountant, or colleagues for a referral. Find someone who is willing to invest the time to answer your questions, search for the best policies for you, and discuss the pros and cons of the various options. In fact, ask the agents you talk with for a spreadsheet with at least four possible packages. This way you can compare the many features of each policy.

Use the insurance checklist with your lawyer and insurance agent. Discuss your needs in each area. If you work from home for someone else, you can review the list with your employer as well.

Putting together an insurance package that meets your needs within your budget limitations is a challenge for you and the professionals who can help you. Develop a plan that can grow with your business.

Whatever package of policies you get, find out whether there are discounts you can qualify for on your insurance. Sometimes discounts are available if you have fire-smoke alarm systems or smoke, heat, or ion detectors approved by Underwriter's Laboratory. Other discounts are available for having deadbolts on your exterior doors. Also, nonsmokers and people who run as part of a regular exercise program can sometimes get lower rates on health or life

An Insurance Checklist

- ☐ Liability Insurance
- ☐ General Liability Insurance
- ☐ Business Property Insurance
- ☐ Policy Limits on Homeowner's Insurance
- ☐ Special Computer Insurance
- ☐ Business Interruption Insurance
- ☐ Disability Insurance
- ☐ Group Health Insurance
- ☐ Worker's Compensation Insurance
- ☐ Employee Benefit Plans
- ☐ Non-owned Auto Insurance
- ☐ Malpractice Insurance
- ☐ Errors and Omission Insurance
- ☐ Product Liability Insurance
- ☐ Commercial Liability Insurance
- ☐ Partnership Insurance

insurance policies. (For more information on such health policies, see the Resource List at the end of this chapter.) As someone working from home, you may be able to save money on auto insurance too. If you drive only a minimum number of business miles, you are placed in a lower-risk category for insurance coverage, and it therefore costs you less.

Then remember that insurance is inherently a gamble between you and an insurance company. The insuror is betting that bad things won't happen to you. So don't wipe out your protection against risks by buying from a shaky company.

Be sure to check out the financial stability of whatever insurance company you're considering. You can look up the company's rating in *Best's Insurance Reports,* available in public libraries. A rating of A or A+ indicates a company that's likely to be able to pay its claims, and less than one in four companies has this high a rating. If you're considering buying insurance from a mail-order company, also check with your state's insurance department to be sure the company is licensed to do business in your state.

And how much insurance do you need? You should insure against what you can't afford to lose, but you don't need to pay for insuring what you can afford to risk.

Once you find the insurance package you need and it is in force, you can work at home knowing you're protected from many of the pitfalls that may occur along the way.

Chapter Digest

1. Business-related insurance costs you less when you work from home than it would if you were operating a business outside the home.

2. We think of insurance as one of three approaches open-collar workers can take to risk-management. Most important is doing what you can to avoid risks and then absorbing those risks you think you can afford. Obtaining adequate insurance will provide the added protection you need to feel secure in your business.

3. Open-collar workers often do not realize that their homeowner's or apartment dweller's insurance and their auto insurance will not necessarily cover losses related to their business. So review your current policies to see if you need to obtain additional riders, endorsements, or policies.

4. Health and disability insurance for the self-employed can be costly and sometimes difficult to obtain, but insurance industry experts are confident that there are alternatives to meet the needs of most individuals.

5. We recommend finding an independent agent who deals with multiple companies to review your home-office insurance needs and asking him or her to develop a number of scenarios for you to consider. To find an even broader range of companies, consult with several independent agents.

6. In the case of loss, it is always the burden of the insured to prove the value of what is lost. Keeping adequate records of what you have on hand, bills of sale, and receipts is therefore important.

Resources

Best's Insurance Report. A.M. Best Co., Ambest Road, Oldwick, NJ 08858.

Buyer's Guide to Insurance. National Insurance Consumers Organization, 121 N. Payne St., Alexandria, VA 22314; (703) 549-8050. Send a self-addressed stamped envelope.

Don't Get Burned: A Family Fire Safety Guide. Gary and Peggy Glenn. Huntington Beach, CA: Aames-Allen Publishing, 1983.

Health Insurance Association of America. 1850 K St., NW, Washington, D.C. 20006. Offers consumer booklets.

Health Insurance Selection Service. (800) 662-0470. Conducts database search for a fee.

The Insurance Almanac. Underwriter Printing & Publishing Co., 50 East Palisade Ave., Englewood, NJ 07631; (201) 569-8808.

Risk Management: A Small Business Primer. Washington, D.C.: U.S. Chamber of Commerce, 1987.

SBA (see full citation under Chapter 3):
  Insurance Checklist for Small Business (#MA2.018)
  Business Life Insurance

Simple Living Investments: For True Security and Adventure in Old Age. Michael Phillips. San Francisco: Clear Glass, 1988.

Support Services Alliance. P.O. Box 130, Schoharie, NY 12157; (518) 295-7966 (free brochure).

Associations

Health Insurance Association of America. 1025 Connecticut Ave., NW, #1200, Washington, D.C. 20036; (202) 223-7780.

Insurance Information Institute. 110 William St., New York, NY 10038; (800) 221-4954 or (212) 669-9200.

National Insurance Consumer Organization. 121 N. Payne St., Alexandria, VA 22314; (703) 549-8050.

Health Insurers Recommended by Open-Collar Workers

Small Business Service Bureau. 554 Main St., Worcester, MA 01601; (800) 356-4032.

National Business Association. 15770 North Dallas Parkway, Ste. 260, Dallas, TX 75248; (800) 343-0939.

Guardian Life Insurance Company of America. 202 Park Ave. South, New York, NY 10003; (212) 598-8000.

MONY. (800) 628-2610.

National Organization of Women (NOW). 1000 16th St., NW, Ste. 700, Washington, D.C. 20036; (202) 331-0066.

Resources for Alternative Health Insurance

Alternative Health Insurance Services. P.O. Box 9178, Calabasas, CA 91372; (818) 702-0888. Locates progressive health insurers that are willing to reimburse for alternative or holistic medical providers such as chiropractors, acupuncturists, etc. They provide policy information and price quotes for insurance plans that fit the individual's medical provider preferences.

Consumers United Insurance Company. 2100 M St., NW, Washington, D.C. 20063. Offers most of the features of mainstream insurers plus alternative medical services like biofeedback, childbirth classes, massage therapy, marriage and family therapy, and nutrition counseling. Individual policies available through the National Organization of Women (NOW). NOW is open to men and women alike.

PART 4

∎ ∎

Managing Your Home Office

CHAPTER
TWELVE
■■■■■■■■■■■■■■■■■■■■■■■

Getting Organized and
Staying That Way

Although the single most frequently mentioned advantage of working from home is the freedom and flexibility to do what you want when you want the way you want, once one lives with the joys of near total freedom, it's not uncommon to hear comments like these.

"My work is taking over the house. There are stacks of paper everywhere and I can't find what I need. I'm not getting as much done as I should and I'm always behind. There's so much to do, I don't know where to start!"

This common refrain has led a few who begin working from home to move back to an office before they drown in overdue projects, missing receipts, and backed-up paperwork. For some, just the fear of such havoc is enough to keep them from thinking they can successfully work from home in the first place.

Those experienced at working from home, however, find that success comes from having a system. With a system, you can get both your work and your home organized and keep them that way. You'll be able to find the things you need in a handy place when you need them. You'll have the time to accomplish your priorities. And you'll be able to enjoy the extra time you've saved by not commuting to work.

If using a system immediately makes you think of clean desks, rigid schedules, and hours of filing, sorting, and cleaning, STOP! Don't confuse having a system with being chained to an inflexible regimen. Rather, think of a system as a way of resolving competing demands on your time and space so that what's most important gets done easily and efficiently.

The routine that people are most familiar with, of course, is the nine-to-five office system. Chances are you've arranged your work and home around this framework for most of your professional life. If so, going to the office organized your day for you. You managed everything else in your life in the time that was left after work and on weekends. This is only one of many possible systems for organizing a workday, however, and it's one many of us want to get away from. Part of the joy of working from home is the freedom to create systems that are more suited to our personal preferences and desires.

There is one stipulation. To work at home successfully without the familiar office routine, you have to become a self-organizer, someone who can create and operate your own systems. In talking with people who work at home, we met some who were natural self-organizers. Organizing their work seemed to come effortlessly. Others we've met have struggled with how to reorganize their lives around their new work schedules and have still come out winners.

In this chapter we want to share with you what these people either knew already or learned along the way. From their experiences, you can glean the essential features of creating your own successful systems.

Becoming a Self-Organizer

As we talked with people about how they organized their work at home, the most obvious self-organizers, regardless of the type of work they did, typically described their routines something like this:

"I don't have trouble working at home because I have a routine I follow every day. I get up at five every morning and run. Then I make long-distance calls from seven to eight. During the rest of the morning I do paperwork. In the afternoon I meet with clients. Every Monday morning I pay the bills and update my records."

"At first I was quite disorganized. Then I realized that if I work just as if I'm at the office, I'm very productive. So now I'm at my desk by nine sharp and I usually quit working by five. If I have lunch I take no more than an hour, but I usually take a short break in the morning and the afternoon."

"I work best with deadlines. Whenever a project is due I count backward from the due date and figure out how much I'll need to accomplish each day. When I've gotten that amount done for the day, I stop."

These more obvious self-organizers are choosing to follow formalized systems similar to those practiced in a traditional office setting. But for those of you who want to break away from formal routines, you'll be glad to know that there are less obvious, but equally successful, self-organizers who do not follow such traditional structures. At first these people sound rather disorganized, typically describing their daily routines something like this:

"I don't like schedules and things like that. I like to roll with the punches and do whatever comes up."

"I don't have any particular schedule. Sometimes I take off the whole afternoon. But then there are times when I work all night too."

"I do the things that need to be done. Some days are very light and I don't do much work. Others are quite busy. A lot depends on how I feel."

When we pushed further about how they decide what to do or when to take time off, we found that, indeed, these seemingly disorganized workers also have organized systems. In fact, their systems are sometimes more complex than the formal ones we're more familiar with. It's not uncommon, for example, for such workers to create a different system for different days of the week or for different aspects of their work. One management consultant and trainer told us:

"People who work in an office may think I'm not organized because they see me with such a variety of schedules. But actually I know exactly what I'm doing. Today, just because it's five o'clock, I don't have to stop working. But tomorrow will be different. Tomorrow I will be training all evening. So to be at a peak, I'll probably take off in the afternoon."

Whether their systems are conventional or unconventional, the self-organizers we spoke with share these characteristics:

1. People who are organized realize they can be in charge of how they do things. After years of too many rules and regulations while growing up, going to school, or working in an office, it's possible to feel you must do things in certain ways whether you want to or not. Too often, the result is that "being organized" takes on a negative connotation. It comes to mean doing things someone else prescribes and may even prompt resentment, rebellion, and a desire to sabotage all efforts at organization.

Self-organizers, however, have discovered that even if it doesn't seem so, they're free to choose how they're going to do things. Also, they are willing to live with the consequences of their choices. Often self-organizers only gain this wisdom after they start working from home. As one man who started a rug-cleaning service told us, "The first three weeks after I quit my job, I goofed off most of the time. Then it dawned on me, I could goof off forever. No one was ever going to tell me I was fired or give me a failing grade. If I kept this up though, I wouldn't be able to pay the rent and I'd have to get another job."

Or as someone who is now telecommuting told us, "I hate to admit it, but I used to try to look busy so I wouldn't get assigned any more work. But after I started working at home, I realized no one was watching me. I was either going to exceed my quota or I wasn't. It was all up to me."

2. Self-organizers keep their priorities in mind and orchestrate their work around these goals. Knowing what's really important to them pervades everything self-organizers do, from the hours they spend working to their choice of tasks. A salesman who started his own sales company expressed his priorities this way: "I want to make this business go. That's the most important thing to me right now. I don't care how many calls I have to make or how many letters I have to send out, I'm going to do it."

A woman who runs a part-time business designing flower arrangements has a different set of priorities, to which she is equally committed. "Being here to nurse my daughter is what's really important to me. I've built my day around her schedule. But I still get my work done."

A graphics designer told us, "Everyone thinks my office is a mess just because you can't see any clear space on the desk. It may not look great, but that's not what's important. When I'm working on a project I need everything at arm's reach."

And a mail-order merchandiser laughed when we asked how he decided what was most important to him. "Knowing how much each item is costing me is what's crucial. Any overage will eat away my profit. You better bet I keep a record of my expenses on a day-by-day basis. I never get behind on that. Knowing what other companies are doing is important too, but if I have to make a choice between keeping my records up and reading the trade journals, there's no doubt which one will have to wait."

3. Self-organizers take responsibility for what happens in their work. Since they realize that they can usually structure their work the way they want, self-organizers have also learned that they're responsible for whatever results they get. If they aren't getting what they want, they realize it's because their approach isn't working. They take responsibility for problems as well as solutions, like the owner of a word-processing service who told us, "My daughter is still interrupting me. I haven't gotten this worked out yet. I'm going to have to do something different."

Or like the consultant who admitted he has a hard time finding things once he's filed them. "It happened again this morning. It took me fifteen minutes to find something I was looking for. So I'm setting up a better filing system."

Or like the bookkeeper who confessed, "I'm always tired in the afternoons, so I make more errors. Now I start a couple of hours earlier in the morning so I can quit around three o'clock."

4. Although self-organizers often don't realize it, they have made a habit of following the basic principles of good systems organization. Natural self-organizers have learned the principles of good systems organization by osmosis. They picked it up from their parents, a teacher, or on the job. The most common way people learn organizing habits is from the way they were taught to clean up their rooms as young children.

Think back to the time you were nine or ten years old, and remember how whoever was rearing you got you to clean up your room. Were you effectively taught how to organize your things? Or:

- Did your parents give up on getting you to clean your room and do it themselves?
- Did they condemn and nag you, saying, "What's the matter with you, anyway? Why haven't you cleaned up your room?"
- Did cleaning your room become a dreadful battle of wills between you and your parents?

- Did your room become an embarrassing shambles that was hidden behind closed doors?

Whatever your experience with cleaning up your room, don't be surprised if you use that same approach with yourself when you begin working from home on your own and want to get organized.

If you weren't blessed during childhood with learning the basic skills for creating and using systems, don't despair. There's no need to struggle through the hazards of learning by trial and error. You can use the principles set forth in this and subsequent chapters to design systems that will work for your home office.

Seven Dynamic Principles for Designing a System That Will Work for You

In organizing a home office, you're actually creating a system that will coordinate many different aspects of your professional and personal lives. Your system should include a plan for using your time, managing your money, keeping track of the information you need or the flow of paper through your office, and getting the help you need to keep everything running. Whether you're setting up a system to handle your mail, manage your schedule, or keep track of your files, the basic principles are the same and you will find them throughout all the chapters in this section.

1. Set Goals

To create a workable system you need to know what it's being designed to help you do. Career counselor Ines Beilke discovered this principle when she began her long-awaited sabbatical. "At the college where I work, I have a very tight schedule. My sabbatical was going to be my chance to do so many things I'd been wanting to do. Two months later, working at home without the schedule I'd been used to, I almost panicked because I'd gotten nothing done."

Ines found that the only way she could get back on track was to remind herself of the goals she had set for the year: to complete a project she had undertaken and to spend time relaxing and going camping with her husband. She told us, "I kept reminding myself every day of what I wanted to accomplish with the time I had. Then I could make a plan to be sure I got it done."

In creating a system for managing both your household and your office, we recommend that, like Ines, you define your goals for both your work life and your personal life. Ask yourself questions like these:

What does success mean to me?

What are the five most important things in my life?

What do I want to accomplish in my work?

What is important to me about my home? My family? My friends?

Make a list of goals you have for your career, your personal development, your relationships, your children, your home. Be specific. Precisely how much money do you want to make? How large do you want your business to be? What skills do you want to develop? What do you want to provide for your children, or for yourself in terms of your own personal development? When do you want to have achieved these goals? What do you want to accomplish this year? Next year?

2. Turn Goals into Tasks

The more specific you are about what you need to do to achieve your goals, the easier it will be to create a system to help you carry out the tasks that will enable you to do it. Once Ines set her personal and professional goals, for example, she realized that to reach them she would have to start turning down requests to do other things people were asking her to do. Instead, she had to set dates for the camping trips she and her husband wanted to take. She had to call and arrange appointments with each of the people she wanted to contact for the project she was doing, and so forth.

In designing a system for your office, identify the specific tasks you will need to do in order to achieve each of your goals. Ask yourself questions like these:

What will I need to do to get this accomplished?

How much money will it take?

How much time will I need?

When do these things need to be done?

3. Set Priorities

The principle of setting priorities is expressed by the familiar adage, "First things first." It involves putting the tasks you have to do in logical order.

If, for example, you have to run errands, make phone calls, do paperwork, and hold a meeting, decide which of these activities needs to be done first, second, third, and so on. If you have ten phone calls to make and only half an hour to make them before you must leave for a meeting, order the calls in terms of importance and make the most essential calls first.

Or when you're organizing your filing cabinet and have ten different types of records to keep track of, decide which ones are most important and which you will use most often. Then place them so they will be accessible in order of importance and frequency of use, saving the lower and more difficult to reach drawers for the infrequently used and least important files.

Or when you have a series of errands to run, save both time and gasoline by ordering the errands in terms of their location in relation to one another. We organize our business and personal errands, for example, into what we call our "standard errand routes." We do errands along an "eastern route,"

Five Proven Steps to Better Goal-Setting

Ken Blanchard, author of the popular *One Minute Manager,* says you set goals so you'll know when you're doing something right. After all, you can't know if you're on course if you don't know where you're headed.

1. Begin by visualizing or imagining in full detail the result you want as if it's already occurred.
2. Then, to state your goal, describe the situation you desire using an action verb in the present (not the future) tense. For example, "I earn $50,000 a year." "I deposit $10,000 a month into my bank account." "I speak to three associations each month and receive my full fee. They are pleased with my performance and invite me back." "I complete twenty pages of reports each day." Write it down.
3. Add a definite date by which you intend to accomplish this goal. For example, "By December 31 of this year, I will have closed six accounts." "By next Friday at 5 P.M. I will have made twenty calls." Best-selling author Harvey MacKay puts it this way: "A goal is a dream with a deadline."
4. Write out a list of the steps you will need to take to accomplish this goal and decide when you will perform each of them. Put them on your calendar.
5. Post your goals where you will see them regularly and review them daily. **Do at least one task related to achieving your goals every day.**

going to the gas station first because it's nearest, then to the printer, and last to the grocery store so perishable items won't spoil. At a different time, we do errands along the "western route," going first to the bank because it closes early, then to the dry cleaner, which is near the bank, and finally to the post office, which is on the way home.

4. Put Like Things Together

Putting like things together could be called the "combining principle." It's not a new idea, either. We've all heard it expressed as "killing two birds with one stone." It's a matter of figuring out what similar things could be done together.

Whether you're planning your day, organizing your files, or setting up a way to handle your mail, put similar tasks together. For example, when you have to go out of the house for a business meeting or to make a bank deposit, do all other activities that need to be done outside the house on the same trip. You can go to the post office and the print shop while you're out, or you can arrange your outing to correspond to the time you have to pick up a child from school.

Other examples of using this principle at work would be keeping all files and materials related to financial record keeping in one place, and setting aside time to do all your paperwork at one time during the day rather than scattering it throughout various times. When you pay bills, you could combine that task with checking your bank statement. Likewise, you can set up one time to place whatever phone calls you need to make for the day and keep all the files you use in conjunction with your calls close to your phone.

5. Create Routines

Quite contrary to the popular belief that following routines is dreary, routines actually bring your system to life. A routine is only dreary when it becomes an end in itself rather than a vehicle for taking you toward your goals.

By structuring your activities into regular routines, you save the time and energy spent making hundreds of little decisions every day and trying to remember today what you decided yesterday. So once you've discovered when, where, and how best to do something, turn it into a routine and you'll find you can operate more easily day in and day out according to your goals.

In setting up our routines, for example, we've found that it's easier to reach people by phone first thing in the morning, so now we have a regular routine of making phone calls from 8:00 A.M. to 9:30 A.M. On the other hand, if we do errands during prime business hours, we miss important calls, so now we have a regular routine of doing errands after 4:00 P.M.

In setting up routines, however, be sure they match your style of working. If you like precise schedules, make yours very exact: "I'll do this every morning at 9:00 A.M." If you prefer more flexibility, make yours less specific: "First thing every morning I'll decide which things to do," or "I'll do my filing sometime during the first week of each month."

Once you've adopted a routine, set up ways to remind yourself of it. Use calendars, timers, tickler systems, "to-do" lists, posters, index cards, or computer programs to help you remember specifics of the routines you've set up. For example, if you have a routine for closing out the end of each week on Friday afternoon, you might keep a checklist posted on your file cabinet to remind you of each of the tasks you need to complete before the afternoon is over. Finally, make your routine a habit by doing it the same way repeatedly until it becomes second nature.

6. Remain Flexible

Although you will need to follow your routines consistently to make a system work, you will soon find yourself wavering from a system that is too rigid. Life is simply too unpredictable for any system to operate flawlessly without at least occasional changes. So allow yourself leeway for emergencies and unanticipated events. But then resume your routines the next time around.

7. Evaluate the Results

At least once a month take a look at the system you've designed and see if it's working. Are you achieving your goals? Can you see daily progress? Are you feeling satisfied with your business and your lifestyle?

Fourteen Signs That Indicate You Need a Better System

1. Feeling as though you never have enough space. (In her book *Getting Organized*, Stephanie Winston claims that 80 percent of overcrowding is the result of disorganization.)
2. Never having enough time for what most needs doing.
3. Finding too much paper lying around and working its way into the rest of your home.
4. Not having any time away from work.
5. Not finding what you need when you need it.
6. Being late for appointments or deadlines.
7. Doubting your ability to manage your work.
8. Feeling things are getting out of hand.
9. Discovering overdue bills.
10. Not knowing your bank balance.
11. Failing to return phone calls because you feel embarrassed that it's been so long since the person called you.
12. Feeling that you have to do everything yourself.
13. Procrastinating.
14. Not getting important things done because of endless interruptions.

Evaluating, however, is not a time for criticizing and condemning yourself. It's a time for acknowledging what's working and what needs attention. We like to take time at the end of each period to review our accomplishments, and the insights we've gained.

In reviewing your efforts, pay attention to whether you're following your system. If you're not, it wasn't designed well enough to meet your needs. A good system is easy to use and should make life simpler, not more complicated. Finally, decide whether or not it's helping you to get the results you want. If it isn't, adjust and revise your system until you can achieve your goals with ease by following it.

Customizing Your System

Below we've identified fourteen decisions you should make to set up a comprehensive home office system that's tailored to your unique preferences and work demands. There's no one right answer, but most people run into trouble if they haven't addressed the issue each of the following questions raises. So decide:

1. **How many hours will you work each day and each week?** If the nature of your work is such that you cannot set a precise figure, define clearly how you will decide on the amount of time you'll spend working from week to week or day to day.

2. **Which hours of the day will you work?** As we'll discuss in the next chapter, unless your work demands it, there is no reason to limit yourself to typical hours. You can work at hours better suited to your circumstances.

3. **How many breaks do you plan to take each day** and when will you take them? Some people like to break for five minutes each hour. Others prefer taking longer breaks after working for several hours. Still others break when they come to a stopping point in their work.

4. **When will you do household chores?** Some people like to take a break for household chores and find that the change of pace allows them to come back to the office refreshed and ready to work. Others find that if they stop to do a household chore, the next thing they know the whole morning has slipped away.

5. **When will you eat lunch and will you snack while working?** Having the kitchen only steps away often becomes a problem for people who work at home. Consciously deciding how you will handle this should make it easier to keep your weight and concentration in bounds.

6. **When and how will you dress?** Some people find that to work effectively they need to get dressed as if they were going to the office. Others relish the freedom to stay in a robe all day.

7. **Will you watch TV during daytime hours?** If so, how much and when? Some people find it's easy to get hooked on game shows or soap operas. In fact, some people claim they work best while watching TV. Others can't work well with the television on but get hooked nonetheless. Even if you wouldn't be caught dead watching a soap, the variety available on daytime TV today can lure you with movies, sports, and news.

8. **Under what circumstances will you take off a day, afternoon, or a morning?** Sick leave and days off take on a new perspective when you work at home. If you're self-employed, establish your own leave policies, consistent with the nature of your business. If you're employed at home, you'll be on your own to coordinate your work with the established leave policies.

9. **When do you decide to get someone to help you with your work?** Many work-at-homers try to do everything themselves. Some can. Others end up saving money by spending it to hire help.

10. **If you have children, when will you be available to them?** Most people find they cannot allow children to have unlimited access to them during working periods. So you will need to make age-appropriate arrangements for their care and set boundaries regarding when you will and won't be available to them.

11. **What information do you need to keep track of?** Usually, in-house office procedures include policies for records you need to keep.

Working at home, however, you will probably have to establish your own record-keeping procedures.

12. **How will you manage your money?** If you're self-employed you will need to establish a system for managing the financial aspects of your business. Even if you're working at home on a salary, you'll have to arrange a procedure for managing your home-office tax records.

13. **What interruptions are you willing to allow?** There will be phone calls. There may be people coming to the door to repair things, sell things, or make deliveries. Neighbors may want to visit. It's easier to have a policy than simply to respond to each interruption as it occurs.

14. **Do the decisions you make in answering these questions apply to every workday or are there exceptions?** This will depend on your work style and the nature of your tasks. A psychotherapist may not allow any interruptions during client hours but may be more flexible while doing paperwork. While working on a deadline, a writer or manufacturer may need to keep very strict hours, but the same person can be much more flexible in slower periods.

Unless you address these questions and incorporate them into your system, you will probably be faced with answering them afresh every day. That can be a tiresome and sometimes disastrous situation. For a closer look at the major issues we've raised, read the chapters that follow. They contain ideas and suggestions that will help you make the best decisions for creating a system that's right for you.

Chapter Digest

1. To work from home successfully requires that you become a self-organizer who can create and operate a workable system for getting organized and staying that way. This does not mean living with rigid, boring, time-consuming schedules and rules. A system is a flexible, easy way of resolving competing demands on your time and for your space.

2. Effective self-organizers set up their day in diverse ways but share several key qualities. They realize they are in charge of how they work. They know their priorities. They take full responsibility for what happens. Although they may not realize it, they follow general organizing principles.

3. Good organizers are made, not born. Often the approach you take to organizing your life is similar to the way your parents got you to clean up your room when you were a child. If you weren't taught the basic skills during your childhood, you can still learn the principles easily. Key organizing principles include setting goals, turning goals into tasks, setting priorities, putting like things together, creating routines, remaining flexible, and regularly evaluating your results.

4. To custom-design your own system for getting organized, ask yourself questions about how, when, and where you want to work. Ask what your policy will be for handling the many aspects of working from home. Identify your expectations and keep experimenting until you find a system that works. You'll know your system is working if you're finding it easy to follow and you're reaching your goals on schedule.

Resources

Books

The Path of Least Resistance. Robert Fritz. New York, NY: Ballantine Books, 1989.

Tapes

How to Stay Up No Matter What Goes Down. 1988. Sarah Edwards, P.O. Box 5172, Santa Monica, CA 90405.

The Goals Program. Zig Ziglar. Carrollton, TX.: The Zig Ziglar Corporation, 1986.

The Psychology of Achievement. Brian Tracy. Chicago: Nightingale-Conant; (800) 323-5552.

CHAPTER
THIRTEEN
■ ■

Managing Time: Working on Purpose

Overwhelmingly, people working from home find they have a greater sense of control over how they use their time. They have fewer interruptions and more flexibility to work in ways that are most productive for them. On the other hand, some also encounter difficulties managing their time, difficulties that they either didn't have at the office or had to a lesser degree. Primarily, we find that three-quarters of the people who have trouble with time report difficulty getting down to work, while the other quarter have trouble getting away from work. We hear problems like these:

"I have a hard time getting started. By the time I've eaten breakfast and read the paper, done my exercises, gotten dressed and put things away, half the morning is gone."

"I can't stick to business. It's too easy to think of something else I need to do when I get tangled up in a tough problem. The plants always need watering, the trash always needs emptying, there are always errands that need to be run instead."

"It's not infrequent to start the morning with a clear day ahead of me, no appointments, no place I have to be, just a whole day to get my work done. Then something will happen. The dog will get sick. The plumbing will break. And there goes the day."

"My problem is just the opposite. I'm always working—morning, noon, and night. The other day I overheard my son asking my wife, 'Why doesn't Daddy every do anything but work?' That got me to thinking, but I don't seem to be able to get away from it. It's always there waiting to be done."

For those who are already working from home, these problems may sound all too familiar. In this chapter we want to address each of them, and provide

---

Diagnosing Your Time-Management Problems

.Place a check by the problems you encounter most frequently:
- ☐ Getting started and sticking to business
- ☐ Organizing your workday
- ☐ Procrastinating
- ☐ Being interrupted
- ☐ Getting away from work
- ☐ Overworking

---

specific recommendations about what you can do to take charge of your time and avoid the problems you're most likely to encounter. You can begin by using the following checklist.

Getting Down to Work and Sticking to Business

It's so easy and enjoyable to sleep in on rainy mornings, spend extra time over the newspaper, take the day off, reorganize a closet or polish the silver, run errands, take your toddler to the park, sign up for a midday tennis class, or work in the yard during the cool morning hours.

The opportunity to partake in these kinds of activities at times of your choosing may be precisely what attracted you to working from home. The question is, with no boss in the office next door and all these opportunities to do something else, can you get to work and stick to business on a regular basis?

Yes. Fortunately, it is possible to have the best of both worlds. You can combine the many activities in your personal life with effective and efficient work habits. But it takes a new way of working. It may require new skills, some fresh attitudes about work, and a few new tricks of the trade. You'll need to set up a work schedule, arrange ways to cue yourself to get started, and master the art of working efficiently.

Five Ways to Set Up a Successful Work Schedule

We've found that only about 10 percent of people who work at home follow the same schedule they had at the office; most people take advantage of the rich opportunity working from home provides by devising their own unique work schedules. The quality of your life can change with a creative schedule, so open your mind to all the possibilities. Don't limit yourself to the old ideas of what makes up a workday.

Here are a variety of ways you can approach designing your schedule.

1. Establish your schedule around the demands of your work. Let the work itself serve to get and keep you going. This may happen naturally or you may have to make it happen by organizing what might seem like an atypical workday.

When psychotherapist Greg Rohan first opened his practice, he found his clients preferred appointments in the late afternoons and evenings, after traditional working hours.

"Since I was home anyway, I began setting up appointments throughout the entire day, a few in the morning, a few in the afternoon, and a few in the evening. I was very disorganized and I wasted most of the time in between. I finally decided to limit all my appointments to between 2:00 P.M. and 9:00 P.M. This way everybody's happy. I'm free in the mornings and very efficient from one o'clock on."

Data-entry clerk Helen Gillis begins her day when her supervisor calls to transmit her workload for the day. "I never have any trouble getting to work, because Marge calls at 8:30 A.M. sharp. So whether I'm dressed yet or not, I'm at my terminal and ready to work through to my first break."

Lynne Frances found that her cleaning service is its own built-in alarm clock. "I have crews at my apartment every morning at the same time. From that point on there are all sorts of demands, people coming in, deadlines, phone calls. The business is a built-in motivator."

Janet and Carl Jeninski, who operate a bed-and-breakfast inn at their home, worked out a more unusual arrangement. When they're at home, they feel as though they work twenty-four hours a day. "We put in eighty-hour weeks. Our work is our life and we love working side by side. But we need time away too, so we work three weeks a month and take the fourth week off at a cabin we own with several other people. We hire someone to come live in our home and manage the inn while we're gone."

2. Establish your schedule around those times of the day you work best. Everyone feels more alert and energized at certain times of the day. During these high-energy periods, it's easier to get to work and produce a higher-quality job. Our high-energy periods come at different times of the day. Paul is a morning person. He's up at dawn and ready to work. By midafternoon, he's running down. He does his prime work during the mornings and saves the afternoons for errands and other less-demanding activities.

On the other hand, Sarah doesn't usually get going until midmorning. For years when she worked for the federal government, she would sit at her desk at 8:00 A.M. nursing a cup of coffee to keep her eyes open until around 10:00 A.M. By 3:00 P.M. she was raring to go, but the workday was winding down. So now she usually reads and does less-demanding activities in the morning and saves her prime work activities for the afternoon or evening.

Thor Thorensen, vice-president of Advanced Computer Techniques Corporation, has a highly unusual pattern that makes having his office at home ideal for him. "I prefer working from late afternoon to two in the morning.

When I was working at other companies, I had to work from eight to five like everybody else. Now I can pick my hours." And since he picks them, he finds it easy to stick to them.

3. Establish your work schedule around the other priorities in your life.
Raising a family, exercising, painting, or some other activity that's important to you can serve as an effective way to structure your workday and make those things you value a regular part of your lifestyle.

Twila Carnes, for example, who works from home on-line with a computer, has established a schedule that allows her to devote sufficient time to other priorities. A single parent, she logs on to the computer at midnight, works until seven in the morning, gets her kids up and off to school after breakfast, and goes to sleep until around three in the afternoon when they come home. "With this schedule, I get to be a full-time mother and still earn a living. That means a lot to me."

Artist Gary Eckart is a marathon runner. He spends up to fifty hours a week training for the races he competes in on weekends. "I schedule my work around training runs. My morning run starts the day. When I get back I begin working at the drawing board. After my afternoon run, I come back and start filling and shipping orders."

One common pattern among people who work from home is to work long hours four days a week so they are free to pursue their personal interests over a long weekend. Engineering job-shopper Kevin Maher loves to ski. He gladly works from nine to nine Monday through Thursday so he can go to the mountains over the weekends. "I'm motivated to get everything done before Thursday night. If I leave early Friday morning, I can beat the crowds to the slopes."

4. Organize your schedule around particular work tasks.   Landscape designer Joseph Turner teaches Monday, Wednesday, and Friday at a university. His time on campus defines the schedule for those days, and he limits everything involved in his teaching to those three days. Tuesdays and Thursdays he works with customers and completes their landscape designs. He finds that by separating these two aspects of his work into different days, he stays focused on the tasks he needs to do for each.

Potter June Wright throws her pots in the morning and markets her wares in the afternoon. "I organize my whole day around these two tasks. I get up, fire up the kiln, and don't even get dressed. Until lunch I'm the artist. At lunch I close down the studio, get dressed, and become the businesswoman. I make calls, deliver work I've done, and arrange for shows I want to enter."

5. Set up an arbitrary schedule.   Establishing any schedule is always better than having no schedule. Whatever schedule you initially set up will help you define the one you'll ultimately want to adopt. Once you begin to adhere to an arbitrary schedule, you'll notice the times you have difficulty working and can then begin tailor-making a more compatible one.

Using Rituals to Make Sure You Get Started

Even with an established and workable schedule, many people still find they need to prompt themselves to get started at the appointed time.

Working from home, you don't have the forced rituals of shave, shower, and dress that millions of office workers experience between 6:00 A.M. and 7:00 A.M. daily as they get themselves off to work. Some commuters have to resort to a full ashtray of cigarettes, a pot of strong coffee, or a shot of vodka to get going. Usually open-collar workers don't have to go to such extremes, but without the pressure of having to arrive at the office on time, they still have to find a way to be sure they get out of bed and into their work.

Of course, for Greg Rohan, Lynne Frances, and Helen Gillis, the work they do provides those cues. Greg's clients ring the doorbell; Lynne's cleaning crews arrive at the kitchen door; Helen's phone rings with work from her supervisor.

If you can arrange to have your business cue you, this is a surefire work starter. Since this is often not possible, however, people create a variety of rituals they use to give themselves the message "It's time to work." Here are some:

- Hearing the closing music of "Good Morning America" or the "Today Show"
- Getting into your work clothes
- Simply walking into your home office
- Turning on the answering machine or calling to switch on the answering service
- Pouring a thermos of coffee to take into the office
- Starting when your spouse leaves for work or when your kids leave for school
- Setting a clock radio to go off at the selected hour
- Hiring a reminder service to call when it's time to start
- Walking or driving around the block and starting to work when you get back
- Starting each day by making long-distance calls before 8:00 A.M.

These rituals can help you get to the desk, the drawing board, or the computer terminal. Once you get there, however, if you're still faced with the horror of the blank page, the overflowing in-box, or the empty computer screen, you may still need an action plan for really starting to work.

If you're still having trouble getting started in the morning, try this tip from business consultant Dan Shafer. "Leave something half done when you quit for the day. That runs counter to your upbringing, right? Like fingers scraping a chalkboard? But it works. As a writer, I've used this trick dozens of times. Just leave off in the middle of a sentence and I know exactly where to start in the morning."

Seven Tips for Getting Started

1. **Take action:**
   Sit down at your desk.
   Clear the desk.
   Turn on the computer.
   Get out the pertinent files.
   Sharpen your pencil.
   Make up or review a "to do" list.
   Dial the first phone number you need to call.
2. **Begin with the most interesting thing** you have to do.
3. **Start asking questions:**
   At the end of the day, what do I hope to have accomplished?
   What tasks am I most concerned about getting done?
   What needs to be done next?
   What will happen if I don't get this done?
4. **Set a deadline** for yourself or tell someone else you will have completed a project by a certain time.
5. **Bribe yourself.** "If I get such-and-such done today I can . . ."
6. **Make a game out of your work.** "Let's see how many of these I can finish before noon," or "Can I make three calls in ten minutes?"
7. **Use positive aphorisms with yourself.** "This is the first day of the rest of my life." "The early bird gets the worm." "The sooner I start, the sooner I'll be done."

Sticking to Business and Working Efficiently

Once you get started, your work can develop a momentum that keeps you going all day. But sometimes it can be as difficult to keep working as it is to get started in the first place. Household distractions and interruptions, poor work habits, lack of planning, or procrastination can thwart your efforts to stick to business. Before we consider these problems, however, let's take a new look at what it means to "stick to business."

Traditionally, it meant sitting at your desk riveted to work tasks without interruption and looking busy even if you weren't. Actually, once people start working at home with no one looking over their shoulders, they're often surprised to find they work better when they don't "stick to business" in such a traditional way. This is how writer Marcia Seligson describes the way she gets her work done:

"When I'm writing intensively I don't sit at the typewriter without moving for six hours. I typically write for half an hour, and then I'll start thinking about something I'm developing and get up and wander around the house, make a cup of coffee, or water a plant. It's part of my thinking process, wandering and pacing around for ten minutes or so and then going back to the typewriter."

Publisher and magician Mike Caveney describes a similar process for using time-out from his office while ideas gestate in his mind. "When I'm working on something, I might go mow the lawn, but I'm thinking about what I was working on."

When graphics designer Nancy Rabbitt started her home business, she was relieved by the change she was able to make in how she keeps herself working. "I discovered that when I'm stuck or my mind isn't sharp, I can go on to something else. We've been taught to sit there and struggle with a work problem. But you go nowhere when you do that. It takes longer if you try to force a solution. And to handle the responsibilities of my business, I have to go on and come back to the problem later when I'm ready."

From reactions like these, we've identified a more flexible work pattern among successful home-office workers which confirms our own experience. Since we began working at home in a more flexible way, we've become more creative and the quality of our work is immeasurably better. We've given birth to some of our best ideas while jogging, reading, or driving somewhere.

Although the flexible pattern we're describing is not the way we're used to thinking about work, management consultant and psychologist Tom Drucker argues that "if they have the choice, most people will work this way. The truth is, most people do. At the office they just have to look like they aren't."

Still, flexible work patterns like those we've described strike fear in the hearts of many supervisors and some workers. Although they may allow that such flexibility might be fine for artists or professionals, they doubt it would be efficient for most office workers. Their fear is, "Will the work get done?" Many home-office workers we've talked to argue that it does.

One telecommuter who does data entry at home told us she had tried working both ways, and "when I take a break at least every hour and go do something totally different, I actually get more done in the same amount of time than if I work straight through to a midmorning or midafternoon break."

Freed from having to stick to business in the strict sense, people generally can find shortcuts to get the work done more efficiently. The secret to doing this, however, lies in being able to make the distinction between breaks and distractions, between shortcuts and diversions. Supervisors can't make these distinctions, because to an onlooker they often appear the same. But *you* can tell the difference, and when working from home you will probably have to.

A classic research conclusion known as the "Hawthorne Effect" has shown that people are more productive when there are changes in their work environment. You can improve your efficiency by occasionally moving around while you work, changing the room arrangement or décor of your home office, or working in a different place for a while. If your work allows you to move around while you work, you can do certain tasks by a pool, in the living room, on the porch, in a restaurant, or at the park. A portable phone, portable dictating unit, portable computer, or portable typewriter are all tools that make it possible to effect a change of scenery.

Steps for Maximizing Your Efficiency

1. Plan the workday.
2. Safeguard your work from unwanted distractions and interruptions.
3. Recognize and sidestep procastination.
4. Set reasonable work goals.
5. Praise yourself frequently for your work.
6. Reward yourself for a job well done.
7. Take frequent, regular breaks.
8. Schedule work so it won't conflict with your favorite extracurricular activities.
9. Arrange for a change of scenery.

Planning Your Day

Planning your workday at home is not much different from planning a day at an outside office, with one important exception. Since your home and office are so closely interwoven, we recommend planning your entire day at one time—work, household responsibilities, social activities, and so on. Otherwise it's too easy for them to interfere with one another.

Time management experts claim that the best approach to planning your day is to use a time-planning system of some kind. There are many systems available at stationery stores or through the mail. They range in price from under $20 to over $100. Three popular systems are the Day Runner, the Day-Timers, and Filofax. Alternatively, you can use an electronic personal organizer such as Sharp's Wizard, Casio's B.O.S.S., or Psion's Organizer, each costing several hundred dollars. With the Wizard system, you can buy add-on program cards that will give you a dictionary, thesaurus, language translator, or time/expense manager.

In selecting a system, make sure to choose one that is more than a simple calendar and address book. A time-management system should include a calendar for the year, month, and week, a daily planner, and pages for setting goals and planning projects. It should also allow you to add, subtract, and rearrange the pages to suit your needs.

We will introduce you to the daily planning system we've developed especially for working from home. It tailors the principles of good time-management to the unique needs of the home office. Some of the systems, like those mentioned above, already contain these elements. Or you can create your own customized system using readily available supplies from stationary stores if you have specialized needs.

The Basic Tools You Need

A ringed binder and dividers. Use a ringed binder to store all your time-management planning activities. Formal time systems like the Day Runner come in various specialized sizes that make carrying your system with you to appointments and on errands easy. The RunningMate system, for example, can fit easily in a purse or briefcase. Having a portable system is vital to effective time-management. It saves you the frustration and wasted time of trying to coordinate schedules and lists between your home office and the many other places your day takes you.

Although you can create as many sections in your planner as you wish, we recommend having a section for calendars (yearly, monthly, weekly), a section for daily planners, one for goals and projects, and one for a "Thought of Everything?" list of the many things you need to do at some time in the future.

An appointment calendar. Choose a calendar that enables you to schedule appointments and events for the week, month, and year. Use only this one calendar. If you are creating your own system, remember the calendar needs to fit conveniently in your ringed binder so you can have it with you and use it for all scheduling activities.

A daily planner. Use a one-page daily planner like our Time Manager (Figure 13-1) that enables you to sort, itemize, and schedule the variety of tasks you plan to do during the day and display them all on one page. This daily planner will serve as both your schedule of appointments for the day and your "to do" list. One frustrated woman told us: "I have so many 'to do' lists, I need a list of my lists." Does her problem sound familiar? A daily planner saves you the hassle of having multiple "to do" lists lying around.

Your one-page planner should fit into your ringed binder and have space for the following categories:

- Appointments and meetings, by time of day
- Correspondence, bills, invoicing, and filing you need to do
- Phone calls you need to place
- Major projects you want to accomplish that day
- Errands to run and odd jobs you plan to do
- Plans you need to make, and things you should read or write

The back of your daily planner can be used to keep track of other tasks you need to do at some time in the future. We call this the "Thought of Everything?" list. You should review this list when planning each day. But in the meantime you can get them off your mind by keeping them on this master list. The Day Runner has a "Memory" section to serve this purpose.

Figure 13-1. Time Manager

Goals and project sheets. Use these sheets to record and track personal and career goals. You will be surprised how much more quickly you can achieve your goals in life when you have them written out clearly and take the time to review them when you plan your daily activities. Breaking your goals down into specific projects that will bring them about also helps keep you organized.

A Surefire Daily Planning Process

Now here's a step-by-step process for putting the system to work on a daily basis. Each day:

1. **Use your daily planner to build one "to do" list.** Find time either at the end of the day or first thing in the morning to fill out your daily planner, listing all the tasks you need to do in each category: appointments, correspondence, phone calls, major projects, errands, reading.

   To be sure you're including everything, go through the day in your mind, review your appointment calendar, go over your list of things to do in the future on the "Thought of Everything?" list, check deadlines in your current project files, and review upcoming-event or tickler files you have.

2. **Screen your items.** Once you have identified the things you need to do, go through a screening process to be sure they need to be done. Ask yourself these kinds of questions: Does this have to be done today? What will happen if it isn't? Can someone else do it? Is this task worth the time required to do it? If not, could I do a scaled-down version that will take less time?

3. **Assign all tasks an "A" or "B" priority.** "A" priorities are tasks that should be done today. "B" priorities are those that might well be done today, but are not crucial.

4. **Identify your top three "A" items** and rank them first, second, and third. The top three "A" items are those tasks you feel are most important to get done before the end of the day. They will take priority during the day.

5. **Plan to do your top three "A" items first.** Block out your day around these three tasks and indicate on the planner the times during the day you will spend on completing them. Leave larger blocks of time for creative work. When possible, schedule these creative tasks to coincide with your peak energy periods.

6. **Plan to do the remaining "A" tasks next.** You can save time by doing the "A" tasks in each category together: making all "A" phone calls at the same time, running all "A" errands together, and so on.

7. **Plan to move to the "B" tasks after you've finished all the "A" items,** again saving time by doing those in the same category together when possible.

8. **Check off the items as you complete them.**

9. **Carry over to the next day tasks you didn't have time to do.** List the tasks you didn't get done on the daily planner for the next day. If you carry tasks over more than a week, consider whether you should drop them.

Magic Timesavers

Once you begin working on the tasks for the day, whatever you're doing—whether it's writing a letter or attending a meeting—your goal should be to "work smarter, not harder." Here are some timesavers to build into your daily routine.

Set up an organized information system for keeping track of names, addresses, phone numbers, and files. The number-one timewaster is not being able to find the information you need when you need it. A simple-to-use filing system that keeps this information at your fingertips will save you more than a two-week vacation. You'll find many ideas for creating such a system in Chapter 15.

Use technology to save time.   Technologically advanced equipment that will enable you to speed up daily tasks include a touch-tone telephone with a redial button and the ability to program frequently called numbers, a fax, a computer, a high-speed printer, a photocopier, electronic mail services like CompuServe and MCI Mail, an electronic postage scale, a postage meter, an electric stapler, a letter-opening machine, a letter folder, and dictation equipment if you have a secretary or use a secretarial service.

Computer software can help you save time. Borland's Sidekick Plus includes among its capabilities The Time Planner, which is a calendar, scheduler, and organizer. It has alarms, and the ability to display your schedule and make "to do" lists. Sidekick Plus can either operate as a stand-alone or memory-resident program. There's a Sidekick for Macintosh computers, too; however, Focal Point II for the Macintosh goes beyond time-management to relate to other office tasks such as billing and ordering office supplies. Specialized programs such as Timeslips III, Time$heet, and the shareware program Time Tracker for IBM-compatibles and Timeslips for Macintosh enable you to streamline billing by automatically keeping track of your time and then billing for it with no additional calculation.

Learn to say "no."   A simple "no" can save you hours of time. Evaluate the request for your time from clients, family, and friends. You may find that many requests are in keeping with your goals, while others are clearly at odds with them. Although saying "no" may be difficult at first, with practice you will find it easier to draw the line tactfully and protect your time.

Make use of idle time.   Take advantage of idle moments, the times you're waiting for a call, an appointment, or a printout. Read the journal articles you've highlighted, change the ribbon you've been meaning to replace, or slip out to put on dinner during these downtimes.

Build a time cushion into your plans.   In estimating how long it will take to do something, include not only the time it takes to do the actual work but also allow time for getting ready, setting up, driving to and from where you're going, and putting it all away. Then add in some leeway for the inevitable delays in getting the job done.

Make quick decisions on small matters.   Decisions take energy. If the stakes are not high you can afford to make snap decisions. When deciding things like which brand of paper clips to buy, save your energy and act impulsively.

Do two things at once. Plan a project or listen to an informational tape while shaving, driving, or cooking dinner. Scan periodicals at night while watching TV.

Keep a list of fill-in jobs or five-minute tasks. When you're between projects and waiting on hold, there are myriad mini-tasks you can do: jot down the agenda for a meeting, write a note, clip an article, sort incoming mail, proofread a letter.

This is not to say you should be working every minute of every day. Breaks and idle time throughout each day and week are important to refresh your mind and spirit.

Now let's talk about specific timesavers for handling those tasks that are notorious for consuming—and too often wasting—much of our time.

Reading. There is more information in even a highly specialized field than any one person can keep up with. To cut the time you spend reading without losing out on vital information, skim tables of contents, directories, and headlines and read only pertinent material. Learn to read more quickly by taking a speed-reading course. Use a clipping service that will clip pertinent articles for you, or subscribe to specialty newsletters or digests that summarize developments in your field.

Meetings. Before scheduling a meeting, ask yourself if the matter could be handled by phone or by mail. To keep meetings efficient, limit their length. If you don't complete your agenda within the allotted time, you can schedule another meeting or follow up by phone or mail. Time limits force people to say what they have to say and hear what they have to hear quickly, with fewer diversions into nonessential details.

If you have meetings away from home, schedule them, whenever possible, so you will not be traveling in rush-hour traffic. When you have business that relates to more than one person, arrange joint meetings, if feasible.

For formal meetings, plan to use an agenda, have a leader who keeps the meeting on track, and generally restrict meeting time to decision making rather than actually working on projects. Have a system of referring such work to individuals or subgroups to do outside the meeting. For more casual meetings, begin by agreeing on what you want to accomplish. When conversation strays from the goals, bring it back politely.

Learn to use body language to signal the end of a meeting or appointment. Shut your notebook, pick up your papers, rise and begin moving toward the door, using closing comments like "I'm glad we could meet," "We got a lot done," and "I'll look forward to hearing from you soon."

Correspondence. Set up an efficient routine for processing your mail. To cut time spent on correspondence, use postcards, response checklists on which people can quickly indicate their answers, and small letterheads for outgoing mail. Write your own responses to inquiries on the bottom of the original request and return it to the sender. Use stick-on notes, standardized forms and form letters, and keep all correspondence materials together in a convenient location.

Use the phone instead of writing a letter when a call will accomplish the same thing in less time. Fax, or use electronic mail, instead of using regular mail whenever you can. Ask for information you need in a hurry to be faxed to you.

To create customized forms for fast action, use Per:Form software by Delrina Technology for IBM-compatible, and Smartform Designer and its companion Smartform Assistant for Macintosh computers. Other software programs, such as Venture by Star Software, contain preformatted standard letters as well as other forms for a variety of businesss purposes. These can be adapted to your needs and can save you the time of having to struggle with what to say. *To the Letter* by Diana Booher is a large handbook of sample letters for the busy executive, and *Letters That Sell* by Edward D. Werz provides ninety ready-to-use letters to help you sell your products, services, and ideas.

To make sending out form letters a snap, computerize your mailing list. Most database programs, such as Symantec's Q&A, can be used for mailing-list management. You may find that a mailing-list management capability is included with your word-processing program. There are also special programs to automate mailing-list management which come as either stand-alone programs or desk accessories. For IBM-compatible computers, Spinnaker's Better Working One-Person Office not only enables you to manage mailing lists but can also be used for expense tracking, invoicing, managing sales contacts, and generating reports. PC Label Master is a well-regarded stand-alone product. For the Macintosh, MacEnvelope is a stand-alone program; Kiwi Envelopes is a shareware desk accessory. In Chapter 15, you'll find a variety of other suggestions for handling correspondence more efficiently.

You can even save time buying stamps by phone or mail. You can order them by phone from 1-800-STAMPS24 and charge them to MasterCard or Visa. To order stamps by mail, use the order forms you can pick up at post offices.

Errands. Keep time spent on errands to a minimum by doing as many things as possible in one trip. Do errands during your low-energy periods. Avoid rush-hour traffic and go when you are least likely to encounter lines and crowds. For example, avoid the post office while the twelve to two o'clock lunch crowd is there. Take other work with you to do while you're waiting in lines you cannot avoid.

Call ahead to make sure the person or material you need is ready and available before you take the time to drive by. If you're spending too much time on errands, schedule biweekly or monthly trips for supplies or consider finding an office-supply store that will deliver goods to you.

Phone calls. Keep names and phone numbers current and within arm's reach so you won't have to spend time looking for the numbers you want to call. Use the auto-dialer feature available on most phones. It holds frequently called numbers in its memory with one-number codes. All you need to do is punch one number to put a call through. Or consider using a software program like Hotline to dial your phone number for you. It's like a computerized Rolodex. You keep the names, addresses, and phone numbers of business contacts in your computer and you can call them up immediately even while you're working in another file. You can also transform your Hotline files into a handy mailing list or use it for mailing-labels.

Keep phone conversations in bounds by having a set time of day for making and returning calls. Use an answering machine or service to protect yourself from untimely interruptions. In fact, you can use an answering machine to screen your calls, only picking up those that are high priority and returning all others at a designated time.

Limit time on the phone by telling callers you only have a few minutes. Rather than discussing points in detail over the phone, ask for or send written materials to be reviewed later. Arrange to call back after you or your caller has had time to think over ideas brought up.

Learn to use closing comments like "Thank you for calling" and "I'll get back to you soon" to bring the conversation to a end.

Projects. To manage large projects efficiently, break them down into smaller tasks and list them in the order in which they need to be completed. Assign deadlines to each task and set up a Project File that will serve as the clearinghouse for the entire project. On the inside cover of the Project File, write the following information, in pencil:

Names, phone numbers, and addresses of all people involved

Tasks to be completed

Schedule and deadline for each task

Dates and locations for project meetings

All correspondence, proposals, and contracts

Keep all correspondence and material related to the project in this file. As work progresses, check off the tasks you complete and note any modifications in your project schedule.

Consider using project-management software. In the planning stage, this software enables you to set goals for the project and divide the work into smaller tasks. It helps you identify the resources you will use, determine the costs involved, track your progress, and evaluate your results. Popular project-management programs include *Harvard Project Manager, Microsoft Project, Super Project Plus, Time Line,* and *MacProject II.*

Staying Cool, Calm, and Collected

Planning your work ahead of time is clearly the best way to avoid the panic of getting behind schedule or becoming overwhelmed with too much to do. Knowing what you have on hand and what you have to do also helps you say "no" to projects and activities that you can't realistically handle.

It's not uncommon for new open-collar workers, eager for business or the opportunity to prove their worth on the job, to leap into every opportunity that comes along. In reality, taking on more than you can do, and do well, sets you up for failure.

The first time Joyce Green started a word-processing service she actually put herself out of business by agreeing to do more than she could. She took on the typing of several doctoral theses simultaneously, thinking this would launch her business. Instead, her son became ill and she ended up being unable to deliver. Trying to juggle the typing and the care of her son put her farther and farther behind. Two months later her customers were furious and demanded their deposits back. They took their business elsewhere and spread the bad word about Joyce on campus. Their deposits, of course, had been spent, and she had to borrow the money to repay them. "I ended up going back to another job. But this time it's different. What I learned from that horrible experience is to take on only what I know I can do. Now I refer business out when I'm busy. I also try to stay ahead of schedule because I know there will always be some unexpected interruption."

Writer and editor Nancy Shaw works with her husband, Jim, from their oceanfront townhouse. She keeps her sanity with her demanding schedule by planning all her meals for the week on the weekend. She gets the groceries in on Saturday and cooks most of the main courses on Sunday. "This way I can relax during the week and just concentrate on the work I need to do. When we're ready to eat, I just go to the freezer, and everything is ready."

In the midst of deadlines, delays, competing priorities, unforeseen emergencies, and demands from family, customers, and friends, even a well-organized day can get pretty hectic. It's on just such days that you realize that you don't actually manage time, you manage yourself.

With the pressures of the day, you can lose precious time stewing, floundering, and storming around the office. There are moments when chaos reigns despite the best-laid plans. So we've collected a list of things you can do to keep your wits about you and stay in the right frame of mind in the midst of it all.

1. **Take a deep breath.** In the pressure of a stressful situation, most people start holding their breath or breathing more shallowly. This leaves them with less oxygen to think clearly, and signals to the body that it's under stress. The adrenaline starts pumping, the heart beating, the palms sweating. By taking a slow deep breath, you bring oxygen into your system and fool your body into thinking it can relax. Immediately you begin to feel more relaxed and at ease.

2. **Count to ten.** This old adage still serves us well. When your mind starts racing and there are more problems than you can handle at once, slowly counting to ten will give you a few moments to recover your perspective.

3. **Use aphorisms.** Studies of highly successful executives show that they have slogans or jingles they repeat to themselves to get through rough situations. In other words, they give themselves pep talks with sayings like these: "Hang in there, Charlie." "You can do it." "Inch by inch everything's a cinch." "When the going gets tough, the tough get going."

   Psychologist Shad Helmstetter calls these aphorisms "self-talk," and his book *Self-Talk Solutions* is filled with many useful things you can say to yourself to get through the most challenging of times.

4. **Project the best.** Instead of worrying about what you fear might happen in the future, use the techniques of Olympic athletes and concentrate on what you *want* to have happen. Actually visualize things going precisely the way you want them to go.

5. **Look for the learning experience.** Instead of worrying about mistakes you've made, think of what you can learn from them. The road to success is lined with mistakes. So rather than chewing yourself out for getting in such a mess, be your own fan club. Congratulate yourself for getting one step closer to success, and cheer yourself on.

6. **Take a five-minute break.** Take a walk, get a hug, play with your dog, or throw a private tantrum. Then ask yourself, "What's the best thing to do right now?"

7. **Slow down and take one step at a time.** Just because things are happening at a breakneck pace around you, it doesn't mean you have to be caught up in the same whirlwind. Concentrate on doing one thing at a time.

8. **Remind yourself, ". . . and this too shall pass."** Nothing lasts forever. You've been through tough times before and you're still here. Tomorrow is a new day.

Taking Charge of Interruptions and Distractions

Even the most carefully laid plans are vulnerable to interruptions and distractions. Like financial consultant Michael Fey, most people find this is even true when they are working at home: "There are interruptions you can't even contemplate."

The most common interruptions and distractions you are likely to encounter fall into three categories: being distracted by household responsibilities, by other family members, and by your own lack of focus. Let's take a look at each of these and some of the things you can do to tackle them.

Escaping from Household Responsibilities

The Problem: When you're working from home, the various aspects of your life can become so interconnected that it can sometimes be hard to tell whether you're working or you're busy doing other activities.

Errands and household responsibilities become part of the workday. They can be insidious, monopolizing the best part of your day before you know it. Writer Marcia Seligson recounts what often happens: "You could spend half a day, every day, doing trivia—the laundry, the errands, taking the car in. You can spend days paying the bills, arguing with the phone company."

Certainly all the trivia Marcia refers to is work. And it needs to be done. Therefore, while you are doing it, you feel productive. Career consultant Marilyn Miller describes this feeling: "Originally I had problems focusing, because whether I was doing household duties or whether I was doing my work, I kept telling myself, 'It's okay, you're working.'"

Many of the business errands you run are the type that someone else would have done at the office—getting supplies, taking out the mail, delivering a package, and so forth. Now, when you have to do them yourself, they fit in naturally with stopping to get a birthday card and dropping off the dry cleaning.

Also, when you were working away from home, all the household responsibilities weren't there staring at you. You didn't know about the broken pipe until you got home. Somehow you squeezed in all the major responsibilities and just let the rest go. And that's what you will have to do when you work from home. It's just harder, because everything is there in front of you.

The Solutions: Your daily planning process and priority system should help, but the best safeguard is your attitude and determination. You will need to cultivate the attitude that even though you are at home, you are at work. You'll need to train yourself to operate as if you were at an outside office.

Calligrapher Jean Hilman handled her problem this way: "When I first started working at home, I'd tidy up the house before I got to work, but I would always find one more thing to do. Finally I decided that come 9:00 A.M., wherever things were, that's the way they would stay until my work was done. After all, that's the way it was when I had a job."

Marilyn Miller found she had to get over the old rule, "you always answer a ringing phone," and turn over her personal line to the answering service. Obviously you don't have to answer your personal phone while you're working. You wouldn't be answering it if you were away at an office.

Simply closing the office door is helpful to many people. Some take coffee and other things they'll need into their office first thing in the morning so they don't have to go out later amid the many household items that need attention. Others are comfortable doing housework during a break or during their natural downtime.

Getting Solid Family Support

The Problem: Since your family is probably used to having you generally accessible when you're at home, discovering they can't talk to you during large blocks of time can be quite an adjustment. "I had to learn to pretend he wasn't here," one wife reported about her spouse. "That took a while, but now I only interrupt him during those times I would have called him at the office anyway."

And what a surprise for a child of any age to discover that Mommy's home, but can't be seen. "I really didn't need to talk to her," one sixteen-year-old told us, "but I kept interrupting her just to see if I could. Now I'm used to it and I only bother her if I need to."

The Solutions: Work out a clear plan with your family and get their support. Let them know when you will be working and what your expectations of them are during that time. The plan should define the following:

1. **How everyone will know when you are working** and when you aren't. How you'll signal your family that this is work time.
2. **When you are not to be interrupted,** the particular hours or activities.
3. **What other expectations you have:**
   Any areas of the house that must be kept neat.
   The sound level you expect in the house while you are working.
   Who is responsible for taking care of household events while you are working.
   Whether you expect anyone else, such as a spouse or an older child, to be responsible for making sure you aren't interrupted.
   Whether you want anyone to answer your business phone.
   Whether you have any particular expectations for them when you have business visitors.
4. **How any young children will be cared for** while you are working.

In setting up your plan, remember, you want to *work* at home, not become a police officer. And when someone is opposed to doing something you expect them to do, problems will usually develop. So most people find that in order to get the support they need, everyone involved needs to be consulted before an operations plan is decided on.

Expect a lot of testing in the beginning. At one time or another, everyone will forget the plan. Everybody will push and explore the limits. Even you will probably forget sometimes. But most people find that if you simply keep your expectations to yourself, the plan will go out the window. "I wasn't able to work at home because of the kids," an entertainer told us. "If I had set and kept the limits in the beginning it might have been different."

Be prepared to discuss exceptions. What emergencies will you want to know about? What type of problems should you be interrupted for even if you're working? What household events will you be willing to handle?

Often family members find it helpful to have cues or signals that remind them when you are not to be interrupted. Here are some signals people use:

- Posting a schedule on the door
- Seeing your office door closed
- Hanging up a Do Not Disturb sign
- Posting an Out sign on the door, meaning "Don't interrupt," or an In sign, meaning "It's okay to come in"

You will probably find you'll have fewer interruptions if you let people know exactly when you are available. When family members hear a vague "Later" or "When I'm done," too often they just make further interruptions to see if "later" has arrived. So if it's "not now," let people know exactly "when."

Some people post the time of their next break on the door. One consultant arranged for family members to knock once when they needed something, and he would come out at the first opportunity.

For small children, a speech therapist suggested a tactic she used with her children. Draw a picture of a clock showing what the face of the clock will look like when you are free to see them. You can also set the kitchen alarm or a clock radio.

When people do follow the plan, let them know how much you appreciate not being interrupted. Be sure you don't make the mistake one advertising executive made: "Every time my ten-year-old would come to the door and interrupt me, I'd talk to him about what he wanted and how he shouldn't be interrupting me. We'd have an out-and-out argument. A friend pointed out to me that he got more attention by interrupting me than he got if he waited until I was free."

Giving a lot of attention to someone who interrupts, even if it's negative, will only encourage more interruptions. So when you're interrupted, keep your responses short and sweet and give family members more attention before and after business hours.

Most families find that by sticking with it, through what is usually a bumpy beginning, they can eventually evolve a creative and individualized plan that will work for them. For more ideas, see chapters 18 and 19.

Keeping Focused on Your Work

The Problem: Many people interrupt themselves. A phone call reminds them of someone else they should call. The dog barking in the backyard reminds them they need to put out the trash. Hearing the kids squabbling, a parent want to get involved.

The Solutions: Set up your environment to help you stay focused on the job at hand. Put temptation out of sight. Close the door. Soundproof your office in one of the ways suggested in Chapter 7. Close off the TV room. Close the kitchen door. Put away books or magazines.

Psychology Today once described a surgeon who was concentrating so intently on his work that he was unaware the ceiling had collapsed around him. When he finished he asked the nurse, "What's all this plaster doing on the operating room floor?" This story highlights how effective the power of concentration can be.

The ability to maintain deep concentration can safeguard you from almost any interruption. Working with psychologist Frederick Robinson's ideas about concentration, we've identified four simple principles for developing improved attention and concentration.

1. **Cultivate a zest for the work you are doing.** Become involved in mastering it, taking it to its limits, finding a new or better way of doing it. Become fascinated with the possibilities. Make the work come alive. See it in relation to the big picture, the difference it makes in the world, in the lives of others. There's nobility in all work; discover the nobility in yours.

2. **Keep thinking about your immediate goal.** Sift out everything that doesn't related to your goal. At other times, seek to find a relationship between everything and your goal. This is how people can be watching TV or reading an article and suddenly find a way to do their job better.

3. **Take it easy. Don't push.** The most economical use of your mental and physical energy is also generally the most effective.

4. **Let your subconscious work for you.** Grapple with whatever you're focusing on. Really get in there and wrestle with it. Then take a break. Often ideas and solutions will appear to come from nowhere. This is the key to how people are able to take productive breaks while mowing the grass or running an errand.

If disruptions continue to be the bane of your workday, despite all efforts to control them, there are several last-ditch approaches you can try. Consider relocating your office to a different area of the house. If your work allows you to move around, work somewhere else during certain periods. Public libraries are a good place to go. College campuses, hotels, or restaurants are other possibilities.

Consider changing your office hours too, perhaps working after the children are asleep or early in the morning before other activities have started. Rearrange your schedule, putting tasks at different times of the day.

Finally, learn how to tolerate the interruptions you can't avoid. Set up reminders or cues to get back to work easily after you've been interrupted.

Leave yourself a short note about where you left off. Mark the page or the file you're on. Leave your work as it was, so you can step right back into it when you return.

Preventing Procrastination

With all the freedom you have working from home, it's a snap to procrastinate. You can easily put off or never get to something you want to avoid. But procrastination arises from a number of causes, and recognizing the reasons can keep you from succumbing to it.

Perfectionism

In the face of impossibly high standards, we're all likely to put off what we fear can't be accomplished. Therefore, to avoid procrastinating, think *performance,* not absolute *perfection.* Set manageable, concrete goals to be achieved at specified times.

Fear

In their book *Procrastination: Why You Do It, What to Do about It,* Jane Burka and Lenora Yuen say the major cause of procrastination is fear of something, whether it's fear of success, fear of failure, or fear of change. Finding out what you fear, and then deciding whether it's realistic, or how you could handle things if your worst fears came true, can free you to go ahead with the task.

Large, Overwhelming Tasks

When what you're doing seems so large and complex you don't know where to start, procrastination is often the result. In a situation like this, break the work into small chunks that will take you no more than ten to thirty minutes each. Take one small step at a time.

Unpleasant Tasks

If you hate doing something, you're likely to procrastinate about tackling it. When possible, delegate or hire someone to do the tasks that are most distasteful to you. If you must do them yourself, think about how good you'll feel when the task you've been avoiding is done. Bribe yourself with the promise of a reward when you finish, and keep your promise. You might offer yourself small rewards for doing each part of a larger task. Also use the tactic of doing unpleasant tasks first to get them out of the way and free the rest of your day.

Creating Pressure to Perform

Some people motivate themselves by creating the pressure of a crisis atmosphere. They procrastinate until the last minute and then dramatically complete the work. Since this strategy actually helps them get the work done, they're often confirmed procrastinators. The emotional expense, however, is great and detracts from the kind of consistent, concentrated effort a successful business needs. So instead, motivate yourself by working at a reasonable pace to finish one step at a time rather than working yourself into a panic to do it all in one last-ditch effort.

Waiting for the Right Moment

People get entrenched in procrastinating by telling themselves they can't start something until something else has happened. Their thought is, "I'll do this as soon as . . ." (For example: "I'll clean out that storeroom as soon as my son moves out.") The way out of this trap is to do it now. Now is not only the right moment, it's the only moment. Tomorrow has a way of never coming, so start today.

A Useful Warning

Sometimes procrastination is a warning signal, a way to tell yourself this is not the right thing to do or that it is a waste of time and doesn't need doing. A potter we talked with, for example, kept putting off delivering a particular pot she had sold. All she needed to do was to take a picture of it for her portfolio and deliver it. After much delay, she realized that if she sold this pot, she would not be able to duplicate its unique and unusual finish. Once she realized this, she knew she did not want to sell it and called immediately to work out a new agreement with her customer.

When, for whatever reason, you find that you continue to avoid important tasks, identify what you're doing instead, and cut off your escape routes.

If you chronically procrastinate and find you can't cut off the escape routes, ask yourself these three questions:

1. **Under what circumstances would you be motivated to do what needs to be done?** Listen carefully to your answer. Don't censor it. Think about what's stopping you from going on with what you need to do. If you're honest with yourself, you may recognize you're not willing to work as long or hard as it takes to get the job done. You may not have scheduled enough free time for yourself. You may not be willing to do some of the tasks your work entails. In any case, now you have to face the truth because you are the boss. But you can't fire yourself. You have to learn to live—and work—with yourself. So you may have to compromise or strike a bargain with yourself about such things as setting up a different schedule, getting additional help, or allowing more free time.

2. **Do you enjoy your work?** If the honest answer is "no," it's no wonder you are having difficulty getting yourself to do the tasks involved. When you work at home, it is particularly important that you enjoy

what you do at least most of the time. If you don't, seriously consider finding different work. As magician and publisher Mike Caveney says, money alone is often not motivation enough to get you to work when you're on your own. "I can't think of anyone who works harder than we do. At midnight or eleven o'clock we'll knock off and watch the news. If we were to do it just for the money, it wouldn't work. You have to love it."

3. **Are you depressed?** If you chronically can't get yourself going, your procrastination may be a sign that you are depressed. Working at home alone, day in and day out, you can be more vulnerable to depression and it can grow on you gradually. Depression can arise from not having enough personal contact, enough excitement and stimulation, or enough structure for doing things. You can also become depressed from too much contact, too much stimulation, and a schedule that is too rigid or overloaded.

The isolation, unexpected interruptions, uncertain financial conditions, loss of regular routines—all these changes people face when they work at home—can lead to depression. In fact, depression could be an occupational hazard of working at home unless you take preventive action. To combat the situation:

- Keep moving. Even though you may not feel like it, stay active. Physical exercise for twenty or more minutes daily is a good way to keep your spirits up.
- Make daily contact with people.
- Set up and follow a schedule that is neither too tight nor too loose.

Whether feeling depressed is related to working at home or other events in your life, if it continues or worsens despite your efforts, contact someone for professional help. It is important that depressions not deepen or continue for weeks on end.

How Do You Avoid Your Work?

☐ Socializing on the phone
☐ Visiting with friends and neighbors
☐ Daydreaming, planning a glorious future
☐ Worrying, but not acting
☐ Working on other, less-important projects
☐ Getting sick
☐ Watching TV
☐ Starting later, stopping earlier
☐ Cleaning out all the file cabinets
☐ Taking longer, more frequent breaks

Closing the Door on Work

If you have more work to do than you can possibly get done in a regular workday (and who doesn't?), how do you put it aside if it's always there with you? At an outside office, you can close the door and go home, but some people who work at home find that's not enough when the door is right down the hall next to the bedroom.

Short of moving the office out of your house, there are several things you can do to get away from the work around you.

Separate Your Office Space

When you have an office space or work area that's as remote as possible from the rest of the house, it's usually easier to "close the door"—literally—the way you would when working away from home. Psychotherapist Richard Nadeau has his counseling practice in a separate wing of his home. "When my last client leaves, I put away the coffee cups, empty the ashtrays, and close the door to that portion of the house. I don't go back in again until the next day when I begin to prepare for my first client."

Graphics designer Mary Stoddard has to walk across an outdoor courtyard to get to her studio in the garage. Lauren Brubaker has his recording studio in the basement so that "downstairs I'm at work, upstairs I'm not."

Whatever you do, if you have a tendency to overwork, *make sure you don't put your office in your bedroom!* Any other room in the house will be easier to get away from!

Set Up an End-of-the-Workday Ritual

Michael Warner, who operates his company, InfoSource, from home, has created a unique ritual to close his workday. "At the end of the day I walk to the garage, open and close the car door, walk in the front door and shout, 'Hello, dear, I'm home.' It gives me the feeling that I don't have to go back into the office until I 'leave' for work the next morning."

Here are some other rituals people use:

- Taking a walk around the block
- Running errands
- Taking an exercise class at the end of the day
- Taking a shower and changing clothes
- Picking the kids up from the baby-sitter or from school
- Having a snack while watching the five o'clock news

Set a Firm Schedule

If possible, set up a fixed "closing hour" and do not compromise except for emergencies. This is usually easier to do when you're salaried than when you're self-employed. In our work, for example, we give many evening speeches and seminars. We have early-morning meetings with our editors. We give all-day seminars too. If we weren't careful in planning our week, we would end up working morning, noon, and night.

For situations like ours when you're working at different times of the day during the week, we've developed two general rules:

1. **Set aside either the morning, afternoon, or evening** of each day as "free" time during which you do not work. As you fill in your appointment calendar, block off either the morning, afternoon, or evening of a day by putting a big "X" over the one free period.

    We realize, of course, that some days will be more hectic than others, but to make this sytem work, we've found we have to be fairly rigid about this rule. When we have X'd out an evening of a fully scheduled day and someone wants us to meet that night, unless it's crucial we have to say, "No, that evening is already filled." And it is. It's filled with time off.

2. **Allow at least one full "free" day per week.** Usually this is Saturday and/or Sunday; however, it can be any day of the week. A family we know operates a swapmeet booth every weekend, and takes Monday and Tuesday off. A professional dog handler works at shows on weekends and teaches evening classes during the week. His free day is Friday, and during the rest of the week he doesn't go to work until one in the afternoon.

Put Nonwork Events on Your Calendar in Advance

There is another simple step you can take to close the door on work when you need to. Use your calendar to prepare yourself to take time off. Most people reserve their appointment calendars for work-related activities or special social occasions. Personal or family activities are usually fit in around business. Writing these activities on your calendar helps give them equal time.

Get Out of the House

When work is home and home is work, people sometimes find they have to get away from the house to get really away from work. They come to feel the way graphics designer Nancy Rabbitt does: "When you commute to work, coming home is like a retreat, a refuge. But when you work at home, it's no longer a refuge. To relax and refresh myself I have to go someplace else, get away for an evening or go off for a weekend."

Getting away isn't always easy, however. Have you ever thought of planning an evening at the theater or taking a short trip, but then waited to see if you'd be free or if you'd feel like it when the time came? What happened? Too often, when the time came, you were too busy or too tired to go.

Genevieve Marcus and Bob Smith, who run an educational foundation from their home, have found that to get away from work they have to make reservations in advance. When they see an event that looks interesting, they buy the tickets right away. If they want to spend a weekend at a vacation resort, they pay for the tickets and the hotel room in advance.

"Then we have to go. We have to drop what we're doing," Genevieve explains. "Right before it's time to go, I always wish I hadn't bought the tickets. I never feel like going. But since I've paid for them, I go and I always end up having a wonderful time. When I get back, I'm glad I got away."

Protect Your Free Time

Home business owners frequently complain that clients, knowing they're at home, call or even drop by any time of day or night. When this is your situation, you'll have to create ways to protect yourself from business intrusions into your free time.

Nancy Rabbitt found a double solution to this problem. Although she had fixed business hours, she kept getting calls in the early morning or having the doorbell ring while she was still in the bathtub. "I now have an answering service, which I keep on before and after business hours. When customers call, they're told the hours they can reach me and asked to leave a message. I also have a box on the front door so if someone comes by before I'm open for business, they can leave off whatever work they're bringing. Or in the evening, they can pick up their work after I'm closed."

If you are one of those people who can't stand to hear a phone ring without picking it up, a phone with a button for turning off the ring may help you turn a deaf ear.

When All Else Fails

Perhaps you're a person who simply can't stop working, a "workaholic." If many of the signs of overworking apply to you, an office at home may aggravate the situation. You don't have to move your office out of the house, however, to escape from overwork. You can get to the root of the problem.

People who overwork often link their self-worth and sense of well-being to whether or not they are being productive. They feel bad if they aren't always doing something. They fear the worst will happen if they let up.

Behavioral scientists have found that the constant drive to work is usually traceable to very basic concepts and beliefs about ourselves and about life. These convictions are related to what we unconsciously believe we must do to survive, to be loved, to succeed, to be worthy as a person.

Often overworkers have gotten the idea they must overwork from their parents, or even grandparents, who were living in more difficult economic times than those today.

One woman we know traced her belief that she had to be working all the time to her immigrant grandparents' struggle to survive and rise above poverty. She recalls her grandmother working from dawn to dusk seven days a

---

Signs of Overworking

1. Do your spouse, children, or friends nag and complain that you need to spend more time with them? Do frustrated children, friends, and other loved ones feel last on the list for your time? Do they sulk, badger, or act up for your attention?
2. Do you have many business associates but few friends? Are you always too busy to get together with people? Do you hear yourself saying things like, "I can't make it," or "Sorry I had to miss it"?
3. Do you work even in nonworking situations? Do you "work" your social gatherings, and talk shop wherever you go?
4. Do you work at your play? Is all your recreation as much work as being on the job, because you play to win every point, improve your every previous performance, and refuse to take losing lightly?
5. Do you feel uncomfortable if you're in a situation where you can't be productive, growing nervous as you wait in a grocery line or for a red light to change?
6. Do you think of nongoal-directed fun as frivolous? Do you feel that "doing nothing" is being lazy, and do you consider those who don't work as hard as you do unmotivated?
7. Do you let the clock run your life? Do you look at the clock often, wanting to cram as much as possible into every minute, or are you frequently late because you had to get just one more thing done before you left?
8. Do you take everything so seriously that you miss or resent humorous comments in a work situation?

---

week. She remembers every family member being sent to work, and how her mother continued this tradition years after they were all affluent.

Similarly, one man recognized how his tendency to overwork arose from growing up in the Depression. His father never lost his job, but those around him did. The father worked long hours during that time and ever after. For years to come, the father would recount how being caught with an idle moment could have cost him his job and the family's livelihood.

In addition to the experiences in our past, societal conditioning also invites us to overwork and rewards us for doing so. Many men have been conditioned to believe that their value lies in how much money they can make or how high up the corporate ladder they can climb—both of which often seem to depend on putting in overly long and difficult hours.

In recent years, many women have found themselves in this trap too, feeling they can't get ahead unless they overwork as much as so many men do. Women also get caught in the "Superwoman" syndrome, working full time and trying to be the perfect mother, lover, and housewife all at once.

If you're self-employed, concern about your economic security can drive you to think that you must keep working all the time or you'll never make it. Sometimes family and friends unintentionally intensify such concerns because of their own fears. Not wanting you to fail or suffer needlessly, parents may subtly suggest that you take another job. Worried about mounting bills, spouses can thoughtlessly comment that you should have kept your job.

Usually overworkers are not aware of such patterns, beliefs, and conditioning, but once recognized for what they are, these factors can be changed. The overworker can develop new values that support a healthier, more balanced, and even a more productive and secure life. If you overwork, here are several steps you can take:

1. Change your ideas about success. There's a difference between hard work and overwork. Success today does not require working yourself into the grave. In fact, success can be easy. A consistent, steady effort proves more successful than a stress-filled obsession. Reassure yourself of your ability to achieve your goals or get reassurance from others who will support you. When sales trainer Harriet Brayton left her job, she was so frightened about whether she could make it on her own that she at first couldn't even sleep. She kept thinking of work she could be doing. She turned to her father for reassurance. "For a while I was calling him every day. A successful businessman himself, he kept telling me 'Harriet, relax, you're doing fine. Just keep going.' And that's what I would say to others. It works. I'm doing fine now and I still take time to play."

2. Have a talk with yourself about the therapeutic effects of relaxing. Convince yourself that you're entitled to relax and that there's more to life than work. In fact, you owe it to yourself. Your life will not only be just as good when you stop working so much, it will actually be better. Studies like the one by Dr. Charles Garfield of the University of California, San Francisco, School of Medicine, show that workaholics not only have more heart attacks and other illnesses, but actually don't get as much accomplished! You may be surprised to discover that you get more done and have more energy after you begin to take more time off.

If this is hard for you to believe, read about others who used to feel as you do. Writer Norman Cousins is a good example. He has written about how, after a near-fatal disease, he learned to change from an inveterate overworker to someone who could relax and enjoy life while he still had it.

3. Find out what drives you to overwork and give yourself permission to stop. Below we have listed what psychologist Taibi Kahler has identified as the four most common messages people use to drive themselves and the messages they need to hear to stop.

4. Explore how you became so driven. Try to discover how you got the idea you have to work so much. If you overwork, look back into your roots to find out what experiences or social pressures influenced you to overwork. Use the Five-Step Change Process (see next page) to recognize what you believe about overworking, why it's important to you, and how you can develop new, healthier, and more rewarding ways to accomplish what you want to do.

5. Set up mini-breaks. Set aside five to fifteen minutes a day to "do nothing." Spend that time doing anything that you enjoy but don't have to do. It's surprising what people call "doing nothing." For example:

- Working in the garden
- Watching TV
- Taking a walk
- Sitting in the sun
- Playing ball with the kids
- Brushing the dog
- Taking a nap
- Reading a magazine

At first you may find these five to fifteen minutes uncomfortable, but make yourself take them. Don't expect "doing nothing" to feel good at first. You're

---

How to Escape What's Driving You

Driving Message	New Beliefs
Be Perfect	You can learn from making mistakes.
	Mistakes take you closer to success.
	No one is perfect.
Try Hard	Do your best and you'll do a good job.
	Doing well doesn't have to be hard.
	You don't have to struggle to succeed.
	Success can come effortlessly.
Hurry Up	You can go at your own pace.
	You'll get more done when you go at a reasonable and steady rate.
	Slow down. Take a breath. Take one step at a time and you'll reach your goals.
Please Others	You can't please everyone all of the time.
	You have to take care of yourself before you can take care of others.
	It's okay to say "no."

going against your conditioning and years of habit. It takes a while to shed the discomfort and develop new habits. To help the process along when you are feeling uncomfortable, take notice of the old beliefs your feelings stem from and mentally replace them with the new beliefs that will free you from over-working.

At first you will probably have to schedule your leisure time by formally putting these five- to fifteen-minute work breaks into your day. Set a goal of taking one break at ten o'clock in the morning and one at three o'clock in the afternoon, for example.

Set aside part of each day for leisure.   If you are now working most of the waking day, build up to enjoying a portion of every day off. For example, graduate from mini-breaks to setting aside a whole hour once a week for leisure time in the evenings. Then add one or two hours a week as free time begins to feel more comfortable. Eventually, you will be able to limit your work to eight or ten hours a day.

Avoid invitations to work on something else.   When you start taking time off, some people may see that you're free, for a change, and try to put you back to work—finally you're available to do some of the things they've been waiting for you to do! Tell them these "free times" are health breaks that will keep you alive longer, and send them on their way.

A Five-Step Change Process*

Step 1. Ask yourself, ''What *positive intention* do I have for working so much and driving myself so hard? What are you hoping to get? What are you hoping to avoid? Here are a few sample answers:

   To make enough money to relax some day
   To be somebody
   To keep from going under
   To avoid hassles in the family

Step 2. Ask yourself if you would be willing to consider other ways of achieving your positive intention besides overworking.
Step 3. Then, using your creative abilities, think of three *other* ways you could achieve your positive intention.
Step 4. Ask yourself if you are willing to use these three new ways instead of overworking.
Step 5. Check to see that you have no doubts about using the new alternatives. If you do, go back to Step 3 and come up with some other ways that will overcome your doubts.

*From neurolinguistic programming techniques developed by Richard Bandleo and John Grinder.

Refuse to let anything interfere with the time you've blocked off for leisure, and avoid the trap of working at your play. Do leisure activities because you enjoy them, not because they will produce some work objective for you. Your leisure time is for doing things that are gratifying in and of themselves. Play golf, for example, because it feels good, not because you can talk over a business deal. If you play golf with a prospective client, that's probably not leisure. If you jog to improve your time, you are probably working at it and not playing. So you'll need to include another way of relaxing.

Finally, as time-management consultant Dr. Terry Paulson advises, spoil yourself when you relax. See that baseball game you've been itching to go to. Listen to your favorite album or radio talk show. Buy yourself that science fiction thriller you've been meaning to read. And read it. Or, in the good doctor's words, "Pamper yourself . . . there are no replacements."

Chapter Digest

1. To make sure you get to work and stick to business while working from home, set up a schedule, establish rituals that cue you when it's time to start, and plan your day.

2. Use a time-management system that includes a calendar for the year, month, and week; use a daily planner with sheets for setting down goals and planning projects. You should also be able to add, subtract, and rearrange the pages of your time system to suit your needs. And it should be small enough to carry with you on errands and appointments.

3. Use a daily planner to outline what you need to do each day and give each item an "A" or "B" priority. Get your top three "A" items done first. Move incompleted tasks to the next day.

4. Throughout your day, work smarter not harder. Use time-saving technology, make quick decisions on small matters, keep a list of mini-tasks that need doing and do them while you're holding on the phone or waiting for a printout.

5. Follow time-saving tips for managing meetings, correspondence, phone calls, errands, projects, and keeping up with reading in your field.

6. Learn mental techniques for staying cool, calm, and collected in the midst of deadlines, multiple demands, and unexpected emergencies. Take a deep breath, count to ten, take a walk, use supportive self-talk, and take one step at a time.

7. Learn to focus on your work as if you were at an office away from home. Get solid support from your family. Let them know what you expect of them.

8. To prevent procrastination, make sure you enjoy the work you do and learn to recognize what's keeping you from doing what you need to

do. Often your reasons (not your excuses) for procrastinating hold valuable messages about what you need to do to work more successfully.

9. To avoid overworking, set a firm schedule; leave your morning, afternoon, or evening free; put personal events on your calendar and get away from the house regularly.

10. If you are a workaholic, someone who simply can't stop working, recognize that fact. Look into what's driving you to overwork and realize that you will actually get more done and be more successful if you work at a relaxed, steady pace with ample time for rest and relaxation. Begin taking small work breaks and then gradually stretch them out to allow yourself time off.

Resources

Books

Anatomy of an Illness. Norman Cousins. New York: W. W. Norton, 1979.

From Burnout to Balance. Dennis T. Jaffe and Cynthia D. Scott. New York: McGraw-Hill, 1984.

The Healing Heart. Norman Cousins. New York: W. W. Norton, 1983.

How to Get Control of Your Time and Your Life. Alan Lakein. New York: New American Library, 1973.

Living with a Perfectionist. Dr. David Stoop. Nashville, TN: Oliver-Nelson, 1987.

Successful Time Management: A Self-Teaching Guide. Jack Ferner. New York: John Wiley & Sons, 1980.

Take Control of Your Life: A Complete Guide to Stress Relief. Emmaus, PA: Rodale Press, 1988.

The Time Trap. R. Alec Mackenzie. New York: McGraw-Hill, 1975.

The Now Habit: A Strategic Program for Overcoming Procrastination and Enjoying Guilt-Free Play. Neil Fiore. Los Angeles: Jeremy P. Tarcher, 1989.

The Self-Talk Solution. Shad Helmstetter. New York: Simon & Schuster, 1987.

To the Letter. Dianna Booher. Lexington, MA: Lexington Books, 1988.

Type A Behavior and Your Heart. Meyer Friedman, M.D., and Ray H. Rosenman, M.D. New York: Fawcett Crest, 1981.

What to Say When You Talk to Yourself. Shad Helmstetter. Scottsdale, AZ: Grindle Press,

Tape

How to Master Your Time. Brian Tracy. Chicago: Nightingale Conant; (800) 323-5552.

Time-Management Systems and Supplies

Day Runner. Harper House, 3562 Eastham Dr., Culver City, CA 90232; (213) 837-6900.

DayTimers, Inc. One DayTimer Plaza, Allentown, PA 18195-1551; (215) 395-5884.

CHAPTER
FOURTEEN

■ ■

Managing Money: Financing and
Cash-Flow Management

If you're like the majority of the people who work from home, whether you're salaried or self-employed, you have neither the time nor the inclination to spend hours doing complicated record keeping. Fortunately there's usually no need to get complicated, but you do have to spend a little time setting up a system for managing the records you need to keep. Otherwise, it's all too easy for your money management needs to slip through the cracks.

Picture this: A check bounces and your credit is marred. It's tax season and you're buried beneath a mound of receipts trying to figure out just how much you spent on supplies and equipment. You're at a party and overhear how you lost out on a way to make your money work for you by earning higher interest rates. With an effective money management system you can avoid these and other problems of money mismanagement, which is the number one reason for small-business failures.

Unfortunately, many record-keeping systems for small businesses are only scaled-down versions of those used in large organizations. They require too much time, too much energy, or too much money for a one-person home office. At the same time, systems for managing household money matters aren't adequate for home business needs, either.

Faced with choosing between two extremes, some home-office people adopt the bookkeeping systems designed for larger businesses. Others, seeking to avoid the hassles of complex systems, fly by the seat of their pants, hoping everything will work out in the end. For too many, both of these strategies produce disappointing results. People frequently tell us:

"I've tried several times to use a formal record-keeping system, but it takes so much time that I get behind after a few weeks. Then for the rest of the year I just try to keep up with what's necessary. The receipts and everything, they're all in a box in the corner of my office. I guess until I can hire someone to do it for me, I'm doomed to trying to straighten it all out at tax time."

To avoid this dilemma, a money management system for a home office should meet four criteria:

1. **It should be simple and easy** enough for you to use in the time you have. In fact, it should be so simple that it's as easy or easier to use than not to use.
2. **It needs to have a fail-safe mechanism** so that if you fall behind, there is a way of picking up again without undue effort.
3. **It needs to be easily expandable** into other larger systems if and when your business needs grow.
4. **It has to do the job for you.**

What You Need to Keep Track Of

The specific financial information you need to keep track of depends on whether you're salaried or self-employed and on the type of business you're in. Here is a checklist of the typical kinds of information you may need to manage. Review it and check off the items that apply to you:

- **Banking transactions:** making deposits as well as keeping track of and balancing your savings or checking accounts.
- **Bills:** paying and keeping track of your personal and business-related expenses.
- **Time and expenses:** keeping a record of time and costs you need to bill to your customers, clients, or employer.
- **Billing or invoicing:** keeping records of money people owe you and sending statements to get paid for services or products you've provided.
- **Inventories:** keeping track of products you have on hand.
- **Sales records:** keeping track of the products you've sold and any sales tax you've collected.

Easy-to-Use Record-Keeping Systems

As with time management systems, there are a variety of ready-made money management aids available at stationery, office-supply, and software stores to help you keep track of the information you need. When you're salaried or affiliated with a sales organization, the company may have a system of its own for you to follow. If so, you'll need to incorporate it into a comprehensive system that addresses all aspects of your personal and business finances.

The right system will enable you to:

- Know how you're doing financially: whether you're making a profit; how far ahead or behind you are each month.
- Keep track of how you are spending your money so you can adjust what you spend in accordance with your goals.
- Determine which of your business activities are the most profitable.
- Be prepared, save time, and avoid stress when you do your taxes, when you seek loans and investors, when you want to sell your business, or any time you need to prepare financial statements, profit-and-loss statements, or balance sheets.
- Provide your tax preparer with everything needed to complete your federal and state returns in minimum time, and therefore save you money.
- Minimize your taxes by enabling you to take the legal deductions to which you are entitled.
- If you're self-employed, estimate your quarterly state and federal tax payments so you can put aside enough to pay those bills.
- Provide adequate records should you be audited by the IRS or state agencies.
- Have everything in one place so you know where to find it when you need it.

In this chapter we provide you with a framework to set up a system that will meet these criteria and provide some guidelines for getting additional help when you need it.

Is Your Money Management System Working?

1. Do you know your bank balance?
2. Are your bills paid on time—without late charges?
3. Are your tax materials already in order when tax time comes?
4. Do your get invoices out within the week?
5. Can you locate a receipt, order, or payment record you need in less than five minutes?
6. Do you know exactly what you're spending your money on?
7. Do you have the money you expect to have on hand when you need it?

Basic Money Management

We find the easiest way to handle your money is to use a personal computer. With the proper software, you can write checks, reconcile your bank accounts, do budgeting and basic bookkeeping, and produce needed financial reports. There are hundreds of financial software programs; we recommend, however, selecting one that meets the level of complexity your business demands, is easy to learn and use, and will enable you to transfer your financial records to more sophisticated software when your business growth demands it. Using these criteria, we recommend the following:

Level 1. One- or two-person business with no employees. Our choice at this level is *Quicken* by Intuit software. It is extremely easy to use and makes keeping track of cash transactions (checks, money orders, and currency) as simple as writing a check.

Level 2. Fewer than five employees, or a need for billing or inventory capabilities. If your business has fewer than five employees or you need to do regular billing or keep track of inventory, we recommend a program like *Money Matters* by Great American Software for managing the financial side of your business. In addition to check writing and basic financial management, *Money Matters* enables you to do payroll and invoicing, pay your bills, and control your inventory. Of course, this greater capability requires greater effort on your part to learn the program.

Level 3. More than five employees and a need for accounts receivable and accounts payable capabilities. If you employ more than five people and your business involves a significant volume of credit purchases or sales, you will benefit from using a software program such as Great American Software's *One Write Plus*. This program is based on the popular paper system of the same name and enables a home business to track significant volumes of open accounts payable and accounts receivable. It does everything the above programs do and in addition provides a powerful general ledger capability.

Many people are also using their computers and modems to pay their bills electronically using a service called *CheckFree*. This service eliminates having to lick stamps and seal envelopes when paying your bills. You don't need to sign checks and you can schedule automatic payments on dates you choose. Currently, this service costs $9 a month for up to twenty checks a month. You can use *CheckFree* in conjunction with many money management programs like *Quicken*.

There are many other fine financial software programs. Others that home-based businesspeople express satisfaction with include *Andrew Tobias' Managing Your Money, MoneyCounts*, and *Accpac Easy*. For Macintosh computers, *Mac-Money* by Survivor Software, and *Bedford Accounting* are recognized as good choices. *Bedford Accounting* is also available in an IBM version. Shareware programs for IBM-compatible computers are available, too. Medlin's *PC-GL* and *PC-Accounting I* and *II* are well regarded by people who use them.

Electronic Spreadsheets

Electronic spreadsheet software provides vastly greater versatility for forecasting and manipulating financial information than is possible with pencil and paper. When you change an entry on an electronic spreadsheet, the software alters all the other affected figures immediately to reflect that change. You can:

- Do financial modeling—play "what if" with numbers
- Do tax planning
- Plan alternative budgets
- Project monthly sales, cash flow, profit and loss
- Do financial problem-solving
- Track and plan your project schedules
- Track your productivity
- Evaluate a stock portfolio

The best-selling spreadsheet program is *Lotus 1-2-3*. Many add-on programs are available for it, such as *Ready-to-Run*. *Quattro,* by Borland, is easy to use and very flexible. If you have an Apple Macintosh, *Excel* is the stand-out product. *Multiplan* is also well-regarded as a spreadsheet.

Leaving a Paper Trail

The Internal Revenue Service still requires a paper backup of all financial transactions. Computer records alone, because they can be so easily altered, will not do. So to make yourself an easy-to-keep *paper* trail, we recommend using partitioned accordian files to keep records of paid bills, and receipts for cash and charge card payments of expenses.

Simply place labels on the partitions of the accordian file to correspond to the categories of tax deductions you take—for example, advertising, automobile, dues, publications, entertainment, and so forth. We keep our accordian files in a room right by our entryway. Then, filing receipts, along with taking messages off the answering machine located nearby, is part of our ritual when coming home. Receipts don't get lost or accumulate for filing at some other time. Another place to keep your accordian file is near the computer with your bookkeeping software. In that way, it will be handy when you enter cash and credit card expenses into your computer records.

Recording Time and Expenses

To keep simple, yet accurate and legal, records of time and expenses, use your appointment calendar or daily planner to write down the times that you begin and end working on billable projects. Note the beginning and ending mileage for billable travel. And enter your expenses as they occur. Enter them in pen, because pencil entries are not acceptable in an IRS audit. Erasures are not acceptable, either. Corrections should be made by crossing out the erroneous entry with a single line, not by obliterating the entry with ink or correction fluid.

You can also use this method for keeping track of business mileage and travel expenses you won't be billing to anyone but need to use in calculating your business deductions for tax purposes. You can also use your computer to keep track of your time for billing purposes with software like *TimeSlips* or *Time$heet.*

Managing Cash Flow

If you are self-employed, having a system for managing your cash flow is a matter of survival. Cash flow is to your livelihood what breath is to life. If the cash doesn't keep flowing, your business doesn't keep going.

We recommend a system that enables you to minimize what others owe you, utilize your cash on hand for maximum benefit, and hold on to what you have.

Collecting the Money You're Owed

For ideal cash management, you should collect on services or products at the time you sell them. Of course, this is not always possible, so here are several ways to make the money come in as quickly as possible.

- Get deposits, retainers, partial or progress payments.
- Offer a discount for cash payment at the time of sale or delivery of service.
- Take bank cards instead of extending credit.
- If you need to extend credit, have clear terms for when you must receive payment. Offer discounts of from 2 to 5 percent for receipt of payment within 10 days from the date of the invoice. Some companies are known for taking 90–120 days to make payment, so negotiate payment terms of 30 days as part of your sale.
- Reduce the risk you take in extending credit to new customers by getting TRW credit reports, just as large corporations do. A home-based business can get access to TRW reports by subscribing to NewsNet, an on-line service that primarily provides business newsletters. For under $50 a report, you can use NewsNet to get the TRW credit reports that contain any derogatory information about a company's credit, a history of the firm's payment for the last six months, and TRW's estimate of the chances that the customer will pay within thirty days of the due date of your invoice.

- Bill immediately upon delivery of a service or product, instead of waiting until the end of the month. A thirty-day payment period usually begins from the date customers receive your invoice.

- Act promptly on overdue accounts. Don't let them slip by. The longer the bill is overdue, the less likely it is to be paid.

Obtaining MasterCard and VISA merchant accounts.

Offering your customers the ability to pay you with MasterCard or VISA will increase your business from 10 to 50 percent, depending on the type of business and your clientele, according to sources in the charge card industry. Unfortunately, home-based businesses have a very hard time getting a merchant account to offer credit cards to their customers. We hear complaints like the following from all over the nation.

Bob Falk is a computer programmer producing computer software products. He told us: "Banks do not take home-based business seriously. If you want to get a credit card merchant account you have to rent office space somewhere outside your home or pay very high charges for guarantees."

Tom Rochford, a business consultant working on very specialized government contracts, has had similar problems. "I have noted some discriminatory practices toward home-based businesses in the world of banking. It's nearly impossible to get a MasterCard/VISA merchant account if you're a home-based business. I got mine only after several lunches with bankers and a lot of cajoling, threatening, and foot stomping."

If you want to offer your customers the ability to pay for your products with MasterCard or VISA, don't be surprised if your bank turns you down. But here are several avenues to consider.

Banks. Even though banks as a general rule are not granting home businesses merchant status so that their customers can pay with MasterCard or VISA, do try your own bank first. You have a track record with them and they already know you as a customer. If your own bank say "no," some people have been successful approaching small, independent banks. This is particularly true in small communities. Many middle-sized banks are getting out of the credit card business, selling their portfolios to the large credit card operations such as Citibank and Household International.

Savings and loans, thrifts, credit unions. Most people think of banks as the only financial institutions granting merchant status to companies. But they are not. Savings and loans, thrifts, and even credit unions increasingly offer merchant status. You may find them to be more liberal in their attitudes toward home-based businesses.

Trade associations. Another alternative is to work through trade associations. Accountant and Working from Home Forum member Barbara Schanker of New York has found that trade organizations will sometimes provide MasterCard/VISA merchant accounts as part of their membership package.

"Of course, there still is a service charge involved, but they are quicker to grant the privilege than banks," she reports. "For example, I am starting a pet supply business, so related organizations I can join include the Retail Merchants Association, Direct Marketing Association, and others specifically related to the pet industry."

To find trade associations in your field, check *Gale's Encyclopedia of Associations*, available in your library.

Chambers of commerce. Ask your Chamber of Commerce for help in securing merchant status. Some Chambers are providing this service or can assist you in gaining access to it.

Companies that specialize in providing VISA/MasterCard. Still another choice for securing merchant status is to work with one of the companies that are serving as intermediaries when banks fail to respond to the needs of home businesses. A current list of companies that will accept home businesses is kept in Library 2 of the Working from Home Forum we manage on CompuServe Information Service. Some companies currently offering this service to home-based businesses are listed in the Resources at the end of this chapter.

Maximizing Benefits from Cash on Hand

Let your money make money for you while you have it. Don't just let it sit in a noninterest-bearing checking account.

- If your balance is large enough, an interest-bearing checking account will make money for you.

- Avoid bank fees. Avoid banks with ATM charges. Keep a high enough monthly minimum balance to avoid monthly fees. If you have both your personal and business accounts at the same bank, arrange to use what's called "relationship banking"—that is, linked accounts, which allows you to save on fees and some minimum balance requirements if you have more than one account in the same bank.

- If your business volume is large enough, you can use cash management services provided by a bank. A lock box, for example, is a program in which you have your customers mail their payments to a box maintained by the bank. The box is located so that in most cases payment is received the next day, and it is immediately deposited by the bank to your account.

- Deposit surplus cash on hand in interest-bearing certificates and money-market funds.

- Invest excess cash. Arrange to have excess cash transferred to funds with a higher yield. Some banks will also automatically transfer money back if your accounts drops below a certain level.

Holding On to What You Have

Cash-flow problems arise because you need to spend money to make money and, of course, to live, while you're providing your services or products. To minimize your problems, you'll want your business to pay for itself as it goes. To do this, we recommend that whenever possible you

- arrange for thirty, sixty, or ninety days of interest-free credit from suppliers.
- use charge cards. They provide you with thirty to sixty days' free use of money. Of course, when you able to spend less by paying cash, you need to balance your cash-flow needs with the need to keep your costs down. Have a separate charge card for business use.
- rent or lease equipment rather than tying up your capital by owning it.
- make timely but not immediate payment of bills.
- keep costs down. Don't overstock on supplies.

If you have debt problems, the National Foundation of Consumer Credit located in Baltimore will refer you to a local credit counseling service. The First National Bank Center in San Clemente, California, offers a secured credit card to those anywhere in the United States who need to rebuild their credit. (See the Resources at the end of this chapter.)

Protect Yourself from Income Fluctuations

The most difficult time to manage your money is when there's too little to manage. There are several things you can do to protect yourself from the woes of feast or famine, peaks and valleys.

1. Keep a reserve of cash on hand.   Bruce Michels, president of Management Advisory Services Consulting Group, advises small businesses to have

---

Paying Bills to Maximize Your Cash Flow

Here's a simple but effective manual system developed by Ray Martin, president of Microcomputer Applications, Inc., of Austin, Texas:

1. Check the day's incoming bills and invoices for accuracy and discounts offered for quick payment.
2. Determine the best date to make payment of each bill so that you will neither be overdue nor early in making payment. Then write a check.
3. Place the check in its envelope; stamp and seal it.
4. Code the envelope in the lower right corner with the necessary mailing date. Allow three days for local delivery, seven days for cross-country mail.
5. File the envelopes in chronological order.
6. Each day, mail those bills earmarked for that date.

$2 of current assets on hand for every $1 of current expenses. Accountant Michael Russo says your cash cushion should depend on your own comfort zone. While some need a $10,000 reserve to feel secure, others require more. Still others need considerably less. Find your level of security and operate within it.

2. Market constantly. Set aside at least 20 percent of your time each week for marketing activities and do this all year long. Don't slack off your selling effort when cash flow is great. There is always a lag time between marketing efforts and marketing results, so keep selling every week.

3. Track your income and expenses. Project your expenses and anticipated income at the beginning of each month. Post all due dates. You'll find that establishing this habit will prove invaluable. You'll always know exactly where you stand and you'll be alerted when you need to take action either by deferring costs or accelerating your marketing effort. You'll also know the moment someone is late with payments.

4. Plan to make the most of slow times. Most businesses go through periods of time that are slower than others. For example, holiday seasons are great for party planners and gift-related businesses but not so good for business consultants or training professionals. Anticipate these periods and devise special marketing efforts to attract business during these periods. For example, private-practice consultant Gene Call, who teaches professionals how to market their services, finds holiday times are slow for him so he runs a year-end promotion. Anyone signing up for his January training program in December gets a juicy discount.

Word processor Evalyn McGraw finds Augusts are routinely slow so she builds up cash reserves in June and July and plans her vacation for August. Before she leaves, however, she sets her late-August marketing plan in motion so that when she comes back there will be business coming in.

5. Create various income sources. Another way Evalyn manages her cash flow is to offer several adjunct services. In addition to straight word processing she provides editing and indexing services. She also teaches university extension program writing courses at a local university. So if one area of her business is slow she can rely on other areas. She finds they are rarely all slow at once.

You'll notice, however, that Evalyn is not offering a variety of scattered services that dissipate her efforts or confuse the public about what business she's in. All these services are related and, in some cases, ancillaries to word processing.

6. Continually upgrade your skills and improve your business. Grow with your business. Don't get caught in the rut of offering the same services and products year in and year out. To spark sales add new lines, offer more advanced techniques. And you shouldn't wait for sales to wane. Every change you make in your business provides an opportunity for promotions and gives you a good excuse to contact present and past clients about what you're doing now.

7. Network, network, network. Make regular contact with colleagues, clients, and associates part of your ongoing weekly marketing. Participate in professional, trade, and civic organizations so you'll be abreast of new market trends and the latest breakthroughs; this will also help you generate referrals and find out who needs you right now. Don't overlook regular congenial contact with your competitors. They may be overloaded just when you're slumping. Offer to help them with business they can't handle on a subcontract basis. More and more independents are forming consortiums to take on large projects and refer work to members. Consider joining or forming a consortium of people you are comfortable working with.

8. Remember, you're in charge. Sometimes it may seem as though your cash flow has nothing whatsoever to do with your efforts. You may feel you are being tossed about at the whim of fluctuations in the economy, the seasons, or your market's fickle passions. In actuality, if you *take* charge, you'll *be* in charge. You aren't dependent on the wishes of a single boss who can fire you on a moment's notice. All your clients would have to fire you before you'd be out of business. You're ingenious, talented, and creative or you wouldn't be in business in the first place. There is always some way for you to serve others and thereby keep the cash flowing in. If you start feeling out of control, just focus on that reality.

Tips for Good Money Management

1. Keep business and personal finances separate. Have two bank accounts— one for business, the other for personal expenses. Have separate bank cards. Keep records and receipts for business and personal expenses separate.
2. Have one place where you keep all of your financial materials, records, equipment, and supplies.
3. Establish a time each day, week, month, and quarter to take care of needed financial transactions.
   - Banking transactions
   - Bill paying
   - Invoicing
   - Tallying monthly and quarterly summaries
   - Filing tax and other necessary reports
4. Establish the habit of filing expense and income receipts immediately after getting them.
5. Keep inventory records as you add to or take from your supply.

When to Get Help

With the tools and ideas suggested in this chapter, you can probably manage your own record keeping while your business is small. Depending on your experience and the size and nature of your business, however, you may want to get the advice of an accountant in setting up your system. Also, you will periodically want to evaluate how well your system is working.

Less expensive alternatives to CPAs are franchised "business counselors" from companies like General Business Services and Marcoin. They advise small businesspeople on a quarterly basis for much less money than the typical CPA charges. They help prepare and analyze financials and do tax planning and tax returns.

If your business expands or is already too large for this system, you will need to set up a more sophisticated system and get additional assistance. You can hire a full- or part-time bookkeeper or use a bookkeeping service. Finally, since many record-keeping tasks involve filing and sorting, you may be able to hire a full- or part-time secretary or file clerk whose duties would include various record-keeping tasks.

Here are some signs that it's time to go beyond a do-it-yourself system:

- When you would make more money by paying someone to keep your records than the money you save by doing it yourself.
- When you are operating under government or other contracts that require you to use a double-entry bookkeeping system.
- When you need to spend more than thirty minutes a day doing financial management tasks.

Even when you have help in keeping your records, you will need to be responsible for providing the receipts, reviewing and evaluating the records regularly, and making financial plans and projections for your business. So you will still need to establish daily, weekly, monthly, and quarterly routines for carrying out these tasks.

Chapter Digest

1. Having a workable financial record-keeping system will provide you with invaluable peace of mind. You will know exactly where you stand, be prepared for tax season, know when you need to take steps to increase your cash flow, be able to separate household and business matters, and be in a good position to plan for continued success.
2. Your financial record-keeping system should be simple and easy to use, have a fail-safe mechanism for catching up should you fall behind, be easy to expand, and do the job you need done.

3. There is a wide variety of paper and computerized systems available on the market to help you keep track of your money. Avoid selecting those which are scaled-down versions of complicated systems used by large companies. As a one- or two-person office, you will not have the time or expertise to keep up an elaborate system.

4. We recommend computerizing your financial management tasks as well as leaving an easy-to-follow paper trail. A simple accordian file for receipts by quarter can provide an excellent paper trail.

5. To help manage your cash flow, collect the money you're due at the time of service or as soon thereafter as possible. Get deposits and cash payment when possible. Take bank credit cards or bill promptly. Don't let overdue accounts add up. Act promptly. And remember you're in charge. You can act creatively to minimize income fluctuations.

6. To receive maximum benefit from the cash you have on hand, use an interest-bearing account or deposit surplus cash on hand in interest-bearing certificates and money-market funds.

7. To put the money you make in your business to work, arrange to get thirty, sixty, or ninety days of interest-free credit from your suppliers. Use charge cards and make timely payment on your bills.

8. To keep up with financial management, incorporate the majority of data entry and filing into your daily business routine. Then set aside thirty minutes a week to handle billing and make bank deposits. Set aside an additional fifteen minutes monthly and quarterly to balance your bank statement, sort and tally your income and expenses, and to do financial planning and projections.

9. When your business grows to the point where you are spending more than thirty minutes a day doing financial management tasks, it's time to consider getting additional help. You can hire a full- or part-time bookkeeper or use a computerized bookkeeping service.

Resources

Books

Basic Accounting for the Small Business. Clive G. Cornish. Blue Ridge Summit, PA: TAB Books, 1988.

How to Borrow Money from a Bank. Don H. Alexander. New York: Beaufort Books, 1984.

Small-Time Operator. Bernard Kamoroff & Steve Steinke. Laytonville, CA: Bell Springs, 1985.

Newsletters and Reports

NewsNet Action Letter, 945 Haverford Rd., Bryn Mawr, PA 19010.

Small Business Administration Booklets (see full citation under Chapter 3):
   The ABC's of Borrowing (#MA1.001)
   Business Loans from the SBA (ask for by title, no order no.)
   Credit and Collections (#MA 1.007)
   Financial Management: How to Make a Go of Your Business (#111W)

Internal Revenue Service (see full citation under Chapter 3):
   Recordkeeping for a Small Business (#583)

Secure Credit Cards

First National Bankcard Center. Financial Access Program, 946 Cable Amanecer, Suite M, San Clemente, CA 92672. (800) 552-8985.

Intermediary Companies (Independent Selling Organizations) Enabling Home-Based Business to Take Charge Cards

ACH Bancard Corporation. 100 N. Barranca Ave. Ste. 1070, West Covina, CA 91791. (818) 858-5711, and for California only, 1-800-273-8679.

Cardservice International. 21122 Erwin Street, Woodland Hills, CA 91367. 1-800-593-3500. (818) 593-3500

Cherry Payment Systems. 4099 William Penn Highway, Monroeville, PA 15146. (412) 858-1040

Data Capture Systems. 231 Quincy Street, Rapid City, SD 57701. (605) 341-6461

Gold Coast Bankcard Center. Ft. Lauderdale, FL. (305) 492-0303. 1-800-777-VISA

Harbridge Merchant Services. 681 Andersen Drive, 4th Floor, Building Six, Pittsburgh, PA 15220. (412) 937-1272

R.E. Mulhern Co., Inc. 1820 East Garry, Suite 213, Santa Ana, CA 92705. 1-800-245-2558

Teleflora Creditline. 12233 West Olympic Boulevard, Los Angeles, CA 90064. 1-800-325-4849 or (310) 526-5233.

US Merchant Services. 775 Park Avenue, Huntington, NY 11743. (516) 427-9700.

CHAPTER
FIFTEEN
■ ■

Managing Information:
Getting Rid of Clutter

One of the non-news events of the nineties is that we're being overwhelmed with information. Compare the amount of mail we receive with what our parents did; the size of the newspapers, the number of magazines, newsletters, even the number of media that bring information to us—cable TV, fax, audiotext, videotext, videotapes, and more. Chances are that if you're reading this book, you have at least one pile of unread or unfiled magazines, newspapers, or mail somewhere in your house. One of the symptoms of this paper avalanche is the question, "Now where did I put that?"

How often this frustrating question interrupts the flow of work! Not being able to find needed information is probably the single most common form of home-office inefficiency. And it's not a minor problem. Think of the missed opportunities when you can't find a business card you need, the lost hours spent searching for correspondence you should refer to, the embarrassing moments when you lose the address for a meeting you're already late for, or fail to return an important call because you can't remember where you wrote the phone number.

Even computer users suffer from this office malady. Forgetting what they named a file or on which disk or directory they put it is as aggravating as misplacing a memo or file folder.

So no matter how small your home-office operation, it's helpful to have a system for processing and organizing the array of information you need at your fingertips. You require a way to easily process your mail, handle phone messages, and store phone numbers, addresses, business cards, and mailing lists. You need a system for recording upcoming events and keeping track of subject matter of interest to you as well as key information relating your clients and projects. And sometimes you have to track this information in both paper and computer files. You also need a way to conveniently store reference materials you want to keep from magazines, books, and tapes.

Since you probably don't have anyone to delegate these administrative tasks to and you're undoubtedly operating in limited space, your system for managing these details needs to be simple, easy to use, and compact. An effective system will provide you with

1. a proper place for keeping the information you need
2. a regular and convenient time for putting the information where it belongs.
3. a familiar routine for organizing and using the information
4. materials that make storing and locating the information easy

In other words, with the proper system you will have a place for everything and will be able to find everything in its place when you need it. In this chapter, we describe a variety of such systems that you can set up and use with a minimum of time and energy. We also provide guidelines for what to keep, where to keep it, when to throw it away, and when to get help to keep everything in order.

A Filing System for Keeping Track of Paper

If you can't find your desk for all the piles of paper, but you have them stacked in descending order of importance, you have a filing system. This kind of system, however, cramps your space and makes finding anything that isn't on top a difficult proposition.

Remember that the primary purpose of a filing system is retrieval, not storage. If you won't use a piece of information again, there is no reason to file it. But if you will need it, first you'll have to find it. So your filing system should be designed to help you *find* information, not just provide you with a place to keep it. Even the walls can become part of your filing system, if they're set up to help you find what you need.

To work effectively, however, any filing system, whether on the walls or in filing cabinets, should group the many types of information you use into clear and simple categories that correspond to the various aspects of your work. The system should enable you to find the information you've filed in a minute or two. Also, it should be easy to weed out and keep current. Setting up the following seven kinds of files and using them as described should provide you with a system that meets these criteria.

Project Files

Create a separate file for every major project you're working on. For example, if you were writing an article on child abuse, you would create a file entitled "Child Abuse Article." In this file, you would put your query letters, content

Using the Walls as Information Organizers

You can turn your walls into calendars, project planners, and information organizers by using:

Blackboards or whiteboards. Columns and lines for permanent headings can be drawn with indelible markers, paint, or tape. Different colors of chalk or markers can be used to highlight different types of information.

Plexiglass panels, plate glass, or see-through plastic. Clear panels of these materials can be mounted on the wall and held in place by a wood molding. Use grease pencils, crayons, or felt-tip markers of various colors and wipe them off easily with a moist cloth.

Movie screens or clear white walls. Using an overhead projector, clear plastic transparencies, and felt-tip pens, you can easily project and work with information displayed on walls and screens.

Newsprint. Sheets of blank newsprint from pads or rolls can be used to outline material you're working on and can then be hung on the walls for easy reference.

Bulletin boards or cork squares. Information can be tacked or pinned on commercial bulletin boards.

Planning boards. Commercial planning boards are sold as wall units made of magnetic material that can be written on with felt-tip markers and wiped off. (See Figure 15-1.)

outline, notes, the contract made when you sold the article, records of interviews, and so forth.

File your Project Files in alphabetical order. On the inside cover of each file, record the pertinent information related to that project—the names, addresses, and telephone numbers of contact people, your deadlines, meeting dates, work schedule, and so on.

If the papers related to a project outgrow one file folder, separate them into additional folders (marked, for instance, "Interviews," "Drafts," "Correspondence") and place them in an accordian file labeled with the name of the project.

Client or Customer Files

If you provide a service, create a file for each of your clients or customers. As with project files, use the inside cover to record pertinent information you want to have readily available. File these folders in alphabetical order by company name or the last name of the individual.

Figure 15-1
Storing information

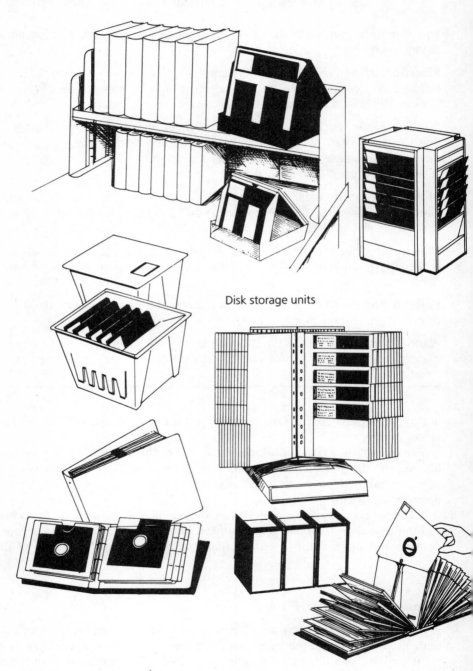

Disk storage units

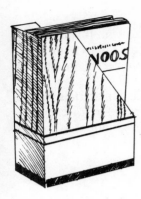

Magazine shelf organizers

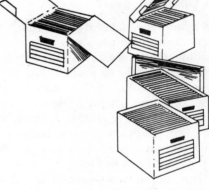

Cardboard storage files

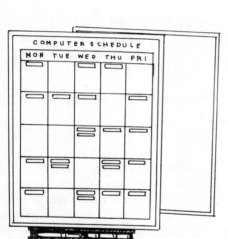

Wall-unit organizers

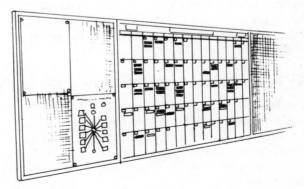

Subject Files

Create a file to keep information on subjects of interest to you. If you will be buying a copy machine in the future, for example, create a Subject File titled "Copiers" for articles you have clipped, brochures on different brands, or notes you've taken when talking with a salesperson.

When you have purchased the copier, clean out the file of materials you no longer need, and relabel it with the trade name of your copier, for example, "Canon Copier." Now you have a place for your instruction manual, warranty information, and supply order forms.

Keep these Subject Files in alphabetical order.

An Upcoming File

Use a file folder labeled "Upcoming" to keep announcements, confirmation letters, convention programs you plan to attend, and so forth. Before you file anything, mark the date of the event in the right-hand corner of the first page with a bright-colored marker. File the material in chronological order, with the nearest event at the front of the file.

By using an Upcoming File you avoid having to create a new file for each event you will be attending. Keeping the file in a desk drawer or somewhere near your phone makes information about upcoming events readily accessible. When you need to look up details or locations for these events, you can simply reach for your file.

Clean this file out periodically, discarding material on events that have passed.

A Tickler System

When you have more activities that need to be acted upon by a certain date than can be managed in an Upcoming File, you can set up a Tickler System.

To set up a Tickler System, label one manila file folder for each day of the month (1–31). Have one extra folder labeled "Next Month" or, for a more extensive system, one for each month of the year (January–December). Then, throughout the workday, you can put materials in the file for whatever day in the future you want to act upon them, whether they're checks to be mailed, letters to be answered, phone messages to be returned, or monthly reports to be filled out.

A Chronological Correspondence Notebook (Chron File)

Instead of creating a new file every time you send out a letter, use a three-ring standard notebook to file copies of miscellaneous correspondence. File the letters by date, with the most recent in the front of the notebook. If certain correspondence develops into a project or leads to a client, you can easily remove it from the Chron File at the time you create a Project or Client File on the matter.

Business-Card Files

There are a variety of filing systems for business cards, names, addresses, and phone numbers. We recommend using a system that enables you to file business cards and other names and addresses in one place. The system you select should be easy to update so you can add to, change, and remove names in alphabetical order. Here are several popular systems:

1. *Rolodex* **filing system.** This is the familiar system of cards on which names, addresses, and phone numbers are noted and attached to the center of a circular column so that you can flip to the one you're seeking. The uncovered versions are easier to use. Color-coated cards are available to easily identify certain clients, suppliers, or other key people. Adhesive dots can be placed on the upper right-hand corner of cards to highlight most frequently used or high-priority numbers.

2. **Metal business-card holders.** Business cards fit into a metal tray that is separated alphabetically. Keeping spare cards in the back of the file enables you to write out a name and address when you have no business card for a client or customer.

3. **Calling-card files.** In this system, business cards slip into soft plastic wallet-like inserts bound in a ten-by-fourteen-inch plastic notebook.

4. **Stapling cards to file folder jackets.** Instead of placing a business card into a filing system, you can staple it to the inside cover of a Project or Client File. This can be an efficient way to keep numbers or addresses you will only be using in conjunction with information in the file.

You may find, as we have, that using more than one of these systems will save time. We keep all client cards in a metal business-card file. These are organized alphabetically by name. We keep cards from our business suppliers and merchants such as printers, photographers, and plumbers in a calling-card file that is organized alphabetically by the service they provide. Names and addresses of the clients whom Sarah counsels are kept on the inside cover of her Client Files because the nature and date of every phone call needs to be recorded in the file.

Whatever combinations you work out for your filing system, follow these simple rules of efficient filing for it to be most effective.

Filing Rules of Thumb

1. **File each folder, card, or record in one, and only one, designated place.**

2. **"If a file is out, use it or lose it."** Every file or record should be in one of two places: in use on your desk or stored in its designated

space. Put files away immediately after use. Don't leave them lying around to get to later.

3. **File material immediately.** Whenever you have new information for your files, add it at the time you get it. Don't create "file piles." When you receive mail, read articles, or take phone notes that you want to save, file the pertinent material as soon as you finish reviewing it. If you come home from a meeting with business cards, notes, or flyers you want to keep, file them when you arrive—at the same time you store your receipts for any expenses you've incurred.

4. **Put the most recent materials in the front of the file.**

5. **Remove all paper clips before filing materials.** They fall off and get stuck inside the files. If papers belong together, staple them together.

6. **Don't overstuff files.** Keep three or four inches of extra space in file drawers so they will be easy to use and the files won't get damaged. When files get overly crowded, clear them of outdated material.

7. **Label all file folders.** Use a file name that is broad enough to cover all the materials you will want to put in the folder.

8. **To keep from misfiling your folders** when you return them, either remove the papers you need and leave the folder itself tilted up, or tilt up the file behind the one you remove, leaving the drawer open as a reminder to return the file.

9. **Separate "active" files from "storage" files.** Active files are those you use on a regular basis. They should be kept in an area near your workspace. Storage files are those you need to keep for legal or tax purposes, but which you no longer use. Keep these in cardboard file boxes in more remote storage areas. (See Figure 15–1.)

10. **When filing accumulates, catch up during "down times,"** while watching TV, or talking casually on the phone.

11. **Don't let file folders grow beyond three-quarters of an inch.** Finding a single paper in a thick file takes too long. Break large files into subfiles.

12. **Reduce legal and large documents to letter size for easier filing.**

Computerizing Your Information

Most home offices can benefit from computerizing many of their written communications. From correspondence to proposals, from invoices to newsletters and mailing lists, managing this paperwork can be done more quickly and efficiently with a computer. There are five basic types of software programs you should consider using to manage the information in your office: word processing, desktop publishing, database management, personal information managers, and pop-up programs.

Word Processing

Word processing is the most frequently used computer program in home offices for good reason. Paul Strassman, author of *Information Payoff*, has found that typing text on a word processor is 23 percent faster than it is on a typewriter. And *Scientific American* found that, besides being faster, word processing lowers the cost of producing documents by one-third over the cost of typing them.

Today, word processing allows you to do much more than type letters, proposals, reports, manuals, and manuscripts. Most word-processing programs come with capabilities to do jobs in minutes or hours that used to take days to accomplish. For example, the index for this book will be created in a matter of hours using the built-in indexing capability of our *WordStar* software, a task that might have taken someone many days to do in the past. Here are some additional capabilities word-processing programs enable you to do:

- Check your spelling, use a thesaurus and, with complementary programs like *Grammatik* or *Correct Grammar*, check your grammar.
- Get a word or character count, useful when you're writing articles or copy for directory listings that limit the number of words you can submit.
- Individualize form letters used for sales or collection, and personalize boilerplate text you created previously.
- Print out multiple originals.
- View and work on two or more documents on your screen at the same time and move items from document to document.
- Make, alphabetize, sort, and maintain all types of lists, including to-do lists and mailing lists.
- Address envelopes and mailing labels.
- Create tables of content and indexes, and organize footnotes.
- Do mathematical calculations inside documents.
- Preview pages as they will look when you print them out.
- Do automatic repagination.
- Use the desktop publishing features to create a newsletter incorporating illustrations and charts.
- Create handouts and overhead transparencies to increase the impact of your speeches and proposals.

If your work involves extensive writing, you'll want to get a versatile and sophisticated word-processing package. Good choices for an IBM-compatible computer are *WordPerfect, Microsoft Word, WordStar, XyWrite,* and *PC Write. Word-Perfect* is the best-selling word-processing program today, and is generally the first to incorporate new features. *WordPerfect* is also available in versions for Macintosh, Apple II, Atari, and Amiga. *Microsoft Word* offers superior typesetting and printing controls. After being bypassed for a while, the once-favorite *WordStar* has now largely caught up as a full-featured program and remains a favorite of touch typists. *XyWrite*, fast and flexible, is the choice of many professional writers. *PC Write* is a shareware product, which is available on-line. For a Macintosh, the leading programs are *Microsoft Word* and *MacWrite*.

If your work involves little more than basic business correspondence, you may feel well served by an integrated program like *Microsoft Works*, which combines word processing, spreadsheet, database management, graphics, and communications programs all into one package. A more sophisticated integrated program with an excellent word-processing capability is Ashton-Tate's *Framework*.

Desktop Publishing

Desktop publishing saves time and money by combining computers, software, and laser printers to design and produce professional-looking documents. Actually, desktop publishing is something of a misnomer. Except for a very small job that can be produced on a laser printer, you will still need a print shop to publish something in large numbers. The key to desktop publishing is powerful computer software that makes it possible to combine text and graphics on the same page and lay it out with the computer instead of pasting it up by hand or sending it out for pasteup. And it often only takes roughly the same time it takes to write the material, once you learn to use the software.

Aldus Corporation, creator of *Pagemaker* software, has identified 350 different types of documents people can create using desktop publishing, but the company reports that two-thirds of their customers use desktop publishing to produce newsletters. Other frequent users of desktop publishing in home offices are producing promotional materials like flyers and brochures, and designing manuals, proposals, reports, and forms for invoices and contracts.

Newsletters are an excellent tool for maintaining contact with customers and getting new ones. Roland Sutton, who operates a parking lot maintenance service in Conway, South Carolina, said the turning point in his business came when he began sending out a monthly newsletter. "I was ready to fold my business when I tried the first letter," he told us. "I had such a great response to it that I knew I had hit on a winning business-getter. Now I'm afraid not to send one out each month. I always get business from them."

The leading stand-alone desktop publishing programs for IBM-compatible computers are Xerox's *Ventura Publisher*, and *Pagemaker* by Aldus. But most home businesses are able to get their desktop publishing needs met with a less sophisticated but easier-to-use program like Timework's *Publish It*. Sophisticated word-processing programs, like *Ami Professional*, *Microsoft Word*, *WordPerfect*, and *WordStar*, include many desktop publishing features and may have all the capability you need. For Macintosh computers, *Pagemaker* and *Quark Express* are the leading programs.

Database Management

A database enables you to turn your computer into a filing cabinet, a *Rolodex* rotary card system, or a box of index cards. Using database management software you can enter any type of information into your computer and then call it up on your screen and review, update, or change it, and then print it out whenever you wish.

Increasingly, open-collar workers are keeping their vital information in computer databases instead of trying to keep up cumbersome and time-consuming paper files. We, for example, have a wide variety of mailing lists, survey results, and in-depth interviews stored in our databases. We find having vital information literally at our fingertips saves time and space. Here are some examples of what you can do with a computer database:

- Organize, store, and retrieve your notes
- Retrieve information on any subject in your files
- Do inventory control
- Budget your expenses
- Keep income-tax records
- Keep track of car maintenance
- Do job-costing
- Tailor individual sales presentations to prospective clients
- Keep sales and client contact memos
- Conduct sale analyses

Database management software can be the heart of an information-intensive home-based business. For example, songwriter Pamela Phillips-Oland uses a database to keep all her lyrics on file. Insurance agent Lewis Mann replaced stacks of index cards by creating a database with *Foxbase* software. Bill Vick, who operates a highly successful executive recruitment business, says his database, which he customized to his needs, is the "core of my business." A database is also the nucleus of Shell and Judy Norris's Class Reunions, Inc.

If information is the core of your business, you'll likely need a highly capable "relational database" like *Paradox, dBase,* or *Foxpro.* Relational databases enable you to update your entire database quickly and make extensive searches and comparisons among data. Simpler and easier to use electronic filing systems, or "flat databases," are completely adequate, however, to keep track of information like customer contacts and mailing lists. The leaders among these simpler programs are *Q&A, Re6ex,* and *PFS:File,* a shareware program. For the Macintosh, *Fourth Dimension* and *Re6ex* are well-regarded database programs.

Personal Information Managers

No single type of software is better suited for cutting clutter than personal information managers. With such programs, you can enter the valuable bits and pieces of information that contribute to clutter and get lost after being written on the backs of envelopes and business cards, stick-on notes, telephone message slips, or anything else that was handy when you got an idea or heard some item of information you wanted to keep.

A personal information management program enables you to locate, analyze, and cross-reference *words*. These words may be ideas, leads for future business, facts and quotes you want to have available for proposals and speeches, as well as business information such as inventory, sales, billings, and personnel records—any kind of information. The strength of this category of software is that, unlike database management software, many of these programs free you from the constraints of formatting information in specified ways using mandatory fields with fixed lengths. Instead, you can enter your information freely, in whatever format or length you choose.

Here are some of the best known of these programs: Conductor Software's *Act*, which is especially useful for sales work; Lotus's *Agenda*, which many people are using to organize their lives and work because of its strengths in managing time, retrieving information, and outlining; *askSam*, which is particularly good at retrieving unstructured information; *InfoSelect*, which is extremely flexible and easy to use and will fit in 6K of memory; Persoft's *IZE*, with which you can organize documents created with different types of programs in a way that enables you to retrieve related information; and *Notebook II*, which we use for interviewing and which is especially popular with people doing bibliographic research. Also falling within the category of personal information management software are outliners like *Grandview* and Brown Bag's *PC Outline*.

Pop-Up Programs

These handy programs are stored in your computer's memory and wait in the background to pop-up whenever you need them in whatever file or program you're working. And what a variety of work they do! For example, with pop-up programs, you can:

- Look up a name and phone number (instead of using your *Rolodex* or the Yellow Pages (e.g., *Hotline II*)
- Dial a phone number
- Use your computer as a calculator
- Schedule an appointment on your calendar or look one up
- Make charts and graphs (e.g., *Graph-in-the-Box*)
- Type an abbreviation and have the longer word or phrase entered automatically (e.g., *PRD+*)

- Locate files whose names you've forgotten by using a phrase or a few key words
- Sort your files by name, size, or date created
- View files while inside another program
- Provide menus replacing the A> or C> prompts on your screen
- Perform maintenance tasks like copying, deleting, and moving files more simply

Organizing Your Computer Files

1. **Create directories and/or disks with the same names as your paper files.** For example, if you have a Projects section in your file cabinet, create a corresponding Projects directory or disk. Keep your computer and paper records related to one another.
2. **Label files with the same names you use on your paper files** to help you find information more easily. To further help you identify the contents of files, use file manager programs to write and view file descriptions.
3. **Back up the contents of your hard disk on floppy disks** or some other storage medium, such as streaming tape or a Bernoulli Box, to avoid costly errors. Just in case of error, have a program like the *Norton Utilities* that will restore many mistakenly erased files.
4. **Erase unnecessary back-up files daily and purge inactive files monthly** to keep your disk uncluttered.
5. **Use file compression and archiving utilities** to expand the amount of space available on your disks. Phil Katz's *Zipware, LHARC* from Japan, and Vern Buerg's *ARC* utilities are either in the public domain or are considered shareware. *Stuffit* and *MacArc* are archiving programs for the Macintosh.
6. **Optimize your hard disk** by using software like the *Norton Utilities* to keep a hard disk operating at top speed.
7. **Use a utility that enables you to find your files,** no matter where they are on the disk by name or key words in case you have forgotten the name of a file or can't locate it.
8. **Use batch files** to do routine and repetitive tasks automatically.
9. **Use macro commands** to use a few keystrokes to perform complex and repetitive operations. Often a macro-making capability is included in software, or it can be obtained in a pop-up program like Borland's *Superkey*.
10. **Use disk organization programs** like *Norton Commander* or *XtreePro Gold* to simplify moving, deleting, copying, and renaming files.
11. **Keep disks you use frequently within arms' reach** of your computer. The cardboard holders that disks are packaged in can be used for storage and kept in desk drawers or on shelves. Special disk storage units, however, are available in multiple sizes, shapes, and designs.

- Change the time and date on files
- Control your printer for specialized tasks like printing envelopes, and selecting and loading fonts

These programs, which range in price from free to several hundred dollars, are technically called TSRs, for Terminate and Stay Resident, and are for computers that use DOS. The most widely used ones are *PC Tools Deluxe,* Borland's *Sidekick* and *SuperKey,* and Lotus's *Magellan.* Control Panel Devices (CDEVs) enable Macintosh users to customize their computers with additional capabilities, such as warning them of possible viruses in their computer systems or letting them bypass the mouse in favor of cursor-movement keys.

Storing Newsletters, Magazines, Books, and Tapes

The best system for storing newsletters, magazines, books, and tapes depends on how many you have. One or two tapes can be kept in a drawer. A few newsletters can be kept in a Subject File. A few books can be placed on a work table or credenza between book ends. But, like file folders, once you get more than a few of these items, they can begin to stack up. So here are some tips for keeping them in order:

Newsletters. Using a three-hole punch, file newsletters in standard-size ring binders, keeping the most recent ones in the front. Some newsletters come prepunched.

Magazines. Instead of stashing magazines in corners or under the bed, keep them in chronological order on bookshelves or in cabinets. For ease of access, standing them on end is preferable to stacking them. You can buy open-style magazine files to keep them standing upright. (See Figure 15–1.)

Books. Books can be kept on shelves in closets or cabinets or, more commonly, on bookshelves. Although there is a wide variety of styles to purchase, we made our first bookcase from three pieces of lumber and some bricks.

You can arrange books on shelves in alphabetical order either by subject or by author, but always place the most frequently used books on the shelves that are easiest to reach.

Tapes. Special plastic trays are available for storing your tapes, or they can be placed in shallow drawers, wood cabinets, or cardboard boxes. The biggest problem with storing tapes is that they are usually labeled on the front rather than on the spine, which makes locating the one you're looking for a time-consuming process. To avoid this problem, you can label them on the side yourself, with adhesive labels, and then organize them as you would books, in alphabetical order by subject or author.

A Daily Routine for Handling Mail

For most at-home workers, the mail brings the biggest influx of information into the home office each day. While some of it is vital business information, some may be personal or for other family members, and much is junk mail you would just as soon not receive. Whatever it is, you have to do something with the mail once it arrives at the door.

The first step is to designate one area where you process all mail, personal and business, incoming and outgoing. Often your desk is the best location. It's usually near both the phone and your files. Sometimes, as in our case, another location is more suitable. Our mail usually includes orders that need to be shipped out, so our Sierra Madre home had a long counter in the family room that we used for processing all of our mail.

Keep all the materials you need for handling both incoming and outgoing mail within arm's reach of the area you've selected. For example, we keep our mailing materials in the cabinets beneath the counter where we handle the mail. These are the materials we find it useful to have nearby:

Manila folders	Postage scale
Stamps	Postage affixer
Mailing labels	Packing material
Envelopes	Postcards
Letter opener	Wastebasket
Filing labels	Marking pens
Stapler	Tape

If it isn't convenient to have these materials near your workspace, you can keep them elsewhere in a drawer-organizer tray, and then bring out the tray when you're ready to deal with the mail.

Set aside about forty-five minutes each day to process the mail. Many people like to handle the mail immediately after it arrives. If your mail arrives at an odd time for you, however, like ours does (2:00 P.M), you may wish to handle it at a more suitable hour. Some people prefer to process the mail first thing in the morning, feeling it's a good way to get the day under way. Others like to do it during what they call the "after-lunch lull." Still others prefer to close the day with the mail.

Which part of the day you set aside for handling mail is less important than doing it at some regular time and not letting it pile up from one day to the next. Avoid the temptation to scatter different pieces of mail hither, thither, and yon. Keeping it in one place and doing it at one time each day will make it much easier to manage. One exception to this is people whose work keeps them out of town or out of the office most of the week. They may prefer to set aside an "administrative day" once a week for processing all mail and other paperwork.

Use the Sort/Act System

Whenever possible, follow the "handle it one time" principle of mail management. Using the system we're about to describe, you can handle every piece of mail once, and trash it or stash it in its proper place within forty-five minutes.

Open the mail, sort it into the following four action piles, and handle it in one of these ways:

1. Throw it away. The wastebasket is our best friend in sorting the mail. We usually throw away three-fourths of our mail, tossing out advertisements and announcements that aren't of interest. In fact, we don't even open mail we know will not be of interest to us.

2. Act on it. Whenever possible, take immediate action. Fill out forms, send any requested material, ship out orders, make out a needed check, call to make a reservation, read correspondence or short newsletters. If the necessary action will take more than a few minutes, however, put the mail into a pile to be filed in the proper place for handling at a later time.

3. Refer it to others. Sort out mail for other family members or employees who are to handle it. Designate some place where this mail will be put on a regular basis. We put our son's mail on the ledge by the stairway to his room, for example.

4. File it. Any piece of mail you have not thrown out should be placed in its proper location by the end of the forty-five-minute period. It should be in one of three places:

- **In the appropriate file.** Put materials that require no further action in the Subject, Client, Chron, or Project files discussed earlier in this chapter. Materials that need further action should be placed in the Upcoming, Project, or Tickler files and flagged for when they need attention. If you wish, you can take this time to add these items to your daily planner or "Thought of Everything?" list (see Chapter 13).

- **In an area set aside for reading material.** Find a place to put magazines, newsletters, and journals you want to read. Places people frequently use include a bookshelf, a nightstand, or a magazine rack in the TV room or bathroom.

- **In your financial record-keeping system** (see Chapter 14).

Some people prefer to create a special place or file for personal mail they want to handle after business hours. We often put our personal mail on the nightstand, for example, since we prefer to read and write personal letters at our leisure.

If you have more mail than you can finish filing in forty-five minutes, you can set up a tray or box on top of your filing cabinet for materials to be filed later. Generally speaking, we don't recommend this, because it's too easy for this kind of "file pile" to get so backed up that it's out of control.

Unless you have someone else coming in to do it, leftover filing is too often something that just never gets done. Then you're always having to scramble through the "file pile" to find missing information and may even overlook vital data that's become buried in the pile.

Managing Phone Messages

Set up an area on or near your desk where you handle phone calls. If you're right-handed, place your phone on the left of your workspace. This will leave your right hand free for writing while you're talking on the phone. Keep the following materials within arm's reach in your phone area:

- **A telephone message pad for writing down messages.** The pink tear-off pads we're all so familiar with are designed for multi-employee offices in which a secretary takes messages for several people. There is no place or need for "pink slips" in the home office.

    Instead, we recommend a spiral-bound steno pad for recording phone notes. Using a steno pad, you won't have hundreds of little slips cluttering the desk and forever getting misplaced. You will always know exactly where all your messages are. Who called, when they called, who needs calling back, their phone numbers, directions to where you are meeting them—this will always be easy to find. In short, all the information you receive over the phone will be in one place.

    Put the date you begin using a particular pad on the front cover of the pad. When it is full, record the date of the last day's messages on the cover also. The pad can then be stored as a permanent record.

    Be sure to write the date beside the messages as you take them each day.

- **Stick-on notes** for writing down information you want to take with you or put into a Tickler File. Avoid the temptation, however, of replacing your time-planning system with little pieces of paper hanging all over your home and office. Besides creating a mess, they're too easy to overlook on the day you most need to see them.

- **Pen and pencil with eraser.** Although this seems obvious, how many times do you end up saying, "Just a minute, let me find a pen"? We've found the only solution to this is to have a pen that does not leave the phone area. There are pens you can attach to your phone with a little cord, special desk pens with a stand, and, of course, pen and pencil holders you can use next to your phone.

- **Business cards, addresses, and phone numbers.** Keep whatever filing system you have selected for storing this information near your phone for easy access.

Calls, of course, can come at any time of day or night, but some people find it easier to manage an office at home if they set aside a time of day for placing and returning phone calls. Often they work alone and don't want the phone

---

Home Office Organizing Shortcuts

1. Use a letter opener.
2. Have a large wastebasket near the area where you process your mail.
3. Use memory-resident calculators on your computer so you can make quick calculations no matter what files you're working on.
4. Use a typewriter instead of your computer for filling out forms and simple response-postcards.
5. If you send out lots of mail each day, use a ceramic wheel or automatic stamp applicator.
6. Use card extenders to turn business cards instantly into *Rolodex* cards.

---

to infringe on their business at hand or, for that matter, on their personal lives.

Writer Kitty Freidman, for example, finds that phone calls disrupt her train of thought, so she places the calls she needs to make first thing in the morning before she starts writing. Then she turns on the answering machine and writes until the end of the day when she takes the messages off the machine and returns her calls.

You are more likely to reach people if you call before 9:00 A.M. meetings, at 11:45 A.M. before people leave for lunch, and in the late afternoon, between 4:00 P.M. and 5:00 P.M.

When working on the phone, record notes and messages on your telephone answering pad. At the end of a phone call, you may want to set up a Project File or Client File relating to the call. Use your notes on the pad to record the necessary information on the inside front cover of the file.

If you need to follow up on a call, use the information on the telephone message pad to write a note to yourself, and stick it on the inside cover of your Upcoming or Tickler File.

What to Keep and What to Throw Away

Deciding whether to keep a piece of paper, a file, a letter, or an announcement can consume undue time and energy. Some people have a tendency to keep everything, "to be on the safe side." Others, not wanting to bother with the decision, throw things away too hastily. We've found the following guidelines useful in making the right decision.

1. **Keep materials you will use in relation to current projects or clients.** When a project is finished or a client or customer is no longer active, cull the file of extraneous material and retire the file to storage.

2. **Review files at least once a year.** If you haven't used a file in the last year, ask yourself whether you have a good reason to keep it.

3. **Keep materials related to work you still do,** if reconstructing them would require a lot of effort. If you currently have no use for the materials but expect you could use portions of them in future work, retire the materials to storage files.

4. **Keep irreplaceable materials.** If they are related to work you still do, materials that are not available elsewhere should be retained if reconstructing them would be difficult, expensive, or time-consuming.

5. **Some documents should be kept permanently.** Keep legal documents, warranties for the life of a product, securities, licenses, capital assets, insurance policies, and so forth.

6. **Keep tax records for six years after you've filed the return.** Records supporting a return filed April 16, 1990 should be kept until April 16, 1996. After filing your return each year, you can retire the material to storage files, discarding materials over six years old. Real-estate records and those relating to stocks must be stored indefinitely since records must be kept "as long as they are important for any tax law." Keep the tax returns themselves permanently.

7. **When in doubt** about keeping something, ask yourself these questions:
   - What will I use it for?
   - When will I need it?
   - Under what circumstances might I need it?
   - What would happen if I didn't have it?
   - Would I pay to rent extra space to store it?

Generally, we agree with what Stephanie Winston says in her book *Getting Organized*: If you haven't used something in the past year, and it has no sentimental or monetary value, but "it might come in handy someday"—then toss it!

When You Need Someone to Help

As your work expands, the first person you hire will probably be someone to help with your information management tasks. When is the right time to get this help?

One general answer we frequently hear is, "As soon as you can afford it." Certainly, having someone else to take over many of those office housekeeping tasks makes life easier and frees you for more creative and profitable uses of your time.

A more direct answer to the question, however, is to think about getting help when you are spending more than forty-five minutes a day processing information. Finally, if you find that you're simply not able to keep your records up to date, investing in the expense of getting someone to help may be the best use of your resources.

Once you do get help, we recommend that you set up a system you can use yourself when you need to, and evaluate its effectiveness regularly. Someone else can handle the files, the mail, and the phone calls, but ultimately you need to be able to step in at any time and handle these things efficiently, because information is the lifeblood of any office.

Chapter Digest

1. You should be able to avoid clutter and keep your office organized if you do four things: establish a proper place for keeping the information you need; set aside a regular time for putting the information where it belongs; create a familiar routine for organizing and using the information; and have the proper materials for storing and locating the information easily.

2. You should be able to manage your paper flow if you create files for each of your projects, clients, and subject areas, and one for upcoming events.

3. A simple tickler system will alert you to when you need to take action on various files.

4. A file should be in one of two places: in use or filed in the appropriate place.

5. In today's home office, computerizing the information that goes through your office will save time and space and make access to it easier. Consider using these four software programs: word processing, desktop publishing, database management, and pop-up programs.

6. Establish a daily "sort and act" routine for responding to your mail which enables you to handle a piece of mail only once. Set up one place in your home office where you handle all mail and keep all relevant materials within arm's reach of this area.

7. Use a steno pad for keeping all phone messages. Record messages chronologically. Use stick-on notes when you need to carry information to other locations.

8. Find compact, convenient, high-quality storage units for newsletters, magazines, books, tapes, and computer software. Don't let these resources lie around haphazardly in stacks.

9. When you are spending more than forty-five minutes a day processing and managing information, you should seriously consider getting part-time or full-time administrative help.

Resources

Getting Organized. See full citation under Chapter 7.

Information Anxiety. Richard Saul Wurman. New York: Bantam, 1990.

The Instant Business Forms Book. Roger Pring. New York: John Wiley & Sons, 1987.

Mastering the Information Age. Michael McCarthy. Los Angeles: Jeremy P. Tarcher, Inc., 1990.

Organized to Be Your Best. Susan Silver. See full citation under Chapter 7.

Records Control and Storage Handbook, with Retention Schedules. Order from Bankers Box, 2607 N. 25th Ave., Fankling Park, IL 60131.

PART 5

....

Managing Yourself and Others

CHAPTER

SIXTEEN

■■■■■■■■■■■■■■■■■■■■■■

Avoiding Loneliness

"Isolated? Me? Impossible!" says Nick Sullivan, a senior editor working from home via modem for *Home Office Computing* magazine. "When I work I work. When I socialize I socialize. Whether I work at home or at the office, it doesn't make much difference. I couldn't isolate myself if I tried. I live in the world."

This expresses the amazement most successful open-collar workers experience when they are asked, as they frequently are, don't you feel isolated? Frankly, most people who work from home don't feel isolated once their business or job at home is under way and functioning. Their world is full of clients, customers, neighbors, family, friends, suppliers, business associates, and colleagues.

Although sometimes there's an adjustment period during which you feel cut off from former office mates, working from home does not mean you will be isolated and lonely unless you are a hermit. It does mean you have to be active and take initiative to be involved in the world around you. Should you begin to feel isolated and lonely, here are three steps to getting yourself back in the swing of things again.

Three Steps to Getting Back into the Action

1. Admit you're missing some type of contact. Admitting you're feeling isolated seems to be the first step to avoiding it. Since people usually start working from home for some important reason, sometimes they don't like to consider that it might not be satisfying to them. Bookkeeper Paulene Smith, for example, left her job because she wanted to be at home with her new baby. "I wanted everything to go well and certainly didn't want to think I'd made the wrong decision. But finally I had to admit to myself I really did miss the old gang at the office. I had to acknowledge that working on my own involved some special problems I hadn't expected."

2. Recognize what you're missing. After admitting you're missing something, the next step in avoiding isolation is recognizing exactly what you miss. Isolation means different things to different people. For free-lance programmer George Broady, not having people around wasn't the problem. "It isn't really people I miss. I work better by myself. What I miss is not knowing what's going on. I don't like feeling out of it."

Marriage and family counselor Sharry Cox agrees that "isolation" means more than being alone. "I'm with clients all day, so it took me a while to figure out that it wasn't really contact with people I was missing. I get plenty of that. I miss seeing a friendly face that understands the challenges of the work I'm doing."

In a *Success* magazine article, Robert S. Wieder described how office gossip and the grapevine make a variety of subtle but important contributions to working happily and effectively. It isn't always easy to recognize these intangible but vital benefits of being part of an office culture. Here's a list of things you may miss.

- The inside information. The vital tips. The scuttlebutt about what's going on.
- Esprit de corps. Exciting news or a lighthearted conversation giving you the feeling of being part of a group.
- Some helpful social pressure, a little incentive, to keep your mind on business and your hands off the potato chips.
- Some help or moral support in the midst of an emergency.
- Immediate feedback on your work.
- A way to test out a new idea.
- A pat on the shoulder, an understanding look, a word of encouragement.
- Someone to complain to about how awful things are or brag to about a job well done.
- A candid evaluation of how you're doing or a warning when you're about to make a mistake.
- A chance to build self-confidence in your work by telling someone about what you're planning.
- The sense of belonging that comes from being part of an organization.
- The sense of importance that comes from having a formal title and a needed role in the organization.

3. Take action to get involved in activities that provide what you're missing. Once you know which benefits you're missing, you can set about finding the best way to replace them. A next-door neighbor can provide a friendly "hello" and possibly even a good ear for the joys and tribulations of your day. But only a respected colleague can give you feedback on what you're doing, share news in the field, or recognize and praise a brilliant effort.

You'll have to take action to replace the particular elements of office interaction you're missing. To stay in touch, you'll have to take the time and invest the energy to set up opportunities for the interchanges you miss. Sharry Cox expresses what so many people who work at home discover: "Unless I work at it, I get out of touch with what's going on in my field. I start missing opportunities, learning the hard way what I could easily learn from someone else. Unless I make the effort myself, unless I dial a phone number or drive to a meeting, I lose contact with the people I've known."

In other words, whatever you're missing from contact at the office, chances are *it* won't find *you*. You'll have to find or create it yourself. Here are steps you can take to create the interaction you need.

Nine Ways to Keep in Contact with Peers and Colleagues

1. Join and participate regularly in community organizations and professional, technical, or trade associations. Volunteer for a committee position or run for office, make presentations, attend local, state, and national conferences.

When sales executive Ray Carlton left a position of fifteen years to start his own sales-training organization, he found he missed contact with colleagues. His solution was to join three professional organizations: the American Society for Training and Development, the Sales and Management Executives International, and the National Speakers' Association.

He became active at local and national levels. "The professionals I meet in these organizations are all doing what I do. We share the same interests and face the same problems. I not only get some business, but, more important, I keep abreast of the latest developments in the field and feel like I'm contributing to my profession."

2. Read and listen. Specialty publications now number in the thousands and serve needs in almost every area of interest. Newsletters, professional and trade journals, and magazines spur creative ideas and keep you aware of what's happening. Audiocassette tapes are now available from many sources on almost any subject. You can even subscribe to a tape library program. Two such programs are included in the Resource List at the end of this chapter. Workshops and conferences frequently come in tape format now too. If your work involves driving, listening to these kinds of tapes is a great way to make the best use of your time.

3. Attend workshops, seminars, and courses in your field, or explore new and related fields. Once you've attended a few of these programs, you will be on mailing lists for many others and receive announcements of the workshops in your area of interest. Begin by contacting the continuing education department at your local college or university as well as your professional, technical, or trade association for workshops they may be sponsoring. Also, look through specialty or trade newsletters and magazines for workshops advertised in your area of interest.

4. Use the telephone. Stay in touch by phone with the people you've known. Call to say "hello," to get an opinion or reaction, or just to share some news. People are flattered when you think of them and enjoy being consulted. Use phone contact to discover what others are doing and when or where you might get together.

Call or write the interesting people you hear or read about. If you want contact with them, ask how you can get involved in what they're doing. We have met several of our most valued colleagues because they took the time to call us after reading about something we had done. We've met other important colleagues because we called when we read about them.

5. Take an electronic coffee break. If you don't have a computer, the ability it gives you to keep in touch with others easily is a good reason for getting one. Asking a colleague a question, sharing a victory, or commiserating about a disappointment isn't a matter of walking to the next office, but it's easier than driving somewhere in your car. It's as easy as using your computer to reach out and be in touch with other people who work from home, not only all over the United States and Canada but increasingly in Europe, Asia, and South America. Using communications software and a modem, people are using on-line services, such as CompuServe, Prodigy, and Genie as well as local and company-maintained bulletin-board systems to relate to other people.

Commercial artist Diane Wessling Blake, vice-president of MicroGraphic Images, stays in touch with fourteen other home-based employees in the organization through a bulletin-board system operated from the home of the company's president.

"Everyone in our company works from home. It's ideal for me because I've always worked better alone, but I stay in touch with people by going out to teach classes and consult. Inside the company, we never feel isolated because with the bulletin-board system we can contact others whenever we need to."

Visitors to the Working from Home Forum we started in 1983 on the CompuServe Information Service can get involved in three different activities:

- A bulletin board that serves as a message center through which people converse.
- Libraries of information and software for specific businesses, such as desktop publishing, information brokering, mail order, and word processing, as well as on general matters such as telecommuting, accounting, taxes, legal issues, and office management.
- "Electronic conference rooms" in which you can communicate in real time with other people, attend meetings, or just take an electronic coffee break to chat with someone else. Recently, private investigators have been meeting on a weekly basis.

Here's what some of the members of the Working from Home Forum say about how computer networking has affected their lives:

Ray Jassin, who operates a service managing law libraries in the New York area said, "I can't say enough about how much I've gotten out of both the serious discussions and the fooling around that we do. I've made new friends."

Linda Stern, a writer in North Carolina: "I've gotten very specific advice—such as whether and what kind of home copier to buy—and more general career guidance as well. I also get inspiration—there are a lot of energetic, interesting people hanging around out there."

David Palmer of Tucson: "Obviously lots of writers (I'm one too) use CompuServe and the Working from Home Forum as an information resource and a national networking system. A less obvious, but perhaps more valuable use is as a sort of social sanity check. When deadline pressure mounts and nothing wants to come together right, I find that I can 'hide' on CompuServe for a while and relieve some of the pressure. Browsing the messages and maybe helping somebody else solve a problem can be great therapy for someone who has spent too many hours in 'work mode' and not enough in 'wander mode.'"

What you'll discover on-line is a shrewd realism that's based on the experiences of people who are making it on their own each and every day, solving problems like getting health insurance or merchant accounts from Master-Card and VISA or coming up with ideas for projecting a professional image. Expertise in countless areas is only moments away. Just how specialized the help can be is illustrated by one request we feared might go unanswered. Someone had left a message asking about how he could get information for a client on *Pursung* horses. But within hours, an answer awaited him. Every day people reach out to share their moments of joy as well. Be it celebrating the birth of a child or closing a big contract, those in need receive support that would do any businessperson proud.

To participate in the Working from Home Forum, join CompuServe by purchasing a starter kit from a book or computer store. There are no dues for joining the forum. The only cost you incur is for your connect-time to CompuServe. Once you log on to CompuServe, enter GO WORK at any prompt.

6. Schedule breakfast, lunch, or dinner meetings with peers. Even though this may mean breaking up your workday, set a goal to meet regularly with peers you want to stay in touch with. These business meetings are 80 percent tax deductible, but to personalize the meal and save money, you may want to host your colleagues at home.

7. Invite others to visit your home office and arrange to visit their offices. You can invite colleagues over to see a new piece of equipment, to sit in on some work, or to talk over a new idea.

When Jane Minogue, a telecommuting technical writer for CompuCorp, found that telephone contact didn't provide enough feedback and interaction, she invited several other telecommuting writers to come over occasionally so they could discuss projects and share ideas. "We've really enjoyed these meetings. They've helped a lot," she says.

Whenever you're doing something unusual or interesting in your field, invite a group of peers to come over and have a look. Get together informally afterward to share reactions. If you hear of someone doing something that interests you, ask if you can go see it in action.

8. Set up a networking group to meet with on a regular basis. Networking groups are groups of people who meet because of a common interest. A network can be a study group where you share ideas, a "leads" group where you trade referrals and business contacts, or a support group where you share horror and success stories and get moral support. Author and publisher Peggy Glenn tells the interesting tale of how she created a network for herself when she began her first home business, a typing service:

"Although I wanted to work by myself, when I began typing at home, I did run up against feeling isolated. There was nobody to turn to when I was having a really bad day, nobody to say, 'Come on, let's go have some coffee.' I was two weeks into my business and one of my customers sent me roses! Who was I going to tell? My husband was at work. My kids were at school. None of my neighbors were home. There was nobody to talk to.

"So I got brave and called a few other people who also ran typing businesses at home and invited them to lunch, dutch treat. Six or seven of them came, and right then and there was the birth of what has become a great network.

"We support one another. We help with overload. There is somebody to call on a bad day, somebody to call on a good day, somebody you can learn from if you've just received a job that is something you've never done, somebody to refer others to if you don't want to take the job."

When we moved to the Los Angeles area and first set up our home business, we felt isolated in such a large metropolis. But we felt certain there were lots of interesting people nearby, who for some reason we weren't getting to know. So we decided to start a Friday night Community Network. Every second Friday night of the month we hosted an open house potluck dinner. We invited everyone we met whom we thought we'd like to know better—our neighbors, our suppliers, and so forth. We asked them to come, bring a dish and a drink—and their friends.

It worked! Each month about twenty people came to eat and talk. Midway through the evening, we had people introduce themselves, explain what they did, and the type of contacts they wanted to make.

Through this network, we made both business contacts and new friendships with people who work at home. We've met a potter, a cartoonist, a word processor, a manufacturer of silk hats, a typesetter, and many more. The people who came also made valuable contacts and friendships. Realizing how much they miss the stimulation of working in a clinic, for example, several health practitioners who work alone at home met at one of our meetings and formed HealthNet, a network for health professionals in private practice.

There are a number of formal networking groups with chapters throughout the United States. You'll find some of them listed in the Resource List at the end of this chapter. If these groups do not have a chapter in your community, you may be able to set one up. For example, business consultant Ivan Misner founded The Network so he could be in touch with other independent businesspeople who could refer business to one another. From that first chapter he now has over one hundred chapters over the county. If there isn't a Network chapter in your location, Ivan will help you begin one and it can be a sideline business for you.

9. Affiliate or form other joint business relationships. Drawing on the contacts you make, set up joint projects with people in your field. Think of ways you can collaborate with them. Do a program together. Write an article. Share the workload.

Two human resource development consultants we know, for example, have an interest in future trends in their field, so they've developed a program they offer several times a year at professional conferences. They've also written joint articles on future trends for professional journals.

We've known several artists who regularly share a booth at art fairs. Two other home-based entrepreneurs, Michelle Whitman of High Tech Humor and Debbie Grosshandler of Bit's and P.C.'s, were able to launch their businesses by jointly renting a booth at an important trade show. These joint ventures not only keep costs down but also provide some much needed moral support and involvement with others for those who are working alone.

Formal partnerships can provide similar benefits. Many husbands and wives, such as ourselves, find that working at home together prevents them from having problems with isolation. Sue Rugge, founder of Information on Demand, credits an early partnership with Georgia Finnigan for the initial success of her business. "Although I enjoyed being president and hundred-percent owner of my company, I doubt if I ever would have made it if I hadn't started as a partnership."

Programmer Lucy Ewell and psychologist Elizabeth Scott came together to do what they couldn't have done alone, and started a software firm to develop computer games for girls. Barbara Elman began her word-processing service with a partner. She says of her initial partner, "He gave me the idea and the confidence that I could do it."

In many ways, a business partnership is like a marriage. You may spend more time with a partner than you do with your spouse. Unfortunately, the divorce rate among partners is even higher than among married couples. So pick a business partner with the same care you would take to pick a mate.

Short of a full-fledged partnership is the buddy system, or what Carol Hyatt calls a "planned partnership," in which you and your informal partner agree to meet at least once a week to help each other achieve your goals.

In her book *The Woman's Selling Game,* Hyatt describes how the buddy system can work:

> The partner you select can be a friend or not, and preferably should come from the same area of expertise as yours so you can understand each other's problems and provide useful mutual assistance. He or she should be someone whose judgement you respect and who respects yours, so there will be productive interplay. The two of you should contract to meet formally and at regular intervals.
>
> Your first meeting may be to define your goals and discuss their reality, with subsequent meetings devoted to reviewing your progress toward these goals. When you miss the fact that you've strayed from your purpose, been vague about strategy or laissez faire about precious time, it's your partner's job to spot what's happening and give you the feedback and constructive advice by which you can work through what you want. You, of course, will do the same in return.

Although planning and participating in such activities does cost valuable time and money, they are worthwhile investments in yourself and your work. Besides preventing the problems of burnout and isolation, they also keep you fresh and competitive within today's ever-changing marketplace.

Networking to Make New Contacts

Establishing relationships, meeting people in a crowd, approaching business contacts you've never met before—these are all important skills for people working on their own.

Networking to make contact quickly and easily with people you don't know involves more than the customary "Hello-how-are-you?" handshake and exchange of business cards. Whether you're meeting people at a cocktail party or through a computer terminal, networking involves making contact with them in ways that enable you to assist one another in achieving your goals.

Here are several tips for becoming a master networker.

First, step into the role of host. Adele Scheele, author of *Skills for Success,* suggests that successful networkers approach life as a "host" instead of as a "guest." Guests wait to be introduced. They feel ill at ease until someone makes them feel welcome. Hosts, on the other hand, assume responsibility for making sure everyone knows who everyone else is and for helping people feel welcome and at ease.

Second, tell everyone you meet who you are, what you're doing, and what you want to do. As consultant William Slavin has discovered, "I never know who my next client might be, so I treat everyone as a prospective client." Likewise, you never know who might be a future resource, friend, or colleague.

Third, make yourself and what you are seeking clear. Too frequently people introduce themselves like this:

"Hello, I'm Ralph Carnes. I'm the senior technical writer for Micro-Productions."

After hearing this kind of introduction, do you know enough about what Ralph does to engage in a conversation? Do you have any idea how you might be able to work with him? It's easy to spend a whole evening introducing yourself this way and wondering why you aren't making any valuable contacts.

But what if Ralph introduced himself this way:

"Hello, I'm Ralph Carnes. I work for MicroProductions, writing instructions for how to use the business software they produce for personal computers. Instead of driving to the company every day, I've just started working from my home. I enjoy it but I'm hoping to meet other people around this area who are interested in computers."

This type of introduction helps people know whether you share common interests and whether you can be of help to one another. Introducing yourself this way is a matter of putting together two needs: what people should know to understand what you do, and what contacts you want to make.

Fourth, be interested in other people. The more you listen to what others are saying and ask questions about their lives and their work, the better you will know how you could be valuable contacts for one another.

Fifth, offer to give people the very thing you want. If you're looking for someone to help with your office overload on occasion, offer to provide backup for them. If you're seeking someone to share a booth with you, offer to share one with those you meet.

Finally, plan a follow-up meeting with people you become acquainted with. When you discover others who share a mutual interest, exchange business cards. Write notes on the back of their cards about where you met them and what your joint interests are. Don't wait for them to call you. Make follow-up calls yourself and propose getting together in person to find out more about what they do.

In summary, staying in touch with others is as important to people working from home as it is for the regular office worker. At the office, it takes relatively little time and energy. For those of us who work at home, it's something we have to plan for and work at throughout our careers. Yes, it does take concentrated effort to stay in contact, but there are ways to do it. You just have to use them.

Chapter Digest

1. Most people who work from home don't feel isolated once their business or job at home is under way. The world is full of clients, customers, neighbors, family, friends, suppliers, business associates, and colleagues.

2. Should you feel isolated when moving your work home, you can get back in the action by first admitting you're missing some type of contact,

recognizing just what you're missing, and then taking assertive action to get involved in activities that provide the missing contact.

3. Social contacts on the job make a wide variety of subtle but important contributions to working happily. You may see many people in the course of a day but still miss such contacts as having access to the inside information of the grapevine or a chance to complain to someone who understands. Once you know just what type of contact you're missing, you can use a variety of means to meet people who can provide it.

4. To stay in touch, participate in organizations, schedule meetings with peers, join or form a networking group, take an electronic coffee break on a computer network, pick up the phone and call a colleague, engage in joint ventures. Be active. Participate and you won't feel lonely.

5. Make new contacts regularly by being interested in others, finding out how you can help them, and staying in touch.

Resources

Books

Is Your Net-Working? How to Receive Everything You Want by Giving to Everyone You Know. Ann Boe. New York: John Wiley & Sons, 1989. Available through Career Network, 435 S. Sierra, Ste. 116, Solana Beach, CA 92075.

Skills for Success. Adele M. Scheele (see full citation under Chapter 3).

Networking Groups

Leads Club. P.O. Box 24, Carlsbad, CA 92008; (619) 434-3761.

National Association of Women Business Owners. 600 S. Federal St., #400, Chicago, IL 60605; (312) 922-0465.

The Network. 1341 Ancona Dr., La Verne, CA 91750; (800) 825-8286.

Directories

Encyclopedia of Associations. Detroit: Gale Research Company (see full citation under Chapter 3).

Sources of Audiotape Programs

Nightingale Conant Audiocassette Library. The Human Resources Company, 7300 N. Lehigh Ave., Chicago, IL 60648; (800) 323-5552. Call or write for a catalog.

Personal Progress Library. A membership club that enables members to rent and turn a wide selection of business and personal development tapes. 19310 Vanowen St., Reseda, CA 91335; (818) 996-0352.

Success Motivation Cassettes. P.O. Box 2510, Waco, TX 76702

On-line Information

Working from Home Forum on CompuServe Information Service, 5000 Arlington Centre Blvd., P.O. Box 20212, Columbus, OH 43220.

CHAPTER
SEVENTEEN
■■■■■■■■■■■■■■■■■■■■■

Staying Out of the Refrigerator and
Away from Other Temptations

At first, working at home can seem like Paradise Island. Life's greatest pleasures are at your fingertips. You can literally eat, drink, and be merry at will. Your refrigerator and kitchen cabinets are only steps away. Cocktails are there for your making. The bed is there for your taking.

You have the freedom to eat your favorite foods whenever you're hungry, to have sex in the afternoon, to share a beer with a neighbor at a moment's notice, or to watch a favorite midday TV show.

Like tourists on a holiday, many people working from home start out living it up, indulging in whatever they want, but by the end of a few weeks, they're a little tired of it all. Then they set up routines, time schedules, and effective boundaries to keep their pleasures in bounds.

Sometimes, however, without the structure of a separate office, even experienced open-collar workers indulge to excess. According to them, the enjoyable fantasy of sipping wine and munching culinary delights while working by the pool can become the ugly reality of unwanted pounds and foggy-headed afternoons. In fact, one question we're sometimes asked is "How do you stay out of the refrigerator?" Some people do find this a problem, and when they do, we hear complaints like these:

"I've gained thirty pounds in the six months I've been working at home."

"When I have to work late into the night to get a big order out, I can eat two bags of potato chips without even knowing it."

"I'm having my 'afternoon' drink earlier and earlier in the day."

"A beer with lunch can become a six-pack by dinner."

"Our last baby wasn't planned. She came along about nine months after I began working at home."

In this chapter we will talk about what happens when excesses get out of control and what you can do to prevent such a situation. We will not talk, however, about chronic eating disorders or drug or alcohol addiction. Conceivably someone could engage in and conceal serious addiction more easily at home, but any such problems are beyond the scope of this chapter and must be solved by seeking professional help.

Avoiding Excesses

Whether it's smoking, eating, drinking, sex, or watching TV, overindulgence is generally related to the stress of having too much or too little happening in one's life. People overindulge most often when they are pressured, overworked, anxious, bored, don't like what they are doing, or are in dire need of contact with other people.

There's medical evidence, for example, that eating causes the brain to release substances called endorphins, some of which act as relaxers on the mind and body. Also, psychologists have found that repetitive, nonpurposeful activity like chain-smoking, finger tapping, drinking, and chewing fingernails, gum, food, or rubber bands helps discharge pent-up frustration and discomfort. So chances are that frequent trips to the refrigerator, munching away on snack food, or reaching for a drink starts out as a way to make you feel better and help you get through the day.

Once someone begins to rely on a particular indulgence to deal with stress, what follows makes it difficult to stop. First, the eating, drinking, smoking, or whatever you're doing to excess becomes a habit. You end up doing it automatically, reaching for a cigarette or candy bar without even thinking about it, raiding the refrigerator without having made a conscious decision to stroll into the kitchen.

To further complicate the situation, many of these activities, like smoking, drinking alcohol, taking drugs, and eating salty or sugary food, produce a

---

The Top Ten Bad Habits

1. Snacking
2. Sleeping late
3. Procrastinating
4. Talking on the phone
5. Watching TV
6. Getting sloppy; staying in nightclothes all day
7. Taking too long to read the newspaper
8. Drinking while working
9. Spending too much time visiting neighbors
10. Working too much

chemical reaction in your body that causes you to crave more. So as you indulge to excess, your body begins to demand greater amounts of what you're indulging in. Then instead of feeling better, you start to feel like you "can't go on without it."

These factors combine to make breaking out of habitual excesses a challenging task. For this reason, the easiest way to avoid problems with excesses is to prevent them from happening in the first place or to catch the problem as early as possible.

Awareness Is the First Step

Take notice right away when you start to exceed a normal or familiar pattern. Most people do notice the difference. "I'm snacking more." "I'm having my after-work drink earlier in the day." "I've eaten a whole bag of potato chips! I don't usually do that."

Act Immediately

Before divergences from your regular pattern develop into a new habit, take steps to deal with the situation. Recognize what you have too much or too little of in your life that is causing stress, and find a different way to handle it. Here is how people working at home have managed to avoid the stressful situations that lead to excesses.

Six Ways to Avoid Overindulging While Working

1. Work at a relaxed and reasonable pace. The best protection against raiding the refrigerator or grabbing another drink is to take good care of yourself. Don't overwork. Take breaks. Learn to relax.

Barbara Bickford found that "the only way I could be sure I wouldn't turn to the junk-food snacks every night was to put an end to working all day and into the night. By taking on so much business that I had to work late, I was really abusing myself. Occasionally, yes, it's okay. But I was doing it as a matter of course. Eating was my way of buying myself off so I wouldn't complain about letting my work consume me."

Don't let your home office become as stressful a place to be as the worst of traditional offices. Take advantage of the fact that you have more flexibility about when and how you work. Use the time you would have spent commuting to relax in one way or another and structure your day to keep the pressures from building up. It can be good for your health. When nationally known speaker and seminar leader Lee Shapiro, known as "The Hugging Judge," went "from the courtroom to the living room," he found his blood pressure went down.

2. Develop what psychologist William Glasser calls "positive" addictions. Glasser uses this term to refer to activities like jogging, swimming, and knitting, which people enjoy and find helpful in handling everyday stress. Glasser found that people who regularly engage in such an activity actually feel as though they were "addicted" to it. They miss the activity when something interferes with doing it at their regular times. They crave it and feel depressed and out of sorts when they're deprived of it. Unlike an addiction such as smoking, drinking, overeating, or taking drugs, however, these activities actually improve your health.

Engineering consultant Jeff Knoghton found himself drinking more when he first started working at home. "I was used to having a drink to unwind when I got home from work. Once I was at home all day, whenever I felt pressure building up, I'd grab a can of beer. Then I started jogging for twenty minutes every morning. I heard it helped you become less tense." If it's a really bad day, he runs again in the early evening. "It just relaxes me, keeps me loose. It's better than beer, because it clears my mind rather than fuzzing it up."

3. Be sure you have enough contact with people you enjoy. An office with other people provides stimulation, company, and someone to share problems with. Working at home can be lonely at first. But the loneliness doesn't have to lead to overindulgence. Instead of heading for the kitchen, reaching for another drink, or turning on the tube, you can head for the telephone. Call someone. Go visit a neighbor. Invite someone to come over. However busy you are, make time in your workday for some kind of interpersonal contact.

4. Treat yourself with something special each day. It should be something you can look forward to as a refresher after work, or once or twice during the day. In this chapter you'll find a list of treats we and others have developed. Build your own list.

5. If you want to snack, set some guidelines. Deepak Chopra, physician and author of the book *Perfect Health*, suggests several such guidelines. He advises eating only if you're actually hungry. Sometimes the urge for a snack is actually a desire for something else, such as taking a break or doing something different. If you are actually hungry, he proposes that you stop whatever else you are doing, sit down away from work with your food, take a moment of silence before you eat, and then eat with the intention of enjoyment.

Psychologist Dr. Nancy Bonus, founder of the Bonus Plan, has developed a nondiet weight-loss program that distinguishes between physical hunger and habit or emotional hunger and suggests eating only when your body actually needs fuel. She also advises eating exactly what you want to eat and enjoying it fully by taking very small bites, chewing them thoroughly, savoring the flavor, and pausing between bites. Then she recommends that as soon as you feel slightly full, you *stop eating* immediately and return to work feeling completely satisfied.

Treats Instead of Sweets:
Positive Ways to Reward Yourself

- Go outside. Walk through your neighborhood or visit your favorite outdoor spot. Notice the grass, trees, wind, sun, clouds, the sounds of birds, barking dogs, and children playing, the faces of strangers and friends.
- Buy yourself some flowers or pick a bouquet from your own garden.
- Take a stimulating shower or a relaxing bath, go to the spa or sauna, soak in a candlelight milk bath with music playing in the background.
- Do something handy around the house. Fix what's broken, build something new, work in the garden.
- Buy yourself a present, something you might not otherwise purchase for yourself but wish someone else would.
- Have a party.
- Enjoy your favorite sport. Take time out for a game of tennis, badminton, golf, or handball, or join a softball or bowling team.
- Curl up in your favorite spot and read an enthralling book or a magazine of your choice.
- Keep a journal in which you write down your thoughts, your feelings, and your goals, make a list of your accomplishments, describe what you've discovered about yourself and your work.
- Serve your favorite meal on your best dishes and invite someone special to join you.
- Take a class you've always wanted to take: photography, modern art, yoga, programming.
- Sit in the sun, take a nap.
- Make a change in your day-to-day life. Rearrange the furniture, get a new hairstyle, go on a vacation.
- Do something childishly carefree. Romp with the dog, turn a cartwheel, buy a balloon, play a video game.
- Dial up a bulletin board on your computer and talk to the world through your fingertips.
- Go to a funny or suspenseful movie, take in a concert, a play, a ball game, a museum, the zoo.

6. Keep whatever you want to avoid as far away from your office as possible. Data entry clerk Helen Willis told us, "I don't keep salty or sugary snacks in the house anymore because they just make me want to eat more. So I have lots of nuts and bananas and dried fruit around now. They're much more satisfying."

This is one of the plusses of working from home. Unlike office vending machines, your kitchen cabinets can be filled with whatever you choose. Here

Guidelines for Snacking

1. Don't snack mindlessly. Snack consciously and only when hungry.
2. Take a break from whatever else you are doing. Go somewhere other than your office.
3. Select exactly the food you want to eat when you snack.
4. Sit down with your food and spend a moment silently relaxing before eating.
5. Eat with the intention of enjoyment.
6. Take small bites. Chew your food thoroughly. Savor the flavor. Pause between bites.
7. Stop eating when you feel slightly full and satisfied.

are a few more "out of sight, out of mind" tricks people who work at home use to keep themselves from overindulging:

"To avoid walking in and out of the kitchen all day for a cup of coffee, where I invariably grab a cookie to eat along with it, I've set up a coffeemaker in my office. I keep all the supplies—the cups, even the bottled water—on a small cabinet in the office closet."

"I close the kitchen door and think of it as a restaurant. It's only open between noon and one and after five o'clock."

"I don't allow smoking in my house. That way I have to take a break and go outside to smoke. This keeps my habit under control."

"We set up a little icebox and hot plate in the office, which is behind the garage. We 'bring' our lunch to work every day and usually don't go into the house while we're working."

"I work at the computer most of the day. I put the computer on a stand that doesn't have enough space to set down coffee cups, glasses, or food. To eat or drink anything, I have to get up and go somewhere else."

Breaking Old Habits and Creating New Ones

But what do you do if you've already developed a bad habit? And what if it's a habit you've had a long time? Again, awareness is the first step, and then comes corrective action. You must find another way to deal with the circumstances that led you to develop the habit in the first place, different ways of handling the stresses of your work. Then you have to replace your old habit with a new one. Here are five suggestions for breaking undesirable habits:

1. **Anticipate when you are likely to indulge in your habit.** Know the actions leading up to an occurrence. Do you snack or smoke at particular times of the day on in conjunction with particular activities?

2. **Create a new and competing habit to take the place of the old one.** For example, if you have a habit of going to the kitchen for a snack between projects or clients, establish a new habit by making phone calls or taking a walk instead.

3. **Interrupt the sequence of the habit or disrupt its pattern.** If you are used to smoking while you sit at your desk talking on the phone, for example, stand up while you talk on the phone. Clear away all the ashtrays. Keep your cigarettes away in another room, so you'll have to go through several involved steps to get to them.

4. **Set up cues or "anchors" that help you remember to change your habit.** Put a No Eating Between Meals sign on your refrigerator. Set the alarm for scheduled snack breaks.

5. **Think about how terrific you'll feel when you no longer have this habit.** Begin imagining yourself as a person without such a habit. Think of yourself as a nonsmoker, for example, or as someone who doesn't snack.

Ending Addictions and Compulsions

If you have a particularly stubborn habit of overindulging, you may be suffering from an addiction or a compulsion—you feel enslaved. Recent findings from the emerging field of psychoneuralimmunology suggest that addictions (whether physical or mental, acquired or inherited) are the result of a fundamental distortion in the biological system. This research indicates that these distortions can be corrected by using your mind and your environment to return yourself to a natural state of health.

You'll find a variety of books and programs available to help you apply the methods from this new field cited in the Resources List at the end of this chapter.

Chapter Digest

1. The most common overindulgences such as smoking, overeating, drinking too much, or watching too much TV are related to the stress of having too much or too little happening in one's life.

2. The best way to avoid overindulging is to enjoy a rewarding, fulfilling life devoid of chronically stressful situations. Working from home is an ideal solution to an overly stressed lifestyle because it puts you in charge and provides you the flexibility to learn new and healthier ways of living and working.

3. The first step in avoiding overindulgence is to notice that it's happening and take immediate action to alter your routines and work habits so they become more satisfying.

4. Avoid stress by working at a relaxed and reasonable pace. Be sure to have ample contact with people you enjoy. Treat yourself each day with events and activities that you look forward to. Develop positive addictions, like jogging or knitting.

5. If you have an established habit of overindulging, take action to break the habit by creating new routines that interrupt and disrupt your old patterns. Restructure your environment and work habits to support the new behavior you desire.

6. Take advantage of books and programs that apply the most recent findings of the medical and behavioral sciences to the cure of addictions and eating disorders.

Resources

Books

Diets Don't Work. Bob Schwartz. Houston, TX: Breakthrough, 1982.

Perfect Health: The Complete Mind/Body Guide. Deepak Chopra, M.D. New York: Harmony Books, 1990.

Positive Addiction. William Glasser. New York: Harper & Row, 1976.

Power Walking. Steve Reeves. New York: Bobbs-Merrill Co., 1982.

Thin Within. Judy Wardell. New York: Harmony Books, 1985.

The Relaxation Response. Herbert Benson, M.D. New York: Avon, 1975.

The Runner's Handbook: A Complete Fitness Guide for Men and Women on the Run. Bob Glover and Jack Shepherd. New York: Penguin Books, 1978.

Organizations and Programs

The Bonus Plan: Non-Diet Weight Loss Home Study Course. Nancy Bonus, 15141 Haynes St., Van Nuys, CA 91411; (818) 780-0222.

Schick Shadel. 12700 Ventura Blvd., #200, Studio City, CA 91604; (800) 322-5796. Alcohol and drug treatment.

SmokEnders. 1430 E. Indian School Rd., #120, Phoenix, AZ 85014; (800) 828-4357.

C H A P T E R
E I G H T E E N
●

Staying in Love and
Saving Your Marriage

"How do I know that if I start working at home I won't end up getting divorced?"

"I'd like to work at home, but how do you two stand being around each other so much?"

"What happened to your relationship when you started working at home? Was there an adjustment period? Did you fight all the time?"

Hundreds of people have asked us questions like these after a speech or at breaks during a seminar. We answer that when you're married, working from home is like opening a birthday present. It may be just what you wanted or it may not suit you.

Our files are filled with stories of couples who, like us, discovered that the best part of working from home is the extra time they have to be together. It's hard to build a relationship on weekends and in the few hours that remain when people get home from an exhausting day at the office. At the very least, working from home gives couples a better chance of building a good life together. Occasionally, however, it doesn't work. Instead of things getting better, they go downhill.

For better or worse, you can count on undergoing some changes in your life and your relationship when you begin working from home. And, as with any degree of change, there will usually be a period of adjustment. The question is how the adjustments will affect your relationship. We agree with Peggy Glenn, who had a new husband and three kids when she quit her job to start a home typing service:

"If a person decides to work at home to salvage a dead marriage or revive a dying one, I think it will kill the marriage altogether. But if the relationship is strong and there is trust between the husband and wife, then they'll get through the change, and working from home will strengthen the relationship."

In this chapter we want to share the principles we and other couples have found for staying in love when you work from home. Although there are many differences in how couples go about it, there do seem to be several key ingredients.

First it's important to get off to the right start. Then it helps to be prepared for the inevitable adjustments you will encounter, to realize they are normal, and to know some positive steps you can take to resolve the conflicts that arise. Finally, it's important to recognize the early warning signs of trouble and know what you can do when things aren't getting better.

Getting Off to the Right Start

Couples begin working from home for many different reasons. Sometimes it's by choice, sometimes it isn't. Sometimes it's an opportunity, sometimes it's a necessity. Whatever the situation, you'll get off to a better start if you both agree that the best course of action is to work at home.

It's virtually impossible to work happily at home without the cooperation and support of your spouse, so a joint decision will most certainly work better than issuing an edict or even simply making an announcement that you've decided to work at home. Even if you already have an office at home, it's not too late to sit down and talk about whether it's working out.

Be honest about how you feel about using your home as an office and encourage your spouse to be honest too. Discuss your concerns openly. If you're worried that your spouse will never leave the office, say so. If you're concerned that the children will be neglected, say so. The potential problems you identify can help you develop a practical plan to guard against them.

Specific Steps You Can Take

Make the decision to work at home a joint one.
Express your reasons for wanting to work at home.
Discuss your concerns openly and encourage your spouse to do so as well.
Thank your spouse for each concern he or she brings up.
Respond honestly to each other's concerns.
Take each concern seriously and get the facts about it.
Think of possible solutions and develop a plan for how to avoid potential
  problems.
Test out your solutions. See if they work. Revise them when they don't work to
  your or your mate's satisfaction.

One woman told us she felt silly bringing up her real concern. She was afraid that if her husband worked at home, the house would always be a mess and she would become a servant cleaning up after him. Fortunately, she did talk it over with him and they decided to hire a cleaning service.

It's ignoring "silly" concerns like these that get us into the worst problems. This very problem did precipitate one of the few marital casualties we know of. The wife who worked in an outside office couldn't stand coming home every day to a messy house. She'd tidy it up in the morning, and when she got home, exhausted from a day's work, she'd find another mess awaiting her. Failing to resolve this incompatibility ultimately contributed to their divorce.

So when your spouse brings up an objection, thank him or her on the spot for sharing it with you. That's just one more problem you can avoid. Once the objection has come up, you can start talking about the facts of the situation and work out various plans for ensuring it won't be a difficulty.

Avoid the temptation to discount the concern by saying, "Oh, that won't be a problem. You don't have to worry about that." Even if it seems as though there would be no problem with a particular concern, explain your reasoning, describe in detail why it won't be a difficulty, even create hypothetical situations to show that indeed there is no need for concern. You may discover something you overlooked.

A radio announcer we talked with, for example, didn't think he'd mind having his mother use his office as a guest room when she came to stay on weekends. His wife wasn't sure. "Since she didn't think it would work, I decided to test it out. Although I wasn't yet working full time at home, one weekend when my mother came up I had just put my equipment and a number of important files in my home office—that is, the guest room. My wife was right. We had to figure out some other solution before it would work for me to move everything home. Even though it required some construction, we decided to set up a basement studio for my office."

Facing Inevitable Changes

The inevitable changes that take place when you start working from home can strain your relationship. The situation doesn't have to become painful, however. The initial stress can be a sign of new and better things to come. But you must be alert and responsive to difficulties that arise while they are still manageable.

Here are some of the healthy reactions a couple can expect. They don't always feel good, but they are a normal part of the process of changing your lifestyle.

Conflicts with New Identities

The decision to work at home is almost always part of a larger decision to change your life, which changes your identity. People who begin working at home are at turning points in their lives.

Assuming a new identity is a major adjustment in itself. Add working from home and the many accompanying changes in daily routine and you can see why people going through so many adjustments may not be easy to live with. You can understand why they may be unsure of themselves, edgy, worried, or struggling to put up a good front.

Even when spouses want to be supportive, and actually think they are helping, they may not welcome all aspects of their mate's new identity. One woman, whose husband quit his job to become a professional entertainer, described the experience this way: "I didn't marry an entertainer. I married a lawyer. I don't know him anymore. He's a different person."

She wasn't so sure she liked this new person. She also wasn't totally sure who she was now, either. Among other roles in life, she had been a lawyer's wife. Now she was supposed to be an entertainer's wife. "He expects me to come to late-night shows and sit with a lot of other entertainers and their wives while he performs. I'm not sure this is something I want to do."

When she started her typing service, Peggy Glenn's identity changed from being someone's secretary in a nine-to-five job to being an entrepreneur and businesswoman. "It was very, very difficult for my husband. Not only was he unsure about the money I would make in this new business—and we needed the money from my work—he was also unsure about this new change in me. All of a sudden I was someone who was in demand by other people. My customers knew him as 'Peggy's husband.' That was kind of hard on his ego."

Disputes over Duties and Responsibilities

Working from home usually means changes in household routines. Many arguments and conflicts can arise over day-to-day arrangements about:

Cleaning. Living and working at home twenty-four hours a day means more mess and more wear and tear. Who does the extra work to keep the house in order? When does it have to be cleaned up or repaired? Do children now have to be neater because customers are coming to the house? If so, who gets the children to clean up? If the packaging department of your business is on the dining room table, how long can it stay like that, and who puts everything away—the person who made the mess or the person who wants it cleaned up?

Meals. Working at home usually means at least one extra meal there. So you need to discuss who plans it, who buys it, who fixes it, who cleans it up. If you have been fixing the meals, for example, will you still have time to fix them all, or to fix the same kinds of meals, now that you're working at home?

Space. Working at home can place certain limitations on what your family can do there or even on other things you want to do. If your family room is now your office, where does everyone go to relax? Can they have company while you are working? Can your spouse walk around the house in a bathing suit during business hours? You'll need to consider issues like whether your family can play the stereo or talk on the phone whenever they want, or if such activity infringes on your office space.

Children.　Children need a lot of attention. They can be a distraction and an interruption that makes work next to impossible. A decision has to be made about who handles this. Does the one working at home take on more of these responsibilities than before? Who keeps the children quiet or out of your office?

Time.　Once your office is at home, you need to determine who gets to spend time with you and when. If you're away at the office all day, you clearly can't take the kids to the park after school. And of course you can't make love before lunch. But what about now? What will you say when someone you love asks, "Couldn't you just take a minute for . . .?"

Money.　Working from home is likely to mean a change in your income. If you've quit your job to start a business, the amount of money you're bringing in could go down at first. What gets cut—theater tickets, your tennis lessons, your spouse's night class? If you've taken a second job or started a new career at home, it could mean your income will go up. In that case, who decides what the additional money is used for?

Adjusting to New Roles

When people decide to work from home, the nature of their role in the marriage often changes. Sometimes they like and welcome the new role; sometimes the new role is thrust upon them without their consent. Let's consider some of the adjustments individuals and couples can encounter.

A man moving his work home.　In our society, while a woman's place is no longer necessarily at home, a man's place is still at the office. As columnist Jim Sanderson wrote, the "Image of the Stay-at-Home Kind of Man" can create some humorous but uncomfortable situations. He found that his wife's friends, the neighbors, and repair personnel who came over either thought he was ill, implied he was lazy, or believed he'd married a "rich dame."

In addition to contending with the perceptions of others, a man moving his office home often finds himself confronted with household or child-rearing responsibilities he's not used to handling. Also, he may have difficulty adjusting to working without the support services he's been accustomed to getting at the office. He may feel angry or depressed about having to do everything himself, from buying paper clips to making copies. On the other hand, he might feel grateful for the independence and new responsibilities.

A woman starting or returning to work.　When a woman who has been a homemaker decides to start working from home, she will have less time for household chores. Housework, meals, laundry, and possibly even children

PERSONAL PROFILE: Michael Fey, Financial Consultant

When Michael Fey decided to leave his hectic downtown job and work from his suburban home, his wife decided for the first time in their marriage to work outside the home.

"With my being at home and her starting to work away from home, we had a real shift in role responsibilities. Since I was there, I found myself handling certain domestic tasks." Now, before he sits down at his desk in the morning, he finds himself doing things he never had to do before: getting the house organized, getting the kids off to school, and monitoring their squabbles.

"It's been a real education. I would say it's been an advantage. The kids have gotten to know me better. My wife is glad that part of the responsibility for child-rearing has shifted to me. It's less of a burden on her and frees her to do what she wants. She's also glad because the kids do need to get to know me now. In a couple of years they'll be grown and gone."

Although Michael hadn't expected the changes that took place after he started working at home, he says, and his wife agrees, "We're happier as a couple."

will not get her full attention. A husband who may be supportive of his wife's new work style may still not like the inconvenience of doing things for himself that she once did for him. He may have to start packing for his business trips, preparing his own lunches, or shopping for his own shirts. He may even have to forgo some of the conveniences he's become accustomed to, like freshly ironed and folded shirts.

The homemaker turned open-collar worker may also have difficulty getting family, friends, or neighbors to take her new role seriously. After all, she's still at home. Everyone may expect her somehow to do everything she has always done. In fact, polls still show homemakers who decide to launch a career do not get much additional help with household chores. They simply add to their existing responsibilities as wives and mothers.

If the woman who begins working at home tries to keep up with everything, she can get caught in the "Superwoman syndrome," trying to be all things to all people, which is a good way to become irritable, overstressed, burned out, or even sick.

The homemaker. The wife who is a homemaker may feel her husband's presence is an intrusion into her domain: "I married him for better or worse, but not for lunch!" She may feel pressure to become not only a wife and mother but also a receptionist and secretary. On the other hand, she may be eager to have her husband home, thinking he can take on more responsibilities around the house and that they can spend more time together. But will he have the time to take on these new roles? If he's like most at-home workers, he will actually work more, not fewer, hours.

Two-career couples. Wherever they work, at home or away, two-career couples face unique challenges and strains on their relationship.

When one spouse works at home and the other works away, it's easy to fall into "the grass is always greener" syndrome. The spouse who works away from home may be jealous of the one who's been home all day. Those at home may seem to have more free time and less pressure. After all, they haven't had to contend with traffic or wait for the train in the rain. Those working in an outside office may even feel disappointed to find the house a mess when they get home. They're likely to wonder why, with all that time at home, their partner wasn't able to get more done.

From the other point of view, the ones who work at home may feel burdened by household interruptions and responsibilities and jealous of their partner's freedom to get out in the business world and socialize with others during the day. Those who've been working at home all day long may be itching to get out in the evening, while their partner is looking forward to getting home to rest and relax.

When both partners work at home, they may have difficulties drawing lines between their roles as workers and their roles as spouses. It's hard to tell your spouse, "No, I can't talk now, I'm in the middle of a project." It's equally hard to resist the temptation to start sharing the events of your business day when you're excited, devastated, or just eager to talk.

PERSONAL PROFILE: Tom Drucker, Management Consultant, and Marcia Seligson, Author

Even when he was an executive for Xerox, Tom was attracted to the idea of working from home. Now that he is self-employed, he feels working at home is a way for him to spend more time with his wife. Instead of trying to play catch-up each night about the events of the day, he enjoys "sharing the day with her while it's happening."

As a writer who had worked at home alone, Marcia likes having Tom home while she's working. "I enjoy his company and it breaks the solitude of writing." At first, however, they were so thrilled to have each other there that they would eagerly interrupt work to talk about what was happening.

"On the job it was easy to create a boundary around myself," Tom recalls. "I had people screen my calls. If I was interrupted I could say, in a straightforward manner, 'Don't interrupt me now.' But when my wife comes in and says she's like me to read this letter, I'm less likely to say those things. I'm just like everyone else, I'd rather go do something I enjoy than struggle with some difficult task I'm working on."

Aware of the problem, Tom and Marcia have learned how to respect each other's workspace. They've begun telling each other when they don't want to be interrupted, and Marcia finds "we're getting better at it now. We save our news for lunch breaks together."

Couples working at home are also susceptible to each other's moods. Usually your spouse is the only one there to talk with about the feelings and events of the day. When one of you is down, it may pull the other down too. When one of you is hassled, the other may pick up the frazzled feelings. When you are angry about something that's happening with work, you may take it out on your partner and disrupt his or her work as well. Or, in order to keep peace in the house, partners may try to hide negative feelings from each other and find there is no place to let off steam.

Partners who both work at home generally feel like getting away from each other once in a while, just as translator Bill Grimes and his partner, Isabel Leonard, do. "We tend to go our separate directions on weekends and evenings. If we didn't, we'd get pretty sick of each other." Bill and Isabel's reaction is a perfectly natural feeling for any two partners to have, but sometimes mates feel guilty about it, or hurt if their partner is the one who wants to get away.

Resolving Conflicts

While these adjustments are normal reactions to the changes that come with working from home, they can produce conflicts that need to be resolved so both your business and your relationship can be successful. Here are a few rules of thumb we and other couples have found useful in resolving conflicts before they become ongoing problems.

Remind yourself the conflict is temporary.   It helps to remember that this is a transition period. Your life won't be like this forever. So make an effort to be understanding and patient with both yourself and your spouse while you work out the initial conflicts. It's only for a while.

Approach problems as opportunities.   Since adjustments and conflicts are an inevitable and normal part of striving to create a new life for yourselves, each of them is truly an opportunity to take another step toward that new life. So regard problems as obstacles to be removed on the way to reaching your goal.

Remember, you love each other.   When your relationship is an important, indispensable element of your life, it's worth practicing restraint to protect it from the corrosive effects of thoughtless arguments. Although you may feel upset at the moment, remind yourself that this is the person you love. This is someone you respect. This person is probably the most important individual in your life.

The many small things married people get upset about are truly insignificant in the shadow of the love they can have between them. Don't overlook what's bothering you or simply put up with it in the name of love, but reach out to your spouse. Try to understand his or her position. Maybe if you can help your partner through the adjustment, he or she will be able to help you. As you discuss conflicts, keep the basic love you have between you in the forefront of your mind and concentrate on how important your relationship is.

Since it's often difficult to keep a positive perspective in the midst of a heated argument, here are a few things you can do to short-circuit flaring tempers. First, when you notice that communications are going from bad to worse, take a break. Go for a walk. Take a deep breath. Remind yourself that the opposite of love isn't hate; it's indifference. And anger is only part of the full range of feelings you have for your mate. Taking a moment to think of the loving feelings will make all the difference in the world in resolving the conflict.

Solve problems so everybody wins. Sometimes in the midst of a conflict, the people involved think someone has to win and someone has to lose. Or they think someone has to be right and someone has to be wrong. In sports events and lawsuits this may be true, but, fortunately, solving problems with your spouse isn't a contest or a trial. It's possible for everybody to win.

Actually, if you approach a conflict as a win/lose contest when you're working at home, nobody will win. The "winner" has to eat, sleep, live, and work with the "loser" every day. Once you've done that, you realize you haven't won much. So whenever you feel that someone must win and someone must lose, know you are on the wrong track. Usually you haven't defined the problem correctly. For example, if there is only one spare room in the house and both spouses want to use it exclusively, it may look like a win/lose situation. Actually the problem is not who gets to use the room. The problem is that there are two people who each need space to do something that's important to them. When you've solved that problem, everyone has won.

When you define a problem in this way, there are almost always options for solving the problem so everyone wins. It's amazing what two creative minds can come up with when seeking a solution that will benefit them both.

Make clear agreements. Making assumptions is the surest route to frustration, disappointment, and unnecessary conflict. When you work from home, the familiar assumptions people make about how things are done at an office no longer fully apply, nor do the assumptions people normally make about how things are done at home. Getting clear agreements about who is willing to do what is crucial, whether they concern how you want your partner to act when the business phone rings, or who will fix lunch.

It's easy to overlook telling your spouse what you expect and then proceed to get angry when he or she doesn't act accordingly. It's also easy to declare what you want and assume it will be done without further discussion. And when you're worried that your partner won't want do something, it's awfully tempting to use coercion, manipulation, threats, shame, guilt, or pressure tactics to get your way.

Thirteen Ways to Keep Romance Alive
When You Work at Home

1. Remember, love keeps you together. Don't dissolve it with acid remarks. Keep the bond strong with small kindnesses.
2. Enjoy each other's enjoyment.
3. Keep the positive regard you have for each other in the forefront of your interactions.
4. Compliment each other liberally every day for your individual accomplishments, contributions, and talents.
5. Solve problems when they are small. Don't let them build up.
6. Commit yourselves to solving problems so you both win, instead of defining problems so that one of you must win and the other must lose, or one of you must be right and the other wrong.
7. Work out clearly stated agreements. Don't assume. State what you need and ask for what you want from each other.
8. When you say "no," explain what you're willing to do instead, and when you're told "no," find out what the other person would be willing to do.
9. Close the door on work at the end of the day. Have nonbusiness time. In particular, separate the bedroom from business. Don't take business to bed and don't go to bed mad.
10. Don't hoard negative feelings. Express them when they develop so you don't have an overflow of bad feelings to unload on each other in an explosive argument.
11. Get out of the house together regularly to do things you enjoy. Take mini-vacations for an afternoon or weekend.
12. Follow the advice of Kahlil Gibran: "Let there be space in your 'togetherness.'" Have and pursue your own interests.
13. Take time out to celebrate and don't let a day go by without at least ten hugs.

Unfortunately, agreements made under such circumstances are either not kept or are kept halfheartedly or grudgingly. Sometimes they're actually sabotaged. Although it's easy to blame the other person for not being supportive, you will nonetheless have to take responsibility for instigating such behavior and will come to regret the day you extracted an agreement under duress.

Agreements that clearly define what each of you will and will not do can make working from home easier and more enjoyable. Here are a few tips for making clear agreements:

- Express precisely what you want and what you expect.
- Make it clear whether you will meet your spouse's expectations or whether you won't.

- Don't say "yes" when you mean "no."
- Accept "no" from each other as okay. A "no" is clearly better than a "yes" the person will not follow through on.

Communicate, communicate, communicate. Besides talking, listen open-mindedly to your spouse's feelings and concerns.

As Peggy Glenn discovered in starting her typing service at home with a new husband and three children, "Communication is the key. If you communicate, you can overcome most of the problems."

You might use the time you once spent commuting to and from the office to listen to each other, not necessarily about problems, but about yourselves, your lives, and your dreams. Chances are that this kind of honest and open communication will strengthen your determination to succeed and keep your romance alive.

Laugh a lot. Laughter is the sugar that can sweeten the bitterest moments in periods of adjustment. It can save the day. Be willing to step back to look at yourselves, to see some of the humor in your behavior and your situation. If laughing amid the pressures of life doesn't come easily to you, make a habit of going to funny movies together, going out with lighthearted people, and watching TV comedies.

What to Do If It Isn't Getting Better

On occasion, the changes and adjustments of working from home seem to precipitate more serious problems than those we've been discussing. The tension and bad feelings build until there is certainly nothing to laugh about and the situation feels intolerable. What happens in a situation like this? What goes wrong? Has working from home destroyed the marriage?

Yes and no. Whether it's a new baby, a new job, or a new house, any new element introduced into a marriage can aggravate existing problems or bring them to the surface. Working from home is like this too.

It's easier to avoid marital problems when you don't see each other very much. When someone is at the office for most of every day, it's simpler to push the difficulties away. Working at home, couples usually see more of each other. This proximity, and the strain of adjusting to the changes involved, can stir up and bring out problems that were kept beneath the surface before.

In a relationship that's suffering from underlying problems, it's difficult to get in touch with the basic loving feelings that brought a couple together. Every little concern becomes a battleground. Even the smallest differences can become unsolvable, because the real problem is not being addressed. In situations like these, it's important to heal the relationship itself before a couple attempts to solve the more peripheral problems of working from home.

If you're concerned about whether the conflicts you're having are normal adjustments to the changes of working from home, or whether these changes are bringing up more general problems, review the five early-warning signals that follow:

1. Your spouse begins blaming all the problems the two of you are having on your work.
2. Your spouse starts to feel jealous of your work.
3. You start using your work as a way to escape talking with your spouse.
4. You start using your work as a way to avoid sex.
5. You talk about everything but what's really on your mind.

If you notice these warning signs either before or after you begin working from home, we suggest you communicate with your spouse about them. Then, if the problems persist or go from bad to worse, get professional help to improve your relationship.

There's no need to settle for less than the relationship and lifestyle you want for yourself. You deserve it and so does your spouse. Don't wait until things have deteriorated to a hopeless state. Act now. You can use the resources listed at the end of this chapter or contact the following organizations for help.

Marriage Encounter programs are offered across the country. You can usually locate them through local churches and synagogues. Otherwise, find out about programs in your area by writing to: International Marriage Encounter, 955 Lake Drive, Saint Paul, MN 55120.

The American Association for Marriage and Family Therapy, 1717 K St., NW, #407, Washington, D.C. 20006, can put you in touch with trained professionals in your community who help couples solve problems.

If your spouse won't seek help with you, go yourself. Sometimes all it takes is one person's having the courage to take the first step and lead the way.

Chapter Digest

1. For many married people, one of the best parts of working from home is the extra time they have to spend together and the opportunity to build a better life together.
2. It is, however, virtually impossible to work successfully from home without the support of your spouse, so making it a joint decision will most certainly work better than issuing an edict that you'll be working from home.
3. Working from home brings changes in routines and roles. Decisions will need to be made about who handles which aspects of managing the household and the office. Typical conflicts are those which arise around

cleaning, meal preparation, space issues, parenting responsibilities, time, and money. Honest communication and win/win problem-solving are the cornerstones of making decisions everyone will support and follow through on.

4. The decision to work from home is almost always part of a larger decision to change your lifestyle and sometimes your identity. Being understanding and patient with fears, concerns, and irritations is easier when you each remember that they are a natural part of an adjustment period that will not last forever.

5. Occasionally, the proximity and strain of adjustments to working from home can bring hidden conflicts in a relationship to the surface. When this happens, it's difficult to get in touch with the basic feelings that brought you together in the first place. Communicating about these buried feelings can help, but if the problems persist or go from bad to worse, get professional help to improve your relationship.

Resources

Books

Do I Have to Give Up Me to Be Loved by You? Jordan and Margaret Paul. Minneapolis: CompCare, 1983.

Embracing Each Other. Hal Stone and Sidra Winkelman. San Rafael, CA: New World Library, 1989.

Love Is the Answer. Gerald Jampolski and Diane Cirincioni. New York: Bantam Books, 1990.

On the Family. John Bradshaw. Pompano Beach, FL: Health Communications, 1987.

Parent Effectiveness Training. Thomas Gordon. New York: Peter Wyden, 1970.

The Working Parents Survival Guide. Sally Wendkos Olds. Rocklin, CA: Prima Publication & Communication, 1989.

Tapes

Creating Positive Relationships. Gerald Jampolski and Diane Cirincioni. Chicago: Nightingale Conant; (800) 323-5552.

Relationship Series. Hal Stone and Sidra Winkelman. Delos Publishing, 5451 Laurel Canyon Blvd., North Hollywood, CA 91607.

CHAPTER
NINETEEN
■■■■■■■■■■■■■■■■■■■■■■

What to Do About Children

Many parents first begin to think about working from home as a way of pursuing both parenthood and a career. This is hardly surprising since studies show that two-thirds of children under age six will have working mothers by 1995, and juggling family and career is already the number one source of stress for women.

Certainly bringing work home holds the potential of making juggling these demands easier for both mothers and fathers and yet often parents and others who want to work from home worry about whether they'll be productive enough, working with children in the house. In this chapter we want to affirm that working from home does indeed offer many rewards for parents. At the same time, we want to realistically address what parents can expect, the difficulties they face, and the practical steps they can take to avoid problems and take full advantage of the benefits.

It Can Be Worth the Effort

Our son Jon was eight years old when we moved our offices home. Having both worked long hours away from the house since shortly after he was born, we felt pleasure hearing him come in the door after school and call out, "Hi! I'm home!" We'd take a break to make him a snack and find out the highlights of his day.

Our being in the house so much was a real treat for him too. Until we started working at home, he had only seen us at night and on weekends. From the time he was tiny, we had asked the baby-sitter to be sure he took a nap in the late afternoon so he could stay up late with us when we got home. So, at first, having us there in the afternoon was like a continual holiday for Jon.

We liked knowing we were more available to him, too. Although at times he had trouble knowing when he could or couldn't interrupt us, we were all surprised to discover that he was often too busy with his own things to pay much attention to us. Jon has graduated from college now and is living in Berkeley. We often think that if we hadn't decided to work from home, we would be looking back on his childhood regretting how much we'd missed.

When financial consultant Michael Fey moved his office home, he found, just as we had, that being with his teenage children was surprisingly rewarding. "Being at home in the morning, helping the kids get off to school, being involved in their squabbles, it's been a real education! My kids know me better now. They may not like me any better, though, because I'm a real parent. I'm putting down certain prescriptions, not leaving it up to Mom. It's changed their image of what a father is. Daddy isn't just somebody who goes off to fight traffic and bring home a barrel of cash for everybody else to spend."

Both men and women who work at home describe this close involvement with their children as a real advantage. And indications are that it's also a benefit for the children. Often the adult world of work is so removed from the lives of children that it's literally a life apart. Alvin Toffler expressed this separation in his book *The Third Wave.* "Most children today have only the foggiest notion of what their parents do or how they live while at work." He tells a poignant story to illustrate his point.

> An executive decides to bring his son to his office one day and take him out to lunch. The boy sees the plushy carpeted office, the indirect lighting, the elegant reception room. He sees the fancy expense-account restaurant with its obsequious waiters and exorbitant prices. Finally, picturing his home and unable to restrain himself, the boy blurts out: "Daddy, how come you're so rich and we're so poor?"

In contrast, when parents work at home a child not only gets to know them better but also experiences their world of work. Management trainers Linda and Bill Belisle have even involved their children in their home business. "Our kids know what it's like to be in business. They've grown up with it. We all work together, and when we have deadlines to meet, the kids pitch in and help. We think it's good preparation for them to succeed in life."

But while the rewards are potentially rich for most parents and children, it is also true that working with kids around is not always easy. Ken and Stephanie Wilson work from home and are the parents of two young sons. They agree that "it's just wonderful for the boys to have both parents here, but it's a real adjustment. It's a real test of living up to what we want as parents and professionals."

Noise, interruptions, and privacy are usually issues parents have to face, as well as knowing what's reasonable to expect of your children and yourself under the circumstances.

Children have an adjustment too. We remember at least one occasion when Jon, feeling frustrated with our ever-present business conversation, asked angrily, "Is this a home or a business?" So let's talk about the different reactions you can anticipate from your children, what you can say to them, and how to make practical, age-appropriate arrangements for their care.

What You Can Expect

Children's reactions to your being at home will vary greatly, depending upon the ages of your children, their personalities, your family, and the nature of your work. In most situations, children are glad to have a parent there more often, but probably will not fully comprehend what it means to have a parent working from home. To them, you are Mom or Dad, and that's it. They probably don't know you as lawyer, doctor, bookkeeper, or whatever else you happen to be. So if you want to make working at home with children both enjoyable and productive, you'll have to introduce them to the career aspects of yourself and show them how to relate to you now that you're more than a Mom or Dad at home.

Whatever their ages, kids will be kids. Don't expect your children to act like grown-ups just because you're working at home. Don't expect them, for example, to be quiet. Remember, by nature children are not quiet, and to be so for more than short periods of time is unhealthy for their development. Constantly trying to hush them will be a losing battle for you in the short run and not good for them in the long run.

A good rule of thumb, applying to children of all ages, is to "child-proof" your home office rather than trying to "office-proof" your children. In other words, let your kids be kids. Let them engage in normal activities, but set up your office and your schedule so that having "normal" children around will not disrupt your work. Here are some examples of how people have "child-proofed" their work while letting their kids be kids:

Programmer William Keen solved his dilemma this way. "I put the business phone and a desk down in the basement because it just doesn't make any sense to try to keep two dogs and three kids quiet when I have a phone call. By putting the desk and phone at the far end of the basement, under the master bedroom, I get very little noise. Even when the TV is going full blast, I don't hear it."

Artist Gary Eckart managed the problem another way. "I set my workshop up in an RV on the side of the house, because cutting stained glass just isn't compatible with having a toddler around. There's too much risk. If even once she crawled into my studio and got cut or put a piece of glass in her mouth . . . well, I couldn't take that chance."

Word-processor operator Barbara Bickford found the solution not in *where* but *when* she worked. "I make my calls and do all my deliveries while the kids are at school. I take my three-year-old to day care in the morning. When they're at home, home is home; when they're gone, it's an office."

If you have sensitive equipment or materials you don't want children to disrupt or damage, we suggest not allowing them to play in your office while you work because they will then think of it as a play area they can use even when you are not there to supervise them. Judy Wunderlich, who runs a temporary agency for graphic artists in Schaumburg, Illinois, found a creative way of solving this dilemma. As her two young children are under five, she needs to have them in sight while she works, but doesn't want them playing around her computer equipment. So she divided her basement in half with a three-foot-high divider. Her office is in the back half; the kids' playroom is in the front. She can see and hear them and they can see and hear her, but the office is still off limits.

So the first step is setting up your work to accommodate the reality of children in the house. Then remember that you can fully expect your children to behave responsibly and appropriately for their age and level of development. They do not need you all the time and can grow and develop very well while you're working undisturbed at home.

Let's take a look at what you can expect at each age level and how you can get work done whatever ages your children are. Since the age groups we discuss are based on typical stages of childhood development, assess your own children's personalities and rates of development so you can adjust these expectations to your family.

Children Under Twelve

Newborn to six years old. With mothers of newborn babies going back to work earlier than ever before and 52 percent of all mothers going back before their babies are one year old, working from home becomes increasingly appealing to parents eager to find ways of avoiding the risks of day care, not to mention the high costs of child-care services.

Research shows that day care poses both physical and mental health risks for children under six and surveys show that more than 80 percent of mothers are unsatisfied with child care for which they pay an average of $62 weekly. One of the most common misconceptions new mothers have, however, is that working from home will be a replacement for child care. Usually it is not a replacement but it does open up many more flexible and rewarding options for combining motherhood and career. Some people can and do work while caring for infants and toddlers but since they need constant supervision, want and demand your attention, and try to be part of everything going on around them, most people find this unsatisfactory.

When working parents care for toddlers and preschoolers at home, the typical result is that little work gets done and/or the parents end up expecting the young children to behave in ways beyond their abilities. This usually leads to a flood of yelling and unpleasantness. It can also result in emotional or behavioral problems in the children.

Barbara Elman was operating a word-processing service bureau when she became pregnant with her first child. Her story is similar to that of many women who begin working at home with infants and toddlers. During the first six months, she found she could work fine while the baby was right there with her. "Then my daughter became mobile. She started crawling and moving around and needing more attention. I couldn't sit and nurse her any more while I was proofing, because she wanted to play with the keys and everything else in sight. I couldn't work when she was around. It was difficult then and it's impossible now that she's two-and-a-half."

Experiences like Barbara's have led most people in this situation to the same conclusion. If they want to work without interruption for longer than 15 minutes, they either need to work at night while the children are sleeping or to get some form of supplementary child care for children under six or seven years.

If you do hire someone to help with your children and your children are wondering why someone else is caring for them while you're at home, it's important to explain that you are working just the way someone works who goes out to a job each day.

Seven to twelve years old.   Once children are over six, they are usually in school for a good part of the day, which leaves parents with considerably more flexibility as far as scheduling uninterrupted work time goes. Parents can arrange their schedules so they are not working while the children are home, or are doing tasks that require less concentration and can more easily withstand interruptions.

PERSONAL PROFILE: Ken and Stephanie Wilson, Writer and Landscape Designer

Ken and Stephanie Wilson have two boys, ages seven and ten. Stephanie began working from home as a landscape designer. Ken left his job at a major utility company to begin consulting and writing from home.

The Wilsons have located their offices so they are less likely to be disturbed by their children's activities, but they believe that children should have free access to their parents. Therefore, the Wilsons take a flexible approach to interruptions.

As Ken explains, "I don't want to make a rule 'No, you can't come in and see me.' I don't want limits on their coming in and saying, 'Hey Dad, what's this or what's that?' That's why I'm here. I'm glad they're coming in to see me. It means we're relating."

The Wilsons have avoided making rigid rules, by letting their boys know in the beginning that an office at home is serious business, and by having frequent family meetings to talk about everyone's feelings. They agree that "it has worked out reasonably well, but it hasn't just happened. It does take effort."

Children over six also require less direct supervision, so it becomes feasible to work in your office while they are playing in their rooms or in the backyard. Another advantage is that children this age often play in the homes of friends, although their friends are just as likely to come over to your house.

Ideally, you would have another adult available for children seven to twelve years of age when you need to work without any interruptions for periods of over an hour or so. This is especially useful if there is more than one child in the family and bickering is likely. However, you can often handle the needs of children this age on short, intermittent breaks and teach them to wait for those break times.

You can usually expect children from seven to twelve years old not to interrupt you when:

- There is some other person over twelve in the house whom they can ask for help.
- You let them know the home office has become your room and they need permission to be there.
- You tell them specifically when you will be available, and you are only unavailable for about an hour at a time.
- They understand that they can and should interrupt you for emergencies. (Beware, though, that what is an emergency to you and what is an emergency to an eight-year-old can be quite different, so you will need to spell out what you mean.)

Children of this age will probably do a considerable amount of testing in relation to these expectations. At first, they may push to find out if you mean what you say and exactly what the limits are. This will be particularly true when you have been with them full time before you began working at home. But if you are both loving and firm, they can usually adjust to your expectations after a few weeks.

In the first few weeks after we began working at home, we told our son not to interrupt us if we were in a session with a client and had the door closed, but he did anyway. We explained that clients came on the hour, and asked him to wait to talk with us until the break between each hour. We would be free once the client had gone out the front door.

Whenever he disrupted a session unnecessarily, one of us would simply say, "I'm in a session now, Jon. I will be done at—," and then we would close the door. Later, on the break, we'd be sure to check out what he wanted. It didn't take long for him to understand he could get his needs met without interrupting us.

Over twelve years old. Children over twelve should be able to carry out agreements not to interrupt your work for specified periods as long as they know:

- When you do not want to be interrupted.
- What emergencies you *do* want to be interrupted for.
- When they will be able to have your attention to deal with their needs. (We've found this is important not so much because teenagers need your time but because they want to know that you are there.)

In fact, with children who are ten to twelve years old, you may find that involving them in some aspects of your work is rewarding for you both. Teenagers in particular have many more talents and abilities than our society provides them with outlets for. They may well be our greatest untapped natural resource. We often had our son help with mailings, newsletters, or big projects of various kinds. We suggest, however, that such help be strictly on a voluntary basis, if not for a set wage; you will get more willing and productive participation that way.

Sandee and Al Burger started an extermination business in their home in 1960, when their two children were toddlers. Sandee says, "The family and the business grew together." When the children were old enough, they got 50 cents to sharpen pencils and do other office tasks. In high school, they worked for the business on weekends. The Burger's daughter, who is now twenty-one, has taken a full-time job with the company, which long ago outgrew their home.

Child-Care Options

The type of care you arrange for your children is a highly personal decision. What suits some people will not suit others. So for working parents, having a wide variety of creative and flexible child-care options is one of the real advantages of working from home. You are no longer limited to only those arrangements which can provide care from 7:00 A.M. to 7:00 P.M. while you commute to work in a downtown office.

For example, the Wilsons find that between the two of them they can work at home and provide the care their two sons need, without additional support. Barbara Elman, on the other hand, finds that in order to be productive, she must hire someone to take care of her daughter part of the day while she's working.

Like so many women, Barbara originally wanted to work at home so she could take care of her daughter herself, and was hesitant at first about making other arrangements. But she discovered that trying to run a business and parent a toddler was too much to expect of herself, so she decided to explore the different kinds of support she could get. Now she urges women to give themselves permission to find child care that will best fit their needs.

In deciding which options are best for you, review the following pros and cons of each and consider your situation, the nature of your work, the ages of your children, and the help available in your home.

Call on another adult in the family. The advantages of having a spouse or relatives care for your children are that these adults know and are known by the children, and are aware of how you want the children to be treated. Often, too, there's no extra cost involved. The disadvantages are that spouses and relatives may not always be available when you need them; they also may resent your asking them to help on a regular basis; and even if they don't say so, relatives may expect to be paid.

If you do plan to use a spouse or relatives, be sure to let them know what you expect of them, and find out if they are actually willing to meet your expectations. You don't want help that's given out of duty, obligation, coercion, or guilt. Chances are these motivations will just lead to resentment and unreliable support for you, as well as possible negative experiences for your children.

Use a sibling over twelve years of age. The advantages of using older siblings are that they are usually close by; their help is free or they'll be earning spending money you might give them anyway; and by helping you, they have the opportunity to contribute to the family. The disadvantages are that they may not want to watch their younger siblings; they may not watch them very well; and they may sometimes even mistreat them. Another drawback is that older brothers and sisters are usually only available at certain times of the day. Also, sometimes younger siblings resent being "parented" by an older sibling, so they become disobedient and create more squabbles for you to police.

If you do use an older sibling, be certain to talk this over with all your children to get their agreement and support. If they really hate the arrangement, it's better—for your own benefit—to respect their wishes and use siblings only in special situations.

We strongly advise against using children under twelve years of age to supervise a younger sibling, because they generally cannot get younger children to respect and obey them. One way you can measure whether a child is effective enough to watch younger children is to observe whether the child can get dogs or other trainable pets to obey him or her. Also, watch the child interacting with younger children from day to day. See if he or she demonstrates the skill and judgment that caring for a younger child requires.

Hire a baby-sitter to come into your home. The advantage of having a sitter come into your home is that you now have someone whose explicit job is taking care of your children while you work. You can also hire a sitter who clearly wants to work and who is available at the specific times you need child care. Having someone come to your home saves you the time of taking the children elsewhere and also provides you with the opportunity to oversee what the sitter is doing.

The disadvantages are that you have an added expense, and since the children are still there at the house, noise and interruptions may continue to be a problem. Because you can probably still overhear some activities, you may have difficulty not going out to see what's happening when disturbances arise. To overcome this problem, some parents take their children out to the home of a private baby-sitter.

Take your child to a child-care program. Although some parents are fearful of taking their children to child-care programs, many people highly recommend them. The advantages are that licensed child-care programs are generally reliable; they're open every day because they are businesses; and since the children are not at home, you can work with total privacy. The disadvantages are that the child may not get the individual attention you'd like; the hours may not be as flexible as you want; and you'll have to make other arrangements when your child is sick.

There are many good child-care programs, including day-care centers, day-care homes, preschools, and after-school programs. Call your county offices for a list of licensed programs in your area. Then visit several of them while children are there. Talk with the operators and teachers and ask how they handle the various situations you're concerned about in child care.

Find out, for example, what the children will be doing during the time they are there. Will they be learning and playing, or only playing? How many children are in the program, what are their ages, and how many adults are present? How is discipline handled? Talk to other parents who have children in the programs you are considering. Find out how pleased these parents are and whether they have any complaints. And be sure to investigate the provider's credentials.

Join a child-care co-op or trade baby-sitting services. In a child-care co-op, you join with other parents and take turns providing care for your children. Sometimes parents provide all the care by themselves and sometimes they only supplement the work of professionals who are hired to provide the care. The latter arrangement is called a "parent participation" nursery.

The advantages of co-op programs are that they usually cost less than other options; you get to participate in the care of your child; and other parents often become close friends. The disadvantages are that participating in a co-op means contributing time that may take you away from work; you also have to invest time in organizing the co-op and energy in caring for other people's children.

When selecting a co-op program, shop for one that understands and appreciates the needs of working parents. This is particularly important if you are a working single parent and will have to contribute all the time yourself. If you cannot find a satisfactory child-care co-op arrangement in your area, do what many parents have done—initiate a co-op by getting together with other working parents in your neighborhood.

On a more informal basis, some parents also trade the task of baby-sitting with friends or neighbors. Although this is more often done on a back-up

Seven Child-Care Options

1. Call on other adults in the family: spouse, aunts, uncles, brothers, sisters, grandparents.
2. Have siblings over twelve years of age watch younger children.
3. Have a baby-sitter or housekeeper come into your home.
4. Take the children to a private baby-sitter.
5. Place the children in a child-care program:
   A day-care center.
   A day-care home.
   A nursery school.
6. Join a child-care co-op.
7. Trade baby-sitting with a friend.

basis when other child-care arrangements aren't available, writer Libby Crowe finds this option works well for her.

Libby started working at home with the birth of her child. At first, working at home with the baby made everything easier. "I worked while she napped or played nearby," Libby remembers. "Now that she's a toddler, she naps less and is less willing to do her own thing." So Libby has worked out a variety of more informal arrangements. "I trade kid-watching with a friend who has a child near the same age as mine, and let my mom help out as often as she will. Occasionally I use day-care services."

Whatever child-care option they choose, most people working at home with children under twelve find that the cost of the care is less than the cost of lost productivity and the stress of trying to parent and work at the same time. Then, too, the financial burden can be partially relieved by taking a tax credit for child- and dependent-care expenses (IRS Form 2441) if you have the proper receipts and the provider's Social Security or tax I.D. number.

Introducing the Idea of Working at Home to Your Children

Whatever ages your children happen to be, when you decide to work at home they will have some reactions to this new way of life. At the very least, they will be curious and have their own ideas about what your being at home will mean. Sometimes these ideas will be unrealistic. For example, children are likely to think you will be as available to them as you have been on weekends or during your other free times at home.

So when you decide to set up a home office, remember to give your children as much information as you can about:

Personal Profile: Nancy and Mark Porter, Importers and Manufacturers

When Nancy and Mark Porter started their home business, the Susquehanna Hat Company, their oldest child had just started school and their youngest was about six months old.

At first they did their best to care for the children themselves. "We worked around the kids' schedule," Nancy remembers. They found, however, that "if you're really going to go for a business, you have to have child care." So as soon as the Porters were making enough money, Nancy found the name of a child-care home from a friend. "I liked the lady. She had a fenced yard, wasn't too expensive, had a boy the same age as mine, and was right across the street from where my older son went to school. It was the biggest relief to have 9:00 A.M. to 2:00 P.M. free for work every day."

Now seven and three years old, the Porter boys are both in "parent participation" schools. The schools require the Porters to contribute forty hours a year working in the classrooms. Sometimes Nancy dreads putting in the hours, but after she gets there she realizes "it's not so bad." For added convenience, they take turns driving the kids to and from school with a friend whose children are in the same schools. They're happy with these arrangements.

Although they are still working in the same home, Nancy and Mark are now divorced, so child care is even more important. Nancy explains, "If you find a school that's aware of your situation as a single parent, the people at the school become like co-parents. It's a nice personal support system that helps a lot now that we're divorced. And being involved in your children's education strengthens your relationship with them."

Are they still working from home? Yes. Although Mark doesn't live at the house anymore, he comes over every day to work. He finds, "It's good for the children to see me every day and provides them with more continuity than if we weren't working together at the house."

And how do the children feel about having the business at home? Of sharing his bedroom with the hat-storage space, their three-year-old says emphatically, "I like it." He loves to carry the hats back and forth.

- When and where you will be working.
- When you will and will not be available.
- Who, if anyone, will be available to them while you are working.
- Exactly what you will expect from them now that you are working at home.
- Who might be coming to the house to see you.

Develop a plan with your children like the one discussed in Chapter 13 under "Taking Charge of Interruptions and Distractions," to provide all the above information. Be firm in carrying out the plan you agree upon, but give your children the opportunity to ask questions about the plan, your work, and what you will be doing each day. Be sure that you do set aside times when you are not working and are fully available to be parents. Make sure your children know when those time are. If problems (crying, frequent interruptions, and so on) develop, talk with your children before you decide to punish them. Search for the underlying need a child may be expressing, and for underlying feelings of fear or anger about changes in your relationship. Offer support and information. Some questions children may be troubled about in connection with your working at home include:

- Am I still important?
- How much can I get away with?
- Are you still available to me when I need you?
- Who is going to be in charge?

Some messages that help children adjust to parents working at home are:

- You and your needs are still important to me.
- My work is important to our family and to the world.
- You can think and solve problems yourself. (For children over three.)
- There is time for you to get what you need from me. (Specify when, and follow through.)
- It's okay for us to be mad, sad, glad, or scared and to express our feelings to each other.
- We can solve problems so we are both happy.

Listen to your children's needs and expect them to listen to your demand for time and space to work. With children over four years old, invite them to propose solutions that will satisfy both their concerns and yours. Propose such solutions yourself.

Books that are helpful in understanding how to listen to children's feelings and still communicate your needs to them appear in the Resource list at the end of this chapter.

Handling Special Problems

A variety of problems can arise when a family tries to combine work with having children in the house. Here are several of the most common problems and some of the things you can do about them.

Getting Off on the Wrong Foot

Sometimes a problem can develop and become entrenched in the family before people know it. Then they not only have the initial problem to handle but also a bad habit to break.

If, for example, you start out allowing children to interrupt you whenever they want, you set a precedent. You will probably then have more difficulty convincing them not to interrupt you than if the problem had been handled the first time it happened. Sometimes, breaking out of bad habits like this one takes a bold approach.

When Peggy Glenn started her typing service, she discovered that her three teenage children expected more from her now that she was at home. They rebelled against the hurried meals and extra chores that they had put up with when she was working away from home. No, not by arguing. Instead, they began leaving everything around the house for her to do. Because she was at home all day, they thought she should handle all the things a full-time mother would.

To put an end to this habit, she proposed two alternatives, either of which would have been acceptable to her: all five members of the family could do an equal share of the work, or they could get a housekeeper and everyone would pay a proportionate share of the cost, based on individual income.

"All of us had some income," Peggy remembers. "My oldest daughter had a job. The youngest was baby-sitting, and my son had his paper route. Not wanting to part with their money, they thought at first they would rather do a proportional share of the work. But when I didn't do anything more than my share, they soon decided it would be better to hire the housekeeper. Then an interesting thing suddenly happened. They no longer left the messes they had been making."

Resentments

At times, children or parents may feel resentful about a working-from-home situation. Children may resent having to pick up their things because of clients; not being able to make noise at certain times; having strangers in the house and being expected to be polite to them. Parents may resent interruptions; kids who seem uncooperative; and the pressure of having to do two jobs at home: working and parenting.

Most of these resentments are a normal part of life. Remember, if you weren't working from home, you and your family would be resenting other inconveniences, like driving on the freeway, getting up early, never having enough time together, and so on. The best way to handle resentments like these is to express them and get on with living and working from home.

Resentments that build up, however, are probably a sign that you need to make some changes. If you hear *frequent* complaining and whining about why you're always working or why your family can't be "normal" like everybody else's, it's a clue that work may be intruding too much on family life. If you're frequently doing the complaining, cursing, and yelling, it could be a sign that the family is intruding on your work.

Don't overlook these symptoms. Instead, sit down and talk about the basic problem with your children and see if you can come up with some practical solutions, like locating the office somewhere else in the house or changing your work schedule.

Acting Out

Occasionally children will use the fact that you are working at home to act out their personal difficulties. For example, if you and a child have a bad relationship or the child is lonely, your working at home may be a chance for him or her to communicate the problem to you by doing things that will clearly get your attention, like being belligerent to business guests or damaging your business property.

Acting out is definitely a sign of a problem that needs to be solved. Talking it out can help sometimes. It may be especially helpful, now that you're home, to follow through on any solutions and keep a more watchful eye on the child. But if your efforts are not working, your pediatrician, family practitioner, or religious adviser should be able to refer you to someone who can help. Some counseling resources are listed in the Resource List at the end of this chapter.

Constant Interruptions

It's not uncommon for people to tell us that even after a few weeks of "testing," a child is still interrupting their work more than they would like. This can occur for a number of reasons. If it happens to you, consider the following possibilities.

First, you may not have arranged for the level of care the child needs. For example, you just can't expect a four-year-old to entertain himself or herself alone for more than a short period. A television set will not substitute for a baby-sitter. Unless someone else is there with the child, you will continue to be interrupted. Sometimes, six- or seven-year-olds are "young" for their age and require more supervision than you initially thought. Making other child-care arrangements can solve this problem, too.

There are other possibilities. You may not be letting your children know when you will be available. Perhaps you're not giving them enough time once you stop working. Occasionally children will keep interrupting you because of personal problems they are having with your working at home. Talking with them about their feelings and arranging to spend nonworking time with children should help when this kind of problem is at the root of the interruptions. Usually, however, continued interruptions occur because parents have not been clear and firm enough. They give double messages like, "I told you not to interrupt me. Now what do you want?" And after responding to the child they say, "Now don't interrupt me again." With children, actions always speak louder than words. In this case, the words say, "Don't interrupt," but the actions are saying, "It's okay."

Thinking they are being firm, some parents get angry at the child and spend a lot of time and energy dealing with each interruption. Teachers and army sergeants have both learned this lesson the hard way: negative attention is better than no attention at all. Briefly notifying children that you are working, telling them when you will be available, and closing the door as if you expected the child to act accordingly is the best approach.

Consistency is important, too. Behavioral research shows that being firm 80 percent of the time, but lax the other 20 percent, only increases the chances of repeated interruptions. From the child's perspective, perhaps *this* time will be one of the exceptions.

Inability to Say "No"

Some parents find it very difficult to say "no" to their kids. If you are one of those people and you want to keep working at home, you will either have to get someone else to manage your children or learn to say "no" and mean it. Otherwise you will probably end up yelling and screaming and wondering why your children still don't do what you want them to.

You can learn to say "no" without sounding harsh or cruel, by practicing with pets or store clerks. When you can use your voice firmly enough to get the pets to obey you or the clerks to accept "no" for an answer, you're well on your way to being able to make your children obey without screaming and physical punishment.

Guilt

"When I'm at work, I feel guilty that I'm not with my kids, and when I'm with my kids, I feel guilty that I'm not working." This is a dilemma many parents face. Certainly, working at home can help ease the discomfort of feeling that you should be in two places at once, but sometimes it intensifies a parent's guilt feelings instead.

As one woman told us, "When my daughter comes to the door and says, 'Mommy, please don't work anymore,' I could just cry." Of course, feeling this way splits her energy between her work and her daughter. The result is that she doesn't get to enjoy either one. With feelings like these, it's very hard to send a firm, clear, and consistent message to your children about the importance of not interrupting your work. So instead of getting their cooperation, you end up getting even more interruptions and feeling even more torn.

But what can a parent do to combat guilt feelings like these? Recognize that pursuing your career effectively is actually important to your children's futures. We don't feel guilty about working, because we've realized that the best thing we can do for our son is to love him and care for him while pursuing fulfilling lives for ourselves. This way of acting shows him that it's wonderful to be alive and to grow up. It says that having children is a joy, that you can love and care for them and live your own life to the fullest, too. For us, working at home has made this all possible.

When It Doesn't Work

If your needs, the needs of your family, and the needs of your business just don't match up, working at home can be more pain than pleasure, and finding another office location is the best solution. Single parent and publicist Kathy Hubbell encountered such a problem. When she opened her public relations firm, she decided to work at home so she could be closer to her children, both of whom were in grade school.

"I never dealt very successfully with my guilt about my not being there when they got home from school," Kathy explains. "I've never particularly liked being a single parent. It usually means one provider, but no parent. So I thought working at home would provide a more cohesive way of life and I wouldn't feel so split."

She felt the kids did benefit from her being at home, but found her own tensions only increased. "It was really difficult for the kids to understand that when I was in my home office, I was at work and couldn't be disturbed. They were so glad to have me home, they'd just launch in and talk away about their day."

The constant interruptions angered her, but she was torn because she felt they deserved her time after not having had it for so long. For her own sanity, she moved her office out of the house. She felt better, but the kids felt worse than ever. She finally found the solution when she placed an ad in a college newspaper for a male student to come serve as a big brother to the kids and adopted family member, in exchange for room and board. When Doug Hagan joined their household, "the kids stopped fighting, chores were getting done, the whole atmosphere changed, and I began to relax about what I'd find when I came home from work."

Does she still like it better having her office away from home? "No, since Doug is here, home has become a better place to be. I want to be here again."

Kathy Hubbell's story illustrates an important point about working at home with children around. It seemed impossible, yet she finally found a solution that made it feasible and even preferable.

When you work from home and live with children, there will almost certainly be adjustments to make and problems of one kind or another to resolve. Yet with firmness and love and time to share feelings, you're just as likely to find solutions that will make working from home rewarding for all of you.

Chapter Digest

1. Working from home holds the potential of making juggling the increasingly stressful demands of career and family easier for both mothers and fathers.
2. Usually if you have children under school age, you will need to arrange for some supplementary child care. You have many more options, however, than when you work away from home.

3. Children react differently to parents' working from home. But whatever age your children are, don't expect them to act like grown-ups with regard to your work. They won't be quiet. They won't always be neat and tidy or polite. So the best rule of thumb is to child-proof your office instead of trying to office-proof your children. Set up your office and your schedule so having "normal" kids around will not disrupt your work.

4. Make your expectations clear to your children and stick to them. Learn to be firm and to say "no." Recognize that you can't be "super-parent" but you can find a way to make adequate time for both work and family.

5. Be sure your children know when you will be available to spend time with them and when you will not. To avoid problems, allow ample time to spend with them.

6. One of the benefits of working from home is that your children learn more about the work you do and the world of business. Sometimes families enjoy working together in the business. We find this works best, however, when it is voluntary instead of mandatory.

Resources

Books

Between Parent & Child. Haim Ginnot. New York: Avon, 1976.

Between Parent & Teen. Haim Ginnot. New York: Avon, 1982.

Growing a Business/Raising a Family. Jan and Charlie Fletcher, eds. Seattle: NextStep Publications, 1988.

Parent Effectiveness Training. Thomas Gordon. See full citation under Chapter 18.

TA for Kids (and Parents Too). Alvyn M. and Margaret Freed. Palos Verdes, CA: Jalmar Press, 1977.

TA for Tots, Vol. II. Alvyn M. Freed. Palos Verdes, CA: Jalmar Press, 1973.

TA for Teens. Alvyn M. Freed. Palos Verdes, CA: Jalmar Press, 1976.

The Third Wave. Alvin Toffler. New York: Bantam Books, 1984.

Classes and Counseling Resources

The Association for Marriage and Family Therapists. 1000 Connecticut Ave., NW, #407, Washington, D.C. 20036.

Parent Effectiveness Training, Inc. 531 Stevens Ave., Solana Beach, CA 92075; (619) 481-8121.

CHAPTER
TWENTY

■■■■■■■■■■■■■■■■■■■■■■

Getting Help When You Need It

Most people who work at home are self-sufficient and self-reliant—perfect candidates for an Emersonian society. Yet in this age of information overload, a jack-of-all-trades can become a slave to his or her own independence.

Alternatively, putting other people's efforts to work for you can extend your time, your money, and your peace of mind. For these reasons, successful people who work at home call upon the skills and talents of a variety of other people to help them get their work done. They build a network of local suppliers who can provide business supplies and services. They build a team of professionals who can be relied upon to handle legal, tax, insurance, and banking needs. They find support staff and personnel to help carry out the day-to-day operations of their work.

In this chapter we talk about how to identify the help you need, where to find it, and how to make the most of it.

When It's Time to Get Help

We recommend getting help from other people in four situations:

- When you don't have the skills and expertise yourself to do a job.
- When it will cost you more to do the job yourself than to hire someone else to do it.
- When the job can't be done by one person.
- When you hate doing a task, but it must be done.

Particularly at first, you may prefer to do most of the things that need to be done in your business yourself. Certainly the more you can do, the easier it will be to get under way. As a matter of fact, in their book *Honest Business,* Michael Phillips and Salli Rasberry identify the desire to handle every facet of an enterprise as an attribute of successful entrepreneurs.

Here are some of the tasks that people working at home often dislike, can't do alone, or find more cost-effective to have done for them. Review the list for the ones that apply to your situation.

Accounting	Office management
Advertising	Printing
Answering the phone	Public relations
Assembly	Research
Bookkeeping	Shipping
Cleaning	Tax preparation
Delivery	Typesetting
Filing	Typing
Marketing	

There are usually some necessary tasks that you don't have the skills to carry out. Some of these skills, like typing, selling, and marketing, you can and probably should learn.

If you don't type, you may be tempted to hire a secretary or a service to do all your typing for you. Resist this temptation. Jeffery Lant, who trains others in how to establish a consultant practice, believes typing is a basic entrepreneurial skill that saves time and aggravation. We agree. You can still use a secretary or service when you want to. But costs mount up when you have to send every little note to a secretarial service and you lose out when you have to wait until Monday to get out an emergency letter.

The ability to type will also open the world of word processing and telecomputing to you. In fact, in telecomputing, a fast keyboard response is as important as being able to think on your feet. And fortunately, with a personal computer, learning to type is easy because there are software programs you can use to teach yourself quickly and painlessly. There's also a simplified keyboard arrangement, the Dovorak keyboard, you can get for most computers that takes less time to learn than the standard keyboard and results in faster typing with less fatigue.

Other skills, like graphic design or accounting, may not be feasible for you to acquire. It's in these situations that you should hire the expertise you need. Studies, like the one done by Thorne Riddell, show that successful business owners recognize when they need professional assistance and get it.

When you first begin working on your own, you will probably have free time to do the majority of things involved in your business. Later, some of those things may no longer be cost-effective to do yourself. Writing and pasting-up a newsletter, for example, can be a good use of your time when you don't have much business. Once your workday is filled with business, paying someone else to do these tasks could actually cost you less.

You may also start out being able to handle all the business you can generate, but a sudden burst of seasonal activity or one big order may be more than you can handle alone. At this point, your choice is to hire help or turn away business. You may find yourself forced to act like Van Von Middlesworth who has a sideline business producing hand-painted toy soldiers. For shows and special orders he has no problem producing what he needs, but when a large chain wanted a thousand soldiers during the Christmas season, he had to hire help to fill the order.

Finally, when there are tasks that you clearly dislike, neglect, or resist, it's very likely you can find others who are willing to do them. Finding someone else to assist you under these circumstances will undoubtedly make your life and your work pleasanter and have a positive effect on your enthusiasm. The time to get help with these tasks is when you see that help will free you to generate the business you need to cover the added expenses involved.

Six Sources for Getting the Help You Need

Working at home can present various roadblocks to getting the full range of help you need. Money certainly is one, since most people start working from home on a limited budget. Space is frequently another. The typical household can take only so much equipment and very few employees before it begins overflowing. Finally, finding the right people to do the work under home-office circumstances can also become a problem. But none of these obstacles is insurmountable. Here are six workable alternatives to doing everything yourself.

Using Business Services

The service section of our economy is growing rapidly. With the increasing number of services available for small businesses, you will be able to purchase many of the services you need without hiring any employees.

Printing services are available in most neighborhoods. In addition to standard printing and duplicating, many of these shops offer artwork, layout, typesetting, proofreading, and design. You can also use secretarial services, bookkeeping services, answering services, messenger services, cleaning services, and research services, to mention just a few. Many of these services are home businesses themselves.

In our neighborhood, we have been able to create a network of small home businesses with whom we trade. Our artist, cartoonist, audio technician, and typesetter all operate home businesses in our area. It's like having our own organization, without the cost of an office building for the workers or the ongoing overhead of employing them.

By purchasing services, you pay only for what you need when you need it. And since businesses that don't provide a good service won't be able to stay in business, they're likely to want to please and stand behind their work.

Because these businesses have overhead to support, you will pay more per hour or per task than if you hired your own employee. You may also have to wait until a service can get to your work. Then sometimes, just when you need them most, they're too busy to help. The service will improve, however, if you become a regular customer. And the better a customer you become, the more willing they will be to extend themselves and help you out in emergencies.

You can locate services through your local business Yellow Pages, the Chamber of Commerce, or networking groups. Once you find a service, try it out for a while. Then, if you're satisfied, keep using the same service so they'll pay special attention to you.

Hiring and Contracting for the Help You Need

When you need someone to come in and work with you shoulder to shoulder, hiring help is usually going to be the answer, and here are several different ways you can go about doing it.

Full-time employees. If you hire the right full-time employee, you have a loyal and hardworking person you can count on day in and day out to get the job done for you. Such employees are worth their weight in gold and may be the answer to ensuring that you'll have the help you need.

Legal Checklist for Hiring an Employee

State and federal regulations for hiring employees vary according to the number of employees or the nature of your business. When hiring an employee, check with state agencies or your attorney to determine how these government laws and regulations apply to you:

☐ Social Security Tax and Federal Income Tax Withholding
☐ Federal Unemployment Taxes
☐ State Withholding
☐ State Disability Insurance
☐ State Unemployment Taxes
☐ Workers' Compensation Insurance
☐ Employee Benefit Plans (ERISA)
☐ Employee Safety and Health Regulations
☐ Employee Wage and Hour Regulations
☐ Fair Employment Practices

However, the primary reasons most people choose to work from home are to keep their overhead low and to simplify their working life. Hiring employees may deprive you of some of these benefits. There are the direct payroll costs to consider, and unless you have enough work for a full-time person, you may find the employee with nothing to do and yourself manufacturing something to keep him or her busy.

One consultant told us, "At first I enjoyed having my own secretary. It made me feel like an executive, but paying her monthly salary really put me behind the eight ball. I had to support someone else before I could support myself! Finally I decided to let her go and hire a secretarial service. It felt like someone had taken a weight off my shoulders."

In addition, you have to provide workspace, equipment, and supplies for your employee. Unless you plan to rent separate space, this means you will have another person coming into your home every day. In some areas this can present a problem with zoning. Certain municipalities allow home businesses, but prohibit having employees on the property.

Finally, as C.P.A. Bernard Kamoroff points out in his book *The Small-Time Operator*, "Hiring employees will just about double the amount of your paperwork." When you become an employer, you must keep separate payroll records, withhold federal income and Social Security taxes, withhold state income and possibly state disability taxes, prepare quarterly and year-end payroll tax returns, pay the employee's portion of Social Security taxes and unemployment taxes, usually purchase workers' compensation insurance, and prepare year-end earnings statements for each employee. The cost of these requirements has been estimated to add 30 percent to the salary you pay an employee.

Once you set up a system for managing the complexities of having one or more employees, these administrative details will be much less formidable than they seem at first. Handling the excess paperwork is a task you can even pay others to do. Or you can always get a payroll service to manage many of the formalities involved in having employees, although you will still be legally responsible for your employees.

Our advice is to consider some of the other alternatives we'll be discussing before you decide to hire. Then when full-time employees are your best answer, consult your attorney and your accountant for help in setting up the easiest and most workable arrangements for handling the responsibilities of being an employer.

Part-time employees. Although hiring part-time employees may pose some of the same problems as full-time workers do, many home-based businesses opt for part-timers, either to save costs or because several part-time employees can do a variety of specialized tasks that no one person could do alone.

Career consultant Marilyn Miller, for example, has three part-time employees. A secretary works three days a week typing, filing, and returning phone calls. A training assistant accompanies Marilyn to seminars and work-

Employee Fringe Benefits and Personnel Policies

When you have employees, you need to determine the fringe benefits you will offer and establish policies for managing them. Common fringe benefits that employees may expect are listed below:

- Health insurance
- Disability income insurance
- Life insurance
- Paid holidays

- Vacations
- Sick leave
- A retirement plan

Written personnel policies covering the following issues are also advisable:

- Working hours
- Lunch hour
- Job description
- Breaks
- Absences from work

- Probationary period
- Termination
- Payroll schedule
- Confidentiality
- Tardiness

shops to manage all the on-site logistical arrangements. And she has a research assistant who does library work for her. None of these employees can do the jobs of the others.

Hiring part-time employees also helps meet short-term high-volume demands. For example, Paul and Gretchen Fava rented a warehouse and hired seventy part-time workers to achieve the high buildup of inventory needed to fill orders for their hand-painted Christmas decorations. After reaching the inventory level they wanted, they returned to the renovated guest house behind their home where they maintain their inventory with the help of only a handful of part-time college students.

Independent contractors. Many people prefer to hire independent contractors for specific tasks and pay on a fee-for-service basis. Independent contractors are self-employed individuals who usually work for more than one client. An independent researcher, for example, will work on projects for various clients and charge individually for each task.

As Bob Baxter's business, Pet Organics, grew from twenty-four accounts to five hundred, he decided to expand by using independent contractors. Instead of mixing, bottling, and preparing to ship his natural flea treatments in his garage, he now contracts with someone to produce, bottle, and ship the products for him. Instead of calling on only those retail stores he could visit himself, he has contracted with independent salespeople to represent his line to retailers.

Rather than hire an administrative assistant, consultant Thomas Kerr has contracted with someone who provides a range of administrative services for him and several other clients. Kerr describes the primary advantage he finds in contracting. "I prefer this arrangement because I can call on the assistance when I need it, which is maybe once or twice a quarter when I have a special project to get out."

As these examples illustrate, using contractors can help you control costs. Also, contractors generally provide their own facilities, supplies, and equipment. Another advantage is that using contractors provides you with the flexibility to find the best services possible for the specific task. Being small-business operators themselves, independent contractors may have a keen understanding of your needs as a small business too. They face many of the same issues you do and may, in fact, work at home.

Since an independent contractor is not an employee, you do not have to withhold taxes, pay employment taxes, or file payroll tax returns for this kind of help. When you pay an independent contractor over $600 a year, you do, however, have to file IRS Form 1099 with the Internal Revenue Service and send a copy to the individual.

A word of caution. Do not think that you can simply employ someone and call him or her an "independent contractor." The IRS position is that if the person is an employee, the label you give that employee doesn't matter. In other words, to the Internal Revenue Service, an employee by any other name is still an employee. To help you understand exactly who is and who isn't an employee, the IRS puts out a free publication, *Circular E-Employer's Tax Guide,* or you can request a ruling on your situation from the IRS by using Form #SS–8.

The disadvantage of using independent contractors is that *your* work may not be their first priority. They may not be available when you want them. There may be delays in getting your work done while they work for others. Also, independent contractors only become knowledgeable about your business needs if you use them frequently. They may fail to produce work done the way you want it, but unless you have a contract that covers this possibility, you may have little practical recourse other than to go elsewhere.

Temporary-help agencies. For certain short-term assistance, you can hire help through a temporary service. Temporary services are primarily limited to secretarial and office management personnel. On the other hand, these agencies have the advantage of being able to provide you with reliable help quickly, without your spending the time and money to locate and select someone. The agency handles all financial arrangements with the employee and bills you for the service. The agency also stands behind the work. The cost is usually somewhat higher than using an independent contractor, and you cannot depend upon getting the same person again.

Contract staffing companies. One way to have employees while saving yourself the paperwork and legal responsibility of being an employer is to lease employees from a staffing company. Doctors and dentists have been using these services for years. You maintain substantial control over the employee, except that if the worker assigned you must be fired, you send the employee back to the staffing company instead of releasing the person yourself. For managing all the legal and administrative responsibilities of your staff, you pay the staffing company a fee over and above the cost of the employees' earnings and benefits each month.

Where to find help. To find employees, independent contractors, and employment services, you can use:

- *Telephone Yellow Pages.* Various kinds of employment services are listed under "Employment." Independent contractors are listed by field—for example, word-processing services. They usually have one-line listings under their own names.
- *College placement offices.* Students seeking part-time work or contracting out their services are often listed with these offices.
- *Referrals from associates.* Associates are good sources of information about independent contractors they have been satisfied with. Part-time employees of associates may also be looking for additional work.
- *Chambers of Commerce.* Temporary services, contract staff firms, and independent contractors in your area may be members of the local chamber. Also, other members may have used services they can recommend.
- *Networking groups.* Networking groups are formal and informal meetings of independent businesspeople who come together weekly for the purpose of referring business to one another. In Chapter 17 we recommend that home-based business owners join at least one such networking group for marketing and affiliation purposes. Finding reliable support services is another excellent reason for participating in such a group. As you get to know the individuals in your group, you may find that using their services can be a highly reliable source of support.
- *Classified ads in local newspapers or specialty newsletters.* Often neighborhood papers or trade papers are more helpful in locating the people or services you need than are larger metropolitan papers. Read the ads under "Business Services" and "Positions Wanted." Sometimes local papers even feature articles on local independent businesses.

    You can also place ads for the assistance you want, but screen applicants by phone or mail and check their references before giving them your address or having them come to your home. Usually you can make arrangements to have applicants forward information through the newspaper.
- *Community, business, and computer bulletin boards.* Read the bulletin boards at banks, community centers, grocery stores, laundromats, print shops, and libraries. Often home businesses and independent contractors will post their cards or flyers in these places. Also scan computer bulletin boards like CompuServe.

Bartering or Exchanging Services

Barter is a cashless exchange of services that some home businesspeople find useful for getting the assistance or the products they need. You offer your services to someone who needs them in exchange for their services to you. Barbara Elman, publisher of *Word Processing News,* has a barter arrangement with her answering service. They answer her phone; she does their mailing labels each month on her word processor.

Barter obviously reduces your costs or enables you to have assistance you could otherwise not afford. However, it may be difficult to find the appropriate person to trade services or products with. Barter clubs enable you to overcome this problem. They keep a credit balance for you, so if you offer a service to one member, you get credit to receive services from any other member. These clubs often require a considerable start-up fee, though, and may or may not have the business services you need in your area.

To barter for services on your own, take the initiative and ask people who offer the work you need whether they are willing to barter. You may be surprised at how many people will consider it.

Marilyn Miller, for example, was surprised to discover that she could barter to have color slides made for her management-training presentations. When she realized she would need slides of higher quality than those she was presently using, to accompany a planned fee increase, she decided to approach an audio/video service about training its staff in exchange for a set of top-quality four-color slides. They said "yes"! So go ahead and ask. You may be surprised at the response.

When bartering, make a clear agreement as to the value of the services you are exchanging and evaluate the trustworthiness and experience of those you barter with, just as you would when purchasing the service. As with all contracts, you're best protected against misunderstanding by putting the agreement in writing.

The IRS considers business services received through bartering as income, and business services you provide through bartering as deductible business expense. So keep records of your exchanges, and make sure the values you claim represent actual market rates.

Affiliating with Others

Affiliating with others whose skills support and supplement yours can be another way to find the help you need. There are at least three different ways you can affiliate.

Calling on customers and clients. Explore the possibilities of using or buying the services of companies for whom you are working. These companies may be glad to see you purchase services like word processing or duplicating to help offset their overhead costs. They may even be willing to let you use company services without charge, or as part of the fee they're paying you.

Sharing expenses or efforts. Pooling expenses with colleagues or competitors can provide you with help you might not otherwise be able to afford. Two women we interviewed share a secretary, each employing her part time. Other home businesses are using what's called co-op advertising, in which several of them share the costs of advertising their related products and services.

Peggy Glenn found she could call on her competitors to take overload work from her typing service and, in turn, she gladly provided backup for them. Lynne Frances found she could share certain expenses with an owner of another cleaning service, and they assist each other when short on cleaning crews.

Joint ventures. By entering into joint ventures with others who have skills or expertise you need, you can accomplish much that would be impossible to do yourself. In a joint venture, you affiliate with others to provide a service or produce a product, and then share together in any profits. No one individual has to make a large cash investment. Each invests primarily his or her own time and talents. But everyone involved benefits when the venture is successful.

A professional development consultant we know arranges joint ventures on all the training films he produces. He writes the material and joins with others who produce the film and still others who market it. They all share an agreed-upon percentage of the profits on the finished films.

Since partners are often investing their time without payment or at a reduced fee, a joint venture usually becomes a side venture. Locating dedicated and honest partners is therefore crucial. You have to rely on their conduct and efforts for the success of your project. Legally, joint ventures are partnerships. This means you will be liable for anything your partners do in relation to the project. Having a written contract or partnership agreement is a necessary safeguard.

The best way to locate people interested in sharing expenses or joint-venturing is through professional or trade associations in your field, networking, and relationships with competitors or other businesses that complement yours.

Getting Assistance from Family Members

Using family members to do jobs that need to be done provides an opportunity for them to share in your work and is a way for you to limit your expenses. You can ask for volunteers or you can offer wages.

Hiring your children has a tax advantage too. When you hire your children to work for you, their salaries are a deductible business expense, while their earnings are taxed at a much lower rate than yours. In fact, there is no tax for earnings below a certain amount earned each year.

The disadvantage is that family members can be unreliable workers. Sometimes they don't want to help or may be too busy doing other things to follow through for you. Other times family squabbles spill over into work activities, and vice versa. So when you hire a family member or ask your family for free assistance, we recommend that it be strictly a voluntary matter rather than something you expect, coerce, or finagle someone into doing.

Calling on Employers or Contractors

If you are salaried, working on a commission, or under a contract, explore the services your employer or contractor can provide for you. At-home workers are still a relatively new phenomenon. Companies are not always aware of their needs. So express your needs and ask for support.

If you are working with a franchise or are in direct sales, explore with the franchiser or the direct-selling organization what additional support services they can furnish you with. Different companies offer different levels of assistance. Many provide extensive training, promotional materials, and displays. If you are working under a contract, contractors are often more than happy to let you use their facilities and support services when doing so helps reduce the expense of the contract or improves the quality of the project.

Making the Most of the Help You Get

Whatever type of help you use, there are several guidelines you can follow to ensure a top-quality job.

Clearly define what you want done. First, before you even decide on the type of help you want, define precisely what you need someone to do. We suggest writing or sketching it out. Sometimes you have to do some research to find out what you actually need.

Producing the covers for some tape albums we created was a good example. Originally we thought it would be a simple process. But before we hired a printer, we decided to talk with several to find out what it would involve. There turned out to be many different ways of doing it, and having reviewed the choices we were in a much better position to hire a printer with experience in the process we preferred.

Find the right people. Finding the right people is usually a matter of looking carefully at past experience and present capabilities. Getting referrals from a satisfied customer in your field is probably the best way. When that isn't possible, getting—*and checking*—references or looking at examples of past work can help provide the information you need.

In talking with prospective help, raise the problems and concerns you have in relation to the work you're hiring for. If you're under a tight deadline, for example, express your concern that it be done in time. If you need the worker to take certain precautions when dealing with customers, explain what they are. Then listen and watch the person respond. Do they have solutions? Are they confident about handling the situations you present?

Don't assume the help you get knows what you want. We discovered the hard way that just because people are good at what they do doesn't mean they know how to do what you want. Be specific. Draw sketches. Write out a list. Bring in samples. Define the end product with care and monitor the progress. Have checkpoints to look at, or talk with workers about the progress they're making. Consider hiring someone for a small job and reviewing the work before hiring that person for larger or more important projects.

Hiring a typesetter to set copy for a flyer is a good example of this process. Writing out the correctly spelled text is only the beginning. Don't leave the typesetter with the job of deciding on layout, size, and style of type unless you're willing to take potluck. Specify your preferences. If you do not know enough to be specific, ask for the typesetter's recommendations and a sample of what the piece would look like. Then ask to see the way the copy will look before it is finalized.

Set deadlines. Set deadlines for when the work is to be completed and get the worker's agreement that will be completed by that time. To be on the safe side, call or talk with the person along the way to see if things are on schedule. The more notice you have of problems, the easier it is to revise your plans.

Get an understanding about what will be done if work isn't satisfactory. The best policy, of course, is to expect the person will stand behind the work and redo it if it isn't right. You do not have to accept less than the quality you wanted, providing you were clear about what you were expecting in the first place.

Also identify who will pay for costs incurred from mistakes. After one costly error, private practice consultant Gene Call now negotiates with all the designers he uses to ensure that if the mailings they design for him don't meet U.S. Postal Service requirements, the designers will be liable for the resulting cost. Added postage on 100,000 mailings, because the piece was oversize, is an expensive error. And more than once a designer has had to pay the extra bill.

Treat the people you hire like people. We've found that when we are considerate, thoughtful, and understanding of the people we hire, they go out of their way to do a better job. Greeting those who work for you, complimenting them when they're helpful, and listening to the concerns they raise are part of the honey that sweetens any business relationship. One sympathetic word that shows you understand the pressures or difficulties can win you work that goes above and beyond the call of duty.

Pay on time. The best way to have people begin dragging their feet or doing less than their best on your job is to delay or overlook payment you owe. Pay immediately in accordance with whatever arrangements you have established.

Reward good work. Reward good work with praise, repeat business, and referrals. Under whatever arrangements people work for you, they generally appreciate recognition for a job well done. Giving it to them is a way of increasing their desire to please you again and again.

With the variety of possible arrangements you can make for getting help, you should be able to find whatever support you need while working from home. Whenever you want assistance, you can review the options we've discussed for getting the help you need, and then use the strategies given to make the most of the help you get.

Chapter Digest

1. You need not become a slave to your own independence. You can extend your time, energy, and money by getting full- or part-time help by one or more of the following means:
   - Using business services
   - Hiring or contracting for the help you need
   - Bartering or exchanging services
   - Affiliating with others
   - Getting assistance from family members
   - Calling on employers, contractors, or sponsoring organizations
2. In hiring employees or using the services of others, make sure you find qualified people, clearly define what you need them to do, get clear agreements about deadlines, payment, and liability, and reward good work.

Resources

Books

Honest Business. See full citation under Chapter 3.

Small-Time Operator. See full citation under Chapter 14.

Newsletters and Periodicals

Internal Revenue Service (see Chapter 3 for full citation):
   Employers Tax Guide, Circular E.

PART 6

Getting Business and Growing

CHAPTER
TWENTY-ONE
■■■■■■■■■■■■■■■■■■■■■■

Pricing: Determining What to Charge

"What shall I charge?" This is one of the most common questions prospective home-based business owners ask at our seminars. If you've ever read anything about pricing or attended a seminar on pricing, you've undoubtedly discovered the question is not so much "What shall I charge?" as "How do I determine what to charge?"

Although you'll encounter a wide variety of "formulas" set forth confidently by business experts, in reality there is no simple answer to what to charge. Even veteran businesspeople often find themselves wondering if they're missing sales by charging too much, or if they could get away with charging even more. That's why the range of advice novice entrepreneurs receive about pricing is often enough to make their heads spin. Here are a few examples of the type of advice we've been given:

"Set your price so low that they can't refuse."
"Never discount your prices."
"Charge the going rate."
"Charge just below the going rate."
"Charge just above the going rate."
"Add up your direct costs, overhead, and profit and that's your price."
"Find out what everyone else charges and position yourself in the middle."

Does this sound familiar? Now add to this conflicting advice what Sonny Blain found out—there may not *be* a "going rate." When Sonny set out to research what to charge for hypercard programming he found programmers who were charging as little as $30 an hour and others who were charging over $100 an hour, and almost every amount in between. So how *do* you know what to charge? The answer is that you don't *know* what to charge, you *discover* what to charge.

Pricing, like marketing, is an experiment. It's like cooking without a recipe. You're balancing many sensitive factors and adjusting the combinations until you get one that suits the palates of your customers. Like diners choosing a restaurant, some customers want a no-frills cafeteria while others prefer only an elite tearoom or a trendy bistro.

In this chapter we want to provide you with a guide to various elements you can consider in determining your own ideal pricing recipe. You'll learn from the experience of many successful home-based businesses how to avoid the most common mistakes open-collar workers make in pricing their services, and discover how taking the time and energy to find the right price can be a key to your success.

Begin with Some Basic Research

Occasionally, the price of a particular home-based product or your service is driven, like the price of hamburgers or gasoline, pretty much by the marketplace. Clothing merchandising consultant Martina Polaski's specialty is such a business. "All the manufacturers pay the same thing for what I do. It's the rock bottom price. They know what they can get it for and that's that." Under such circumstances, pricing is a matter of finding out how you can run your business successfully at the prevailing price.

Most home-based ventures, however, tend to be more personalized and customized by nature. This means you probably won't be unduly constrained by what someone else is charging. More likely you'll have a great deal of flexibility, as we described above. Therefore, to find the right price, you need to begin by doing some investigation to determine the following:

How much is your product or your service really worth in concrete terms? Value, like beauty, is in the mind of the beholder. It's highly subjective. The value people place on what you offer will vary according to their needs and their perceptions of what your product or service will do for them. So the more concrete you can make the value of your work, the easier it will be to determine your price, and then get it.

Here are several ways to concretize the value of what you offer. Can someone get this product or service elsewhere? How much are they paying now? What would they have to pay someone else? Does your product or service save or produce money for your customer? For example, if you're supplying dried-flower gift baskets to local hospitals, the hospitals save the costs of having them shipped in from out of the area. Or, if hiring you to design a direct-mail campaign will generate $25,000 of income for your client, you could be a bargain at $5,000.

When the benefits of your business are more intangible in nature, think in terms of how much they are worth relative to other things people buy. For example, people might spend $50 for an entertaining evening at the theater. Paying $50 to attend your evening workshop on real-estate investing, however, could be profitable and might even be entertaining. Parents might pay $65 or more for a pair of sports shoes for their junior highschooler, but paying you that for two tutoring sessions could help their child catch up in math.

What will people actually pay?   No matter how much a product or service may be worth, if people won't pay that much for it, it won't sell. A good example of this problem is Carol Hartager's beautiful hand-painted greeting cards. Since they could each easily be framed as a work of art, she thought $10 was a fair retail price. Greeting-card store buyers didn't agree. They thought $10 was too much. When Carol placed them on consignment in a local store, she discovered that the customers thought so too. They didn't sell until she had reduced the price to $3.

So perception of value can be as important as the actual value. If the customer perceives the price as too high, you'll end up without work or with a garage full of inventory. At the other extreme, if buyers perceive something as too cheap, they either won't buy it or they'll worry about what the "catch" is. Many new entrepreneurs are surprised to discover they can actually sell more by charging more. A book, for example, that wasn't selling at $19.95 sold briskly when repackaged as a workbook at $99.95; a particular software package sold much better at $69.95 than it did at $30.00.

So don't rely on your own perceptions of what people will pay. Your perceptions are limited by your particular upbringing and experience, and may be outdated or at least different from those of your market. Find out what your clients and customers are accustomed to paying and match your price to their expectations.

Shirley Glickman learned this the hard way. As a teacher, she knew what public school systems paid for outside consultants. So when she left her teaching job to conduct values-clarification workshops for corporate training departments, she set her fees based on her experience in the school system— and had a lot of trouble closing sales! Prospective clients seemed interested until she mentioned her fee. Then their interest cooled. She feared her price was too high. By asking around at professional associations for trainers, however, she was amazed to discover that companies were used to paying almost double her fee for outside consultants. With such cut-rate fees, they weren't taking her seriously. When she raised her prices to what was expected, she closed sales.

Underpricing is one of the most frequent mistakes home-based businesses make. So as desktop publisher Matt McCaffrey advises, "Don't sell yourself short—I landed a typesetting contract recently at a rate 35 percent above the prevailing wage in my area because I valued my time appropriately and was firm in my requirements."

Programmer Kristi Wachter agrees. She says, "I still feel weird telling people I'm charging $75 an hour when this little voice in my head keeps reminding me of all the jobs I've worked on at a salary of $5 an hour. But companies are used to paying this kind of money for the consulting help they need. And remember, they're paying for all the time you've put in to develop the expertise you have. You are not an employee any longer, you're supporting yourself. No one's paying for your coffee breaks, benefits, or anything else."

A rule of thumb you can use in setting your initial fees is to determine the salary an equivalent job would pay, divide by 2,000 hours (40 hours per week for 50 weeks) to get your hourly rate, and then add 30 to 45 percent for overhead. This gives you a figure equivalent to what it would cost per hour to maintain an employee to do the same job. Of course, if you can only work ten months out of the year, you'll need to add another 20 percent.

Are you charging enough to make this worth your while? You can make a million dollars but if it costs you more than a million to make a million, you've lost money. As graphics designer Todd Minor found out, making money can be deceptive. He had two major contracts his first year in business that produced over a quarter of a million dollars. Things seemed to be rolling along. But by year's end, he was in debt. In his eagerness to be the low bidder on these contracts, he had unknowingly run his company into the hole.

So in setting your prices, make sure you'll have more coming in than you have going out. That means charging a price that covers your direct and indirect costs with some to spare. In fact, a commonly used pricing formula is *direct costs + overhead + profit = price.*

Direct costs refers to costs you incur as a direct result of producing your product or providing your service. For example, if you are doing word processing, the paper you print a job out on is a direct cost. If you provide a mobile computer-repair service, the cost of driving to your customer's office is a direct cost. So is the cost of any parts you replace for them. If you are doing public relations, costs of telephone calls you make to book a client on out-of-town talk shows is a direct cost as is the cost of printing and mailing media kits on their behalf. And so is the time you spend on these projects!

Yes, your time is a direct cost. For purposes of doing business, you have to factor in the cost of your time as if you were an employee of your business. For the single-person service business, your time is all you have to sell. You can't make any more money than you can bill out. For example, as a psychotherapist, you only have so many hours a week in which to see clients. As a trainer, you only have so many days a month on which you can train people. Even if your business is manufacturing a product, your time is a labor cost.

To determine what to charge for your time, consider what you would have to pay if you had to hire someone with your background and experience to do what you do. Or if you are doing the same thing as you did on your last job, calculate your salary *including the fringe benefits* into your current rates. Many new home-based venturepeople underprice themselves by leaving out the value of their time or by forgetting to include the cost of their fringe benefits when calculating their fees. Also remember you can't possibly bill out every hour of the business week. Some portion of your time must be spent marketing and administering your business. So you have to set the cost of your billable time high enough to compensate you for your time that isn't billable.

Overhead refers to all the costs of doing business that are not directly attributable to a specific product or service. For example, the cost of your computer equipment, your software, utilities, office supplies, an 800 number, advertising and marketing costs, tax preparer's and attorney's fees, even bank charges and other administrative costs, are all overhead costs. Everything you must spend to stay in business counts as overhead.

Profit is any money that's left over after you pay all your direct and indirect expenses. Many business experts advise adding 15 to 20 percent or more to your price over and above all your costs. This is considered your reward for the risk you take to be in business or as an allowance for development. Many home-based businesspeople, however, do not include profit in calculating their prices. Often this is because they aren't aware they could be adding in profit or because they fear that to survive they must cut their margins to a bare minimum. Others, however, feel that being self-employed is more a benefit than a risk. They reason that if they have charged adequately for their time, they're being compensated sufficiently. Viewed this way, profit is more like a tip. It's what you get because you haven't paid yourself enough.

Ultimately, the important thing in setting your price is that one way or another you are earning enough to provide yourself with a comfortable enough lifestyle to make running your business well worth the effort. If you can't command such a price, then you should rethink your business choice.

Can I make more money doing a little for a lot or a lot for a little? And how much volume do you want? Often pricing requires that you face directly just how you want to structure your business, how much you want to work, and what type of role you want to play in your business. If you want to make $65,000 a year as a psychotherapist, for example, you could see twenty people a week for $65 each. Or you could see thirteen people a week for $100 each. Or you could have five groups of about twelve people each, who pay $25 apiece each week. Which would be easier and more cost effective: getting sixty people who would pay $25 each, or finding thirteen people who will pay $100 a week?

If you are a public speaker and want to make $100,000 a year, you could give just one speech a week if you charged about $2,000 a speech. Whereas if you could only get $1,000 a speech you would have to give two speeches a week in order to make your goal. How much effort will it take you to book that many speeches? How much will it cost?

If you have a pool-cleaning service and charge $50 a month, you can serve sixty clients yourself and make $3,000 a month. Or you can hire, train, and supervise three employees and pay them $25 a client. Then, by keeping your fee the same, you could serve 180 clients and make $4,500 a month. Which work style and lifestyle would suit you better—the challenge of supervising three employees for a possible additional $1,500 per month, or the quiet satisfaction of working for yourself?

Pricing Products vs. Pricing Services

Although many of the principles are the same whether you're pricing a product or a service, some factors involved in pricing a product differ from those involved in pricing a service. For example, in pricing a product, you'll need to attend to manufacturing costs, setting wholesale versus retail prices, and providing for markups and discounts. In pricing a service, you'll need to consider whether to charge by the hour, the day, the project, the piece, or the head. Some service businesses may have virtually no costs of doing business, but when you sell a product, it invariably involves paying for your product up front and keeping an inventory on hand.

Products, however, hold the potential for *passive income*—that is, income that comes to you whether you're working or not. In providing a service, your income is directly wed to how many hours you can work. If you're ill or take a vacation, there's no income. And unless you add employees and the added costs they bring, you can only reasonably work some fixed number of hours a week. Products, on the other hand, can be selling while you sleep. For the details of pricing a product, we recommend reading *Homemade Money* by Barbara Brabec. For details on pricing a service, we recommend *How to Set Your Fees and Get Them* by Kate Kelly or *The Contract and Fee Setting Guide for Consultants and Professionals* by Howard Shenson. Both these books are listed in the Resources at the end of the chapter.

Various Pricing Strategies: Pros and Cons

What to charge is a popular topic on the Working from Home Forum we manage on CompuServe Information Service. Here are a variety of strategies people have shared for setting fees.

Value Added

Steve Singer owns a small business-forms company in the Chicago area. He advises considering three factors in setting your prices: (1) How available your product or service is: the more common the service or product, the less you can charge; (2) the value you add to what is normally provided: the more you've added, the more you can charge; and (3) the prevailing price range in the industry. He points out that you need to walk the tightrope of being neither too high nor too low. Being too low hurts your credibility. But being too high invites competition. Singer has found that the more value you add, the more you will sell, and the less price will be a factor in the final sale.

Top of the Line

Programmer Tim Berry advises that the best time to charge top of the line prices is when you are consciously trying to create a buyer perception of high quality à la designer jeans, BMWs, and fancy resort hotels. If you go top of the line, however, you have to maintain a top of the line image and have entrée to circles with top of the line budgets. And of course you have to have something special. You may have heard the Depression-era story about the man who was standing on the corner with a tray of apples marked $500 each. When asked if he had sold any, he said, "Not yet. But when I do, I'm going to make a *killing*!"

Percentage of Results

Sometimes when you're introducing a new service you'll meet with skepticism and resistance. One way to overcome this resistance is to set your fee based on a fixed percentage of the results you will achieve for your client. This has been referred to as "impact pricing." People whose business is doing telephone audits, for example, could charge a percent of the savings the audit produces. Or a sales trainer could charge a percentage of the increase in gross sales revenues for a specified number of months after his training program. Or a safety engineer might contract for a percentage of the money saved after his safety program is initiated. A variation of this would be to bill for your direct costs up to a specified amount in addition to some percentage of the results you produce. Be sure when using a percent of results strategy, however, that you have a clear written agreement as to how the results will be documented, measured, and validated.

The Bargain Basement Special

You've heard the old joke, "I may be losing money on every sale, but I'll make it up in volume." Well, of course, losing 10 cents on every sale means losing $100 on every 1,000 sales and $1,000,000 on 10 million. Discounting your service can be such a trap, especially for a home-based business, because even though you may have lower overhead as a result of working from home, your volume is usually limited. Home businesses usually can't handle sufficient volume to make only pennies on every sale.

Yet often out of eagerness to get in initial customers, a desperate new entrepreneur will be tempted to price him- or herself as a bargain basement special. He or she thinks: "After all, work does beget work and therefore it's important to get work whatever the price. Which would I prefer: sitting on the porch reading a novel or being underpaid for working?"

Should you be tempted to try pricing yourself as a bargain, keep this in mind: once you set your price, your clientele will beget clientele from the same economic strata. It is difficult to change upward once you have set your prices. When you up your prices, your business will show slow or no growth because you've priced yourself beyond the budgets of your old customers.

Stanton Kramer is the person who first pointed out this phenomenon to us, and he should know. He's changed customer bases three times on the way to getting to the price range he wants to be in. Interior designer Lillian Hamilton also discovered this phenomenon, but to help bridge the price gap as she raises her prices, she continues to serve previous customers at the original price for a full year. She calls this her "preferred client" price and let's them know its a courtesy she offers to her valued customers.

If you decide to start outpricing yourself on the "low" side, remember that you'll never know how much more you could actually have charged. In reverse, this is the same as buying something, knowing for sure you'll find it at a lower price sometime in the future. Setting prices is like fording a river; you never step in the same water twice. The important thing is that you feel sufficiently compensated each step along the way. If you're feeling resentful and taken advantage of, you need to raise your prices.

A Start-Up Price

Rather than entering the market as a bargain basement special, you might consider this approach to establishing a novice-business rate: Determine what established businesses in your field are charging. Calculate what you would be paid if you were doing this same work on a salary. Then pick the difference between the two and make that your start-up price.

Staying in Budget Without Cutting Your Rate

Many business experts will advise you: *never* cut your rate. In radio, the saying is "never go off the rate card." Obviously, you won't present a very substantial professional image if you quote a price and then agree to do the work for less when you meet price resistance. The solution is to offer a range of services or products and to break down the price of your service by type of activity. Then you can essentially cut and paste a customized price that fits your client's budget.

For example, career coach Marilyn Miller offers private consultations, one-day seminars, a six-week workshop, a two-tape audio program ($29.95), and a six-cassette album at $69.95. With this menu of products and services she can meet her range of clients at a price point each can live with. You can do the same with your services. Consider having such price distinctions as a full-day rate and a half-day rate; a rate that includes a final report and one that does not; an in-town price and an out-of-town price; a price for rush service (24 hours or overnight); a price that includes workbooks and one that does not; a price for working from typed copy and another for working from handwritten copy; a price for short-term work and another for long-term projects; a paid-in-full up-front price and a 30-day credit price.

In other words, give your clients a range of options that in essence says:

you can have it fast, you can have it cheap, or you can have it great, but you can't have all three. This "price-options" approach gives you lots of room to negotiate your price, and any reductions you make can be directly related to the effort it demands of you and the value your client receives. So you are always compensated fully for what you provide.

Hourly Rate vs. Flat Fee

It's customary for many service businesses to charge by the hour. And, on the face of it, that seems fair. Sometimes, however, customers and clients become nervous as they imagine the sound of your clock ticking. They have very little idea of what's actually involved in your work and envision their bill mounting out of control. You certainly *never* want clients to be shocked when they receive their bills. So here are several ways to avoid the time-clock jitters:

1. Make a bid that reflects your estimate of the number of hours you think the work will take and call the clients before proceeding beyond that estimate. If you come in under the estimate, they'll be pleasantly surprised. If you run over, you're giving them a chance to remain in charge of their cost before proceeding. As Kristi Watcher found, estimating how long something will take to do is an art in itself, but she suggests "try doubling or tripling the amount of time you think you'll spend and that way you may come close."
2. Establish a flat price to provide price stability in your client's mind but in your contract make it "subject to any change in orders." This will protect you from unexpected demands that would put you in the hole because they would take more of your time.
3. Set a fixed price, but designate a specific allowable percentage of overage. That is, 100 hours at x number of dollars with a possible variance not to exceed 15 percent. Or offer a fixed cost plus expenses not to exceed a specified amount.
4. Establish an assessment stage for a project during which you are paid either a flat fee or an hourly rate to define the scope of the work to be done. Essentially under such an arrangement you are being paid to prepare a proposal that will outline the scope of the work, the detailed costs involved, and the work to be accomplished. Be sure to get a clear up-front agreement in writing that specifies what you will deliver by when.

Adjusting Your Pricing Strategy to Your Business Situation

As you can see from the above discussion, there are three factors that affect what you can charge: your image of yourself, your reputation, and the market for what you have to offer. Each of these factors is subject to change over the lifetime of your business. Therefore anticipate the need for adjusting your pricing strategy to different stages of your business.

Novice businesspeople, for example, may enter a field at a moderate price and raise it gradually as their reputation and self-assurance grow. But let's consider a less obvious evolution. If you're introducing a new product or service and discover that the response to it is strong, you may be able to charge a premium price right from the beginning because you have no competition. When others notice your dramatic success, however, they may well jump into the field and undercut your price. Then you may face having to adjust your price down in order to remain competitive.

Coleen Sager encountered such a dilemma as the developer of one of the first customer-service training programs in the country. She found companies were eager for her information and the dramatic increases it could mean in their bottom lines. Her seminars and video programs sold briskly at a premium price. Over the years, however, many other trainers, seeing her success, added a customer-service training program to their offerings at much lower rates. Ultimately, her products and programs cost much more than everyone else's.

Of course, she still had her reputation as one of the leading authorities, but eventually cost sensitivity won out in the marketplace and her sales began to decline. So Coleen was presented with a monumental challenge. Obviously she couldn't just cut the price of her existing programs without damage to her reputation and stature. The situation called for an innovative new pricing program. And that's exactly what she initiated.

Instead of promoting her three-day seminars, Coleen began marketing herself as a corporate speaker. Because of her reputation she could command top speaking fees and still save her clients money. By bringing her in to speak they could get the best for less. They got her most important information in a condensed form for less than the cost of the lower-priced multiple-day seminars on the market. When the speech went well, she could then work out customized follow-up seminars.

Another stage of business involves retraining long-term clients. We've already mentioned making provisions for guaranteeing some period of price stability for preferred clients. Another way to price for retention is to add on value to existing services when you raise prices, or retain your existing price but add on charges for additional services.

What to Do When Told Your Price Is Too High

When you're told that your price is too high, marketing consultant Laura Douglas advises simply asking, "In what way is it too high?" Then ask, "What price did you have in mind?" You do this not in order to lower your price, but to get a better idea of what the people you're talking to really want done. Remember, you can always offer reduced services for what they want to pay.

Keep in mind, too, that people usually have no idea how much time is actually involved, much less the expertise required to do what you will be doing. Douglas suggests preparing a small graph that illustrates how much more it would cost the company to do the job in house. Include factors such as how much more time it would take an inexperienced person, and other costs they may not think of. Such comparisons provide your prospective clients with a more realistic idea of what they need, and their response provides you with a better means of knowing if and how you could help them.

Making Friends with Money

Many of the problems people have in pricing their products arise from limiting attitudes and beliefs they have about money. Often, we are not even aware that we have these attitudes and beliefs. Many arose during our childhoods from the assumptions our families held about money, and they can interfere with our charging what we are actually worth.

Speech and diction coach Saundra Keen, for example, was barely surviving on the fees she charged for her private consultations. Even though as an actress Saundra had studied with the top speech coaches for many years and had crafted a beautiful voice for herself, she believed that no one would want to pay very much for her coaching because she didn't have a college degree in speech communications. With our help, her self-esteem grew, and she began to notice that her clients were improving dramatically. She finally realized that actual results were the bottom line, not academic degrees.

She remembered that throughout her childhood her father had always told her that if she ever wanted to make any money, she would have to go to college. Little did she know that, once she'd decided to pursue her acting career directly from high school, her father's old admonition about making money would prevent her from earning a decent living twenty years later.

Saundra decided to raise her prices but still was fearful that no one would book an appointment once they heard what she was asking. You can imagine her surprise when she finally worked up the courage to state her new price and the response was "that's very reasonable."

In reality, close examination of one's attitudes about money show that they are often self-fulfilling prophecies. Those who believe in themselves and their product and expect people to pay gladly for it are infinitely more successful than those who expect to have difficulty earning a living. Examples of common negative beliefs that prevent people from setting prices that enable their businesses to flourish include:

■ People hate to part with their money.
■ Making money is hard.
■ You have to work your fingers to the bone to make even a meager living.
■ Rich people are dishonest. They rip other people off.

- Anyone can do what I do, so how can I charge very much for it?
- The work I do is so much fun I really shouldn't charge anything.

Have you ever noticed, however, that when someone really wants something, he or she will pay almost any price for it? They can't get the money out of their pockets fast enough. Or have you ever noticed that truly successful people almost always love what they do and talk about it as something they would do even for free? Also think about how many of the most successful people achieve the success they do because they enable others to enjoy life more. And can anyone else ever really do exactly what you do?

To identify other limiting attitudes and beliefs about money that may stand in the way of your setting a price that will enable your business to thrive, we suggest making the following statement out loud. Say it several times and notice your internal reactions.

People will gladly pay me well for the work I love doing.

If you have a negative reaction to believing any portion of this statement, think about what you believe instead. How did you come to hold these beliefs? What would convince you to believe this statement? In being able to agree fully with each aspect of this statement, you'll find setting and getting prices you want to be much easier.

A Simple Step-by-Step Pricing Guide

Although, as you can see, there is no one pricing formula that will work for everyone, we offer the following process for determining what approach might work best for you at a given time.

1. Work out several possible pricing strategies from those mentioned in this chapter.
2. Test each alternative with several prospective clients.
3. Select the alternative that gets the best response.
4. Remember, pricing is an experimental process, so continue fine-tuning until you're satisfied with the results.
5. Keep track of your income and expenses and evaluate your pricing every quarter. Make changes when the numbers or any of the following indicate the need to adjust:

   - Many complaints about your price.
   - Many other complaints that may be dissatisfaction with your price in disguise.
   - A downturn in sales or the fact that people lose interest after hearing the price.

- People saying, "Boy, that's a bargain."
- Your prices have been the same for a long period of time.
- You're turning away business because you don't have time to do it.
- Sales are fine but profits are low.
- You feel resentful about working so hard for so little return.

Pricing is like the pulse of your business. When it's working, you're working. And that means that life's working!

Chapter Digest

1. Although you'll encounter a wide variety of "pricing formulas," in reality there is no simple answer to what to charge.
2. Pricing is a matter of experimenting until you find a price that enough people will pay and that will cover your expenses with some money left over.
3. In calculating how much you need to charge, determine your direct costs and your overhead. Be sure to include your salary and fringe benefits. Then add your profit.
4. Underpricing is one of the most common mistakes home-based businesses make in setting their prices. Often this happens because of the limiting beliefs and attitudes we've learned about money. Actually, people will gladly pay for quality products and services they need. So don't sell yourself short.
5. Recognize that different stages of your business may well call for different pricing strategies. Remain alert to signs that you need to adjust your prices and respond appropriately.

Resources

Homemade Money. Barbara Brabec. (See full citation under Chapter 3.)

How to Set Your Fees and Get Them. Kate Kelly. Visibility Enterprises, 11 Rockwood Dr., Larchmont, NY 10538. 1982.

Money Is My Friend. Phil Laut. New York: Ivy Books, 1989.

MoneyLove. Jerry Gillies. New York: Warner Books, 1978.

The Contract and Fee Setting Guide for Consultants and Professionals. Howard L. Shenson. See Chapter 9.

Newsletters and Reports

Small Business Administration (see full citation under Chapter 3):
　　Pricing for Small Manufactures (#MA 1.005)
　　What's the Best Selling Price? (#MA 1.002)

CHAPTER
TWENTY-TWO
■■■■■■■■■■■■■■■■■■■■■■■

Successfully Marketing
Your Home Business

If you're working from home in your own business, you know that unless you bring in some business you won't be working at home for long. Without customers or clients, you'll soon be back out looking for a job. So let's take a look at how you can get the business that will make your home entrepreneurial ventures profitable. In other words, let's examine how you can successfully market your product or service.

The Number One Marketing Mistake

The greatest mistake in marketing is thinking that because you have a good product or service, people will buy it. For example, most people think that Christopher Columbus or Leif Ericson discovered America. But 2,000 years before Ericson, Basques, Phoenicians, Druid priests, Libyans, and Egyptians may have visited our shores. Instead of becoming famous for discovering America, Columbus achieved his fame by *marketing* his discovery of America!

Like Columbus, you will need to get your name associated with whatever field you've chosen. Your job is to let everyone who needs your product or service know about it, and to do so in a way that convinces them to buy it *now*.

Large corporations spend munificent sums from doing this. So how do you, as a self-employed individual working from home, give yourself and your product or service the marketing strength you need? In the past, we recommended reaching potential clients by selecting from the wide variety of common avenues used by all start-up businesses. After seven years of talking about their marketing experiences with thousands of people on Working from Home Forum on CompuServe, however, we've discovered that some approaches work much more effectively than others.

In the course of conducting in-depth interviews with over a hundred successful home-based businesses, we found that the most successful home businesses—those grossing over $100,000 a year—use five basic marketing strategies. As a result, we now believe these strategies are much better suited to home-based marketing than the many other possibilities.

The Five Marketing Strategies of $100,000-Plus Home Businesses

1. Taking Your Reputation with You

A small number of the most successful home-based business operators are so good at what they do that they have to do very little to market themselves. Letting other people know informally they are in business is enough. Their reputation with satisfied customers takes care of the rest. Mike Greer is a case in point. Mike is an instructional designer. He had worked for several instructional design firms over the years and his reputation as an outstanding designer had grown. When he opened his free-lance business he had clients waiting in line. Not only was his work excellent, but, as a home-based free-lancer, he could charge considerably less than larger firms and still triple his income.

Collections negotiator and consultant Bonnie Barnett also parlayed her reputation into a smashing business success. Bonnie had worked in the collections field specializing in the medical market. One of her contacts told her that if she started a business on her own he would be her first customer. So she took him up on it and started on solid ground. The outstanding work she does keeps business flowing in.

You could use this strategy if you are already a leader in your field or are willing to stay on your job, consciously honing your skills until you become known as an authority. You can then be in demand when you open your business. Since a reputation of this nature does not transfer easily to another field, you must be willing to stay in the same field, however, when you start your business.

A computer entrepreneur we interviewed used this approach. He worked for over twelve years with major electronics firms with the intention of mastering every aspect of the business from sales and marketing to management and accounting. By the time he left to begin his business he had all the expertise and contacts he needed to succeed the first day he stepped out on his own.

2. "Nichemanship"

A number of the most successful home-based men and women select a specialized market niche to serve, from which they draw all the business they want. They thereby need to spend only a modest amount of time and money on marketing themselves.

Ray Jassin used this approach in building his library-management business, having targeted only law firms. Ann McIndoo also targeted law firms when she launched her computer-training business. She helps law firms computerize their offices and trains their legal staffs in how to use the appropriate software. Chip Morgan, a construction and remodeling consultant, concentrates his business on projects for large radio stations. He says, "There's only one person in the country who does what I do. It's just as easy to market and do a project for a large station as a small one. And on large projects they're more likely to give me more creative freedom and have more realistic budgets."

We've found that home businesses are generally more successful if they can identify such a market niche for themselves, a segment of their market that they are uniquely qualified or situated to tap. When Nancy and Tom Nichols started a billing service, they decided to specialize in serving an often overlooked market that desperately needed their services—freight billing departments.

The Nicholses found that marketing to this small market was easier and less expensive than serving the entire business community. They were quickly able to build a reputation and a referral network. They also discovered an added benefit of "nichemanship": the more specialized your business, the more you can charge. As a result, they turned a profit more quickly than their most optimistic projections.

3. Relying on Gatekeepers

A third method used by successful home-based businesses is to build relationships with one or more key influencers in your field who provide you with all or most of your business. These people are your "gatekeepers." Woodworker Robert Livingston used this approach when he started a cabinet-making business as a way to support his work in the theater. He obtains his business from just a few key architects who refer their clients to him. Graphics designer Tom Dower gets all the business he needs from his publicist wife, Kim Freilich. Janell Besell's husband is an anesthesiologist, so when she opened her billing service his office became her first client. Through referrals to his colleagues her business has grown rapidly.

At first glance you may think these entrepreneurs are unusually lucky to be so well connected. Actually, if you begin thinking about those you know who hold your work in high regard and value your talents, you'll undoubtedly find that you, too, have key connections. If you don't already have them, you can probably get them by volunteering your skills for charity or civic activities that will attract such supporters to you.

4. Positioning Oneself as Preeminent

Another strategy of successful home-based business owners has been to position themselves as preeminent in their fields by writing books and columns, appearing on conference programs, and using radio and other means of personal publicity to develop a high profile that brings business to them.

When Shell and Judy Norris began Class Reunions, Inc., they thought that managing college and high school reunions would be a part-time venture. Because of the novelty of their business, however, *The Wall Street Journal* wrote an article about them. It began a landslide of publicity that has kept them busy full time ever since.

When Dan Cassidy started his computerized scholarship-matching service he had very little money for marketing so he arranged to appear as a guest on a local radio station. He got a hundred calls from that first appearance and now successfully markets his business primarily by making free guest appearances on radio and TV.

Helen Berman is another good example. She wanted to become a consultant and sales trainer in the publishing industry but the competition was tough. There were already a number of well-known consultants serving that industry. How was she to break in?

She was sure that the cost of what she calls "push marketing"—that is, trying to get through to the thousands of her potential customers by telephone—would be too high. If she called a list of people who didn't know her, she was going to have to call a lot of people before she'd be able to make even one sale. So instead, she chose to use what she calls "pull marketing"—building a high profile for herself with interested and qualified individuals. Then when she calls, these individuals already know who she is and the same calls will lead to a higher ratio of sales.

To implement her strategy, she contacted the meeting planners for upcoming conferences in her field and proposed that she offer a seminar on her particular sales expertise. She got several bookings. Simultaneously, she began calling the trade magazines in the field to talk about writing a sales column for them. Soon she was writing a column for *Folio*, the leading trade magazine in the field. With this credibility and name recognition she now gets business from both her calls and her mailings. She's also writing a book and creating her own seminars, which are not only profitable in their own right but also provide a source of funds for a direct-mail campaign.

You've heard the saying "Success attracts success." Positioning yourself as preeminent in your field operates on that principle. It assumes that if you create enough momentum around yourself and your business and then provide a quality service or product, your business will grow. Another way of thinking about it is that people are attracted to a bright, shiny, fast-moving object, something that stands out in a crowd.

Here's another example. When aspiring director David Beaird came to Los Angeles to make movies, everyone told him Hollywood didn't need another director. And indeed he found the studio doors closed tight. Having taught acting classes in Chicago he decided to find another way in. He rented a theater and began teaching classes. Soon he put on a play he'd written and invited the press and industry representatives to come. The momentum was building, and, based on the response to his play, he was able to attract backing for a low-budget film. Although the film was never commercially distributed, it received critical acclaim at the Cannes Film Festival and that led to further financial backing. After his second low-budget film, he reached his "critical mass" and was placed on the list of directors of a major studio.

5. Premier Marketers

Finally, some home-based businesspeople have achieved their success by expertly pursuing aggressive, multi-faceted marketing techniques that include direct mail, telemarketing, preview seminars, advertising, brochures, networking, stimulating referrals from clients, and appearing at trade shows.

Private-practice consultant Gene Call is an outstanding example. Southern California-based Call offers seminars that help professionals learn how to market their private practices. He began his business with a background in marketing and sales, as do many of the premier marketers we've met. For him, getting business is an art and a passion. When business is slow, he views the downturn not as a problem but as a challenge that gets him charged up, an intriguing puzzle to be solved with new, fresh, and more creative approaches.

An avid networker, he built a mailing list of prospective clients and invited them to a free preview evening. Fourteen professionals came to his first preview. From this small group he filled his first day-long workshop. Through clever, well-designed direct-mail pieces and further networking, his previews grew. Now more than sixty people attend his five-week program every month. He holds events for graduates, offers advanced classes and private consultations. Even his answering machine message is a master sales tool, communicating the benefits of More Business for Professionals, the name of his consulting business.

Linda Jagoda of Scottsdale, Arizona, is another premier marketer. She's used her superb marketing skills to promote her own marketing firm and is now grossing half a million dollars a year from her 2,500-square-foot home. She too is an avid networker and started her business by giving seminars to attract clients. In addition, she uses a half-page ad in the Yellow Pages from which she got General Telephone as a client, advertises in four print publications, and makes frequent use of direct mail. She says, "Consistent marketing saves you when times are the toughest. It causes people to call you out of the blue. You never know what new business the next week is going to bring."

If you can recognize possibilities for yourself in any of these successful marketing strategies, you will find marketing your home business much easier than you may have thought. Should none of them fit you, however, you need not be concerned because, like us, many of the successful home-based business owners we interviewed had little or no marketing background when they opened their businesses. Many were starting a business in new communities or in a brand new field. They often didn't have immediate access to a gatekeeper. And while they were competent at their work, many were not initially outstanding. Yet, by developing a marketing mindset, they were able to start and build their businesses successfully.

Developing a Marketing Mindset

Approaching your business with a marketing mindset is not only a matter of focusing on providing a quality product and service but also in determining why your product or service is unique, how it benefits those you serve, and how you will spread the word about these benefits to those who need them. It involves three steps:

1. Find your market niche.   Ask yourself who needs what you have to offer. These people are your market. What are they like? Where do they live? How much money do they have? Find out as much as you possibly can about them. You may even want to conduct a market survey—it doesn't need to be elaborate or expensive. (See the Resource List at the end of this chapter for helpful materials.)

Once you know as much as possible about your market, you can determine the best way to let potential customers know about your product or service.

2. Position your product or service.   What product or service do you provide? Who else is offering something similar? How is what you offer different? Why should someone buy it? Why should they buy it from you? What features do you provide? What benefits are there to using your service or buying your product? Briefly describe (25 words) what you do in terms of these features and benefits. Try out your description with several people and find out if they understand what you do. You'd be surprised at how what seems so clear to you is a puzzle to someone who doesn't have your perspective.

3. Find the best way to let your market know about your business. Once you are clear about the benefits of your product or service and have a thorough knowledge of your market niche, you can then learn how to reach your customers through the many available marketing avenues, such as direct personal contact, telemarketing, mail, advertising, agents, brokers, or manufacturer's reps.

To get your business going, you will need to seek ways to match your customers' needs and habits with your business by using the various marketing avenues open to you. For example, if you are selling handmade dolls, you have several options for getting them into your customers' arms. You can sell directly to gift shops or you can use distributors or reps to carry your line

Positioning Your Product or Service

People buy for gain or to prevent pain. In other words, they buy for the benefits they will receive. Which do you provide? To which of these needs does your product or service appeal?

1. Pleasure: Appearance
   Novelty
   Uniqueness
   Comfort
   Convenience
   Time
   Service/Availability

2. Profit: Economy/Price
   Savings
   Terms of Sale

3. Confidence: Durability
   Guarantees
   Safety
   Security
   Accuracy
   Control
   Proven results

4. Self-Esteem: Prestige
   Quality
   Exclusivity

---

of dolls. You can sell them through a direct-mail catalog, advertise them in women's magazines, or exhibit them at trade shows or local arts and crafts shows.

But how do you decide which avenue will be best for you? Choosing between them can lead to the second most common marketing mistake: putting all your marketing efforts in one basket and hoping for the best.

If your home business is like most, you don't have a lot of money to invest in marketing. But don't let lack of funds trap you into spending all your limited capital on one marketing approach and hoping it will draw in the business you need to get going.

Successful marketing is an ongoing and active experiment that involves trying several different avenues until you find one that works. Therefore, by trying only one approach at a time, you're apt to run out of money before you find one or two effective approaches.

Instead, follow the advice of marketing consultant Cork Platts, who urges new businesses to undertake several approaches to marketing simultaneously on a small scale until they hit the ones that produce results.

But how do you decide which avenue will be best for you?

Seven Fast-Start, Low-Cost
Marketing Methods for a New Business

Our research shows that, fortunately, the best ways to let potential customers and clients know about a home business are not the most expensive. Far too many home-based start-ups try to rely on more costly methods of getting business, such as advertising and direct mail, and are disappointed with the response. Consequently many start-ups run out of money or just give up, figuring there is no market for what they do.

Advertising and direct mail produce the best results as follow-ups to a multi-faceted campaign when you're selling a service that people need and think they can get only from you. Judi Wunderlich hit such a nerve when she started her temporary business in Chicago with a mailing offering graphic arts personnel as temporaries to print shops and graphic arts companies. Judi's was the first such service in Chicago. Her mailings told companies they could get skilled graphics personnel on demand. Since this new service met a pressing need, she got an immediate response.

More commonplace businesses with existing competition don't find that mailings and advertising pay for themselves in immediate business, however. Why not? Primarily because prospects have little way of knowing how you could serve them better than all the other similar services around. They probably won't even read your print ad or direct-mail piece. And when you think about it, you really don't know how you can serve them better until you talk with them and find out how they are being served now and what unmet needs they have.

Since home businesses are usually offering a personal service or a customized specialty item, we've found that the best ways to let people know about you, at least initially, is through an equally personal and customized approach. As a home business, you are your own best promoter. The best methods of promoting your business initially will tend to require a high investment of your personal time and energy but a relatively low investment of cash.

Here are seven low-cost fast-start methods we've found to be the most successful for getting a personal home business under way quickly. You'll recognize many of them as elements of the marketing strategies used by the $100,000-plus home businesses we described above. We recommend that you select two or three of these approaches and begin experimenting with each. As your business grows and you have ample customers to fill your time, you may want to shift the balance of your marketing efforts and select approaches that may cost a little more but will save your time for billable activities.

1. Networking: Leveraging Your Contacts, New and Old

Networking is the single best way to start and build a home-based personal or professional service business. Networking refers to using face-to-face contact to establish relationships that can lead to business. Professional-practice consultant Gene Call of Los Angeles calls networking "word-of-mouth marketing" because it's based on talking with people about what you do and listening to find out how you might serve them.

Once a business is established, "word-of-mouth" comes to mean getting referrals from satisfied customers who talk about you, but until a business is self-sustaining, "word-of-mouth" means moving *your* mouth, telling people about your business, speaking with everyone you already know (family, friends, vendors, and colleagues), and making a determined effort to meet and talk with lots of new people, too.

Family and friends are the oldest networks of all. They have launched many businesses as have members of civic and professional organizations. Now, electronic networks are available, too. Membership in professional and trade associations is another way to find out what others are doing, what's working, what isn't, and where there are holes in the market that you might be able to fill. You can also join associations and groups where your potential buyers might gather.

Today there are networking organizations, business guilds, and "lead clubs" whose sole purpose is to generate business leads for their members. These groups usually meet at mealtimes, and membership is usually limited to one person in a given type of business. For example, as the only member of her women's network and her breakfast leads club to offer executive secretarial services, Dorothy Baranski was able to build her business from these two sources.

Telecommuting consultant Gil Gordon summarizes how networking has worked for him: "Everything in business, whether it's getting an article published or finding a distributor, is a result of networking. I keep in contact with old friends, past co-workers, sales reps who used to call on me. I've joined a couple of carefully chosen small associations or discussion groups composed of the people I need to meet for my business and I'm fortunate enough to know a couple of people who pride themselves on being "matchmakers." They love to get people with common interests together. I can't stress this enough. Just as in job-hunting, your friends and contacts are your best assets."

Despite the fact that most successful home-based businesses are built on word-of-mouth marketing, we've found that networking is frequently overlooked and sometimes even consciously avoided. Yet networking gives you a chance to show personally that you are interested in meeting your prospective clients' needs. It gives you the opportunity to find out what they need and show how you can serve them better. In the process, prospects also have a chance to discover that they like you, and almost everyone likes to do business with someone they like—particularly when dealing with a service business.

Follow-up, follow-up, follow-up. They key to successful networking is following up on the contacts you make. We suggest setting aside a specific time period each week to follow up on networking contacts. Arrange follow-up meetings within the week of making a new contact. When they're hot, they're hot. Nothing is colder than a long-forgotten contact.

To keep your name ever-present in the minds of prospective clients you meet, build a mailing list from the cards you collect. Thumb through your card file periodically for names of contacts you haven't spoken with recently.

Call them or send clippings, thank-you notes, or newsletters. The old saying "out of sight out of mind" definitely applies here. Send regular mailings to everyone on your list. Hold a party or open house occasionally. Here are several other follow-up options:

Direct mail. Experience proves that following up mailings with a personal phone call does improve response. A similar result can be obtained with a triple mailing—all different pieces. The first mailing should entertain. Send an amusing clipping from *The Wall Street Journal,* for example, and include your logo but no name or address. The second, mailed a week later, should further pique the recipient's curiosity with an elegant solution to a problem that he or she may be having. No name and no address on this mailer, either, but do include your logo. Finally, send a third mailer, which has your name and address and logo on it, and includes a brochure that lists your services. This campaign can be tricky because you have to know what kind of solution to offer. But if you know the problems people on your mailing list are having and target those, you can get results, especially since they already know who you are.

Using newsletters. Newsletters filled with informational tidbits of interest to your clients and customers can be great as ongoing follow-up with networking contacts. Whereas brochures are often tossed out, newsletters are often read and even filed away.

If you're thinking you don't have time to publish a newsletter, you have several options for making it easier and less time consuming. You can hire someone to produce it for you. Many companies, including home businesses, will write and publish your newsletter. Another option is to use a personal computer and desktop publishing software to publish the newsletter yourself, quickly and inexpensively. A third choice is to develop and write the newsletter yourself and then have it printed professionally. Using an electronic printing service will speed up this process. By entering the proper print commands into your copy on a computer, you can send it directly to the service via a modem over your telephone. See the Resource List at the end of this chapter for further information on publishing a newsletter.

Personal letters and thank-you notes. Sales trainer Steve Maier advocates writing personal letters to prospective clients. He told us, "I could never isolate a job I got because the client was attracted by a brochure I sent out. I've discovered that a brochure is something you use to ensure that your name is in someone's file after you've talked to them."

So instead of mailing out brochures to attract business, Maier focuses on personal mailings. "I write letters to the people I want to talk to, trying to provide value in the letter, addressing to the extent possible the particular problems they have and offering ways they might solve their special problems."

Maier's strategy works. He has found that the simple thank-you notes he writes to follow up contacts he makes generate enough business to pay his $5,000 annual printing bill.

While you cannot depend on networking to produce immediate prosperity, compared with other business-getting methods, the investment is smaller and the return, surer. So if you want to get more business, get your mouth moving and have a good time while you're at it!

2. Cold Calling

The dreaded words "cold calling" can send a shiver down the spine of even experienced salespeople. But we've been surprised to find that many home-based businesses have used it successfully by placing informal, personal exploratory calls to acquaint themselves with the needs of the people in their market niche.

When David Goodfellow decided to provide and sell mailing list services to small businesses, he got started by going through the Yellow Pages and calling small companies in his community to determine whether they needed his services. He started with "A" and never got past "K." He generated a steady flow of business from the first half of the alphabet!

Bob Garsson did cold calling for years and found that the first call of the day was the toughest one. He says, "I could find hundreds of excuses not to make that first call, but once I got that one out of the way, I could go strong the rest of the day."

To warm up his cold calls, a financial consultant we interviewed looks at nameplates on the desks of the businesses he visits. Or he calls the company and tells the secretary, "I'm supposed to mail something to a man I met at your company and I can't remember his name. He was about 35 and his name was something like—" The operator offers 20 names, while he takes notes to call them back.

Since a sale usually isn't made until after the fifth call, the key to selling by phone (or to any other form of selling) is to keep at it. You can figure that every "no" you hear brings you that much closer to a "yes."

3. Sampling

Sampling means letting people experience a sample of your work as a means of getting them to buy. Debbie Fields and Famous Amos both launched their cookie businesses by letting people sample their cookies. Famous Amos told us that when he opened his first store, he carried fresh hot cookies everywhere he went. Debbie Fields started her business at home and told us that the first day she opened a shop, no one came in. There she was with trays piled high with cookies and no customers. In a moment of desperation, she carried a tray of piping hot, freshly baked chocolate chip cookies down the sidewalk, giving away samples. The story goes that people followed her back to the store the way children followed the Pied Piper.

The effectiveness of sampling is not limited, however, just to gourmet delicacies. Gene Call, Helen Berman, and Linda Jagoda all used sampling to launch their businesses. They offered a free introductory seminar to give people a sample of what they would get if they signed up for a series of seminars. The way Ted Laux began his book-indexing service with a TRS Model I computer is another excellent example of how to use sampling to get business. Laux looking through bookstores for books that didn't have an adequate index. To demonstrate how much more effective these books would be had the publishers used his services, he indexed the books and sent copies to the publishers. Several liked the results and he was in business. His indexing software gave him his unique advantage, and the sample became his platform for showing off just what he could do.

Participating in trade shows is an excellent way to get customers to sample your product or service. It's not unusual for such shows to attract from 20,000 to 100,000 people. And, at many of them, you can not only generate leads but actually sell products and services.

A moonlighting artist launched a new line of greeting cards at one trade show. She booked over $10,000 worth of orders from gift shops. An independent publisher attended the American Bookseller's Association convention with her newly published book on word processing and got orders from stores across the nation.

In addition to exhibiting at a trade show, you can speak or conduct a seminar there. If you speak, show promoters will sometimes give you free booth space in lieu of a presenter's fee. If your reputation warrants, you can sometimes be paid a presenter's fee and also get free booth space. You can also sell your books or products from the back of the room after your presentation.

Speaking at a trade show workshop, speech pathologist Dr. Roger Burgraff sold over $2,000 worth of books on communications to a group of health professionals. Marketing specialist Carol Dysart sells business opportunity packages during her trade show presentations. One sales trainer offers to do free sessions for exhibitors on how to work a trade show. These exhibitors often become his new customers.

Besides attracting customers, trade shows are good avenues for reaching retailers, wholesalers, reps, and buyers. And exhibiting is also a good way to test a new product, build your mailing list, and do informal market surveys.

If you haven't exhibited at a show before, attend some in your field first. Talk to exhibitors about how worthwhile exhibiting has been. At the same time, ask if any exhibitors are interested in carrying your product or sharing future booth space.

Consult the Resource List at the end of this chapter to locate trade show information. Think about the various platforms you could use to show off your products or service.

4. Strategic Pricing

The way you price your service can be a route to quick business. When Arlene Daily started her business promoting restaurants on the radio she used a discount pricing strategy. She offered restaurant owners the opportunity to come on her show and promote their restaurants at a price they couldn't refuse. She gave lots of service for the price. She prepared their commercials. She featured them in live personal interviews and invited listeners to meet her at the restaurants for various publicity activities.

This approach enabled her to break even immediately and, since she now had satisfied advertisers, selling to new ones at a higher price was much easier. For more information about pricing strategies, see Chapter 21.

A photographer offered an apparently absurd service to advertising agencies: a huge (30"× 40") color print in an hour for $150. Obviously, if two customers took him up on it, one customer would get his color print on time and the other would get his print two hours later. But the photographer knew that the chances were that no one would order a rush color print of that size. However, the psychological impact was powerful. The idea was not to sell huge color prints fast but to instill in the minds of art directors that here was a photographer who could deliver photographic services unmatched by any other photographer.

5. Using Free Publicity

Author and business expert Jack Lander claims that, square inch for square inch, free publicity is more effective than paid advertising. We agree.

To take advantage of free publicity, however, you have to qualify for it by making yourself and your business newsworthy. Then you have to invest some time and energy in contacting local newspapers, magazines, and radio and TV stations, or hire a publicist or public relations firm to do this for you.

Public relations consultant Michael Baybeck suggests regularly setting aside a specific amount of time, preferably five hours a week, for "PR" efforts. He also advises treating PR like an investment account in which you send out one news release a month, make five PR-oriented phone calls a week, and have at least one PR lunch a month.

Becoming newsworthy. To make yourself "newsworthy," you have to have something to say or offer that is different and of interest to others. The fact that Susan Smith is starting a mailing-list service on Tenth Street isn't particularly newsworthy. But if Susan's new business opens by announcing the results of a survey she conducted showing how retailers can cut the mailing cost of sales circulars in half, that could be newsworthy. Armed with this survey she'll have a much better chance of getting news coverage.

At times, becoming newsworthy is a matter of taking advantage of a moment's opportunity. Joseph Cossman, author of the book *How I Made a Million Dollars in Mail Order*, and an expert at self-promotion, once found a mallard duck in his swimming pool. He called the local newspaper and TV station, who covered the story. The newspaper syndicated the report nationally and each time it appeared Cossman was identified as the author of the book *How I Made a Million Dollars in Mail Order*. Not bad publicity for just one phone call.

News releases.   Effective publicity is not just a matter of getting your message out, however. That message has to reach your market. Sending a news release to selected publications can result in a product review or announcement of your business in the particular trade and professional publications, newsletters, magazines, or newspapers that you know your customers will be reading.

A news release is usually a one- to two-page statement of some newsworthy event. It announces a new product, releases the results of a survey, or reports on an upcoming promotional event such as an all-day art exhibit at a local shopping center or a free evening seminar on how to save the most money under a new tax law. Editors and producers expect news releases to appear in a standard format. See the Resource List at the end of this chapter for further information on publicity.

Interviews.   News releases or calls to local radio, TV, and print media can lead to appearances on radio or TV talk shows or to feature or news articles about you and your business.

A good example is Charlotte Hartman, who designs beautiful custom-made bridal dresses. To attract more business for the upcoming spring season, she scheduled a February fashion show at a nearby shopping mall. After reading an article about how more marrying couples are opting for elaborate weddings, she began calling local radio and TV stations to suggest a story on new trends in wedding gowns.

Her strategy paid off. She appeared as a guest on several radio and TV programs and, of course, talked about her upcoming fashion show. Before her PR event, she sent press releases to local papers and got news coverage of the show, complete with photographs.

Cable TV opportunities.   An easy way to get TV exposure is to volunteer your product or service for a TV benefit auction. Producing your own TV shows by taking advantage of "local origination" or "public access" programming will bring you high local visibility and give you valuable on-camera experience.

Acting and media coach Judy Kerr generates business with her cable show "Judy Kerr's Acting Class." Hair stylist Ed Salazar builds his reputation and clientele with his beauty and style show "30 Minutes with Salazar." Financial consultant James Irwin has developed a following in the business community with his "Business in the News." To find out about cable TV possibilities in your area, contact your local cable station.

Writing articles. With 6,108 business and trade publications available today, you can probably find a way to have an article you've written published in a magazine or newsletter that your customers read. This builds your credibility and establishes you as an expert in your field.

To get an article published, send it to publications that your customers respect and read, or send a query letter proposing an article you could write. Remember to include a picture of yourself and a brief biographical sketch along with your name, address, and telephone number to be included at the close of the article.

You can sometimes get paid for your articles, or you may be able to trade articles for advertising space. But no matter what arrangement you make with the publishers, always make sure they will include a brief description of you, and your name, address, and telephone number.

Teaching courses and seminars. Adult education is growing at a rate of 35 percent per year. Teaching adult education classes is another way to enhance your reputation, meet prospective clients, and make business contacts. You'll find opportunities to teach courses in college continuing education programs, adult education organizations, churches, YW-YMCAs, and even department stores and hotels.

When management consultant Marilyn Miller wanted to expand her business into the gift-buying industry, she offered to do a seminar for the industry's annual convention. Her topic, leadership skills, turned out to be popular. Several hundred managers attended. Many asked for her card at the conclusion of her presentation, and, by following up on their interest, Miller landed several consulting contracts. You may be surprised at some of the paying business opportunities that arise from offering seminars.

Books, workbooks, and anthologies. Writing a book or pamphlet, developing a workbook, or contributing a chapter to an anthology will not only increase your credibility but can also become an ongoing source of income. You can sell your books at seminars, use them as promotional items, give them away as incentives for people to buy your product or service, or use them to help you get appearances on radio and TV programs.

Writing a book saved Patricia Massie and Pauline Link's fledgling catering service, Adam and Eve. When business tapered off, they decided to write a book on how to cater a party and use it to get appearances on local talk shows. It worked, and it gave them the exposure they needed for the phone to start ringing again.

Getting a book or workbook published doesn't have to be an arduous affair. You can publish a small, simply-bound version yourself using desktop publishing software and following the ideas presented in *The Self-Publishing Manual* by Don Poynter. Or you can send an outline and two chapters of your book ideas to established publishers. Another alternative is using book packagers who, for a fee, will sell your book to established publishers.

Thirty Free or Low-Cost Ways to Promote Yourself

Producing brochures and flyers
Posting on-line notices and listings
Networking at social events
Giving speeches
Writing articles
Getting articles written about you
Sending personal letters and notes
Mailing announcement cards
Placing periodic telephone calls
Making slide presentations
Submitting unsolicited proposals
Joining professional and trade
   organizations
Exhibiting at trade shows and
   conferences
Guesting on radio and TV talk shows
Sending out news releases

Placing yourself in directory listings
Carrying your product with you
Wearing a symbol
Bartering
Donating and volunteering
Writing a newsletter
Teaching classes
Giving away samples
Offering discount coupons
Contacting past customers
Putting up signs and posters
Joining others in promotions
Being active in civic clubs and
   churches
Placing classified ads
Hosting your own cable talk show

If you don't have time to write a book, but could squeeze in time for a chapter (that's only about 3,000 words, or twelve double-spaced typewritten pages), you can reap the benefits of a book by contributing a chapter to an anthology.

For example, Dottie Walters, who heads Royal Publishing from her home in Glendora, California, publishes two anthologies every year, each on a different theme, from sales power and effective communication to stress management. A different person contributes each chapter, which includes a full-page biography and picture, along with the address and telephone number of the author. Authors buy copies of the anthology wholesale and sell it retail. The best part of this arrangement is that while you're promoting yourself with the anthology, every other author using it is promoting you, too.

Since insurance specialist Wayne Cotton contributed to one of Walters' anthologies, he has used it to increase enrollment at his high-priced business seminars. He gives the book away free to each registrant. The "gift with purchase" concept can be used to build any business. Estée Lauder, the famous cosmetics mogul, built her entire business on this promotional concept.

Speaking. You can also promote your services or product by speaking before civic, trade, or professional groups. There are more than 9,000 daily speaking opportunities in the United States. Speaking on subjects related to your business is a particularly useful sales tool in such personal-service businesses as real estate, child care, consulting, or counseling, where people like to feel they have a trusted relationship with the professional.

Consultant Bill Slavin finds that speaking and leading seminars provide him with the high profile he needs to attract business. "You never know for sure who will be a client in the future," he says. "So I've found that you have to treat everyone you meet as a potential client. You can convert the acquaintances you have made at speeches or seminars into clients with a follow-up call and an appointment. But be sure you focus the follow-through conversations on your business or they will think of you as a speaker or seminar leader instead of as a business."

Making impressive visual aids and handouts to accompany speeches, seminars, and proposals is easy with desktop presentation software. Use this software to create 35mm slides, overhead transparencies for speeches, and charts for proposals. Leading programs are *Harvard Graphics, Freelance Plus,* and *Persuasion,* by Aldus. An economical and easy-to-use choice is Spinnaker's *Pinstripe Presenter.* You can print what you create on your printer, a plotter or, using a modem, you can transmit your work over a phone line to a service that produces color slides, overhead transparencies, or color prints for you. Services generally ship your order back to you within twenty-four hours by air courier.

Actually, in a small business virtually every contact you have with others is free promotion—for good or for bad. So it's important to convey the right image of yourself and your business in all your interactions. Pay attention to:

■ Appearance
■ Voice
■ What you say
■ What you write
■ How you dress

6. Creative Advertising

Creative, well-positioned advertising can not only put your business in the minds of your buyers but can also help you locate wholesalers or retailers who see your ads appearing month after month in trade-related publications, and thus will be more likely to respond positively to direct sales contact from you.

Here are some tips for low-cost advertising strategies.

Classified and display ads.   You can advertise your business in newspapers, magazines, or newsletters through either display advertising or classified ads. Display advertising is expensive but can be worth the investment if properly targeted.

When Elizabeth Scott and Lucy Ewell launched their software company, their primary marketing effort was to take out a full-page color ad in *SoftTalk*

Magazine, which was being offered free with the purchase of Apple computers. Their big, brightly colored ad was designed to attract the interest of preteen girls, the primary market for their software games. The ad was very successful.

Display advertising can be expensive, however, and is not a wise investment for everyone. Many entrepreneurs begin by placing classified ads in targeted magazines and then buying display ads in those magazines that produce a good response. This is an excellent way of testing a market.

Barbara Elman used a similar approach in getting business for her word-processing service, which is targeted to scriptwriters. "I advertised regularly in the best places to reach my clients—the Hollywood trade papers," she says. "In the legal field that forum might be in the local law journal; in the academic field, the local university newspaper.

"You don't have to use a big ad. In fact, the small ads I ran regularly drew more business than the enormous, several-hundred-dollar ads I ran once. I found that having an ad run regularly and having some kind of logo or copy that was catchy and showed I knew what I was doing drew best. When people suddenly needed typing, they remembered my ad from having seen it six months ago. Now, sure enough, when they look today, there it is again. They know I'm a serious business."

It's tempting to advertise only when you need business. Still, Jay Levinson, author of *Guerrilla Marketing,* quotes studies that show nine impressions are necessary to make a regular customer and the ad must run three times to be seen once. So he concludes that twenty-seven runs of a new ad are needed to make a new regular customer.

Direct mail. While many start-up service businesses mistakenly rely on direct mail to produce business, a simple, creative campaign using postcards can produce outstanding results. For example, Heidi Waldman launched her desktop publishing business by sending double postcards, cards with tear-off return postcards, to 250 businesses and organizations carefully selected from the Yellow Pages. The number of return cards she got produced so much business that she has not had to do any further advertising in two years. Repeat business and referrals have kept her going.

Cheryl Myers, who operates a word-processing service, used a postcard, too. She sent cards the same size and color of those her community garbage collection company sent. Thinking they were their garbage bills, people saved the cards and Sharon got business.

What's important, says Heidi Waldman, is that "the bi-fold postcard doesn't look cheap." She advises, "Have it designed and typeset by people who know what they're doing. Provide return postage. Getting a postal permit will be cheaper than using stamps because you won't be paying for stamps on unreturned postcards." Also, use quality paper and laser-printed mailing labels in a matching typeface. Clear labels that can be laser-printed are available and will look better than white labels on colored stock.

Computer bulletin boards. You'll find advertising opportunities on both local and national computer bulletin boards. These boards, which list services or referral networks, provide information via the computer keyboard. For example, BuyPhone in Los Angeles lists local businesses from alarm installation to zipper repair. Using a modem, people can phone the listing and call up on their computer the services they need. Each business listed pays a fee.

To learn about local boards, inquire at computer stores and at computer-user group meetings. To use such national services as CompuServe, Source, and Delphi, you need to subscribe to the service and pay for the time you use on the system.

Fliers and tear-off pads. A simple way to reach buyers when your market is limited to a particular geographic area is to use fliers or tear-off pads. For example, if you offer a résumé service, you might want to produce a colorful flyer to display on college bulletin boards or hand out at college events. Or you might place these flyers on cars in employee parking lots of companies where there recently have been large layoffs.

7. Service: Giving More Than the Competition

Nothing sells like service. If your results are "extra-ordinary," if your service is outstanding, people will quickly take notice and want to tell everyone they know. Suddenly you have the equivalent of a volunteer sales force. When Nathan Pritikin started his first Pritikin treatment program, he didn't even intend to go into business. He wanted to demonstrate the dramatic restorative effects of diet and exercise on seriously ill individuals. His results were so dramatic, however, that he found he had opened a floodgate of new clients.

Charlotte Mitchell's business is literally based on going the extra mile. As Notary on Wheels and Fingerprinting on Wheels she goes where her clients need her. Medical transcriptionist Vickie Fite believes her success is the result of the following business philosophy: "I go the extra mile for people. I work harder than I would for an employer." And home-based marketing consultant Linda Jagoda puts it this way: "Treat your clients, no matter what size, to royal service. Your smallest customer can bring you one of your biggest clients later on."

Norm Dominquez's success also demonstrates that service beyond what's expected is a low-cost but effective means of marketing. Dominquez operates Unicom Paging, Inc., a mobile communications service in Phoenix, Arizona, and says of his marketing approach, "The name of the game is service. Phoenix is highly competitive. So I focus on the smaller companies who need only fifteen- to sixteen-pagers, and we provide an incentive to our customers too, so they'll want to refer us to other people. Besides our seven-day-a-week, twenty-four-hour service, our incentive offer is eight months of free service credited to their account. We also have a philosophy of trust. I don't do extensive credit checks and I don't get burned anymore than the norm."

Becoming Your Own Marketing Manager

Whatever marketing avenues you choose, learn as much as you can about them before using them. If you want to be successful, you will need to become your own marketing manager. Fortunately, all the information you need is available. Read pertinent books and articles, take adult education classes, and talk to other successful entrepreneurs. Begin with the references in the Resource List at the end of this chapter. If necessary, hire a marketing consultant to sit down with you for several hours. The investment in time and money will be worth it.

Before sales trainer Helen Berman left her job and started her business, she signed up to take a university extension course to learn the basics she knew she needed. But when the class started, she found weekly evening classes too time consuming for her already tight schedule. She needed the information at the beginning, not the end, of the semester. So she hired the instructor as a consultant and met with him each week until she had the expertise and experience she needed.

Like Berman, you should feel free to do whatever it takes to get all the information and assistance you need. For instance, to get free feedback on the effectiveness of your promotional material before you go to the expense of printing and distributing it, you can contact a faculty member in the marketing department of a university school of business. College professors are always seeking "real world" examples for their classes. Explain that you would like ideas on your marketing campaign. Bring your brochures and material to the class. You'll get plenty of ideas.

Once you have developed your marketing plan and know which strategies you will use, set up a system for implementing it on an ongoing basis. Your systems should include:

1. **A defined marketing effort.** Here are some examples: Call two businesses from the Yellow Pages each day, run a classified ad in the local paper each week, attend two networking groups per week, and send a monthly newsletter to your mailing list.

2. **A defined follow-up plan.** For example: Set up appointments each week with people whom you've called or met, send thank-you notes and newsletters to all the people you meet with, and set up a tickler system for following up on all pending possibilities.

3. **A procedure for tracking how every new client or customer heard about you.** For example: include this information on every order form, code your mailing address for different publications or mailings, and include this information on each client file.

4. **A scheduled time to review your marketing effort.** This would include at least a quarterly review of how you got your business, what type of business you got, and so on, to help you revise and plan for the next quarter.

Some management software can also help you follow up on contacts you've made and keep business relationships alive. An example of this type of software is *Act*. Some of the tasks it automates in one package are the ability to keep track of customers and prospects, maintain records about them, write letters, keep track of expenses and schedule and remind you of follow-up activities.

Keeping up your marketing efforts month after month, year after year, will make the difference. Once you identify the strategies that produce the most results, continue them even after your business is thriving. If you sometimes generate more business than you can handle, you can subcontract the work to others and still make a profit. Or you can refer it to reliable colleagues with or without a referral fee.

Ultimately, your happy, satisfied customers become your greatest source of new business. Marketing consultant Cork Platts reminds us that "referrals are golden. Do something special for each customer or client and they'll remember you to everyone else who needs you." In business, as in all of life, what goes around comes around.

Chapter Digest

1. The marketing methods used by large businesses often do not work well for home-based businesses. The most effective methods for home-based businesses are also often the least expensive.

2. The most successful home-based businesses build their business on their reputation; by carving out a specialized niche; by gaining access to business through a gatekeeper; by positioning themselves as preeminent in their field; or by being what we call a premier marketer.

3. By developing a marketing mindset to your business you can successfully market your business even if you do not have a background in marketing and sales. A marketing mindset is not only a matter of focusing on providing a quality product or service but also in determining why what you offer is unique, how it benefits those you serve, and how you will spread the word about these benefits to those who need them.

4. Once you have defined your product, you need to find a market niche, position your product or service, and experiment until you find the best ways of letting your market know about your business. People buy for gain or to prevent pain. In other words, they buy for the benefits they will receive. Benefits include pleasure, profit, confidence, and self-esteem.

5. Networking is the single best way to start and build a home-based personal or professional service business. Also called word-of-mouth marketing, networking involves face-to-face contact to establish relationships that lead to a steady flow of business.

6. Networking itself is not selling. But a most important aspect of net-working is following up with those you meet to see whether they need your service, and signing them up if they do. Build a mailing list from your networking contacts and stay in touch with them regularly by phone or mail, because out of sight is out of mind.

7. Other effective low-cost start-up marketing methods for a home business include cold calling, sampling, strategic pricing, free publicity, creative advertising, and exceptional service.

8. Unless you have the funds to hire marketing professionals to work for you, you will need to become your own marketing manager. Feel free to do whatever it takes to get the information and assistance you need to create a defined marketing plan and a procedure for following through on that plan on a weekly basis. Don't let up when business is good. The marketing you do when business is good is what will sustain you when it slows down.

Resources

Books

Better Brochures, Catalogs and Mailing Pieces. Jane Haas. New York: St. Martin's Press, 1984.

Consultant's Guide to Proposal Writing. Herman Holtz. New York: John Wiley & Sons, 1986.

Direct Mail Copy That Sells. Herschell Gordon Lewis. Englewood Cliffs, NJ: Prentice-Hall, 1984.

Do-It-Yourself Marketing Research. George Edward Breen. New York: McGraw-Hill, 1989.

Getting the Most From Your Yellow Pages Advertising. Barry Maher. New York: Amacom, 1988.

The Greatest Direct Mail Sales Letters of All Time. Richard S. Hodgson. Chicago: The Dartnell Corporation, 1987.

Guerrilla Marketing: Secrets for Making Big Profits from Your Small Business. Jay Conrad Levinson. Boston: Houghton Mifflin, 1985.

Homemade Money. Barbara Brabec. See full citation under Chapter 3.

How to Make Newsletters, Brochures & Other Good Stuff Without a Computer System. Helen Gregory. Sedro-Wooley, WA.: Pinstripe Publishing, 1987.

Influencing with Integrity. Genie Z. Laborde. Palo Alto, CA: Syntony Publishing, 1987.

Letters That Sell. Edward W. Werz. Chicago: Contemporary Books, 1987.

The Marketing Sourcebook for Small Business. Jeffrey Davidson. New York: John Wiley & Sons, 1989.

Marketing Warfare. Al Reis and Jack Trout. New York: McGraw-Hill, 1986.

Marketing Without Advertising—Creative Strategies for Small Business Success. Michael Phillips and Salli Rasberry. Berkeley, CA: Nolo Press, 1986.

Positioning: The Battle for Your Mind. Al Reis and Jack Trout. New York: Warner Books, 1986.

Publicity: How to Get It. Richard O'Brien. New York: Barnes & Noble Books, 1977.

Words That Sell. Richard Bayan. Chicago: Contemporary Books, 1984.

Directories

Direct Mail List Rates and Data. Standard Rate and Data Service. Available in the reference sections of public libraries.

Directory of Directories. Detroit: Gale Research Inc.

Directory of United States Trade Shows, Expositions and Conventions. U.S. Travel Service, U.S. Department of Commerce, Washington, D.C. 20230.

Encyclopedia of Associations. Gale Research Inc., published annually.

MacRae's Blue Book. 817 Broadway, New York, NY 10003; (212) 673-4700. Directories of companies and products.

The National Directory of Addresses and Telephone Numbers. General Information Company, 401 Parkplace, Kirkland, WA 98033; (800) 722-3244.

The Self-Publishing Manual. Dan Poynter. Santa Barbara, CA: Para Publishing, 1989.

Trade Shows Worldwide. Gale Research Inc., Book Tower, Dept. 77748, Detroit, MI 48277.

Audiotapes, Newsletters, and Reports

National Mail Order Association. 5818 Venice Blvd., Los Angeles, 90019; (213) 934-7986. Mail-order sales record sheets.

More Than a Dream: Raising the Money; and **More Than a Dream: Running Your Own Business.** U.S. Department of Labor, 200 Constitution Ave. NW, Washington, D.C. 20210 (free).

The Professional Consultant & Seminar Business Report. Howard L. Shenson, 20750 Ventura Blvd., Ste. 206, Woodland Hills, CA 91364. Shenson is also the source of audiotapes including **How to Start and**

Promote Your Own Newsletter as well as books and computer software on all aspects of the consulting and seminar industries.

Small Business Administration (see full citation under Chapter 3):
Marketing Research Procedures (#SBB-9)
Planning Your Advertising Budget (#4.018)

Sommer & Gibofsky's Do's & Don'ts—30 Proven Rules to Help You Develop Cost-Effective Brochures and **How to Develop a Cost-Effective Newsletter.** Elyse Sommer, 110-34 73rd Rd., #3E, P.O. Box 1133, Forest Hills, NY 11375 ($1 + SASE for each ordered).

Miscellaneous

Newspaper and radio advertising departments. Not only can they provide you with advertising rates, but their advertising kits often have important and useful demographic information.

CHAPTER
TWENTY-THREE
■■■■■■■■■■■■■■■■■■■■

Moving On: What to Do When Your Business Outgrows Your Home

Sooner or later, the day comes when you think about whether it's time to move the office away from home. Perhaps your business has grown so much it's bursting at the seams, and working from home feels more like living at the office. Or maybe you've had an intriguing job offer or promotion possibility that promises to take you back to a corporate skyscraper. Whatever the reason, many people who work at home eventually face the question of whether they should move on.

For some, the decision is easy because working from home is only a stepping-stone on the road to another goal. Computer consultant Bill Slavin explains that his dream had always been to build a big organization, so "as soon as it was financially feasible, I moved my business to a downtown office."

In contrast to Slavin, there are those for whom working from home is a cherished way of life they refuse to give up. They share the sentiments expressed by mime and typesetter Tina Lenert when she declared, in unequivocal terms, "I wouldn't want to work any other way." Tina and others who feel this strongly about their home offices will do whatever must be done to keep working from home, even if it means moving to a larger house or restricting the growth of their businesses.

For most people, however, deciding whether to stay or move out is less clear-cut. When faced with the choice, the great majority of people who work from home feel torn between opportunities to grow and expand on the one hand, and the convenience, comfort, financial benefits, and flexibility they get from working at home on the other. Medical transcriptionist Georgia Hahn, for example, sought our advice about her situation because she had the opportunity of taking on a large account that would require hiring several staff members, and she feared this would mean moving her business out of her house.

"I've become very spoiled having the business here at home. I make enough money to live comfortably and I've been with my kids since they were little. They're in school now and I'm a successful businesswoman. I've had the best of both worlds, but now I have to make a painful decision. What's it going to be, my easygoing life or a bigger business?"

Fortunately, moving on doesn't have to be the either/or decision Georgia fears. For us, working from home started as an island of relief from high-stress careers that has turned into a satisfying lifestyle. And there's no need to move out just because the business is growing. We have a spectrum of options to choose from if we want to expand without leaving home.

In this chapter, we'll talk about how you'll know when it's time to move on, and the full range of options you have. We'll also share some of the creative solutions others have found for preserving the benefits of working from home while taking advantage of promising career and business opportunities.

When to Move Out

When Gerald and Sandy McDevitt consulted with the Small Business Administration about their home business, they asked, "How will we know when it's time to move out?" The representative simply told them, "You'll know," and we would agree. When it's time for a change, the signs will be impossible to ignore.

As the McDevitts discovered, the issue is usually a matter of space. Two years ago accountant Sandy McDevitt was having difficulty using the software she had purchased for her computer. There were too many commands to recall. In her frustration she had an idea: what if there were a template she could lay over a computer keyboard that would display all the commands she needed to remember in using various software?

With part-time assistance from her husband, Gerald, a computer analyst for the U.S. Navy, Sandy turned this idea into a home business called Creative Computer Products. The object was to produce "keyboard templates" for the major lines of personal computers.

Sandy and Gerald ran the whole operation from their family room and kitchen, taking orders by mail or phone and then packing and shipping them out. For shipping, they rented a mailbox and had daily UPS pickup. Then, by the time they began getting twenty-five to thirty orders a day, several things happened that made it clear they had outgrown their home.

First, the mailbox service told them they had too much volume for it to handle. At about the same time, the McDevitts ran out of storage space at home, and the family room and kitchen started overflowing with materials. There wasn't enough space for eating, let alone working.

So Sandy and Gerald rented a space they thought would be large enough to meet their needs and moved most everything out of the house. A year later, they had to rent a second space the same size as the first one, and now they still don't have enough room. Their printing press remains in the garage, where they produce all their in-house literature, and they have a fifteen-foot camera on order but no place to put it. The next step came later that year when the McDevitts bought a building of their own and consolidated the whole business in one place.

Aside from outgrowing the confines of a home, the quest for a different business image is the next most common reason for a change. In the early days of our consulting business, our firm, Public Affairs Assistance, won a major federal contract. Although we could do most of the work at home, the officials would not allow overhead expenses for a home office. Besides, we needed a place for the contract officers to preview the materials we were developing. The basement office we had in our first home was next to the laundry room and just wouldn't convey the right image.

Since we wanted to keep as much of our work at home as possible, we considered several options short of moving the office out. The final answer was to rent a professional suite temporarily, but there were other possibilities we could have chosen. In fact, here are twelve solutions we and other people have found for these dilemmas. Some may be totally inappropriate for your situation, but others should be catalysts that will help you resolve the issue of how to grow while working from home.

How to Keep the Benefits of Working From Home

1. Rent a professional suite.   If you find you need a place where you can create a highly official business image, hold conferences, or get more extensive office services, consider renting a professional suite from an organization like Headquarters Suites. Such suites are part of a complex that includes small offices, central conference facilities, and a full range of secretarial services available to anyone subleasing space from the complex.

When we rented a suite while working on the federal contract, we had a small office, a separate phone, and a receptionist at the complex to take our messages. The conference room there was useful for making presentations and holding meetings with the contract administrators. The cost of such suites varies by community but is generally less than renting a separate outside office and hiring the equivalent office services.

2. Rent private office space.   Renting an office doesn't necessarily mean you have to say good-bye to working from home. Some people have rented a second office for certain activities (receiving mail or phone calls, working on large equipment, holding meetings) while still maintaining a home office where they can do creative or detail work.

Hypnotherapist Nancy Bonus holds her weight-loss groups in office space she sublets from a private clinic, paying only for the hours her group uses the space each week. She sees individual clients and does all the management of her business at home. Bob Weil runs his part-time picture-framing business from his apartment, but rents workshop time on Saturdays from a large picture-framing company. Marjorie Dahl does image consulting from her home, helping men and women "dress for success." However, when she holds workshops or brings together several clients to look over a number of garments, she rents a hotel suite.

Many homes simply can't accommodate the additional equipment and furniture involved in hiring staff. When necessary, entrepreneurs often rent space for their employees and continue to work at home themselves, either full or part time.

Writer Collin Gribbons, for example, who publishes eight newsletters and magazines for Canadian labor unions, needed a secretary and wasn't comfortable with having one come to his home. His work was generating a seemingly endless parade of air-express trucks, and his loud daisy-wheel printer was clattering away hour after hour, so he had begun to worry that his business would bother his neighbors. His solution was to rent outside office space where his secretary now works full time.

Having an office doesn't preclude his working from home; it just provides another option. Collin says he still works at home, using his computer and modem to link up to his outside office. "I can always send material to the office by phone when I don't want to go in, but a lot of the more office-oriented tasks, like courier pickups and telephone messages, are now handled away from home."

3. Contract work with other businesses. Instead of moving his business to a warehouse, Bob Baxter hired a company to bottle and package his pet health-care products, jobs he once handled in his garage. When developing a large marketing program for a customer, consultant James McClaren subcontracted with several small businesses rather than renting office space and hiring employees for the duration of the contract. Using a free-lance writer, a packager, and an office-services company, he got the program done without leaving home.

4. Move to a bigger home. Whether you buy, lease, or build, a new and larger place to live may provide the added or specialized space you need to continue working from home. Husband-and-wife team Theresa Arnerich and Tom Morrell operated a seminar firm from their condominium, but space was tight. Their shipping department was in the garage, and the one office they shared also doubled as a bedroom for Tom's daughter when she visited on weekends. Theresa threatened to find an outside office, but they decided to build a new house instead. It would be tailor-made to working from home.

Theresa says, "I'm actually glad we worked from the condo for a while, because we found out what we needed before building. We learned, for example, that we want the offices on a separate level, away from the kitchen and other household activities. We want to be able to close the space off from social events and from household maintenance personnel who come in. We also want the offices near the bedroom so we can work late and make early morning calls without having to go across the whole house." For Theresa, the best part about the new house will be the luxury of having an office she can call her very own.

5. Hire employees who will work from their homes. Some companies, like MicroGraphic Images (software) and Escrow Overload (temporary escrow employees), have expanded by adding personnel who work from their own homes.

Commercial artist Diane Wessling Blake of MicroGraphic Images says, "By having our employees work at home, we can expand as rapidly as we need to and keep our costs to a minimum. In a fast-growing industry like ours, this is very important." The founders and chief executive officers of these companies all still work from home, too.

6. Rent storage or warehouse space. When potter June Wright had the chance of filling an order for over two thousand goblets to be used at a special benefit, she knew she'd have to hire helpers. She also knew they wouldn't all fit in her studio behind the house, so she found a warehouse to rent and hired ten students, part time, for one month.

This arrangement worked so well that if she can get more orders on such a grand scale, she wants to keep it up. She would continue running the business and creating pots from her own home, but would have a supervisor overseeing operations at the warehouse.

7. Add on to your home. There are many options for adding on or converting unused areas of an existing house into extra business space. Many of these options are described in Chapter 6.

We added on to two different houses in order to work from home. We bought our first house so we could move from a two-bedroom apartment and start working at home, but it didn't have a suitable place for Sarah to see psychotherapy clients. So we enclosed a side porch, providing a separate entrance and complete privacy for her clients.

Then when we first moved from our home in Kansas City to California, we tried sharing one office in part of our living room. It didn't work. Each of us needed to have our own private office space, so once again we added on. This time we built a second story.

8. Rent an adjacent apartment or buy a second condo. When lawyer Mark Cane passed his bar exam, he worked from his apartment but rented an office from a group of lawyers in a professional building where he could meet with clients. The cost of prime commercial space was high, however, and his overhead was consuming most of his income. When the studio apartment next to his became vacant, he talked to the landlord about renting it for his law office. He explained that his work was very quiet and would not disturb other tenants. The landlord agreed to the idea, and Mark's net income rose in his first month at the new location.

9. *Buy a duplex or apartment building.* Although this may seem like a rather extreme solution, it can be a successful one. Lynne Frances started Rainbow Cleaning Service from her apartment. She ran the business from a bedroom that also served as sitting room and office.

"I enjoyed it until the business just got too big," she recalls. "I had to hire a secretary, and then the number of my cleaning crew employees kept increasing until finally I had worked my way up to twenty. Of course, they were all coming to the apartment for work assignments. Even then it wasn't such a nuisance until it got up to twenty-eight. Then if I'd have one of my kids or my folks come to visit, it was just people around at all hours of the day and night."

After five years of this, she decided enough was enough and rented an outside office. She was running the service from this office when we met her, but she wasn't happy. "People just don't realize what a great way of life it is to work from your home. To move out is a terrible shock!" She had forgotten what a chore it was to have to get dressed up in the morning and rush off in a car to be at the office before the first crew arrived. "And," she told us, "it seems I never get anything done at home now that I have an outside office. When I get home at night the dishes are waiting in the sink, the bed's unmade, and the trash is overflowing."

The next time we saw Lynne, she had reached what was for her the ideal compromise: she had bought an apartment building. She lived in one unit and ran the cleaning service from another. "Now," she says with satisfaction, "I've got it all."

10. *Negotiate to keep a job at home.* A tempting job offer or promotion can lure you back to the office, but if you're ambivalent, consider negotiating to take the position while working at least part time at home. Develop a plan that demonstrates how this would benefit the company and increase your productivity without jeopardizing vital communication with the office. Suggest perhaps two days in the office and three at home, or propose a schedule for regular meetings in the office.

11. *Limit your business growth.* Sometimes staying at home means making a hard decision. What is more important to you—a larger business or the particular work style that only a home office can provide? A surprising number of people are opting to limit their businesses to ones that can be contained within the walls of their homes. Some people we've met have scaled their businesses back in order to return to a home office after moving out of their homes.

Perhaps this is not so surprising after all when you consider a Robert Half International Poll which showed that two out of three men and women said they would be willing to reduce their salaries an average of 15 percent in order to gain more family and personal time.

When collections negotiator Patricia Lineman's business grew to ten employees, she finally realized she had to move to an outside office. She found, however, that she didn't like the added pressure, inconvenience, and responsibility of supervising others. She discovered she wasn't a manager at heart, so she consciously decided to cut back her business, close her office, and return to the more comfortable lifestyle of being a one-person home-based business working one-to-one with her clients. She's making less money, but enjoying it and her life a lot more.

12. Raise your prices; refer or franchise additional business. Raising your prices can enable you to continue your income growth without adding clients, personnel, or space. Or instead, consider referring business you can no longer accommodate to a competitor for a referral fee. When you consider that marketing costs can run 40 percent in many businesses, a referral fee is not unreasonable. Licensing or offering a franchise to others to carry out your business in other geographical locations is another way of expanding financially without necessarily expanding your space.

A Future of New Options

Establishing the right work arrangement at home is often like raising a family—you have to keep making adjustments for new developments, some of which can be foreseen and some of which can't. If, like many we've met with, your intention is to continue pursuing your career to the fullest and to do so from the luxury of your own home, combining a little determination with a little ingenuity should enable you to find a way to do both.

With the desire to work from home growing at such an accelerating pace and the cost and size of sophisticated office equipment shrinking every year, we're beginning to see new housing and community developments that open new options for those who want to pursue thriving careers from home.

So often when people talk about the "electronic cottage" of the future, science-fiction movies come to mind, with images of chrome and steel modules, hermetically sealed and controlled by a master computer. Consider the possibility that the electronic cottage will not look like that at all. In our opinion, the electronic cottages of the future will look more like Rohn and Jeri Engh's wood cabin on their farm in isolated Osceola, Wisconsin, where they produce a newsletter for photographers; or like Doug Hansen's second-floor apartment in West Hollywood where he writes screenplays for a living; or like Vicki McLane's ranch-style house in a Kansas City, Missouri, suburb where she works for Hallmark Cards.

Gradual updating of zoning ordinances and continuing telecommunications advances will make it increasingly possible for you to live and work in almost any location of your choice.

New living arrangements like "Hoffices," part of a real-estate development in Oak Creek, Wisconsin, and "Workman's Mill" in Frederick, Maryland, allow families to conduct business from first-floor offices and shops while living in pleasant condos above. In the future we may see the emergence of rural housing developments linked electronically to urban metropolises. Perhaps ultimately our home offices will be staffed by robotic employees who will tend to both our home and office needs.

Before laughing too hard about such possibilities, consider a few of these "famous last words" compiled by the editors of *Science 84* magazine:

"What can be more palpably absurd than the prospect held out of locomotives traveling twice as fast as stagecoaches?" (*The Quarterly Review*, 1825)

"The ordinary 'horseless carriage' is at present a luxury for the wealthy; and although its price will probably fall in the near future, it will never, of course, come into as common use as the bicycle." (*The Literary Digest*, 1889)

" . . . as a means of rapid transit, aerial navigation could not begin to compete with the railroad." William Baxter, Jr. (*Popular Science*, 1901)

"While theoretically and technically television may be feasible, commercially and financially, I consider it an impossibility, a development of which we need not waste time dreaming." (Scientist and inventor Lee De Forest, 1926)

So who knows what lies ahead? Much of it will be in or beyond the realm of our imagination today. Perhaps orbiting space stations will be among the home offices of tomorrow. As an open-collar worker, you could find yourself ideally prepared for the new frontier of living and traveling in space.

Whatever lies ahead, in the meantime you can enjoy a comfortable, rewarding, and productive life by working from home. And in moments of frustration, when the cat has eaten the corner of your latest report, you haven't seen another human being in four days, or your two-year-old has just hung up the phone in the middle of a business call, take heart.

Think of the tax benefits of working from home. Consider the overhead you're saving. Reflect on what you can do in the time that used to be wasted commuting. Think about how it feels to be there watching your children grow. Recognize how much more control you have, not only of business but of your life in general. Remember, most of all, that working from home is a ticket to realizing a new American dream for personal and professional success, a way to have your cake and eat it too! Someone's going to do it; it might as well be you!

Chapter Digest

1. For some, working from home is a stepping-stone to the larger business of their dreams, but for many others, once they've worked at home they simply never want to leave and will metaphorically go to the ends of the earth to stay there.

2. There is a wide variety of options for managing to expand your business or career and continue working from home. Finding the right one for you involves responding to your changing needs with determination and ingenuity. And the future will undoubtedly hold many innovative new options for living and working under the same roof.

Resources

The Franchise Advantage: Make It Work for You. Donald D. Boroian and Patrick J. Boroian. Chicago: Prism Creative Group, Ltd., 1987.

A P P E N D I X

Home Businesses from A to Z

Accounting Service
Advertising
   Agency
   Brokering
Aerial Photography
Aerobics classes
Affixing company logos to baseball caps
Alarm Service
Animal Show Judging
Answering Service
Antique
   Locating service
   Repair
   Refinishing
   Restoration
Apartment Finders
Appliance
   Refinishing
   Repair
Appraising
   Personal Collections
   Precious Metals
Architectural
   Designer
   Model Maker
Art
   Instruction
   Repairs
   Show Promoting
   Studio
Athletic Equipment Repair
Auctioneer—Real Estate

Auditing services
Audio/Video
   Editing
   Engineering
   Production
Auto
   Brokering
   Detailing
   Upholstery Cleaning
Baby-sitting
   Agency
   Referral Service
Badge and Button-Making
Balloon
   Decoration
   Bouquet Delivery Service
Bartering Service
Basement
   Cleaning
   Finishing
   Waterproofing
Bed and Breakfast Inn
Bicycle
   Custom Construction
   Repair
Billing & Invoicing Service
Book
   Indexing Service
   Packager
Booking Agency
   Entertainers
   Models

Bookkeeping Service
Breakfast-in-Bed Service
Bridal
   Consulting
   Makeup Service
Bronze Work
Building Design
Building Inspection Service
Building Restoration & Preservation
Business Broker
Business Cards—customized (holograms, "pop-outs," photographs)
Business Consultant for small and start-up business
Business Services for small communities
Button Sales
Cabinet Making
Cake Decorating
Calligraphy
Camp Consultant
Caning Repair
Car Pool Service
Career Counseling
Carpet & Rugs
   Cleaning
   Dyeing
Catering
Ceiling Repair
Certificate Hand Lettering
Chartering Services
   Airplanes
   Yachts
Chess Instruction
Chimney Sweeping
Claims Adjuster
Cleaning Services
   Aquariums
   Signs from Store Windows
   Ships
   Venetian Blinds
Clipping Service
Closet
   Design
   Organizing
Clothing Alterations
Clown for parties, promotions
Coin-Operated Equipment Maintenance
   Dry Cleaning
   Laundries
   TV
Collection Agency
Color Consulting

Computer
   Animation
   Bulletin Boards Systems
   Consulting
   Debugging
   Graphics
   Programming
   Repair
   Room Installation
   Tutoring
Concierge Services
Construction Cost Estimator
Consultant Broker
Contest Organizer
Copying Services
   Audiotapes
   Computer disks
   Photocopies
   Videotapes
Copywriter
Costume Rental
Dancing Instruction
Data
   Converting Service
   Entry Overload
   Processing Service
Dating Service
Daycare
   Adults
   Children
Debt Negotiation Service
Debugging Software
Deed Investigator
Delivery Services
   Candy
   Flowers
   Parcels
Dental Practice Management Consulting
Deposition Digesting
Desktop Publishing Services
Desktop Video Services
Diet Counseling
Discount Contracting
Disk Formatting Service
Disk Jockey Service
Dispatcher
Dog Grooming
Doll
   Clothing Making
   House Building
   Repair
Drafting Service

Dressmaking
Economics Research
Editorial Services
Educational
    Consulting
    Record Keeping Service
Electric Hair Removal
Embroidery
Employment Application Checking
Employment Agency
Enameling Repair
Energy Consulting
Entertainment
    Belly Dancing
    Magic
    Mime
    Musician
    Singing
Errand Service
Escort Service
Escrow Temporary Agency
Etiquette Consultant
Event Clearinghouse
Executive Director Services
Executive Search Service
Exercise & Physical
        Fitness Instruction
Expert Location Service
Exporter
Eyesight Trainer
Facialist/Skincare Specialist
Family Historian
Fashion Consultant
Film Processing Service
Financial
    Consulting
    Planning
Fishing & Hunting Information
Flower Arranging Services
Food
    Crafting
    Mail Order Sales
    Service Management
    Special-Diet Delivery
Form Designing
Fountain Pen Repair
Free Classified Advertising Newspaper
Fund-raising
Furniture
    Custom Made
    Repair
    Stripping

Garage Door Service
Garden Care
Generating Sales Leads
Genealogy Research Service
Gift
    Basket Service
    Buying Service
    Wrapping Service
Glass
    Etching
    Repair
Goldsmith
Golf Handicapping Service
Gourmet Cooking School
Government
        Bid Notification Service
        Form-Filling Service
        Procurement Consultant
Grant Writing
Graphic Designer
Greeting Card
    Artist
    Writer
Gunsmith
Hair Salon
Handicraft Making
Handwriting Analyst
Hauling Service
Health Enhancement Product Sales
Herb Growing
Home
    Delivery Beauty Service
    Historian
    Inspector
    Repair Service
    Security Analysis Service
    Security Patrol Service
Horseback Riding Instruction
Hospital Utilization Authorization Service
House
    Cleaning Service
    Painter
    Portrait Painting
    Sitting
Housing Consultant
Image Consultant
Importer
Independent Insurance Adjuster
Information Brokerage Service
Instructional Design
Insurance Agent
Insurance Inspection & Audits

Interior Design Services
Interpreting Service
Interviewer—Print or Radio, TV
Inventor
Inventory Control Services for Businesses
Inventory Household Effects
Investment
    Advisor Referral Service
    Counseling
Janitorial Service
Jewelry
    Appraisal
    Design
    Making
    Repair
Job Placement & Referral Service
Knitting
    By hand or machine
    Instruction
    Selling supplies
Landscape
    Contractor
    Design
Language Instruction
Laser Cartridge Remanufacturing
Laundry Services
Law
    Library Management
    Office Management Consultant
Lawn Care Service
Lawyers Aide/Freelance Paralegal
Leatherwork
Lecturing/Public Speaking
Legal Transcription Service
Letter Writing
Lighting Consultant
Library Management
Limited Edition Book Sales
Limousine Service
Lingerie Sales
Liquidated Goods Broker
List Broker
Literary Agent
Loan
    Broker
    Packager
Locksmithing
Lost Pet Location Service
Mail Order Business
Mailing List Services
    Compilation and rental
    Maintenance

Mailing Service
    Hand Addressing
    Pre-Sorting
Makeup Artist/Consultant
Management Consultant
Management Training
Manicurist To Go
Mantel Repair
Manufacturer's Representative
Manufacturing specialty products
Manuscript Editing
Marketing
    Consultant
    Research
Marriage Broker/Matchmaker
Massage
    Instruction
    To Go
Mechanic To Go
Mediator
Medical
    Management Consultant
    Records Review
    Transcription Service
Meeting Planning
Memory Training
Messenger Service
Miniature Items for Collectors
Mobile Communications Service
Model Making
Monitoring TV, Radio
Monogramming
Murals
Mushroom Growing
Music
    Arranging and Composition
    Instruction
    Instrument Repair
Name Creating Consultant
Nameplate
    Engraving
    Making
Needlepoint
    Instruction
    Supplies sales
Networking
    Classes
    Organization
New Age crafts
    Astrology
    Channeling
    Numerology
    Psychic Reading

Notary Service
Nursery of rare and unusual plants
Nurses' Registry
Nutrition
   Analysis
   Consulting
Office Automation Consultant
Office Lunch Service
Order Fulfillment Service
Out-of-Town Business Service
Package Design & Development
Paging Service
Parent Guidance Instruction
Parking Consulting
Parking Lot Maintenance
Party
   Entertainment
   Planning
   Production
Patio Construction
Payroll Preparation Service
Personal Services Broker
Personnel Consulting
Pest Control Service
Pets
   Breeding
   Identification Service
   Sitting for Unusual Animals
   Portraits
   Training
Photography
   Blow-Up Service
   Color Correction, Retouching,
      Restoring
   Unique Local Landmarks
Picture Framing
Plant
   Care
   Interior Plant Design
   Doctor
   Rent-a-Plant Service
Plastics
   Laminating
   Recycling
Political Campaign Management
Postmark Service
Portfolio Preparation Service
Potter
Power Wash Service
Presentation Support
Pricing and Estimating Consulting and
   Services
Printing—Quick

Printing Broker
Private Investigator
Process Server
Professional Organizer
Proofreading Services
Public Opinion
   Analysis
   Polling & Surveys
Public Relations Service
Publicity Service
Publishing
   Books
   Catalogs
   Directories
   Guides
   Newsletters
   Small Lots
Purchasing Agent Service
Quilting
   Making
   Selling by catalog
Rare Book Finding Service
Reading Service
Real Estate
   Appraisal
   Sales
Record Searching Service
Recording Studio
Record-keeping Service
Referral Service
   Tradespeople
   Roommates
Relocation Consulting
Reminder Service
Rental Services
   Books
   Office Equipment
   Pictures
   Robots
Repair Service
   Appliances
   Mobile Homes
   Shavers
   Snow Blowers
   Umbrellas
   Watches
Repossession Service
Research Analysis
Research Service
Restaurant Consultant
Restoration Services
   Photographs
   Furniture

Resume Writing Service
Retirement Counseling
Reunion Planning
Reupholstering
Reweaving
Roof Inspector
Safety Consulting
Sales Training
Script Preparation Service
Script Writer
Second-Hand Products Broker
Second Medical Opinion Referral
    Service
Security Consultant
Selling
    Ideas to Businesses
    Odd lots of merchandise
    Old Currency and Stock
Seminar
    Leader
    Producer
    Promoter
Septic Tank Pumping
Sewing Machine Repair
Sharpening Services
    Ice Skates
    Knives
    Lawn Mowers
    Saws
Shopping Services
Show Promoter for Consumers or Trade
Sightseeing Guide Service
Sign-Making Service
Singing Telegram Service
Skylight Installation
Small Business Convenience Services
Software
    Writer
    Location Service
Songwriting for special occasions
Sound Studio
Specialty Retail Shop
Speakers Bureau
Speech
    Instruction
    Writer
Sports League Statistics
Square Dance
    Calling
    Instruction
Statue Repair
Stock Market Analysis

Stock Portfolio Management
Stuffed Animal Vending
Swimming Pool/Spa Maintenance
    Service
Tax Preparation
Taxidermy
Technical Writer
Telephone Repair Service
Telephone Sales
Temporary Employment Agency
Tennis Instruction
Terrace
    Design
    Repair
Textile Design
Tool Repair
Tour Operator
Toymaking
Trade Association Operation
Trade Show Exhibit Builder
Training Broker
Transcribing
    Court Reporter Notes
    Radio and TV Programs
Translation Service
Travel Agency
Tree Service
Tropical Fish Care
Trophy
    Engraving
    Making
Tutoring
    Academic
    Achievement Tests
Typesetting
Upholstery
    Cleaning
    Installation & Repair
Urban Planning
Used Computer Broker
Vending Machine
    Operation
    Repair
Video
    Editing
    Production
    Transfer Service
Videography
Vinyl Repairing Service
Visiting Service
Wake-Up Service
Wardrobe Consulting

Washing Services
Water Treatment Service
Weaving—using a computer
Wedding Planning
Weight Loss Instruction
Welding and Soldering
Window Washing Service
Word Processing/Secretarial Service

Writing
   Company Newsletters
   Computer Documentation
   Trade Publications
Yacht Broker
Yellow Page Brokering
Yoga Instructor
Zipper Repair

INDEX

■ ■